# As I Recall

Memoirs

by

DONALD M. EWING

*Dedicated to Esther Ewing, my darling daughter, who has—
edited this work for over two years;
has never let me forget that the enterprise was worth-while;
has conceived, sourced, and organized the voluminous end-notes;
has contributed a couple of choice passages herself;
has applied wide experience in working out with Jessica Heald
the practical details;
has managed to find time for all this in a busy life;
and has always kept you, the reader, in mind.*

Editor: Esther Ewing
Text and book design: Jessica Heald

Copyright Year: 2008

Copyright Notice: by Donald Ewing. All rights reserved.

The above information forms this copyright notice:
© 2006 by Donald Ewing. All rights reserved.

Printed in the United States of America.

ISBN 978-0-578-01275-9

To contact Don Ewing: AsIRecall@gmail.com
To contact Editor, Esther Ewing: EwingChange@gmail.com
To contact Designer, Jessica Heald: Jessica@DigitDigital.com

# Contents

## Part 1—The Early Years

| | | |
|---|---|---|
| 1. | Introduction—Beginnings | 3 |
| 2. | Childhood—A Child's View of Britain | 5 |
| 3. | Dad | 9 |
| 4. | Mother | 13 |
| 5. | Galt | 19 |
| 6. | Alec | 24 |
| 7. | Oshawa | 28 |
| 8. | Early Musical Development | 31 |
| 9. | High School | 34 |
| 10. | University—Change of Course | 40 |
| 11. | University—Music in Those Years | 44 |
| 12. | University—Residence | 47 |
| 13. | University—The Student Christian Movement (SCM) | 51 |
| 14. | University—Politics | 55 |
| 15. | University—Ontario College of Education (OCE) | 58 |
| 16. | Muldrew Lake—The First Year | 61 |
| 17. | Muldrew Lake—1929-1942 | 66 |
| 18. | Muldrew Lake—Canoe Trips | 76 |
| 19. | Muldrew Lake—Openings and Closings | 86 |
| 20. | Muldrew Lake—The Sleeping Cabin | 88 |
| 21. | Brechin | 91 |
| 22. | The United Church of Canada to 1946 | 96 |
| 23. | Dr. J. R. P. Slater | 100 |
| 24. | The CCF to 1950 | 102 |
| 25. | By-election, 1942 | 104 |
| 26. | Eleanor, Before Marriage | 106 |
| 27. | Marriage | 109 |
| 28. | World War II | 113 |
| 29. | BC Forest Service (BCFS)—Part One | 115 |
| 30. | BC Forest Service—Part Two | 121 |

| | | |
|---|---|---|
| 31. | War-Time Supporters | 125 |
| 32. | Train Journeys | 128 |
| 33. | Lemon Creek | 131 |

## Part 2—The Middle Years

| | | |
|---|---|---|
| 34. | Teaching in Lemon Creek, Sault Ste Marie and Regina | 142 |
| 35. | Teaching in Ottawa and Goderich | 147 |
| 36. | Teaching in Burlington | 152 |
| 37. | Summer Courses | 156 |
| 38. | Life in Sault Ste. Marie | 159 |
| 39. | Life in Regina | 161 |
| 40. | Life in Ottawa | 166 |
| 41. | Life in Goderich | 172 |
| 42. | Dad and Mother, 1945-1983 | 180 |
| 43. | The United Church 1946-1955 | 186 |
| 44. | The CCF-NDP, 1950-1980 | 187 |
| 45. | The CCF-NDP, Locally | 197 |
| 46. | Life in Burlington—Part One | 203 |
| 47. | Burlington Part Two—Esther and Morrey as Children | 211 |
| 48. | Books That Were Read Aloud | 217 |
| 49. | Burlington (3) | 221 |
| 50. | Overseas—1968 (1) | 226 |
| 51. | 1968 (2) | 234 |
| 52. | 1968 (3)—Switzerland | 237 |
| 53. | Commuting, 1964-1969 | 241 |
| 54. | Outers Camp in NW Ontario | 245 |
| 55. | Muldrew Lake, 1942-1997 | 248 |
| 56. | Cars We Have Owned | 256 |
| 57. | Supervising Music in the Separate Schools | 266 |
| 58. | The Separate School Concerts | 270 |
| 59. | Our Homes in Guelph | 274 |
| 60. | A Tale of Two Churches | 284 |
| 61. | Other Friends | 291 |

# Part 3—Retirement

| | | |
|---|---|---|
| 62. | Presbytery | 296 |
| 63. | Conferences | 299 |
| 64. | The Big Issue of Ordination of Gays and Lesbians | 302 |
| 65. | Chair of Presbytery (1) | 307 |
| 66. | Chair of Presbytery (2) | 310 |
| 67. | General Council (1) | 313 |
| 68. | General Council (2) | 317 |
| 69. | General Council (3) | 321 |
| 70. | General Council (4) | 325 |
| 71. | Prayer Cycle | 329 |
| 72. | "Pack-Ratting" | 333 |
| 73. | The Bob Rae Government | 338 |
| 74. | Cabinet Ministers | 343 |
| 75. | The USA and Me | 349 |
| 76. | The UK and Me | 357 |
| 77. | Recent Use of the Piano | 364 |
| 78. | Pianos I have Known | 368 |
| 79. | Music That Has Touched Me | 374 |
| 80. | The Glasgow Orpheus Choir | 384 |
| 81. | Bach's B Minor Mass | 386 |
| 82. | Musical Activities since Retirement | 389 |
| 83. | Overseas, 1983 | 392 |
| 84. | Trinidad and Tobago, 1989 | 395 |
| 85. | Norway, 1990 | 400 |
| 86. | Scotland, 1997 | 404 |
| 87. | British Columbia, 1999 | 411 |
| 88. | The Danube-Main Rivers, 2001 | 417 |
| 89. | New York City, 2003 | 421 |
| 90. | Britain, 2005 | 424 |

## Part 4—A Few Considerations

| | | |
|---|---|---|
| 91. | The New Cottage | 428 |
| 92. | Animals and God's Other Creatures | 432 |
| 93. | Eleanor & Our Many Moves | 435 |
| 94. | What If? | 440 |
| 95. | Second Thoughts—After the Event | 445 |
| 96. | Money | 447 |
| 97. | A Loner | 451 |
| 98. | Books | 454 |
| 99. | The Stratford Festival | 460 |
| 100. | The Roll-top Desk | 463 |
| 101. | Letters-to-the-Editor | 465 |
| 102. | 2000—Celebrating 75 Years of the United Church | 468 |
| 103. | What Lies Ahead | 472 |

## Part 5—Family

| | | |
|---|---|---|
| 104. | Esther and Morrey since 1970 | 476 |
| 105. | Aunt Mary | 484 |
| 106. | Breffney Jane | 492 |
| 107. | Caitlin Anne | 496 |
| 108. | Alexander Mactaggart | 499 |
| 109. | Margaret Anne | 502 |
| 110. | April 12, 2003—Gala Anniversary | 505 |

## Epilogue

| | | |
|---|---|---|
| 111. | I—July, 2008 | 509 |
| 112. | II—Politics | 511 |
| 113. | III—Recent Celebrations | 513 |
| 114. | IV—Jim Allen | 514 |
| 115. | End Notes | 516 |

# Part 1—

# The Early Years

CHAPTER 1

# Introduction—Beginnings

Friends tell me I should write my memoirs, and that my plea that I'm too busy living won't wash because I seem to remember so much. So here goes with the first beginnings.

*Don Ewing, age 1*

I need to stress at the outset that memory is very selective. Ask me how I felt on first arriving in one of my places of residence, and I can't answer you. It depends on one's degree of interest at the time of the events in question, and also on the frequency with which one thought of those events. These processes must have been more active in the earlier years. Why else can I tell stories that happened 70 years ago and name participants whom I have not seen or heard of since? Yet the name of someone I see frequently now will sometimes escape me when I need it. Friends claim this is not a matter of age. What do you think?

Memories of my earliest years are sometimes my own, but very often these are mixed up with what I was told when I was a bit older.

My parents were married in January, 1916, and, as my father enlisted in the Canadian army and was posted overseas shortly after that, I was born in his absence and didn't meet him till I was two-and-a-half. When that happened, he felt it his duty to discipline his child. But I was old enough to object strongly and didn't come to appreciate him for a considerable time. As I grew older, I would typically respond to any demand for obedience with the query, "Obedience to what?" How much this was due to my first relationship with my father remains an open question.

I was born in Cobourg hospital, but my first home was the farm two miles north of there called Kenmore. This was my mother's home and her mother's. This household of three

*Grandma Haig, Don, Aunt Mary, Isabel and Alec*

(a grandmother, a mother and me) became what I found normal—me, living only with women. So when Dad came home from the war, I didn't at first feel that he belonged there. However, I must have begun to appreciate him fairly soon, for I vividly recall sitting on his knee at the piano around the age of four while he played the slow movements of Beethoven sonatas by reaching his hands around me to the keyboard. I never heard an assessment of his playing. He insisted on quitting when, as a teenager, I overtook him in technique. What is certain is that he gave me a love of good music early on.

CHAPTER 2

# Childhood—
# A Child's View of Britain

My childhood memories are very spotty. We moved to Winnipeg a few weeks after the famous General Strike of 1919. We lived within a block of a major street-car barn, and I was fascinated with the regular comings and goings of the vehicles. On at least one occasion, a neighbour rescued me from being run down by a street-car. On another occasion, we watched a large flotilla of canoes on the Red River, paddled by local natives. The term Indians, was then in common use.

I remember little of the year that Dad taught at Oakwood Collegiate in Toronto, but it seems that we lived across the road from Dr. Aitken of the College of Education. Dad had had him as a professor during his first year in Canada when he discovered that his Scottish teaching certificate would not be recognized in Ontario. Decades later in Burlington, Fran Tovee, Dr. Aitken's daughter, became one of our closest friends. She and I had been neighbours as babies!

People who grow up in one country and live in another often feel a strong need to re-visit the old land. My father was one of those people. His ties to Scotland and his family there remained strong. From 1920 to 1960, he crossed the Atlantic a number of times. For financial reasons, he couldn't always take his family along. But in the summer of 1922, when I was six, Mother and I were included.

In those times, crossing the ocean meant using steamships called ocean liners. The steamship companies advertised the comforts that passengers could enjoy. But the effects of North Atlantic waves could rarely be avoided, and the question of whether you were a good sailor was always appropriate—

*Four distant Ewings with Charles Ewing in the back and Donald in the front*

something those who fly today don't have to consider. Dad was a good sailor but I don't remember about mother and myself. I suppose we must have been since I have no memories to the contrary. Our baggage usually included a trunk which had a tray at the top for smaller items. I remember a flat green one that had my father's initials C.M.E. printed boldly across the lid. And of course trunks were heavy and often made us depend heavily on porters at each end of the journey. After a train trip from Galt, we sailed from Montreal aboard the CPR ship called "The Scotian." It had one large smoke stack and seemed impressively large until we pulled into Southampton harbour in England beside the "Aquitania" which dwarfed us with four. Mother remarked about our ship, "Did we come over in that little thing?"

I have two memories of our descent of the Saint Lawrence River. The first had to do with passing under the Quebec Bridge. As we approached the bridge, I thought that our high masts could never clear the bridge—an optical illusion that has bothered many. The other memory concerned life-boat drill in which all passengers were taught what to do in case of disaster. We had to practice putting on our life jackets and assembling beside the life boats. Later, we passed through the fogs of Cabot Straight where we moved at a very slow speed and sounded the horn at regular intervals in case of icebergs. I'm sure that I had not been told about the Titanic by then. I am equally sure that the drills were instituted following that disaster. In any case, the drill seemed very real to me and I asked my parents, "When are we going down?"

Of that summer, I am not sure of the exact sequence of events. I know that we visited "Tanhurst," the country mansion of my Aunt Mima's Aunt Janie Rea whom she looked after. Aunt Mima was one of my father's sisters. She took me out to the beehives that were part of the estate, to get some honey. We had put on elaborate netting. But, on our way back, we had taken it off too soon and I was stung at the back of the neck.

While we were staying there, one night, I was put to bed in one of the many bedrooms while the family had dinner at the other end of the house. During dinner, a servant interrupted proceedings to tell Mother that I needed to speak to her. Fearing the worst, Mother made the long journey to my room, only to hear me exclaim, "Mother! I've just remembered. The dog's name is Sport!"

Then there was Seahouses, a small fishing village on the east coast in Northumberland, where my Grandmother was living. Typical of the houses of the village, the "front door", the one strangers would use, was at the back! And in the kitchen there was a row of bell-pulls, whereby the maid could be summoned from any room in the house. As I don't recall a maid, I can only conclude that the equipment was left from a time when there had been one.

I was left with "Granny" while my parents toured the Scottish Highlands. I have no specific memories of Granny, only of a very kindly old woman. One day, a cousin named Elliott showed me the village life-boat. It was large with several banks of oars to allow the crew of volunteers to get quickly to where they were needed—often in heavy seas. The boat was kept on a runner for quick launching.

On other occasions, when my parents were present, we took trips by rowboat on different days, to the Farren Islands and to Holy Island. It was my introduction to the tides, as we once had to land on the mud bottom of the harbour and climb a ladder to get to the top of the dock. Recalling Holy Island, I have only a jingle that I made later, "I took a stitch and fell in the ditch while they went on to the castle."

Toward the end of the summer, Dad had to be home for the

re-opening of school. Mother and I stayed a few days' longer and visited friends in Liverpool. While there, we watched a passenger being taken in a small boat to a liner that was anchored well out in the harbour. Subsequently, we took the train (blue engine and white cars—what a thrill!) to Glasgow. We stayed the night with friends—I think the name was Stewart. In their living-room was a magazine with a cover photo of Mount Everest, and I was given a toy consisting of coloured boxes telescoped in size, so that, as you took the lid off each, a smaller box was revealed inside. The next morning, we boarded the "Cassandra" which proceeded to sail to Liverpool before heading into the Atlantic! Mother always wondered why we couldn't simply have sailed from Liverpool.

The return journey was very rough with lots of sea-sickness. Since the inside rooms became unbearably smelly from people's condition, we sometimes went on deck, even if it was raining. I remember huddling with her under a blanket (called a steamer rug) which was in use many years later at our cottage. At Quebec City, I was ill in my cabin. But the doctor who became available that day insisted on my being brought on deck to be viewed. My mother, a trained nurse, was not impressed.

*A British train at the time*

CHAPTER 3

# Dad

My father, Charles Mansfeld Ewing, came to Canada from Scotland in 1912. He brought a letter of introduction to a second cousin, Thomas Haig, in Toronto. A Haig-Ewing marriage in Scotland in the early 19th century had been followed by the couple's early migration to Canada. In the intervening years the Haigs in Canada married younger than the Ewings in Scotland, and Thomas Haig was a generation older than my father. Through him Dad met and married a handsome niece called Isabel. Thus my mother and I were third cousins!

My father was the youngest of five children of Reverend Alexander Ewing of the Wee Frees (Presbyterian) Church in Scotland and Carrie Ewing. His siblings' names were Oswald, Mima, James and Daisy (Margaret). When he was six months old, his father, minister in Broughty Ferry (now part of Dundee) died of a heart attack. His mother moved the family into Edinburgh where she managed to put all of her children through university. They lived in row housing on Thirlestane Rd. Family life seems to have been happy, for each child had a monosyllabic nickname. Dad's was 'Bim'.

An incident illustrates the atmosphere of that home. When Dad was about twelve, he was

*Charles Ewing*

*Above: Rev. Alexander Ewing*
*Below: Carrie Ewing*

walking home from an event and happened to catch up with a girl of his age named Sally who chatted at some length about recent happenings in the neighbourhood. On reaching home, he started to repeat some of these bits of information to his mother who listened in silence and then remarked, "Charles, I don't suppose that Sally ever gave you a thought in the world."

Dad's family did a lot of walking. He once told me that his mother would march them off on a Saturday morning, walking seven miles to the foot of a mountain—which mountain I never heard—another seven miles up the mountain and the whole distance back. The story seems a bit vague. What is certain is that Dad took me on long walks when I was a child, and that as a teenager, when our house was near the northern boundary of Oshawa, I walked on every road within a radius of ten miles of our home. (There still exists a diary by one of my father's brothers of one of those highland holidays with details of their daily activities.)

Dad always loved his native Scotland. As I was growing up, my Aunt Mima who lived for some years with a wealthy aunt, then married a wealthy cousin, was fond of slipping my father small sums of money, especially to make it easier for him to visit the Old Land and see his family. Sometimes Mother was included in this largess. But in 1938 she wasn't. Since this proved to be hurtful, Dad wrote her long letters during his trip. In one of these letters, Dad tells of going into the lower highlands. At one point, the clouds had dispersed and, he wrote, "The full glory of the Grampian mountains came into view!"

Another year, when my mother was with him, they took a bus trip. The driver, supposedly the expert, kept making comments through his microphone. But, as Mother told me on her return, Dad moved to the front of the bus where he could correct the driver and supply additional information.

In 1947, Dad named their retirement home, Ledcriech. I knew that the name came from a place in Scotland which he remembered fondly. But I never got round to asking him before he died just where it was. On my first subsequent visit to Scotland, in 1968, I tried to find out. It was not listed among place names in a guide book of Scotland that was supplied by Tom Dale. But, during a visit with Morrey and his cousin, Danny to Loch Voil, one of the lochs from which Glasgow gets its water, I walked around a small cemetery at Balquhidder and noticed on a tombstone a name of a person identified as a Ledcriech farmer. No one seemed able to tell me more. So we drove three miles along the Loch and had our picnic by the water.

But three weeks later, as I was having dinner with my cousin Ian in London, I learned from him that Ledcriech was the farmhouse on Loch Voil where Dad's family used to holiday in the early years of the 20th century, and that it was four miles up the loch from Balquhidder. We had been so close. Years later, an ad for Ledcriech appeared in a copy of the English magazine, Country Life. I wrote the realtor in the town of Perth, explaining my background and received from him a set of coloured photos of the property. These included a gardener's residence and an establishment far grander than my father's family would ever have been able to rent, and far different, I am sure, from the place after which he named his Canadian home.

Dad's profession was teaching classics in high schools, Latin, Greek and Ancient History. He taught in Wingham before the First World War, and in Winnipeg, Toronto, Galt (now Cambridge) and Oshawa after I came on the scene. He always made a great effort to justify, with the public, the teaching of Latin. This sometimes involved letters-to-the-editor of the Toronto Globe. His mind moved in the systematic channels that constituted that language, and he would encounter in later years former students who hadn't scored brilliantly in class

*Charles Ewing with his peaches at Ledcriech, Font Hill, Ontario*

(the kind teachers can so easily forget) but who appreciated his teaching because of his lucid explanations.

He was once offered a principalship in Collingwood. But A. E. O'Neill, his principal in Oshawa, persuaded him that he was needed to keep that school staff strong. He stayed in Oshawa until he retired.

During his last year of teaching in Oshawa, Dad's migraines became more frequent. Most week-ends, he would suffer on an empty stomach from Friday night till Sunday afternoon. It induced Mother to redouble her efforts to arrange his retirement in the following June. They moved to the edge of St. Catharines, where Dad had an acre of peach trees to tend. He had never in his life grown anything but grass. However, after visiting the nearby experimental farm and carrying out their instructions to the letter, he produced the best peaches on the street. And the outdoor exercise enabled him to avoid headaches almost entirely.

CHAPTER 4

# Mother

My mother, Isabel Haig, was the oldest of her family of five and grew up on a series of three farms near Cobourg, Ontario. My Grandfather, Andrew Haig, was at first unlucky in the quality of the soil he tried to work, and he moved twice for better farming opportunities. Life on the farm was primitive compared to that of the city, but Mother's generation learned skills that were then essential for survival, and these proved useful on many subsequent occasions. Travel through the country was usually by horse and buggy or horse and cutter in winter. During my first ten years, I often got to visit Kenmore, my grandfather's and later, my aunt and uncle's, farm and three other farms belonging to uncles, Charlie Rutherford, Fred Nixon[1] and James McLeod[2]. I remember being intrigued by the mysteries of the harness room and the piles of bedding that we used in winter to keep warm in unheated bedrooms. Being allowed to hunt the eggs with Aunt Muriel was always special.

Mother's family had birthdays at interesting times of the year. Aunt Mary's occurred on August 23rd. She died seven weeks short of her hundredth. Mother's came on January 31st, and the rest were even closer to Christmas. Aunt Muriel arrived on Boxing day, while the twins, Aunt Helen and Uncle Don, turned up on

*Isabel Ewing holding Don*

*Grandma Haig, as a young woman*

Christmas Eve. Santa brought Mother a new doll, and when she ran in to show her mother what Santa had brought her, her mother exclaimed, "See what Santa brought me!" The twins were in her bed.

Around 1926, two of my uncles, Don Haig and Charlie Rutherford, sold their farms, and after that, we went elsewhere for our holidays. Sometimes, it was to Brechin, near Lake Simcoe, where my Aunt Muriel and Uncle Don ran the village general store. But our summers came to be spent mainly on Muldrew Lake.

My parents both grew up Presbyterians. But, from my early childhood, they became interested in modernism, getting away from the literal interpretations of the Bible and embracing new interpretations. During the 1930's, I picked up from them an admiration for three great preachers we listened to by radio at every opportunity. One was Dr. Harry Emerson Fosdick[3] of the Riverside Church in New York who broadcast regularly on ABC. The other two had Toronto churches. Dr. George Pidgeon, of Bloor Street United Church, had been the first Moderator of the United Church and was a fellow cottager at Muldrew Lake. Getting a cold was not always bad news for me, since it gave me an excuse to stay home from our Oshawa church and hear Dr. Pidgeon! The other, Dr. J. R. P. Slater, of Old Saint Andrews United, had migrated from Edinburgh and was part of a great preaching tradition of that part of the world.

It was also my parents who first got me interested in the Co-operative Commonwealth Federation (CCF). They accepted an invitation in the early thirties to attend a CCF meeting in Oshawa with Ted Garland. He was a Member in the House of Commons first, as a member of the Alberta Federation of Agriculture, and then, with the CCF. Then he had lost his seat in the Social Credit sweep of 1935. He was subsequently appointed national organizer of the party. In 1935, my parents, formerly Liberals, cast their first votes for the CCF. And when I went to university in 1936, I quickly gravitated to the CCF and had a big part in organizing the U of T CCF club.

I think I was more influenced by my mother who constantly argued for the poor at family gatherings. I remember her arguments with her Uncle Fred Nixon who said, "Isabel, hard work never killed anybody." And another with her brother Uncle Don who proclaimed "Let them open a peanut stand." Occasionally, my father would join in, "A business has to make SOME profit."

Mother was also the big influence (along with Harry Emerson Fosdick) which led to my stand as a conscientious objector during World War II. Dad respected my convictions, but was much worried about possible repercussions during my time at college. On the campus, male students were expected to take part in the COTC[4]. Participation would have meant regular drilling and wearing the uniform and joining up. COTC volunteers put in two weeks of training at the army base at Niagara-on-the-Lake. Along with other pacifist friends, I refused to participate and registered as a conscientious objector. Instead, we took a course in first aid and gave blood to the Red Cross. There was some debate among the university powers about whether the conscientious objectors would be allowed to receive their degrees even though they had successfully completed all the work. In the end, a deal was struck. We had to do civilian duties at a two-week military camp at Niagara-on-the-Lake and then, in the week following, while we had been excluded from the official graduation ceremonies, we were allowed to go to the registrar's office to pick up our diplomas. When the registrar had

*Isabel Ewing*

given me my BA diploma, my father was greatly relieved!

My life-long habit of writing down each expenditure came from my mother, one of whose account books is still around. Typically, butter was 20c a pound! It was also my mother who did the careful planning that made it possible for Dad to have a comfortable retirement of 16 years, despite having retired before the age of 65. At one stage in my upbringing, my parents responded to an agency which asked parents to fill out a questionnaire about their son or daughter after which they would recommend an occupation. The answer for me was banking with music as a hobby!

My father came to Canada in 1912 with a letter of introduction to a Canadian cousin, my great Uncle Tom Haig, who was my grandfather, Andrew Haig's brother.

Mother used to speak frequently of the tendency of Ewings to 'slip into a minor key'. Was it really true that we all took a jaundiced view of life? Or was it just Dad?

My mother had trained as a nurse, graduating from the Toronto General Hospital in 1912, two years before the lady who became my mother-in-law—Madeleine Dillon. Upon graduation, she was offered the chance to go and do special duty nursing following some mine disasters in Sudbury and did, in fact, go for a few months. Shortly after she had arrived, she heard that her father was not well and that her nursing skills were needed back home. Esther remembers her telling a story about the decision to leave Sudbury. One of the other nurses had told her that she should stay in Sudbury because there were so many men. But she did go home and the first man she met when she got home was my father, newly arrived from Edinburgh!

From then on, her nursing skills were chiefly used on her family. Dad suffered from chronic migraines and indigestion. My younger brother Alec was a delicate child who died at the age of ten from catching a streptococcus infection. (They didn't have antibiotics back then.) And my maternal grandmother, Maggie McLeod Haig, lived with us during her final illness.

Mother, herself, sometimes had to watch her diet. I was the healthy one with a corresponding appetite. I remember a stage when Mother had to cook different meals at the same time for all four of us.

Our family holiday of 1925 was rather special. Dad rented one of a row of cottages on Presqu'ile Point that faced Brighton Bay, and a row-boat to go with it. Across the bay we looked at Prince Edward county. One night we could see that someone's barn over there was going up in flames.

Near the cottages, a small point, about 100 yards long, enclosed a small bay. Sometimes, after a strong wind had blown in surface water, the water level of that bay rose a foot or so. One such morning, we woke to see several boats drifting free.

*Group at Presqu'ile Point: Charles holding Alec, then Don, & Bob Nixon*

Soon neighbours came asking us if they could borrow our boat to get theirs. My father, having experience with North Sea tides, had pulled his boat higher on the beach than anyone else and it was still safely grounded when the water rose.

Bob Nixon, a 10-year-old cousin who had played with me on the farm, was our guest at Presqu'ile. We used to go out frequently in the boat. There was a chicken-pox epidemic that summer and a case or two had occurred among the cottagers. When we were in the boat, Bob would insist that we keep away from possible contamination from other boats. Once when he saw another boat, he exclaimed excitedly, "Row, Donald, row."

These were the days of prohibition in the United States and smuggling from Canada was common. We became aware that a large boat set off with this purpose every afternoon in time to arrive on the American side after dark. One evening, as a family, we all rowed to Brighton. There, riding at anchor when there was a dead calm on the lake, was the above-mentioned boat. With my piercing soprano voice (I was eight), I exclaimed, "Is that the rum-runner?" My mother told me afterward that several crew members poked their heads out when they heard me.

Bob's biggest activity that month was collecting fossils on the beach. He had so many by the time he left that his suitcase was heavy with them. But when he got home, he discovered that fossils were plentiful on the farm. He just hadn't noticed this before.

CHAPTER 5

# Galt

I recall much more about our five years in Galt than about the earlier years. In 1921, Dad became Head of Classics in the old stone Collegiate that overlooked the Grand River beside the bridge of the CPR railway. We lived for two-and-a-half years in a narrow red-brick house across Water Street from the School. During that time, I was able to indulge my passionate interest in trains which my father shared. The CPR, the main line between Chicago and Montreal, ran through Galt, and at holiday time we traveled on it as a family when visiting Mother's relatives near Cobourg. We would get up in time to catch the 6:42 am. After passing through Toronto, we were able to see the CNR track on which another train was racing us!

On the west side of the Galt railway bridge, the tracks climbed a hill—not steeply by road standards, but steep enough to require extra power for the trains to get up. A shunter engine was kept at the station to assist in this process. And I would sometimes hear the shunter return over the bridge after its job was done. One night my father told me excitedly, "The 5:25 went out tonight with five engines!

The railway bridge was always a temptation for pedestrians, especially as the nearest road bridge was a good mile downstream. The shop teacher at the Collegiate did a lot of private jobs after hours. One night he was late in getting home, and after listening carefully for approaching trains, he started across the railway bridge. But he had not heard the freight that caught up with him as he was about half way across. He lay down flat beside the track, which would have kept him safe, except that the side door of a box car was not fixed down and flapped open and shut. He was lucky. As it passed him it was open. His tools were knocked into the river. But he lived to

19

tell the tale.

I had a brief thrill one day when I was about 7 and Dad had taken me for a country walk. Hearing a train whistle, Dad realized that we were close to a level crossing that was far enough out of town that the train would be going at full speed. To reach that crossing in time, Dad grabbed my hand and ran with me faster than I had ever realized people could run. We were just in time to see the train dash through the woods.

My mother used to relate how I would have an accident just before we would depart on holiday. One morning, the day before we were to depart, the milk-man broke a bottle at the side door of our Water Street house and on going out to bring in the milk, I gave myself a gash. Another year, while Mother was at a women's meeting in a member's country house, I played around a stone fence and managed to pull a loose boulder onto my hip. The other remembered incident happened in a hardware store. In those days, ceilings were very high and huge rolls of linoleum were stood on end at the back of the store. Somehow, I managed to pull one of these rolls over on myself. How badly I was hurt, I don't remember.

Of personal friends in Galt, I recall just three. One was Jean McCallum who lived far enough away across town that each of us had to be transported to visit the other. The other two each had the name Stanley. Stanley Goodwin was something of a bully, while Stanley Birchall was friendlier. During my college years, I went back for a weekend to see Jean. Otherwise, there has been no contact with any of them in the succeeding years.

Our family belonged to Central Presbyterian Church, just across the Grand River from the downtown area. The organist was a brilliant musician named Bert Cutt. If memory serves, he had just one leg. Sometimes, he would get someone else to play the organ while he sang tenor solos. I have always tended to be claustrophobic, and I remember a Christmas concert when a platform was built over the choir pews. This was done before someone realized that they would need hymn books from the choir racks. Of course, little people like me were sent under to get them. I was glad to have that job finished!

The minister of Central was a Dr. Davidson who was sensitive about worshippers who thought he preached too long. One Sunday without warning, he broke off in mid-sentence to announce, "It's twelve o'clock," finishing his sermon as if nothing had happened.

In 1925, when Presbyterians were voting on church union[5], my parents found themselves in the minority as Central voted to stay out. They decided, however, to remain at Central because of their admiration for Dr. Davidson. A year later, we moved to Oshawa where we joined Saint Andrews, the only former Presbyterian Church in town that had joined church union.

The argument over union was fierce. I remember some of the words that were exchanged in people's living-rooms. In our day some conservative members of the United Church have advocated getting back to the Basis of Union as a reliable statement of our beliefs. That document served to unite three denominations in 1925 and was a combined statement of belief. But many Presbyterians attacked the first moderator, Dr. Pidgeon viciously for producing such a radical document. They felt he should have been content to use the document that had united the Presbyterians in the 1880's. But Dr. Pigeon believed that the Christians of every era should state their faith in the language of their day. And were he here today (he lived to be 100!) he would probably consider the Basis of Union as an historical document only.

Most of my parents' best friends were either members of Central Church or were teachers. In our last year in Galt, we lived on a short street near the west shore of the river. We had lived on Blair Road. Two of our friends on Blair Road were the Nairns—Edith of the collegiate staff and her father, a retired Public School principal—and the McKees who lived on the side of a hill. One day, the McKees phoned to say they had extra beets in their garden and wouldn't Mother send Donald over with his wagon to get some. I dutifully set off, but I had not paid enough attention. I went to Nairns, instead of McKees. The elderly Mr. Nairn rose to the occasion by digging some of HIS beets. But I forget whether Mother was more amused or embarrassed by my mistake.

My schooling began with first book[6] in Manchester School. Since that school didn't have a kindergarten, I never attended one, a fact to which I have often attributed my lack of some every-day practical skills like cutting and pasting or drawing which might have been useful.

When we moved west of the river, I walked to Dixon School for the next book. I had a teacher I remember as elderly. At the side of the room, a cloakroom ran from the back of the classroom to the entrance of the classroom itself. Once the teacher scolded a boy severely, whereupon he headed into the back of the cloakroom announcing that he was going home to tell his mother. The teacher was able to head him off by entering the cloakroom from the front.

Around that time, I was diagnosed with hay fever (the word allergy was coined much later) being subject to June grass and Timothy. I was given weekly needle shots, though I doubt now whether they did any good. But the doctor's office was a mile from where we lived and since she had to stay home with Alec, Mother made me walk the distance. As a reward, I received five cents, which I regularly spent on four boxes of candy midgets and an all-day sucker!

I believe my father was highly regarded for his teaching in Galt. I recall that he took part in the Staff Players. Once he played a character that died on stage just before the final curtain. Of course, he had to get up before the curtains opened for applause. One night there was an awkward moment when the boy doing curtains opened them too soon!

Another teacher, Mr. Challen, was sensitive about his oversized feet. Sometimes he would walk around the classroom to inspect the students' work. The students believed that they had only to stare at his feet to induce him to move on.

Decades later, in Guelph, I met a school nurse who claimed to have been taught by Dad in Galt. She told me that when a student had failed to do his homework and used the excuse of a lack of time, Dad used to retort that the student had just as many minutes in the day as the rest of us.

As a child, I was obsessed with maps and with the populations of cities. Dad had a special interest in geography, and there was usually a good assortment of maps around. In those days, population growth was slow and the numbers remained very stable. I recall that London, England, with 7 million, was the largest city in the world; New York was second, with 6 million. In Ontario, Galt had 13,000, Guelph 16,000, Kitchener 22,000, Cobourg 7,000 and Oshawa, 25,000.

CHAPTER 6

# Alec

My brother, Alec, was born in Galt, and was seven years my junior. My first vivid memory of him was of Hallowe'en in the year we lived on Blair Rd. when he was just about eight months old. We shared #77 with a Mrs. Lash who occupied the front part of the house. Our entrance was at the side, so that the only kids who knocked there were those who knew us. One such boy, from my class in school, turned up wearing a particularly scary costume. Mother answered the door, carrying Alec in her arms. When he saw the costume, Alec burst into tears.

Our last house in Galt had a bay window in the living-room, surmounted on the second floor with a tiny platform with ornate metal borders at the outside just four inches high. One very warm day, Mother had left the bed-room window wide open, and I arrived to find our two-year-old Alec walking around on this tiny platform. I quickly brought him in, lest he fall over the edge. But my father wouldn't allow me to act as a hero. "He'd have come in eventually," he said.

*Alec in Cub Scout uniform*

One incident may have occurred in Galt though it may have been Oshawa. Alec must have got up before me, because by the time I reached the kitchen, he was relating a dream to Mother. Curious enough to want to hear the whole dream, I asked him to start again. But Alec gave me the most scornful look. "You know," he said, "You were there!"

The only time I got really angry with Alec had to do with the illustrations of books. Soon after we moved to Galt, one of my overseas relatives gave me a subscription to "The Boys' Own Paper", an English monthly magazine edited by Arthur Mee. It had several regular departments, including one having to do with railways. In one issue, there were colour plates of the different lines in Britain. Before nationalization in 1947, every private line had names like "The Flying Scotchman" (London to Edinburgh) and distinctive colours. For instance, the Caledonian railway had blue engines and white cars. The next issue had coloured pictures of trains across the British Empire. With my passion for trains at the time, I valued these pictures very highly.

After 34 issues of the paper, two issues came indexing the 34, after which my parents had it all bound into ten volumes called "The Children's Encyclopedia." One day I came home to find that Alec had the volume with the train pictures on the floor where he had torn out and torn up the coloured pictures. You can imagine my reaction.

A picture that Mother took showed Alec with Doug and Jack Langmaid, the sons of our Oshawa dentist, all on their tricycles. Another shows Alec with his violin—he had joined an after-school class with Mr. Richer, the local music supervisor.

*Top: Alec with Doug and Jack Langmaid*
*Bottom: Alec with violin*

When I used to go for my dentist appointment, I would hear the mellifluous voice of the receptionist saying, "Just a few minutes, Donald." Then I remember Dr. Langmaid picking up the drill and assuring me, "This will make a lot of noise but it won't hurt." Since this process was never preceded by freezing, the assurance could not have been true, but perhaps Dr. Langmaid was relying on the strength of expectations to overcome any pain.

Alec and I slept together at 602 N. Simcoe Street and I seem to remember that Dad often needed to discipline us after we had been put to bed. At one point—naughty me—I put together a jingle: "Close the door, put out the light, and carry on with all our might!" Alec laughed uproariously.

The year we moved to Oshawa my parents briefly owned a car. One day when our parents had left us alone in the car, I moved into the driver's seat and put my hands on the wheel. Alec, in the back seat, was most alarmed. He shouted at me, "Donald, don't drive it!"

Alec was classed as a delicate child and seemed to pick up every disease that was going around. What finally killed him at the age of ten was a streptococcus germ which galloped through his head before the doctors could stop it. They operated at home on his sinus. Soon afterward, they had to go into his frontal lobe. But by that time it had entered his brain. One Sunday night, Alec had been put to bed on a couch in Dad's study. Mother went up to check and found that Alec was in a bad way, and called me to phone Dr. Donevon. In the next room, my Grandmother, who had been very ill, had one of her attacks and figured out how to take the necessary pill rather than bothering Mother.

Two days later, I was called out of high school class to go to the hospital where Dad informed me that "Alec is unlikely to recover." The brain specialist had come from Toronto and done the operation, but by then it was too late. The next year, a drug came on the market which our doctor told us might have saved Alec.

One thing that I could never explain was that, unlike Mother and Dad, I never cried over Alec's death. I don't think I was callous. I just didn't seem to be able to express my grief that way.

Aunt Mary in Japan had been expecting to hear of her mother's death, and, when she received the cablegram telling her of Alec's death, she thought at first that it was Grandma. Grandma died two months later.

The wife of one of the high school teachers claimed that she could communicate with relatives who had died. Mother told her of her fears over Alec and how he might cope with the next life at his young age. Her friend asked her Dad who had passed away some time previously how Alec was getting along. The answer was prompt and enthusiastic, "He's alright." Mother had had doubts about the process. But she was greatly comforted by this message.

CHAPTER 7

# Oshawa

My last four years in elementary school were reasonably happy. About Miss Stevenson (junior third), I recall only that I must have had good teaching for I learned my stuff. Miss Lick (senior third) lived up to her name. She was the only teacher from whom I ever had the strap. I was one of six in a row where she thought someone had misbehaved. Miss Ford (junior fourth) was special. I remember a grammar lesson in which the word "verb" was first mentioned. "That's your action word," she said. Miss Garrow doubled as principal and teacher of the "entrance class[7]."

Visiting all the classes on a regular basis was our charming music supervisor, Leonard Richer (who had taught Alec) and who had only one leg. He had played viola in the Toronto Symphony Orchestra but had left that in order to get into school music. I remember him correcting the note of a song in front of Miss Garrow. This was probably memorable to me because I had known she had it wrong before he came.

I recall two schoolyard bullies, one named "Farmer", and the other named "Cece." Most of the time, there was little unpleasantness. It was just understood that you didn't cross them. I never distinguished myself on the ball teams. But one day I caught two flies in a row and suddenly gained favour. I also remember damaging a finger in an attempt to catch a ball—on the day I had a piano lesson!

My elementary school was near enough to our house that I sometimes waited till the bell rang before crossing the road. High school was ten minutes away. But that was the count at the rate I walked. Mother used to say that if I fell I would be late. I rarely left extra time for that, and I usually passed everyone as I went. Referring to the time I took to finish homework, Dad once asked me with some exasperation in his voice, "Is there anything you do quickly?" I answered "Walk". That was definitely not what he had in mind!

When we listened to our favourite radio programs, the power of the station made a huge difference. CFRB which carried Dr. Pidgeon's services from Bloor St. Church and the Philharmonic broadcasts in the afternoon, and CKGW which brought in the music appreciation broadcasts both had 50,000 watt power and could be heard clearly in Oshawa. Some Toronto stations, however, including CKCL which carried Dr. Slater's sermons, were much weaker and could be heard only if atmospheric conditions were right.

*Don, class picture*

One Sunday my parents had dinner guests, and proceeded to have a game of bridge in the evening. This didn't fit with the concept I had learned from them about what might legitimately be done on the Sabbath day. So I proceeded to glue my ear to the radio in the next room to hear Dr. Slater's sermon on this weak station. I couldn't hear it very well. But I was feeling very virtuous, when I was probably being a pain in the neck!

In those days, families were quarantined whenever a case developed of a communicable disease. One winter there was an epidemic of mumps. Being a nurse, Mother stayed in Brechin after our Christmas visit to help combat the disease in that area, while Dad brought Alec and me home. But on Mother's return, she got mumps. Alec and I were then quarantined for three weeks. That period was almost over, when Alec came down with the disease. I was kept in for another three weeks. I returned to school to write a set of exams, and then got mumps myself. (Teachers' strikes didn't happen then. But a quarantine of nine weeks could be just as devastating.)

A letter from an overseas relative tested out the efficiency of Canada Post. The letter was addressed to "602 Simcoe Street,

N, Ontario, Canada" and was delivered on time. Perhaps none of the other Simcoe Streets in Ontario towns ran their numbers that high.

At 602 Simcoe Street, the storm windows were a challenge. To hook them into place in the fall, or to lift them free in the spring, they had to be swung well out so that you risked losing your balance—they were heavy.

The furnace, which burned coal, was conscientiously stoked twice a day by my father. The coal was delivered down a chute which ran in the window. Sometimes some hard ash would develop into a clinker which blocked the passage of ashes into the lower area. Ashes, of course, were a regular part of the garbage that had to be put out each week. The dampers that controlled the fire's vigour were adjusted by a chain that hung in one of the dining-room registers. To humidify the house, Dad cut food cans and wired them to the inside of each register, and filled them with water. Once, after Dad had gone down to shovel coal into the fire, we heard him groaning loudly. He had suffered an attack of lumbago. Somehow Mother got him upstairs and to a couch. Occasionally we would hear of wealthy people in Oshawa who could afford oil furnaces. We were envious but those kinds of furnaces were way beyond our means!

Every year on Victoria Day, fireworks were set off in Alexandra Park. We didn't need to go there as we could watch it all from our back yard.

CHAPTER 8

# Early Musical Development

It wasn't until we moved to Oshawa that I began piano study. From the age of ten, I was taught by a wonderful person named Elizabeth R. Emsley. She believed in me enough to get me past the usual hazards that children face. At one stage, she laid down the law that one third of my practice time was to be given to technique which I came to understand meant scales, chords, arpeggios and octaves. At another, she reacted to a rumour that I would quit piano by describing the possibility as a major tragedy. There was a stage at which I was tempted to give it up. But I was thankful a year later that I hadn't. By the end of high school, I would have gladly practised for eight hours a day. But not wishing to earn my living as a private teacher, I went to university.

There was no music on the high school curriculum in those days, and I used to find occasionally that if I was sick enough to stay home on a Friday morning, I could listen to the *Music Appreciation Hour* that was regularly broadcast from New York. Walter Damrosch[8], one of the leading American conductors of the time, was the director, and he would introduce school children (where school boards approved) to many of the great classics.

On Saturday mornings, I would tune in to *Morning Melodies* on CKGW, the station that was owned by Gooderam and Worts Brewers, which was later taken over by the CBC to become CBL. The program actually featured recordings of the great symphonic works. I also was a regular fan of the Sunday afternoon concerts of the New York Philharmonic Symphony Orchestra which broadcast from Carnegie Hall on CBS. I quit Sunday school to hear this stuff, but later I had to choose between hearing the end of these concerts and switching to ABC for Dr. Fosdick's sermons.

The intermission commentator on the Philharmonic broadcasts, for many years, was Deems Taylor[9]. I recall three of his talks. In one, he explained how rarely valued violins actually turn out to be genuine Stradivarius instruments. On another, he discussed activities that listeners might engage in while listening to the concerts without being distracted. Above all, they shouldn't include reading books! On another occasion, Taylor almost caused an international incident. César Franck's *Symphony in D Minor* was on that day's program and Deems Taylor told of the reception the work had been given on its first performance. On two successive Sundays he told parts of the story, always finishing without actually revealing what the audience thought. Finally, after being accused of causing an international incident, on the third Sunday, he revealed that the performance had been a great success.

Two concerts stand out. Both involved me because Miss Emsley regularly organized car loads to Toronto concerts, to broaden the experience of her pupils. In 1931, we took in one of Paderewski's[10] appearances in Massey Hall. The performance was, of course, brilliant. Where did we get the idea that he was constantly "pawing the air"? And he played many famous works, including the *A flat Polonaise* of Chopin. But what raced through my head on the way home was not the Chopin but the Mozart *G Minor Symphony* which I had heard for the fourth time on the radio that afternoon!

Paderewski spent ten months as President of Poland from January 1919 to December 1919. During that time, he found that his practising suffered. He would say, "When I miss a day's practice, I know it. When I miss two days, my family knows it. When I miss three days, my commissars know it. But when I miss four days, the whole world knows it!"

In the spring of 1936, we went to the Eaton Auditorium to hear Artur Schnabel, the world-renowned authority on the works of Beethoven. From my balcony seat, I got the idea that he moved like a mouse. But Schnabel's hands never seemed to leave the key-board. And his program is one I have never forgotten. I'm not sure which Mozart sonata came at the beginning. But the program did include Schubert's posthumous *Sonata in B flat*. Within the next year I had purchased the score of the Schubert work. Since then, I have studied the first two movements and still (in my 90's!) want to learn the very quick last two movements that remain.

Third on the program was Beethoven's *Appassionata* Sonata. In the fast third movement, he played whole phrases as single thoughts. Then there was the *Opus 111*. He began the finale at a very slow tempo, which led Augustus Bridle, music critic of the Globe, to criticize the master in the next day's paper in a way that I found very disturbing.

Schnabel's tempos are a subject all by themselves. In the early 40's Eleanor's parents gave her a complete set of the Beethoven piano sonatas in the Schnabel edition, a set I have since had rebound. He gives a metronomic marking, not only at the beginning of each movement, but at frequent intervals where he recommends changes in speed. Of course, I find his tempos in the Allegros and Prestos to be quite impossible to play. So I use the intermediate markings to speed up or slow down from what I had used to start with.

As I write this, I've been reading Walter Pitman's *"Music Makers"*, his biography of Harry Friedman and Mary Morrison. These names have long been familiar. But, in Walter's hands, they have become wonderful people. In some ways, this was an antidote to Schabas' history of the Toronto (later Royal) Conservatory which I found quite depressing in its content. Harry and Mary endured constant problems. But they were never deflected from the tremendous contribution they made to Canadian cultural development.

CHAPTER 9

# High School

Oshawa Collegiate and Vocational Institute (OCVI), the only high school in Oshawa when I attended, was built around a large auditorium with open corners which made for very difficult acoustics. But A. E. O'Neill who became principal the same year Dad joined the staff, knew how to be heard in the place. A colonel in the First World War, Mr. O'Neill held a daily assembly every morning at nine o'clock for the whole school. As he started up the centre aisle, most students were busily chattering. By the time he was mounting the stage, almost all of the buzz had ended, and he had their attention from the first words he spoke.

By the mid 1920's, several members of the Oshawa Board of Education happened to be graduates of Queen's University, in Kingston, and with few exceptions, they appointed other Queen's grads to the high school staff. These teachers then became like missionaries for the cause, strongly encouraging students to go to Queens. One of those "missionaries" was Violet B. Smith, reputed to be the finest French teacher in Ontario. In intercollegiate football, the Varsity (U. of T.) team nearly always beat Queen's since they had so many more students to draw from. But on one Saturday, Queen's beat Varsity. Miss Smith told us that she had gone straight to the piano and played the Marseillaise! When it came time for me to choose my university, I decided on Toronto because of its musical opportunities. But three other students in my block were going to Queen's. I was the black sheep!

While I was at OCVI, Llewellan Hall was being maintained as a residence for the children of overseas missionaries who wanted their offspring to attend a Canadian high school. These students tended not only to be good academically but were especially appreciative of teachers like Dad. One of them,

Norm MacKenzie, who became a minister, was addressing a meeting in Chalmers Church during the 1970's, and made a point of observing, "Don's father taught me my Greek." Norm and other Llewellan Hall people have served the United Church well.

Two of them were recognized especially in their last year. Every year, Murray Johnson, a downtown merchant, presented a cane to the boy judged to be the best all-round male student. At the same time, Gladys Edmonston of the French department presented a pair of books to the best all-round girl. That year, these honours went to Stanley Best and Katherine Bryce, both of Llewellan Hall. These two eventually married.

*Alec and Don*

The following year, I attended a reunion of OCVI students who were studying at the University of Toronto. We had dinner at India House. Katherine, who had started life in India, began eating with her fingers as was done in that country. But Stan, who had come from China, held up his serviette in front of Katherine, saying, "Will someone hold this up while I eat?" That typified the fun we had that night.

I vividly remember many of my OCVI teachers. There was Mr. Brown, my first form (grade 9) zoology teacher, after whose lesson on snakes I had a dream in which I played with them happily; Mrs. Hazlewood under whom I got 100% in a grammar exam; Miss Laura Jones, of Cobourg who taught German and other subjects, who exclaimed one day on finding that a class had not noticed birds in their own yards, "What do you do with your eyes?"

I also remember Norman McLeod who taught Canadian and British History, telling us about Napoleon, who said to his army in Egypt, "Gentlemen, I'm going home. You get home as best you can!" I later had him as a critic teacher at the Ontario

College of Education (OCE).

I remember Mr. McGirr, of the Commercial Department and Miss Savage, teacher of Mathematics, who had a strange manner, but got good results. And what should I say about Mr. Glass? He was certainly colourful, but not a very effective teacher of Latin. To get us to remember the sign of the future tense in the four conjugations, he would recite, "A, E, I, I" so loudly that I could hear it in the classroom below. "I'm not worried about (and he'd name several of us), but O'Rooney, you're slipping."

Dad, his head of department, was sometimes embarrassed when a student of Mr. Glass's would drop in after school to get a point explained, and, before Dad could tell the student that he/she should have gone to his own teacher, Mr. Glass would appear and ask the student, "What are you doing here?"

Maurice Kirkland, teacher of history and geography, was a special friend, while his wife, Jesse, was a constant friend of Mother's. A cottager and one-time ranger in Algonquin Park, he was later the principal of a new Oshawa Collegiate. Mr. Harrison Murphy, head of English, headed another new school at the same time.

Then there was Flossie Armstrong who taught me English in third form. She had a dry wit. When getting us started on oral compositions, she mentioned that she was tired of students who chose to speak on "the making of pins". So Malcolm Young chose to use that subject but made it funny enough that she couldn't object.

She taught me much about writing good English. Once, after being ponderous and long-winded, I scored with a brief, pungent composition about why I loved Muldrew Lake.

In my day, the school was rigidly divided into the academic department, for students expecting to proceed to university, and, socially, where elite families sent their children; the commercial department where typing and shorthand would prepare students well for business jobs, and the technical wing, where boys learned carpentry and motor mechanics, and girls were taught home economics. Students had to spend all of their time in one department and had to totally leave one to enter another.

At that time, also, the quality of city aldermen had hit a new low. In a discussion of students, one teacher asked, "What are you to do with a student who fails in the academic department, fails in the commercial department, and can't make it in the technical department?" "Don't you see?" said another teacher. "Make him an alderman!"

I think I must have been an embarrassment, sometimes, to my father. He was on the staff of Oshawa Collegiate while I was a student. One day the school scheduled a cadet march at a public park. As a budding pacifist, I stayed away. The next morning at assembly, Mr. O'Neill asked all who had not attended the event to stand, then for those with a clear conscience over it to sit. I took my seat. But it hurt my father to see his own son singled out.

I didn't have Dad for Latin till I reached my last year. But in Fourth Form (now grade 12) I had him for Ancient History. I was impossibly slow as a student, and at one point I got behind in Dad's assignments. He took me aside at home and told me, "Students who get behind are just not in my class." "Put me out," I said. "Oh, no, I couldn't do that to my own son!" I caught up.

During my high school years, there occurred a development among the churches that proved hard to ignore. This development was known as the Oxford Group (not to be confused with the Oxford Movement which applied to Anglicans who were leaning towards Catholicism). The Oxford Group[11] comprised church people who pledged "absolute honesty, purity, unselfishness and love". They undertook to start each day with a quiet time in which personal discipline was considered. An essential part of that discipline involved spreading the message so that the world would eventually be brought into the fold.

The whole thing became visible one Sunday when an Oxford Group team, clergy and lay, arrived from Toronto to speak, one per pulpit, in most of the Protestant churches in Oshawa. This was followed by a series of meetings at which individuals laid bare personal experiences and encouraged others to get involved. I recall one enthusiast declaring informally, "All this was simply God."

United Church leaders were very much divided about the Oxford Group. Dr. Pidgeon, our first moderator, was a strong advocate who spent a lot of time promoting it across Canada. At one of the summer services at Muldrew Lake, he talked of this and mentioned that it was "well rooted in Calgary." His activities sapped his strength and led to serious problems of his health.

After one of the Group meetings in Oshawa, an elderly gentleman asked me in a very serious tone of voice whether I were a member of the Oxford Group. I had to say that I was unaware of such a thing. When I mentioned this to another activist, she assured me that there was no such thing, that the OG was an organism, not an organization. Nevertheless, the emphasis on individual behaviour gave it an evangelical flavour.

One aspect that I could not endorse concerned the "trickle down" evangelism process. The theory was that if you converted the mayor of a city, he (most were men in those days) would then convert his aldermen, who, in turn, would bring city employees into the fold, who would then work on their families. This theory was the subject of much hilarity among opponents of the Group.

In balance, I can imagine that much good resulted when Oxford Group leaders brought enthusiasm to Christian practice. But the social gospel was missing from what was said, and eventually it changed into something called Moral Rearmament and was supported mainly by wealthy people and others who didn't apply the gospel to social action. In 1968, when we visited Lac Lucerne in Switzerland, we were shown the luxury estate of the man who at that time was world president of Moral Rearmament.

When I was in the entrance class (grade 8), I first fell in love with a girl in my class. I had a warm feeling every time she came into the room. I "had it bad." But I had witnessed so much teasing of youngsters in that position—some of it cruel—that I determined to keep it all to myself. The only way I might have let the cat out of the bag was by turning up at the back door of her house during her birthday party and encountering her father who commended me—a boy—for braving, at the back door, a girls' party!

But I tell people who don't understand about sexual orientation that, if anyone had asked me why I was attracted to a girl, rather than another boy, I could only have answered that this was the way I was made. Certainly, I never made a conscious decision that it would be that way.

Later, of course, there were other girls, though I remained shy about it for years. Once I got a notion of taking a girl to a concert in Toronto. I got as far as to discuss it with Mother and Dad, who didn't make major objections though they may have pointed out practical difficulties. In the end, I never asked the girl!

In fifth form (grade 13), I had a rather uneventful date. I invited the girl in French and she replied in kind ("Je serais enchantée[12]"), and we went to a movie. But I doubt if I made good on the expectation of enchantment!

Also in fifth form, I attended a school dance. But I don't recall actually dancing. That happened the next year when I was living in Gate House, Burwash Hall at U of T. The leaders felt it was essential that all members of the residence attend the autumn formal dance. I don't remember who my date was, but I do remember being given lessons in dancing on the common room floor by older students.

But I remember thinking at first that I should not ask the same date out twice lest I run out of things to say! I soon got over that, but not before I was guilty of some awkward moments.

CHAPTER 10

# University— Change of Course

Everyone's life is a combination of successes and failures. Some are perceived and some real. Some loom larger than they should while others seem less important. In public school, I probably thought it important that I never had enough physical coordination to be accepted onto the baseball field, and that, wearing glasses from an early age, I got the nickname "Professor." In fourth year high school, I failed an English exam, the only one I remember failing. It was very long, and I made the mistake of taking half the time on the first question and got only two-thirds of the paper done. However, I redeemed myself in English in my fifth year.

My first major failure was that I did not pass first year in University. There were a number of factors—some would call them excuses. I've mentioned that I tried to study piano before I had learned that studying lecture notes didn't sufficiently prepare one for university exams. The pass history course covered Europe from the Crusades to the French Revolution, and my habits of slow reading didn't allow me to cope. Life in Gate House of Burwash Hall was especially hectic with a virtual civil war taking place between the freshmen and sophomores over initiation.

That year I found out the hard way that serious practice on the common-room piano was not appreciated. No one said a word about it. But I found one day that someone had taken

*Healey Willan*

the trouble to weave newspaper in and out of the strings, so that no notes would sound! I didn't immediately get the message, and another day, I discovered the instrument lying on its back!

The following year, I enrolled, with seven others, in the first year of a new Music BA course. It proved to be too academic as preparation for teaching school music. But, as a liberal education, it was great. Along with the music, we took two other honours and two pass courses. In English, we had Northrop Frye[13], John Robbins[14], and E. J. Pratt[15]. In French and History, we had equally great leaders. And in Music, we had Leo Smith[16] and Healey Willan[17].

Healey Willan gave us memorable sayings: "Music is 10% inspiration and 90% perspiration" or "Down with church music and up with the music of the church!" With this latter saying he was asserting that the music used in the church should be well written and come from the church's musical tradition rather than any old thing that someone wanted to use in the service.

He also had an endless fund of stories. One morning before he left England to come to Canada, he was waiting for a train at Waterloo station in London in a dense fog. He heard someone whistling the theme of Bach's organ fugue in G minor. He tried answering with the response, but somehow he could never get nearer the other whistler. A few weeks later, he got talking with the violin soloist at a concert in Liverpool. The violinist told of a procedure he and a friend had to make contact in London's Waterloo station when it was foggy. They used the Bach theme with good effect, except for one morning when "a blighter" got in the way. Willan said, "I guess I must have been the blighter."

One day at University, Dr. Willan appeared after being off the previous day with flu. "I always believe," he said, "that if you haven't got a fever, you're much better up and around." I answered, "But shouldn't you get extra sleep?" "What do you mean old man?" "Well, nine hours instead of eight." "HOW

MUCH SLEEP do you need? My grandmother brought us up on the dictum, "Six for a man, seven for a woman, eight for a fool, and heaven help anyone who needs more than that!"

Willan has been called the "dean of Canadian composers." I have always felt that his choral music was more easily enjoyed than his instrumental. Perhaps this is natural since his practical leadership was most tellingly exercised as director of music at Saint Mary Magdalene Anglican Church, a post he kept for most of his years in Canada. In that setting, he could try out his ideas as they occurred to him, and revise them as necessary.

His sense of humour was special. Once two harmony students came to a scheduled 4:10 pm lesson with Dr. Willan but were disappointed to find that he was not there. They left a message on his door:

> *"Roses are red, violets blue,*
> *We were here, but where were you?*
> *Twas twenty past four by all of the clocks,*
> *And we had to leave early, your two little Bachs."*

Willan promptly replied,

> *"Twenty past four, by all of the clocks,*
> *And you had to leave early, my two little Bachs?*
> *The rose may be red, the violet blue, but*
> *I got my unpunctuality from you!"*

The girls, in reply, imitated Wordsworth[18] with "Lines composed on the occasion of the misapprehension of a piece of modern verse." But Willan had the last word. He came back with a magnificent parody of Longfellow's *"Hiawatha"*, in which, as Hiawatha, he related his day "In the dim Con-ser-va-to-ry". It is one of the disappointments of my life that that poem has been lost.

Leo Smith, first cellist of the Toronto Symphony for many years, had a personality unlike anyone I have ever known. He managed to combine gentleness with authority. He once compared the culture of the Baroque era with the mountains of Wales. "Most visiting mountain climbers in Wales go up Snowden as the tallest peak. But when they get to the top, they realize that several other peaks are almost as high". So any baroque composer who stood out must be seen among many others who were almost as good.

Leo Smith was also an active executive in the Musicians' Union. He once told me that he regretted the introduction of instrumental music into high schools since the students thus involved might grow up to take the jobs of adult musicians then in the field. It never occurred to him that these students would become enthusiastic audiences for the very concerts the union would support, which is what later happened.

CHAPTER 11

# University— Music in Those Years

When I went to university, Miss Emsley sent me to the teacher she had studied with, G. D. Atkinson[19]. For a few months, I studied with him and sang in his church choir at Sherbourne United (now Saint Luke's) and learned a lot from him, for instance, the importance of thinking in longer phrases. However, the big lesson of that year was that university requires study habits that are different from those that get you through high school. And studying piano just didn't fit that kind of schedule and had to be dropped. But I did manage to do some special piano study one summer.

In July of 1939, I traveled to Chautauqua[20], NY, to study with Austin Conradi. The experience was valuable from other viewpoints as well. Students practised in Piano village, a collection of about 19 huts each of which contained a Steinway upright. I drew a fairly good one. But I learned that Steinways were not all grands, nor were they all of high quality.

Then there were the concerts in the Chautauqua Amphitheatre. This unforgettable place had been literally dug from the side of a hill and seated 7,000! The Chautauqua Symphony, composed of members of leading American orchestras, and conducted by Albert Stoessel, gave four concerts a week. I joined the 200-voice Chautauqua Choir, which, besides local concerts, joined with other choirs from Erie, Pennsylvania and Jamestown, Ohio to perform Mendelssohn's Elijah. I'll not soon forget the sound that 600 of us made with the opening, "Help, Lord." During that summer, Austin Conradi performed with the Toronto

*Austin Conradi*

Philharmonic Orchestra in Varsity Arena. Dad attended and was most impressed.

One other activity during university kept me active at the piano. I was invited one Sunday to take the place of an accompanist at one of the Hart House Songsters. That men's institution scheduled these events on alternate Sunday nights in the Music Room. Sixty to a hundred men would sit in the dark and sing with accompaniments on a Steinway grand piano and an upright, and with the words projected on two large screens. Some people dubbed the events as glorified sing-songs. But what made them special was the leadership of J. Campbell-McInnis, a leading baritone soloist and an expert on British Folk Songs. We used a preponderance of songs from the British Isles—a natural result of McInnis' leadership. But I recall Beethoven's The Heavens are Telling and the American folk song, Carry Me Back to Old Virginny.

The programs were carefully planned by McInnis, in cooperation with the two accompanists. As one of the two over four years, I learned a lot about the art of accompanying. I soon left behind my bad habit of stopping to correct wrong notes. Often accompaniments had to be transposed down to accommodate amateur men's voices. Sometimes the only printed music was a melody that we had to harmonize. Sometimes the melody appeared only on the slides, and we would have to crane our necks to read it from the screen—while harmonizing and transposing at the same time. Eventually, we would develop some facility at playing simple accompaniments by ear.

Once, McInnis had me to lunch at his apartment on Dupont Street so that we could plan the next Songsters' session. He called my attention to a certificate on his wall that indicated that he had been knighted by the King of Italy for his artistic endeavours, and asked me if I felt different having seen it. I responded by telling him that my father's sister had married late in life Walter Rea, son of Rt. Hon. Russell Rea of the Asquith

*Russell Rea*

cabinet in Britain during World War I. He almost exploded. "You don't know what you're saying. Russell Rea gave me my first public audition." I could only guess at the nature of the occasion.

In my last year, I became the Music editor of Acta Victoriana. That involved reviewing such concerts as I managed to take in, but especially, of course, the activities of the Victoria College Music Club. In any other year, that would have meant a production of a Gilbert and Sullivan operetta. But Thomas Crawford decided that he needed a change and chose instead a thing called "San Toy". I don't think that I quoted Norrie Frye's comment that it was "laundry Chinese." But my comments were along that line. I don't remember stirring any complaints. People obviously preferred the Gilbert and Sullivan productions which had usually been spectacular.

Another event I covered was a recital in the Eaton Auditorium of a young Polish pianist named Poldi Mildner. I remember quoting another listener whom I happened to overhear say something to the effect that this program was aimed at other professionals, rather than the general public.

CHAPTER 12

# University—Residence

One reason for my first year's failure was the nature of Gate House in Burwash Hall, where I spent my first year. The official yell of a residence didn't always reflect its prevailing atmosphere which in this case was, "Hit 'em in the wishbone; sock 'em in the jaw; Gate House, Gate House, rah, rah, rah". But it comes close.

There was a long-established tradition that had allowed second year students ("sophs") to dominate first year students ("frosh"). For one thing, Frosh had to do all phone answering. For another, Sophs had the right to discipline Frosh by "tapping" them—carrying them to a shower in the middle of the night, and by using other physical means of enforcing initiation. The students of our year were particularly spirited in their resistance to this treatment, and Sid Gould, the don, later took both groups aside and talked about the "civil war" in the house. None of this was conducive to good study habits.

The matter of room keys illustrated the goings on. Theoretically, each student or pair of room-mates had the only keys to their rooms. In fact, one senior always had a master key, though not, of course, officially. One of our Frosh cleverly converted his key into a master, using a file. Sometimes, the occupant of a room put a pin in the lock of his door at night, so that an intruder's master wouldn't work. But a determined intruder would then kick out a door panel, reach around and unlock it from the inside. A senior in North House was once heard to brag that one night there were as many as 17 door panels out.

One Saturday afternoon when my room-mate was out of town, I heard hammering outside my door and found that it wouldn't open. Shortly afterward, a gang of five students appeared and forced me into my closet while they "set up" my

*Co-op Residence; Don Ewing, 2nd from right, 2nd row from back*

room. Besides messing up my belongings, they dismembered my bed and told me that I would find it in the garden of Annesley Hall, the girls' residence. After they had gone, I tried straightening things up and noticed a string tied to my window with an inviting bow. Unsuspecting, I pulled on the free end and heard a crash as my bed-frame hit Saint Mary Street below. Miraculously, it still fit together when I recovered it, and got the mattress back from the phone booth!

Students from the four houses that made up Burwash Hall ate in the Great Hall, while faculty members ate at a long table on a raised platform. At the long student tables, there was special lingo used for having things passed. For tomato catsup, it was "Blood up", while "mud up" brought Hp sauce. Regardless of the weather, students not wearing ties would not be served. I wonder how long that rule survived.

After that first unsuccessful university year, I not only refrained from piano study, but I made a change in my living arrangements. I left Burwash Hall, the official men's residence of Victoria College and took a room in a private house. Distant relatives, Percy and Grace Sutton (related to the Haigs) kept a rooming house on Walmer Road just north of Bloor Street. My room on the third floor was heated by a coal stove, the coal being stored in rough canvas bags in a hall cupboard. It worked fairly well, except that it sometimes gave off gas fumes that forced me to choose between heat with foul air and pure, but cold, air from an open window.

For food, I used Moore's restaurant for full course meals bought twice a day for 25 cents each, and for breakfasts in my room, I bought muffets, canned milk, and oatmeal date cookies—at 12.5 cents a day. Thus I used depression prices to exercise my Scotch instincts. I used to calculate that $600 would cover the total expenses of each college year!

After two years of using a coal stove, I moved into the Campus Cooperative Residence. The year before, I had told my mother that the CO-OP was for poor students. "How poor do you have to be?" she asked. My room was in "Kagawa House", named after the great Japanese Christian leader who had promoted co-ops for inner-city residents in Tokyo. The house was a modest building on Spadina Ave. We had our meals in Rochdale House on the second floor of a building on St. George's Square, the original location of those who had started the co-op two years earlier.

All members did four hours of housework a week, in the kitchen or in the halls and wash-rooms. There were regular meetings, for education in cooperative principles and for democratic decisions about the running of the residence. The only employee of the coop was the cook. We were proud of our membership in the Cooperative Union of Canada, which meant that we fulfilled all the Rochdale principles of cooperation.

In succeeding years, the CO-OP acquired three more houses north of Bloor Street. In my last year, I lived in Thompkins House on Admiral Road named after a Catholic priest who founded co-ops in Nova Scotia. My roommate was Ulrich Goldschmidt, one of a number of German Jews who had fled to Britain to escape Hitler, but had not lived there long enough to acquire citizenship by the beginning of World War II. They had been incarcerated as enemy aliens, but were subsequently allowed to come to Canada if sponsored by a Canadian.

To avoid prejudice during the war, these people went out of their way to ape English manners. Thus Ulrich had a teapot in the room and made tea each day at "precisely" four o'clock! At one point during that year, other German Jewish refugees arrived in the residence. "Just think," Ulrich said. "There are now six Englishmen in the house!"

In those last years of my stay at the CO-OP, meals were served in a larger house on St. George Street I remember that a square dance was held there. And, each year for a number of years, a Sunday afternoon tea was held in the fall. The members would bring girls as guests. For several years in a row, Dr. Cody[21], the university president, accepted the CO-OP's invitation to attend. Considered a "stuffed shirt" by many, he nevertheless took advantage of this way of getting close to the students. On the occasion, he would systematically speak to everyone present, beginning with the greeting "How do you do?"

At one stage in the CO-OP's history, the Warden of Hart House made available to the CO-OP a set of 144 prints of famous paintings from Giotto to the 20th century, with ample notes on the significance of each. The CO-OP created the post of "Art Director", whose job it was to mount a dozen paintings in available frames each month and to give a talk on them at dinner. After the first Art Director left, they chose me as someone who was taking a one-hour-a-week course in Fine Art. Since I was taking the course to relieve my colossal ignorance of the subject, I felt ill-prepared. However, I went through the motions. My "baptism of fire" came one month when I had to introduce some nude paintings. I should have realized that, for many students from the science faculties, a nude woman was merely a sex object. In the event, the don of the residence had to restore order!

CHAPTER 13

# University—The Student Christian Movement (SCM)[22]

The period of 1936 to 1942 was a great time for students to be sorting out their ideas and forming convictions about the world around them and the people among whom they moved. The years leading up to the war and the first years of World War II brought out the best and the worst in young people's expression. The transition from depression poverty to war-time prosperity changed many people's attitudes to society. And the application of Christian principles to these changes led many of us to take positions that influenced the rest of our lives.

The Student Christian Movement attracted many brilliant leaders who took the organization a long way from what had constituted Christendom at this point. The annual, week-long conferences which the SCM organized for early September were a joy to attend. I enrolled in three different years and traveled to Geneva Park on Lake Couchiching, sometimes from Muldrew Lake, sometimes from a different direction.

At worship on my first morning at Lake Couchiching, I was astounded to notice that almost all of the 100-odd students were singing the hymns in spontaneous four-part harmony. Music was always a big part of those gatherings. The choir would give a concert on the last day with 80% taking part! One year, Russell Ames Cook[23] from Massachusetts led us in a program that included *Hallelujah, Amen* from Handel's *Judas Maccabeus*. The parts answer each other, and often as some of us were out for an evening walk, if one group started that number, another from the darkness would spontaneously respond.

The SCM had its theme song, written to parody our critics.

The first verse and chorus will show the flavour:

> *The SCM has found its true vocation*
> *It is poisoning the student mind.*
> *Its leaders, by astute manipulation,*
> *Are poisoning the student mind.*
> *And pious souls are sure that we will go*
> *To toast our toes at furnaces below,*
> *If we give heed to leaders, who, they know,*
> *Are out for poisoning the student mind.*
> *Poisoning the student mind!*
> *Poisoning the student mind!*
> *Bad men, bold men, villains double-eyed,*
> *'Neath their smiling countenances hide*
> *Spiritual arsenic, moral cyanide,*
> *For poisoning the student…*
> *Poisoning the student…*
> *Poisoning the student mind.*

Other verses began:

> *"But let us not forget the theologians,*
> *For they're the finest in the land…"*

And:

> *"There's just one thing that we forgot to mention…*
> *The student hasn't got a mind…"*

One year, our study theme was the book of Amos. By the end of the week, the words had become familiar. From day one, we had been wakened each morning by a student whose name was David Scott as he did the rounds hitting a frying-pan with a spoon. And, in a parody read out at our closing event, the words, "Shall a trumpet be heard and the Lord not have done it?" became, "Shall a frying pan be heard and a Scott not have done it?"

I can't begin to list the big names who shared their talents at these gatherings. In the 70s, Wilbur Howard[24] became the first and only black moderator of the United Church. At Couchiching, nearly 40 years earlier, he was a tremendous sing-song leader. Then there was E. A. Corbett[25] who was very popular for his poetry recitations. I remember at one of our mealtimes, those at one table were heard to chant, "E.A. Corbett, we want the baseball game," after which the said Mr. Corbett who worked in Adult Education, stood up to recite with the accent of an Habitant a famous entertaining poem[26].

Because of the great freedom of thought that was accorded, the campers included a lot of socialists (the majority probably accepted the social gospel), one or two very vocal communists and enough conservatives to keep our thinking real. One night I heard one of the communists asking his room-mate to make the supreme sacrifice—to drive him to Orillia at 5:00 am the next morning so that he could begin hitch-hiking to Toronto. We had some great philosophical arguments, the Communists tending to believe that the end justifies the means, we responding that the means determine the ends.

Returning to the campus, where classes resumed in the last week of September was like coming down off the mountain to the real world. In contrast to the SCM, the Varsity Christian Fellowship[27] (VCF) was preferred by many students for its literal interpretation of the Bible, and for the emotional testimonies that characterized many of their meetings.

One VCF enthusiast used to appear often in my room in Burwash Hall during my first year. My room-mate was Sam Henderson who had grown up on a farm and who subsequently had a career as a United Church minister. He had a Presbyterian friend who was a former jail inmate, a born-again Christian who loved to preach to anyone within earshot. "He changed water into wine," I remember him saying in our room with a tone of voice that suggested that this was Jesus' chief claim to fame.

Each year, the SCM used to hold a service in Convocation Hall with a distinguished guest speaker, and President Cody was invited to conduct the service. If the main address didn't please Dr. Cody, he would feel free to reply to it before the end of the service. One of these services was reported by the Varsity[28], the student newspaper. The article mentioned the reading of scripture by Dr. Cody and it appeared as follows, "In my father's house are many mansions. If it were not so, I would have told you," said Dr. Cody.

CHAPTER 14

# University—Politics

Many parents of university students worry about the amount of time their sons and daughters spend on extra-curricular activities, time they suspect is needed for regular studies. I believe I somewhat countered those fears by being successful in my second year. By the time of my graduation, my father had become thankful that, as a result of my activities, I had learned to think on my feet.

I first participated in a CCF activity when I went door-to-door in a federal by-election in Toronto Broadview. I doubt that I was very effective, not having been trained by the Lewis family. But I wanted to support Prof George Grube, who was to become the favourite convention chairman in future years, and whose family we got to know on Muldrew Lake when they rented the old green cottage[29] just south of Indian Landing on North Lake. He never had a chance against former mayor Tommy Church who enjoyed a wide personal following which had little to do with his political ideas.

On campus, we formed a CCF Club. We were courted by the CCYM (The Cooperative Commonwealth Youth Movement). But after attending a meeting at which several CCYM leaders acted in an immature manner, we opted for the senior body. I was the first secretary, Ken McNaught the first president. We held meetings, free of charge, either in the Women's Union or in Wymilwood.

We had trouble over one meeting. Charlie Millard[30], later an MPP and head of the Steelworkers, was at that time head of the Autoworkers and had just been chosen President of the Ontario CCF. We invited him to a public meeting at which he was to speak on "Why Hepburn[31] must go."(Hepburn was the reactionary Liberal Premier of Ontario at the time.) We put notice of the meeting in the free bulletin board of the Varsity well in advance. But, due to crowding, the notice didn't appear until the day of the meeting. Late in the afternoon, a member of the club came to tell me that President Cody had cancelled our meeting. Subsequently, he called Ken and me onto the carpet. At that meeting, he gave three reasons for his action: we had failed to ask his permission to bring a speaker from off campus. That was quickly dealt with when Ken reported that he had asked a friend in The Conservative Club if they had sought permission to bring in George Drew[32] in the recent past. They had not. But Dr. Cody hastened to remark that, if they had, he would have said, "Certainly"!

Well the CCF did not have a leader at that time and Charlie Millard, as our president, was the closest thing we had. But Dr. Cody had a story a business man had told him that Millard had used bankruptcy to avoid paying debts. Only later in the day did Ted Jolliffe explain that the story was not true. Following the crash of 1929, Millard's lumbering business had failed and a creditor had forced him into legal bankruptcy. But Dr. Cody didn't consider Millard a fit person to be addressing students.

But his third reason was the real one. Dr. Cody had been summoned to Queen's Park to explain the Varsity notice and had been warned that the incident had put at risk the Government grant to the University. "Do you realize, Mr. Ewing, that this university has a deficit of nine million dollars?" That would have been our fault! We held the meeting off campus the next week. It was well attended, but it was not reported in the Varsity.

When Ken McNaught graduated, Dudley Bristow became our president. He used to tell people that the CCF was Christianity applied to politics but he didn't inspire people by the way he ran a meeting. Some folks thought we should have elected Al Schroeder, though he was unable to finish his college courses for want of money. Schroeder was a CCF candidate in St. Catharines in 1945. I next saw him in Ottawa in 1971 where he was supporting David Lewis[33] for national leader of the New Democratic Party, successor organization to the CCF.

Dudley had a career teaching high school, but worked hard for the party over the years. Ted Jolliffe[34], whose father had been a missionary in China, became the first Ontario CCF leader in 1940 at the first convention I ever attended. He had been a frequent speaker at our campus meetings. Once, Agnes Klinck (later Agnes Herbison) who was a good university friend of ours asked him, "What are we to do with people who refuse to work?" and was told that it was a fundamental socialist principle that he who doesn't work, doesn't eat!

CHAPTER 15

# University— Ontario College of Education (OCE)

During my last year in Arts, several people who had gone on to the College of Education warned me against that institution. They said that it didn't allow students any freedom of expression. When I got there the following year, I found this not to be true, and concluded that these advisors must merely have proved to be unsuited to teaching.

We five graduates of the Arts music course (Eleanor Dillon, Buck MacMillan, Donald Kennedy, Irene Haffey and I) were enrolled in the course for specialists in high school vocal music, and, as such, spent considerable time in the tiny office of Leslie Bell[35]. Bell was, at that time, conductor of the Harmony Symphony Orchestra, an organization of musicians waiting to be accepted into the Toronto Symphony. More famously, he directed a ladies' choir that began as an Alumnae Choir of graduates of Parkdale Collegiate where Bell had taught, and that was later re-named the Leslie Bell Singers that appeared frequently on the CBC. I particularly remember their rendition of the Spiritual, *Rock a' my soul.*

Bell gave us a lot of useful information for our future careers, such as the importance of cultivating the support of the school janitor, and the way the copyright laws affected the copying of music.

We got involved in assisting in the preparation of the Gilbert and Sullivan *Trial by Jury* in the neighbouring University of Toronto Schools[36] (UTS), an experience that was helpful, eight years later, when I produced it in Regina. A lead soloist of UTS was a boy with a bad stutter. I found that the rhythm of a song overrode this condition completely.

In learning to do music appreciation with average boys, one trick was to play a number without comment repeatedly as a class was assembling, until students began asking what it was. By that time, the music was familiar enough that the discussion would have some meaning. We were also introduced to music useful for this purpose in grade 9—stuff like Tchaikovsky's *Nutcracker Suite*, Saint-Saens' *Dance Macabre* or a jazz fugue called *Bach goes to Town* by Alec Templeton[37].

After Christmas, we were sent to different schools in Toronto for practice teaching. First, I went to Malverne Collegiate at the east end. When we got there, the kids were higher than kites because of a special event. But, while I didn't learn discipline there, I got some good advice from John Wood, the music teacher, on how to entice the students into enjoying the serious classics.

At that time, the Toronto Symphony held a series of concerts for high school students. The program would always include a stunt number. With the older established music, Wood would play a recording of what was coming up. After one concert, the students were asked what they enjoyed most and almost unanimously answered the *Mozart G Minor Symphony* which, by then, they knew, rather than the stunt number which was unfamiliar.

My second practice school was Lawrence Park where I had Harvey Perrin[38] as a critic. He assigned to me the arrangement of a hymn tune (*Dundee—French*) four ways for his school orchestra—straight, with a faux bourdon, with a flowing bass and with a descant. I was given a month to get it done, and was told I could get any help I wanted. After a time, when completion on time seemed doubtful, he told me that its purpose was to see whether I had "the guts" to get that much work done. I got Buck MacMillan's help and we produced a very good piece of work. He had his orchestra read it and he pronounced it very good, excepting one note we had written for oboe that

*Don, graduation photo*

was below its range.

Perrin told us a story to illustrate the kind of parental prejudice you can encounter. When teaching the history of mediaeval plainsong, he invited in a Catholic Priest who happened to be an expert on the subject. A parent criticized him for calling the man, "Father"!

Back at OCE, our "guts" were tested by another professor. About January, Prof Cornish of Geography gave us all a major assignment: we were to do a contour map of our home county, plotting an economic feature like the incidence of cattle or the occurrence of mines or industries. So we slaved away and finally got them in, only to be told that we would not be marked on the quality of our effort. The assignment was to be something we would NEVER assign to high school students! We finished the year with the relevant certificates. But my good fortune was that I was able to complete the year at teachers' college by June, 1942, when I got called up for alternative service and was ordered to board a train for New Westminster, BC one night at midnight. If they had called me earlier, I might have had to interrupt my schooling.

CHAPTER 16

# Muldrew Lake— The First Year

In the last 74 years, I have moved nineteen times. But, in all that time, one thing remained constant and that was the cottage. The length of time spent there has varied. But there has been only one year—1943—in which I was never at Muldrew Lake. I hope the reasons for this consistency will become evident in what I have to tell.

In my early years, I became aware of a club in Toronto called the Watsonian Club which held annual dinners in January where graduates of Watson's School in Edinburgh could be nostalgic. I remember the discussion Dad, an old Watsonian, used to have with Mother as to whether or not to go that year. He must have gone from Oshawa in 1927, because in the following September, another Watsonian, Prof. E. A. Dale, made a visit to Oshawa with his son, Tom, to make a proposal.

The proposal was that we rent a cottage from him the following summer. In 1919, he had built a second cottage on half of an island owned by an eccentric professor named Sam Hook. In 1927, Prof. Hook moved to England, and sold his half of the island to the Dales. Thus the Dales had an island to themselves and two cottages, one of which they wished to rent. As a result, we found ourselves, near the end of June, 1928, pulling into the landing for the first time, in an open touring model Ford driven by my Uncle Charles Rutherford with my Aunt Helen. As the lake came in sight, my uncle said, "There's a boy," who was soon

*Tom Dale*

*Using the Mantlepiece for Dale rowing lessons*

identified as Tom Dale who had been sent to meet us.

It is doubtful if any other family could have done a more thorough and successful job of introducing the Ewings to life on Muldrew Lake than the Dales. The bonfires on Wash Rock; the picnics up the lake where use was always made of the billycan to make tea, and Mrs. Dale's oatmeal date squares nearly always finished our meals; the canoe trips on the Severn River; the open air services; the walks to Gravenhurst; and the games of Mahjong were just a few of the activities that enriched our two-month stay in Northerly, the old Hook cottage.

In those days, we went everywhere either by rowing or by paddling canoes. The Mantlepiece, a flat-sterned boat that Mr. Dale had acquired for a motor that never ran, was the craft with the most floor space and was frequently rowed with two banks of oars.

One day, while the Rutherfords were still visiting, some of us took the Mantlepiece to the dam and back. Aunt Helen decided to troll as we went. She had no significant tugs on her line, but on our return as we approached the island, she rolled it in and finding a small fish on the line, she squealed. My brother Alec, then four years old, thought her squeal meant fear, and, from then on, was afraid of fish. When someone brought in a fish he had killed and laid it on the kitchen counter, Alec would notice a wiggle and give the thing a wide berth.

The row boat we were assigned was smaller with pointed ends. One day, Dad and I had an errand at the landing, and, in returning, found the NW wind somewhat challenging. We used the two banks of oars and afterward, Dad told Mother that "Donald had pulled like a man!"

At the age of 11, I had not yet experienced an area with such open rock until that summer. On the day we arrived, I had very soon explored the entire coast of the rocky island, about an acre in size that we had come to inhabit. Every shore had a different rock formation and I believe I got a bit lost in following the shore. But I was higher than a kite in reaction to the terrain.

I also had to get used to Muldrew paths. I had become accustomed to the kind cows made on the farms in Southern Ontario when the ground was soft. I once asked Mr. Dale how he knew where to go, and he called my attention to some quite unfamiliar markings. In the paths at Muldrew, it was the concentration of old pine needles that marked the paths rather than the footprints of the cows.

It was that summer that I learned to swim. On previous visits to Rice Lake or Lake Ontario, hay fever had affected my breathing and I hadn't persevered. At least that was my excuse. I may, however, have been influenced by the fact that my friend Tom, who was just three months older than I was in 1928, had already, become a good swimmer. Another factor had to do with the rule that only swimmers were allowed to use a canoe by themselves. Keeping up with Tom in the water and being allowed the freedom from adult supervision in the canoe were strong incentives to learning to swim.

That summer, a bee was organized to help Dr. Pidgeon put on a new roof. Bees, of course, were most commonly used on farms for cooperation in harvesting or barn-raising. This is the only example I have been aware of on our lake. On this occasion, Prof Dale, my father and Tom all went up to help. It was while they were gone that a violent storm occurred which had nearly disastrous results. The Lavell Smiths were arriving on the lake and they stopped at the island to deliver mail. Mrs. Dale urged them not to continue because the sky was black. Undeterred, Lavell insisted on going on since he wanted to get to his cottage in good time.

The Smith flotilla was complicated. Lavell was rowing a flat-bottomed punt, while a student sat in the stern with Margaret, aged 3. Towed behind the punt was a canoe with Emily (Mrs. Smith) paddling in the stern and Dorothy in a basket in front of her. Behind this canoe, a turtle-decked canoe was being towed. Each craft was loaded with baggage.

They had achieved about ten boat-lengths away from the island when the storm struck in all its fury and brought the whole flotilla quickly to the island in front of the boathouse. We, the four younger Dales, our mothers, and I hurried down to help. At one point, Lavell was standing in shallow water trying to get Margaret out of the boat, but was prevented from acting because waves kept pushing the boat against him. By the time we got all the people ashore, both canoes had capsized spilling their contents in the lake. The second canoe had broken its painter and been blown over to an area of deep water.

Over the next week, divers and grappling irons were put to work to retrieve the Smith's belongings from the lake. I remember going with Prof Dale each evening to the Smiths with stuff that had been recovered and being treated to chocolate bars!

When the storm had begun, Lavell had taken off his vest to

*Don & Alec with homemade boat*

get control of the oars. A few hours later someone picked the vest out of the lake and claimed that a watch was still ticking in a pocket. Many years later, I was trying to put this story together for the Muldrew history. Members of both the Bartlett family (that year in the Ozburn log cabin) and the Scovil family claimed that one of their ancestors had found the vest. But I checked with Lavell about the watch. He remembered that item being in his pants pocket! Thus stories grow in the telling. I hope that my memory of other details has been more accurate.

What convinced my parents that Muldrew was where we must continue to holiday was the fact that it had been the first July that I had been free of hay fever. They set about looking for a cottage site. They chose a property that jutted out into the western end of the lake with a morning view of the sunrise to the east and an afternoon view of glorious sunsets. In that choice, they had a piece of luck. That same day, only half an hour later, Fred Bartlett approached Professor Unwin about the same property and Professor Unwin had to tell him that my father had already spoken for it. Our property had two rock projections at the end of the point. This was, then, the source of the name the Dales had given it. That night at supper, Tom told his family with great excitement, "The Ewings have taken Twin Point!"

CHAPTER 17

# Muldrew Lake—1929-1942

John McPhee came to the Muskoka area early in the 20th century to farm. It was only after he arrived that he found that he had almost no arable land. But he acquired a herd of cattle, his wife developed a small vegetable garden, and, to add to his income, he did jobs for cottagers. Shortly after World War I, he met the Dales at the train at Kilworthy with a horse and buggy. Later, he and his energetic son Ken did many taxiing trips by car. It was long before the days when milk had to be pasteurized and he sold milk regularly to the cottagers within a short time of the milking.

A few cottagers had ice-houses to keep their food cool. The best way to organize this was to have a bed of sawdust in the bottom of the ice house upon which the ice would rest. If they had sawdust and didn't open them up all that often and if they had enough ice delivered, some people's 'cooling system' would last until fall. In winter, for $25 each, John McPhee would fill each of them with ice from the lake.

He and Ken delivered messages since his was, for some time, the only phone on our arm of the lake. And, though he had no training as a carpenter, he built cottages. I believe that our first cottage building, plus the outhouse, cost Dad around $400 (multiply by about 25 for today's values). The place consisted of one large and two small rooms, one of the latter a screened-in porch. It sat on a bit of land seven-eighth's of an acre in extent though the shore line was much more extensive than the distance from the rocky shore in front to a sand bay at the back.

The place was named Thirlstane Point since Dad had grown up in a row house on Thirlestane Road in Edinburgh while Mother had been raised on a farm near Cobourg, Ontario, named Thirlstone. Mr. McPhee also planted 200 pine trees on

*The old cottage, built in 1929*

the property, a number of which are now tall and healthy.

Since some kind of water craft was a necessity, we took some excellent advice and ordered a 17-foot cedar-strip skiff from the Brown Boat Co. at Lakefield, north of Peterborough[39]. Dad made the order in plenty of time, but he received a letter from them in June promising delivery of the boat 'in early July'. A long distance phone call (in those days, you made one of these only on very serious business) got results so that this burlap-covered boat was waiting for us at the landing when we arrived late in June.

This boat and a very few like it were the envy of many cottagers, partly because it rowed so easily, partly because of its appearance, and partly because, whenever it was entered into a race at the annual regatta, its occupant was almost always the winner. At the beginning of the season when the boards were dry, the boat leaked badly, and had to be soaked full overnight, and then kept on the sand beach in contact with the water. Our primitive dock was at the front. Therefore, when the family was going anywhere, Mother would ask me to bring the boat 'round. (Like James and the horse).

In the three years before we got our first canoe, I also used the skiff to learn to paddle, sitting in the stern with the bow in the air. In our second year, the Corbens, friends from Oshawa, rented the Ozburn cottage where the only craft was a canoe. As Mr. Corben had rowed in England, but had no experience of a canoe, we exchanged our skiff for the canoe in the two weeks of their stay. During that time, I received some expert lessons in rowing and learned to master the canoe.

Those early days on the lake were very different from what it became some years later. Every night, we cottagers went to the landing to meet one of the McPhees—usually Ken—who would bring our mail (our address was c/o John McPhee, Kilworthy, ON) and our milk, still warm from the cows' udders. The timing of the McPhees' arrival would vary with the season, and we would visit, sing and sometimes dance to take our minds off the mosquitoes! We learned that, to find pasture, these cows would wander farther west as the season progressed, so that we could sometimes gauge our departure time from the cottage by the volume of the cow bells.

Water for all purposes was brought to the cottage by pails from the lake. Dishwater was thrown out the back door. Cooking was done on a wood stove, with a three-burner coal oil stove for hot weather. Lighting was done by coal oil lamps, the luxury being the Aladdin Lamp which gave a better light when the wick didn't carbon up. Cans from much of our food were sunk in mid-lake after being either washed with the dishes or incinerated. For the latter purpose, Dad had two fire-places, one on each side of the point depending on the direction of the wind.

Not being in possession of an ice-house or having access to ice, our only refrigeration was obtained through a hole in the ground. The deepest we could dig in that rocky land was about 18 inches. But we lined the hole with lumber and made a wooden lid to fit. Butter remained amazingly firm in this hole. But, of course, we just didn't get food that needed to be kept more than a day or two.

Most of our food—we had no car in those days—came to the landing when Grove's store in Gravenhurst brought our orders to the landing while taking our orders for their next visit. They came two or three times a week.

There were always mosquitoes inside the cottage, and we used to plaster our faces and arms with Citronella or Mosquito oil. We were using the latter one night when my Grandmother Haig was with us. Her eye-sight was very bad, and she went to bed with this stuff handy. The bugs got bad again in the night and she reached for the bottle and smeared herself with considerable relief. In the morning, it was the Castor oil bottle that was open!

The cottage was also the boat-house in winter. The first three winters, the skiff lay on its side between the front porch and the kitchen. The year we got the canoe, it rested on the boat in the same doorway. The following year, a porch was added to the cottage across the SW side. From then until 1961 when our present boathouse was built, this porch took both boat and canoe.

Some cottagers had cars, but they rarely just came for a week-end. The highway from Toronto passed through all the little towns and villages and involved lots of curves and hills. The trip took upwards of five hours each way.

Bird life was more in evidence in those years. It was not unusual, in the evening, for night-hawks to fly in great swooping motions above the lake making a 'ssst' sound; while their cousins, the whip-poor-wills, would later sing their names outside our windows. The loons were very leery of a human approach then, but have become much more used to us over the years.

One evening in our first year, we four went for a row and encountered a loon, some distance away. When she saw us, the mother loon frantically tried to teach her baby to dive. The baby seemed to pay no attention for a time. Then he finally went under. But when he didn't immediately re-appear, the mother frantically tore across the lake in search of it. But the baby had learned its lesson well. It came up a long distance from the site of the lesson.

In those years, there were no cottages farther up the main channel than the one belonging to the Pidgeons. With Tom and Hugh Dale, and sometimes others, I would explore every cranny of that end of the lake. Dewdrop Island, the trail into Big Eagle Lake, Patterson's Bay, Laurel Island, Lamaze Landing which led one to Bear Lake and Turtle Lake—these constituted a park where we could picnic, swim, pick blueberries, put up a tent for the night, or hike into other lakes that, at that time, had no human habitation. We always had fun.

But the most important aspect of life on the lake at this time (not to mention later times) was the friendships which we renewed every summer. One of our lake neighbours, Walter Moorhouse, taught Latin at Jarvis Collegiate and led a boys' group at Islington United Church which he used to bring to his cottage for a week-end each summer. He also had a column in the New Outlook, the United Church organ of the time. He had one of the first motor boats on the lake—an outboard which he ran on the Beth, a punt which he had made and named after his youngest daughter. I could recognize the sound of that motor even before it came in sight. Mr. Moorhouse also had one of the first movie cameras, and he sometimes showed his film at the Muldrew winter parties in the city. It happened once in the early 50's, when the young people had started to go everywhere in motor boats, that he showed pictures from the thirties when these kids' parents went around in row-boats and canoes. I wasn't there, but I heard it was a real revelation to the teen-agers!

Of the Moorhouse family, the oldest was Wilson. His cleverness can be gauged from what he once did to me. I took him out in our canoe one calm evening and, with a box between us, proceeded to teach him chess. (He at least contended that he had never encountered the game before). But he beat me by fool's mate!

Ruth Moorhouse was a blue-eyed blond who married and

moved to Edmonton in 1940 which was the last time she was at the lake. Now she enjoys a large number of descendants from her residence on Vancouver Island. Noreen, who lost a husband in World War II, now lives in Toronto. Wilson and Beth are no longer living.

Archdeacon Scovil of St. George's Church in Guelph holidayed alternately in New Brunswick and Muldrew. His son Coster, who died in 2003, played chess, Chinese checkers and other games with me in our early years. We took lectures together in History at U of T, and in our later years we discussed theology, without total agreement but with mutual stimulus. His older sister, Frances, married and lived in British Columbia.

Fred Bartlett held positions as Director of Physical Education for the Department of Education, and later for Queens University. During the Second World War, while I was practice-teaching at Malvern Collegiate, a detachment of cadets were being drilled on the school playground. I was easily able to recognize Fred's distinctive voice as it rang out far beyond the most distant cadet.

At Muldrew, we would often sit in his cottage living-room while he proclaimed his views on the state of Ontario affairs. He once called George Drew "a dandy Minister of Education" because, knowing he wasn't an expert, he knew where to find the expertise he needed. I can still picture Fred's paddling stroke as he moved steadily up the far shore of our channel, and hear his two-note whistle when he paused at our rock. Dad was greatly impressed one day at the regatta when a young girl had dumped her canoe. Fred lifted the girl's canoe over his own canoe and balanced it while he paddled to shore. His daughter, Rosemary Bartlett, one of our very best friends, was born later.

The Dales, of course, remained special, and we did more things with them than with anyone else. An event that was always celebrated in big style was Tom's birthday on July 27th. One year, the Dales limited the people invited for supper, with more to come later for the bonfire. When the day came, there was doubt in our family as to whether parents were invited to supper. So we watched down the lake and noticed that, with the Scovils and Moorhouses, only children were going. So I set off alone. On arrival, I was asked what I had done with my parents. When I explained our confusion, Billy, Tom's younger brother, was dispatched in a skiff to get my parents. He pronounced from the lake in a real Scottish brogue, "Ye're to come to the pairty!"

Another time, Mother was giving Mr. and Mrs. Dale dinner. She put the dinner plates on the back of the cook-stove to warm. But the Dales arrived quietly and, suddenly realizing they had arrived, Mother sent the plates crashing to the floor. I don't remember what we ate from, that day. But Mrs. Dale revealed that someone had left her an extra set. "We'd like you to have them," she said.

But the place where one was probably most keenly aware of the quality of Muldrew people was at the open-air services. Started by Prof. McLaughlin on his cottage porch in the early years of the 20th century, the services, held at the south end of what we used to call the Middle or Hook portage, were well established before I arrived at the lake. After trying various sites, the community finally settled on Memorial Pines, donated to the community by the descendants of Professor Potter.

*Open air service, Dr. Pidgeon looking at the camera*

The rock formation of the site was natural for the purpose. The speaker behind the lectern faces a rock wall in front of which people are seated on benches and above it where people sit as if in a gallery. To the left of the speaker, people are seated on a slight elevation, again in front of a higher rock wall. Sometimes, teen-agers or younger children would sit above this wall, and drop acorns on the folk below. To the right of the speaker, some people used deck chairs.

A different speaker or group of speakers would conduct each service in July and August. Some were clergy, some lay. At one time, it was recommended that lay people do this work to give the clergy present a rest. But lay leaders usually had to spend much more time in preparation, compared with ministers who could often pull out an old sermon from a barrel. Dad sometimes took a service, but usually had a migraine afterwards from having to get up in front of all those Doctors of Divinity. I once told this to Reverend Lavell Smith who pointed out that Dad probably had never had a more sympathetic audience. And the ministers usually felt that their preaching should be special for this community.

Typically, most of those attending these services would spend as much time visiting as in worshipping. On a lake where friends have often brought friends, the people we knew often introduced other interesting visitors. There would be people we knew but had not seen for a long time and needed to catch up. Social arrangements were often made on these occasions since no one yet had telephones in their cottages.

I can't possibly do justice to the array of leaders we had. There was, of course, Dr. George Pidgeon, the first moderator of the United Church, who gave us an annual sermon until his wife started to be protective of his health and told the organizing committee that he had to be saved for Bloor Street Church in Toronto. Once I remember his theme was, "It couldn't be done, but he did it!" On another occasion when, for some reason, no one had brought a Bible, he asked the congregation to repeat from memory the 53rd chapter of Isaiah, and, with a little prompting, they managed it!

The Smith brothers, Lavell and Lloyd, could always be counted on to preach. They started from very different viewpoints, but each had something special to give us. Reverend Donald Solandt, steward of the United Church Book Room, used the phrase, "Helped, just helped," though I don't remember the context. Reverend Mr. Beecroft once preached on stretching our minds. He had a knack of stopping in midsentence in such a way that you would know just what the rest of the sentence would have been. Once, when Aunt Mary was home on furlough from Japan, Dad took the service while she preached. Another year, Dad spoke on the beauty of nature. He took as an example the sound of the whip-poor-wills. Alas, Mrs. Robb, a tenant of the Scovils, objected strongly because a whip-poor-will had kept her awake for half the previous night. Professor Irwin, ancestor of many on the lake, spoke each year. Once, at least, he tackled the problems of Job. Reverends Harold Hendershot, Art Waters, and Arthur Cragg were regular preachers. The latter once described Joseph's coat of many colours beach towel. His sister, Millie Norris, used to tell wonderful children's stories. Sometimes they were easier to remember than the sermons!

Archdeacon Scovil led some memorable services, and tended to encourage the ecumenical nature of the services. In those days, Anglicans seemed to prefer worshipping in a building more than United Church folk. But many came to our services over time. I remember the day Dr. Scovil announced the departure of Coster and Mary for China, a journey that lasted only sixteen months[40] because of Mao Zedong activities.

It was during one of Aunt Mary's visits when home from Japan that Tom Dale and I got interested in Loon Lake, which was parallel and North of our North Lake, and which at that time was totally uninhabited. The biggest attraction was the string of seven islands which Tom proceeded to name after islands of the Hebrides. The largest, of course, became Skye.

The first time, Tom and I went to Loon Lake and built a raft. The next day we brought friends and relatives along for a picnic on one of the islands. The raft was used to ferry those who were not strong swimmers. I can visualize Wendy Jones' mother, sitting on the raft, and wondering how long it would take us to get her to the nearest island. Aunt Mary, who, the year before, had swum a mile on the Japanese Lake Nojiri, chose to be one of the swimmers.

The next year, we built a boat of galvanized iron, planks, and tar with dimensions 6 feet long, two-and-a-half feet wide and one-and-a-half feet high. It was for something light to carry the mile-and-a-half to Loon Lake from the North Lake Landing. Aunt Mary called it the Cha Wan or rice bowl. It got us all to Skye but it was slow as only two people could get aboard at once. Aunt Mary used to value the effort expended more than the result of such projects. Perhaps it was the process of building it that we enjoyed most.

*Alec and Don in the Cha Wan*

Then there were the people we used to see at the landing when we used to the landing to come and go. There was the Middlebrook family who had descended from original immigrants. The McPhees seemed not to like them. But, one day I noticed Dr. Pidgeon addressing one of them with the same respect he gave to others. I told this to Mother who replied, "Your father does that too." It was a valuable lesson.

Hermie Middlebrook was a son who never grew very tall and had a very endearing way of expressing himself. One day the family lost a pig and was fearful that, like most pigs, it would cut its throat with its sharp toenails while swimming. After weeks, Hermie excitedly announced the animal's return, "And he's as fat as a pig," he cried.

Then there was Frank Ford who inhabited a one-room building by the lake. In the evening, he could be heard singing with a persistent croak. He was an excellent fisherman who told us that the best fishing hole in the lake was just off our point.

CHAPTER 18

# Muldrew Lake—Canoe Trips

In 1932, our family got its first canoe. Because it was purchased (for $50) with money Dad had received from his sister, Mima, we called it the Jemima. It was another cedar-strip product of the Brown Boat Company but since it had been used for livery purposes, it had been painted green. A few years later, a man who claimed expertise in boats told me that canoes of the shape of Jemima hadn't been made since 1899! But it would have been interesting to have kept track of the mileage the canoe had covered in the intervening decades.

At that time, our lake was an ideal location for canoe trips. Through the creeks—Muldrew Creek, Morrison Lake and Morrison Creek—we had access to the Severn River and the whole Trent Canal system. And from the North Lake landing it was just a two-mile carry to Muskoka Lake, one of the three large lakes of the area, and, through the North and South Muskoka Rivers, one had access to a large number of lakes and rivers to the north and east. Now, alas, camping sites—even picnic sites—are very hard to find.

I was introduced to the creeks in 1928 by Professor Dale who took Dad, Tom and me on a one-day trip to the Severn, around a large artificial island in the river, and home. We used Oriole, the Dales' cedar-strip canoe. Professor Dale was always in the stern. Dad and Tom shared most of the bow paddling, while I, as the least experienced passenger, got to paddle just between two portages.

The first portage, on the way down the Muldrew Creek, took us around the rapids that are below the dam. Then we paddled for about ten minutes, often in view of both pickerel weed and cardinal flower. This brought us to the falls, which occasioned a short, but rough portage. The next obstruction was a farmer's bridge. Depending on the amount of rain in the creek, one could pass carefully under the bridge, or would have to carry around it either because the water was too high or too low. Farther down, there was a ridge of rock, and farther still, within sight of the Road 13 Bridge, a short rapid that could sometimes be floated over. Then, there were rocks to be avoided under the bridge; soon there was a hair-pin turn and suddenly you were in Morrison Lake. Doing this creek would normally take about 45 minutes.

In Morrison Lake, one had a choice of going east or west of the main island. In the Morrison creek, more than half the distance is straight sailing before the first, short carry and the second, longer one. We used to allow about two-and-a-half hours to get from our place to the Severn. Between 1930 and 1941, I followed the Severn down at least once a summer. Two miles down the Severn from the Morrison Creek, you paddled under the bridge of the transcontinental CNR near the Hydro Glen flag station. Two miles further, there was the first large hydro dam, called Swift's. There was a marine railway there. A large conveyance at the end of a cable took boats over, upstream or down. If we were lucky, we would arrive just as a boat was about to be taken over and we would share the ride. The operators wouldn't make the trip just for one canoe, though they sometimes did it for two canoes, especially if women were involved. Another two miles brought us to Severn Falls, a flag station on the CPR, where there was also a store. Then it was about four miles to the Big Chute Dam and another marine railway. A mile farther down, one came to the Little Chute, a narrows where

*Left to right: Charles Ewing, Isabel Ewing and Don*

the current was strong—manageable with power boats, but challenging for canoes going up, especially in a rainy season. Just below the Little Chute one entered Gloucester Pool, at the south end of which the river enters Georgian Bay at Port Severn.

But we rarely entered the Bay that way. North of Gloucester Pool is Six Mile Lake which can be accessed at any of five places. Also, from Gloucester Pool, one could portage to a channel leading to Honey Harbour. So we never took the same route twice.

The first trip to Six Mile Lake involved Mr. Dale, Tom and (I think) Hugh, Dad, Selwyn Griffin, a history teacher at Jarvis Collegiate who was renting a Dale cottage, and me. We stopped for dinner at the Warbick Hotel near Severn Falls, and we camped at least one night on an island on Six Mile Lake. I remember Dad had a migraine during part of the journey.

Another trip to Six Mile Lake involved Mother and Bill Stevens. Bill was a longtime schoolmate from Oshawa, whose father was the sales manager of General Motors for Canada. Accordingly, Bill tended to discuss things from a big business point of view. He once told me that socialism wouldn't work to which I responded that capitalism wasn't working. Nevertheless, we must have found a lot in common, for we palled around for most of our high school years.

*Don with Bill Stevens*

On this occasion, Bill had an expensive fishing kit, and, on the first day, as we left Six Mile at Crooked Lake in the north-west end of Six Mile, Bill managed to leave the box behind. The second day took us into Georgian Bay and back to Six Mile via Honey Harbour, Baxter Lake, Gloucester Pool and White's Dam. That night the mosquitoes got the better of us, and we were glad to get up at 6.00 am. From this island to Crooked Lake was at least an hour's paddle. But Bill and I left

Mother and went there, retrieved the fishing tackle and got back for Mother's breakfast by 8:30. How she coped with the bugs in our absence, I will never know. But that breakfast was greatly enjoyed.

In 1935, Tom, Hugh and I paddled to Algonquin Park and back. An early start brought us to Muskoka Wharf before the wind got too fresh on the large lake. At Bracebridge, we carried down the street to get around the rapids. The north Muskoka River, which widens to form Mary Lake and then Fairy Lake, is a very pleasant river. Once at the evening meal, our varied upbringing showed in our treatment of food. After Tom served a helping of rice, I horrified him by asking for milk and sugar. I don't believe Mother had ever used rice as a vegetable, as I remember it only in puddings!

From Fairy Lake through a short canal to Peninsula Lake, a one-mile carry into Lake of Bays (we didn't use the little train), and we reached the village of Dwight. The Ox Tongue River is mostly rapid in its lowest five miles. But we crazies attempted it. For much of the way, we waded and pulled the canoe till we reached Ox Tongue Lake. On later occasions, we got taken that far by truck. But, from Ox Tongue Lake to South Tea Lake, the way was good and at the top we experienced one of Algonquin Park's campsites. Because of the density of the Park's forests, rangers had established a number of campsites where one could camp in reasonable comfort. From South Tea Lake, we used Smoke Lake, Kootchie Lake (just as tiny as it sounds), Little Island Lake, Beaver Pond, and Tanamacoon, to Cache Lake where we visited Maurice Kirkland, a teacher of mine in Oshawa and a former Park ranger.

I think that we had done just enough roughing it by that time, and we were determined to use a different route home. I doubt whether the way was easier. But the variety helped. We returned by Head Lake, where Tom broke one of our three paddles by missing the well-blazed trail, the Boncheres and a chain of lakes to Kawagama Lake. All morning it rained heavily, but as we reached Kawagama the sun came out and we found a beach where we could dry things out and camp. The next day, we followed Kawagama Lake and the river of the same name. In the river I lost my running shoes when we dumped while trying to shoot some rapids. That meant a one mile walk in bare feet along a gravel road to the village of Dorset to acquire new running shoes. I vividly recall the headline in the Toronto Globe, displayed outside the store, "Liberals win all 30 seats in PEI!"

From Dorset we entered Lake of Bays and paddled south to Baysville where we entered the South Muskoka River where the current was a big help. This river joins the North Muskoka River below Bracebridge which then flows into Lake Muskoka. As with many other trips with Tom, we covered a long distance on our last day and reached home late at night. Our last Portage was the Middle Portage on Muldrew. Hugh carried a flashlight while Tom carried the canoe. Evidently, Hugh didn't always shine the light in a helpful way, because at one point, Tom lost his patience, "Hugh, do you realize that if I make one false step, I'll break my neck?"

The same year, there was a trip that involved Bill Stevens, Mother, and Agnes Brown, an old nursing colleague of hers who was a lot of fun. She was heavier than the rest of us, so that I doubt whether Jemima had a great amount of freeboard when we were loaded.

This time we descended the creeks and headed for Sparrow Lake. I don't remember whether we went on to Lake Couchiching. But I do recall that the ladies spent a night at the Port Stanton Hotel on the west shore of Sparrow Lake, while Bill and I used his pup tent on an island. In the morning, when we went to pick up the ladies, we saw a Globe heading, "Stevens forms New Party." H. H. Stevens, of the Bennett Cabinet bolted to organize the Reconstruction Party. At the time, Mother waxed enthusiastic, while Agnes thought they should stick with the CCF. At the election in the fall, they reversed. Mother voted CCF, while Agnes reported, "I voted for Stevens because our CCF candidate is just a bag of wind."

We breakfasted on the island where Bill and I had slept, cached our dunnage in the bush of the mainland, and started up the Kahshe River. We found that ascending this river took longer than we had estimated, there being nine portages and a lot of curves. On reaching Kahshe Lake, we headed for the cottage of Oshawa friends of Bill's. Since it was already almost 4:00 pm, politeness prevented us from revealing that we had had no lunch. So we accepted lemon-aid and cookies! However, our hosts offered to drive the ladies to Muldrew. We accepted this, and Bill and I headed back down the river, making much better time with a reduced load.

Near the mouth of the Kahshe River, after we had collected our dunnage, we found a farm where we asked for glasses of milk which we thought would staunch our hunger till we got home. The farmer would have given us the milk free, had we not made a faux pas. When he had asked us which lake our cottage was on, we said, "Muldrew Lake." He appeared not to have heard of it. Bill blurted out, "It used to be called Leg Lake." The farmer retorted, "Leg Lake? Leg Lake! What are they going to think of next?" We had to pay for our milk.

It was already too late in the day to use the creeks before dark. We left the canoe on North Bay of Sparrow Lake and walked the three miles to the landing, where the ladies met us after a long wait. They gave us dinner at midnight, including fried potatoes. We ate ravenously. The next day we went back for our canoe.

About 1938, Bill Stevens and I planned a trip that I'd long wanted to do. It would take us to Algonquin Park as the Dales and I had done three years earlier, down the Petawawa and Ottawa Rivers, by the Rideau Canal to Kingston, Lake Ontario to the Bay of Quinte and home to Muldrew by the Trent Canal and our creeks. We departed on the 9th of June and made good progress as far as Ox Tongue Lake. What we forgot was that this was the best time of year for the black flies. We had planned to meet our mothers in the Park and receive fresh provisions. But the Ox Tongue River had black flies in millions.

When we camped at South Tea Lake, by morning Bill was ill and his neck was swollen to twice its normal size. So when we met our people, it was to rush Bill home to a doctor and drop me back at the cottage. Allergies are different with different people. My arms and legs were a mass of blotches. But I never felt any of them. Naturally, my mother worried about having left me so alone on the lake. But such was the mail service that I couldn't get word to her in less than four days.

About two years later, I had a Georgian Bay trip in early September with Tom Dale and John Coleman, subsequently a professor at Queens University. We took the Dales' 17-foot canoe because of its higher gunwales. From the Honey Harbour Area, we set off to Porte au Baril, north of Parry Sound. Encouraged by a gentle SW wind, we went outside the islands and made great time. The problem was the mosquitoes. At Muldrew these insects vanished from about the end of July. But on the Georgian Bay islands, they bred as long as the warm weather lasted. I can remember hastily serving myself a plate of beans at the fire, running with it for 100 yards before taking a bite, and another 100 yards before the next, etc. On one of these movements I slipped and got slime on my pajamas. I remarked, "It'll dry off." John Coleman replied, "It will probably dry on!"

*Tom & Don, grown up*

At Porte au Baril, we were welcomed and hosted for two nights by Dorothy Fleming, one of Tom's SCM friends. The next day was very wet. When coming in like drowned rats, his friend asked, "Was this being gentlemen?" "Yes," said Tom, "Gentlemen of the first water!"

The next day, a strong north wind came up, and blew us

back—inside the islands this time. We repeatedly had all to paddle on one side to avoid being swept broadside by the long waves. But this wind also swept away the mosquitoes. So that night we slept without our tent. We each found the softest bit of ground on which to rest our sleeping bags.

I spent my summer in 1941 as a counsellor at Camp Ahmek on Canoe Lake in Algonquin Park. Counsellors had a weekly day off, during which we could borrow a camp canoe. I had one such day while my parents were visiting the Kirklands on Cache Lake. To get there, I had to paddle from Canoe Lake to Smoke Lake, with portages to Koochie Lake, to Little Island Lake, to the beaver pond and to Tanamakoon Lake, which is on the same level as Cache. My timing for returning had to involve making sure that I got over the last portage before dark. I fear I was not scintillating company that day, for I remember wanting to sleep the day away, and having to be wakened in time to depart.

"Before dark" probably meant before sundown in my plans. But, of course, dark happens sooner in the forest. In any case I was carrying my canoe across the second of the four portages when a half-grown bear appeared on the trail in front of me. When I growled at him, he got out of my way. But then the trail went in the shape of a horseshoe, and when I got round it, the bear was again in my way. So I growled at him again, and soon reached the end of the portage. I thought I had finished with him but as I launched the canoe and began to unleash the paddles, I turned around and there was the bear standing right behind me, watching my progress. Curiosity is evidently not confined to cats!

I found that many people at Ahmek were quite aware of the history of Tom Thomson, one of Canada's leading painters and a great frequenter of Algonquin Park. Tom had died mysteriously in 1917. Theories about his death abounded. One theory went that, as his body had been found with fishing line strung around it, he must have stood up to land a large fish, overbalanced, and drowned when the fish swam around him to escape. Other theories involved foul play.

Part of the Ahmek site is a natural bay. A stage would be set up at the head of the bay and campers would form an audience in canoes. One night, the presentation featured the life of Tom Thomson. Just as the presentation began a possible explanation of his death, a violent thunderstorm began, forcing the rest of the drama to be cancelled. There were also stories that a canoe with no people in it would be spotted drifting some moonlit nights. Not, of course, that that proved anything.

In one of Tom Thomson's writings, he mentions needing a new supply of Klim. On our early canoe trips, Klim, the backwards spelling of Milk, was standard equipment. Powdered whole milk, it was considered the most healthful form of milk, and it met many needs. Nowadays, powdered skim milk is favoured in its place. Then, I found raw oatmeal, plus a little water and Klim, stirred up, quite delectable.

Some of the campers at Ahmek were war guests—children sent to Canada by British parents for greater safety. One camper was a Herridge, son of R. B. Bennett's brother-in-law. One day he was writing to his uncle, who had moved to Britain after leaving Canadian politics and had been created a viscount. A war guest was looking over his shoulder and asked him whom he was writing to. When told, he exclaimed, in a high voice, "Oh, have you got an uncle who is a viscount? You lucky fellow." Another boy from Rochester, NY, asked in a scornful tone, "What's a viscount?"

I'll now skip forward to 1948. Eleanor and I were married in December, 1947, but had our real honeymoon by way of a canoe-trip in Algonquin Park the following August. There were still trains to the park then and we managed to check our canoe through to Joe Lake. On arriving, we met Louise Colley, an old friend of Eleanor's sister, Marg. Louise was at that time recreation director in Barrie, and was visiting her brother's cottage. She invited us, should the next day's expected rain materialize, to spend the day with them. It did rain and we helped the Colleys poke oakum into the cracks of a log cabin

*Don & Eleanor*

while settling the affairs of the world. The next day, we paddled through Joe Lake, Little Joe, and Baby Joe to Burnt Island Lake. Unfortunately, it was the week in which the summer camps had their last trips. And as well, an American family had set up camp for two weeks in one of the more prized sites. Consequently, camping for us amounted to improvising.

When we started on this trip, Eleanor had pointed out that I was not going with Tom Dale, who had a habit of racing from a great distance on the last day of trips in order to get home quickly. But the plan had been to end our journey at the Dillon cottage on Cache Lake. And guess who suggested that we go all the way from Burnt Island Lake to Cache Lake on the last day? As we paddled on a very calm surface of Canoe Lake in the late afternoon, we got singing the Green Grow the Rushes O or the Twelve Apostles as we used to call it. Some strangers passed us at a little distance. But they called back from half a mile, "Hey, what's eight?"

It was imperative that we get across the last portage before dark. We just managed that, but it darkened as we crossed Tanamacoon and pulled in to the Dillon dock. Eleanor's, "Is anyone home?" was answered by her father's loud but cordial, "Huh!"

## CHAPTER 19

# Muldrew Lake— Openings and Closings

Nowadays winterized cottages require minimum attention in spring and fall. But in the days of the early, primitive cottages, a lot of hard, and often heavy, work was required. In the fall, all watercraft had to be safely stored, screens had to be replaced with shutters, and bedding had to be stored in mouse-proof containers. In our case, upright two-by-fours were wedged into place to shore up the almost level roof of the porch to prevent it caving in if there was a very heavy snowfall; chemicals had to be put down our privies (outhouses) and pieces of tin had to be put around the pedals of the piano in a sometimes vain attempt to keep mice out of the instrument.

From my first university year, I was able to be at the cottage in June and September while my father was teaching and was able to do the honours. But it meant sleeping alone a lot. I recall hearing porcupines under the cottage at night making spooky noises. Porkies loved salt and would often chew cartons we had left there because of the saltiness of the food they had contained.

Part of the job was getting to the cottage from the landing. When we first arrived in the spring, we used a key which all Cottagers Club members carried to open the community boat-house and take out the community row-boat. We then rowed to the cottage with our stuff, got our own boat or canoe into the water and then rowed back, towing our own craft. If there was a heavy wind, this took a lot of energy to accomplish. In the fall, all this had to be done in reverse. We hoped, of course, that we had got back before anyone else needed the community boat. If no one was waiting, we then returned the boat to the boathouse and locked the door.

In one of the summers in which I worked in Uncle Don's store in Brechin, I had to close the cottage on a weekend before going to one of the September SCM conferences at Lake Couchiching. On the previous Thursday, a truck had arrived at the back door of the store with a load of white sugar in 100 pound bags. There were about 30 bags involved. In my haste to get the truck unloaded quickly, I forgot the basic rule of lifting with my knees rather than my back, and soon I was on a couch in the house seemingly unable to move. However, by the next day I felt recovered sufficiently to start hitch-hiking to Muldrew.

On my way, I arranged for a local merchant (Mr. Roach of Kilworthy) to meet me at our landing at 1:00 pm on the Monday. Then I set off for the cottage. At that time, by mid-September, the lake was completely deserted. Mr. and Mrs. McPhee, a mile from the landing, were the nearest people around. And I had no phone by which to change my plans.

On the Saturday morning, I had started to work and immediately felt my back give way. So I made a plan: I would work for fifteen minutes, and then lie down for fifteen minutes, all day Saturday and Sunday. The plan worked, whether because I was careful about my posture, when lying so frequently, or for some other reason. I only know that I was at the landing by 1:00 pm on the Monday with everything completed. Would that necessity were always the mother of invention.

CHAPTER 20

# Muldrew Lake— The Sleeping Cabin

Soon after the first cottage was built in 1929, Mother acquired a big square tent through her family connection. It required a floor if there was to be enough flat space on our property to erect it satisfactorily. So the lumber was bought, and two neighbours offered to make the floor. A neighbour, Professor McLean of the Ontario Agricultural College (OAC) whose cabin was later taken over by the Garrards, and a guest of his who happened to be the bursar of McMaster University, turned up one afternoon to do the job. A thunder storm was threatening, but they thought they could finish before it struck. This led to some rapid nailing and a rather unstable result.

The tent had nine poles—a tall one for the centre, and shorter ones for the four corners and the mid-points of the sides. I got to sleep in this tent. I'd go to bed by flashlight and wake in the daylight to read, in several places and in large lettering: *THE TENTS THAT DON'T LEAK OR ROT ARE MADE BY THE OWEN SOUND TENT COMPANY!*

I also recall, on more than one occasion, being upbraided for sleeping in by Tom Dale who would have arrived for one of our planned expeditions. "Up to your old tricks," he would say. Interestingly, after another sleeper-in, Grace, arrived on the scene, Tom's tune was different. "I've noticed that people who need a lot of sleep have kind dispositions," he said.

In 1932, a memorable storm occurred. Sunday church service was held at 5:00 pm at that time. This one was well attended, but, as distant thunder recurred throughout the service, people skipped their usual visiting and ran for their boats as soon as the benediction had been pronounced. The storm didn't strike for another 50 minutes. But when it did, it was one of the most severe I can remember.

That night, I showed my ignorance of tents. To let the tent take the wind, I should have loosened the guy ropes. Instead I had tightened them. In any case the tent was torn beyond repair. Mother was able to salvage enough of the canvass to make me a small tent for canoe trips. It was a lean-to affair with mosquito netting falling across the open end and weighed down with fishing sinkers. We needed two trees to tie the open corners and rocks to fix the canvass at the ground. I didn't keep track of the miles that tent travelled.

That left the floor, the condition of which Mother must have forgotten over the next winter. The following spring, when asking Mr. McPhee to add the west porch to the cottage, she also had him build a cabin on the tent-floor. These were depression days when one penny was being made to do the work of two. Otherwise the floor might have been rebuilt before the cabin had been erected.

As I was growing up, Mother would have breakfast ready by 9:00, and at five to, she would call me in the cabin, "Yoo-hoo." One morning I got up at 7:30 am and fulfilled a dream—that of walking completely around South Lake. At that time, there were few cottagers through whose property I would have had to trespass, and, that late in the season, I could walk through all the swamps. In the event, when Mother called me to breakfast, I was sitting on a rock across the front channel. I called back, "I'll come if you can come and get me," whereupon Dad got out the boat.

The cabin was always well used. In 1939, Norrie and Helen Frye chaperoned a week-end of three male and three female students from Victoria College. I don't recall which group slept in the cabin. But, in those days, it would not have been mixed!

Morrey was conceived in the cabin. I never knew whether that had anything to do with Sharon's par-

*Helen and Northrop Frye*

tiality for the place in later years.

Later, when Esther and Morrey were 8 and 5, a thunderstorm came at about 2:30 am. Eleanor had the wisdom to have us both join the children in the cabin till it was over. Was that why they never seemed to acquire a fear of thunder?

Over the years, there were various efforts to improve the cabin. Of course, I became accustomed to having to clean out a mouse's nest above the door. But, in the 60's, I took up a piece of linoleum that had been tacked down. Underneath I found a layer of newspaper which turned out to have been taken from *The Globe*, years before 1936 when that paper (a Liberal organ) took over the *Tory Mail* and *Empire* to become the *Globe and Mail* (far from Liberal).

In the early 80's, Esther had the cabin jacked up and a new floor installed. For the first time it ceased to rattle as you walked over the floor. For the first time, the floor was in better shape than the walls.

In 1998, when the new cottage was being built, the cabin was used for storage. But Esther managed to have the fridge stored and plugged in, in the cabin, so that while she and Jim were camping in the boat-house, they could put the fridge to good use.

In 2000, when Esther had her harmonic convergence, we needed all of our accommodation. Among the visitors were the Cory family from Oshawa with two girls, ages 13 & 10, the only children present. They were given the cabin as their space, on the understanding that, while their quarters would not be inspected till they left, they would then leave the place as they found it. They carried out their end of the bargain admirably.

The cabin has evolved into a wonderful storage facility. Shelves have been built so that stored items can be easily found, and in 2004, the floor was painted blue. The building that began as a tent floor now has its floor respected!

CHAPTER 21

# Brechin

In 1926, my Uncle Don appeared at our house in Oshawa to announce, "I've taken the store in Brechin." Brechin was a village on Highway #12, two miles east of Lake Simcoe, and served by two CNR railway lines. It was a general store of the chain of "Superior Stores", a wholesale supplier. Uncle Don and Aunt Muriel ran the store jointly, usually with the help of a hired assistant. They did this until well into World War II.

One such assistant, Charlie Hurtibees, regularly "graded" the eggs brought in by farmers. He would hold each egg up to a light and judge the quality by what he saw. I was told at the time that this was a special skill. Who in today's society would have such a skill?

The store hours were long and, as the house was attached to the store, it was sometimes difficult to avoid being bothered by customers at times when the store was closed. They would say something like, "We forgot to get butter and company is coming this afternoon." On Saturday nights, people would treat the store as a place in which to catch up on local gossip. As 10 o'clock approached, and people seemed to have left, Aunt Muriel would say, "Quick, lock the door." Otherwise no one would get their necessary sleep.

Brechin happened to be about midway between Oshawa and Muldrew Lake. This, and Uncle Don's desire to get away from possible Sunday customers, meant that he usually provided us with transportation to the lake. Sometimes, he would drive us as far as Brechin in one trip. Sometimes, he was busier and we would meet him in Sunderland, on the Toronto to Peterborough bus line. Then, two or three days later, he would take us the rest of the way. I don't believe we ever had to go to the lake via Toronto.

*Brechin Store*

Dad once remarked that the one aspect of store-keeping he could never have managed was tying up parcels. The food packages that today swell our garbage containers didn't then exist. Typically, a huge roll of brown wrapping paper would sit in a roller on the counter by the till, and a run of string would hang from a roll of it somewhere near the ceiling. When time afforded, people would be busy weighing out packages of sugar or flour in lots of 2 pounds, one pound, or half pounds. A large circle of nippy cheese was also in sight and it would be cut and wrapped to suit the customer.

Canisters and barrels that we used in our kitchen at Muldrew would arrive at the Brechin store filled with bulk foods. The pail, in which we got three pints of fresh milk each night from the McPhees, had originally held lard. These were depression years, and my uncle had his share of complaints about prices. One father of a large family kept asking for food at prices which would have been a loss for a store-keeper. Once it was the price of butter. My uncle decided to call his customer's bluff. He said, "I make only one cent on a pound of butter. But I won't see your kids starve. I'll feed them." That ended the complaints of the moment.

For two summers while I was in high school, I worked for my

uncle for $1 a day plus keep. I would bring hundred-weights of white or brown sugar from storage to dump in the barrels behind the counters. I would report on supplies in that storage area, I would sweep the floor on Sundays, and many other things that I don't recall. But I do remember my uncle arriving from somewhere announcing the jobs he had just done, with the implication that I should have done them. As I had not been specifically assigned these jobs, I put this down as evidence of a less-than-perfect employer.

There were two churches in Brechin, a large Catholic Church and a small United Church. Aunt Muriel was a pillar of the latter. She would tell me about the succession of ministers who would be called there. Some would leave a lot to be desired. One developed a mental condition and his congregation decided to give him a summer off. They arranged for a student to do the preaching for that period. Aunt Muriel enjoyed his fresh ideas. But at his last service, the regular minister got up to give the announcements and declared that he would get to the bottom of how the student had been brought in! At the Catholic parish hall, not far from Aunt Muriel's open window, there was a noisy dance every Friday night that lasted till the "wee, small hours." This is, of course, how I was told about it by a Protestant!

Uncle Don had two cottages on Lake Simcoe to rent. Sometimes we got to swim there. In contrast to swimming in Muldrew, where one dived in off a rock, here one waded out a long distance to find enough depth to swim.

For security reasons, they always kept a dog. One of them was especially clever. He liked nothing better than to go on a long ride in the car. When he saw Uncle Don taking down his keys from the sideboard in the dining-room, he would beg to be taken on the intended journey. But he was always refused at night. One night, Uncle Don was driving to Oshawa, and, somehow the dog realized there was no use begging. When the keys were taken, he just slunk away. A mile down the road, the car lights picked out a little dog barking at the car. The dog somehow knew that Uncle Don wouldn't go back once he had gone that far!

Another instance of cleverness on the part of the dog was this. Early in the 1930's in Brechin, my grandmother was there and my mother was nursing her. Grandma didn't like seeing Mother get tired and would find ways of doing jobs she wasn't supposed to do. One day Mother laid down the law with her mother before going upstairs for a rest. Grandma started to do something she wasn't supposed to do and the dog bounded up and barked until my mother came down.

Canoe trips sometimes involved Brechin. One summer, Mother and I set off in Jemima from the cottage even though it was heavily raining. I remember Mother hugging herself to keep warm as we descended the creeks and followed the Severn to Lake Couchiching. About three-quarters of the way down the eastern shore of that lake, we took shelter from an approaching thunderstorm in a cottager's boathouse and got invited up for tea. We also phoned Brechin, with the result that Uncle Don drove up with a second cousin, John Josie, a bit younger than I, in tow. Mother then drove to Brechin while John and I paddled the rest of the way. Once, in Lake Simcoe, we had to take shelter in a cottage from another storm. When we started off again, the wind had died, but the waves were large. I remember that the sensation was a bit like horseback riding.

Later that summer, Tom Dale came to Brechin to use our canoe for another trip with me to Georgian Bay. In the morning, we tried to get launched in the shallow water with waves coming in. But we realized that this was too difficult, and waited till the wind had gone down at night. The sun was setting as we departed. The ten miles we paddled up Lake Couchiching featured the best display of Northern Lights I've ever seen. They extended right across the zenith and showed us every conceivable shape. I remember feeling very cold in my shirt as we carried around a lock in the Severn River. Rather than attempt the creeks in the dark, we left the canoe at the North end of Sparrow Lake and walked the three miles to the Muldrew Lake landing. The sun was rising as we reached Dales' Island where we got several hours of much-needed sleep. The trip resumed the next afternoon.

Uncle Don had a great fund of stories. He told me once that, during the 1930's, someone advertised in the Farmer's Almanac that he would pay $5.00 for the largest potato that he received by a certain date. Evidently, the response was enormous. Some farmers sent two or three potatoes, being unsure which was the largest. The advertiser got a winter's supply for $5.00! Uncle Don was greatly impressed and amused by the advertiser's ingenuity.

CHAPTER 22

# The United Church of Canada to 1946

I am sure I was taken to church at an early age, but I don't remember Sunday school in Galt. However, I do remember a favourite hymn. It ran,

*Standing by a purpose true,*
*Heeding God's command,*
*Honor them, the faithful few!*
*All hail to Daniel's band!*
*Dare to be a Daniel!*[41]
*Dare to stand alone!*
*Dare to have a purpose firm!*
*Dare to make it known!*

As a youngster, I would often request, "Daddy, sing 'Purpose Firm'."

From Sunday school at St. Andrews Church in Oshawa, I have three memories. There was Gordon Maxwell, the minister's second son, who told us a story of how he had deceived his father. For some reason, his Dad was against his making trips to Toronto. After learning to drive the family car, he announced that he was heading east of Oshawa, then headed north and got to Toronto anyway. His father was not deceived. The moral was that God always knew where we were and what we were doing! Then there was Mr. Young, the superintendent, who led us in vigorous gospel hymns like *Bringing in the Sheaves*[42]:

*Sowing in the morning, sowing seeds of kindness,*
*Sowing in the noontide and the dewy eve;*
*Waiting for the harvest, and the time of reaping,*
*We shall come rejoicing, bringing in the sheaves.*

I suspect that he was a good example of what Leslie Bell would later characterize as 'aquatic conductors', people who swung their arms from the shoulders, reminding Leslie of swimmers. It was also Mr. Young who ushered us through a flimsy-looking gate painted with flowers to receive our Robert Raikes[43] certificates as we were promoted to the next grade.

My fourth memory was that I quit that Sunday school when I was around 12 or 13, (a) because I didn't want to have the teacher of the next grade, and (b) because Sunday school was at 3.00 pm, when the New York Philharmonic Symphony Orchestra was broadcast over Columbia and CFRB. I was allowed to do that!

St. Andrews had three successive ministers while we attended there. Mr. Maxwell was a fundamentalist whose sermons were full of archaic expressions like "God's mercy seat." He had four children, all somewhat older than I, and all Sunday school teachers. Frank Maxwell was a much sought-after accompanist for sing-songs for which he used a style involving chords that were repeated from range to range. He married a Miss McLeod of the collegiate staff, but succumbed to a terminal disease at an early age. Greta Maxwell later married Orville Hossie, a minister in Kitchener. My father used to be greatly bothered because both Frank and his brother, Gordon, made executive visits to a number of members as they were gathering for worship on Sunday morning.

Mr. Robb was more modern but tended to be somewhat superficial. After some time, people got tired of his children's stories about Billy, Bobby and Betty. At one evening service, he singled me out because he had learned that an associate of his in the First World War was Allister Haig, a cousin of mine. I remember a story about his car. Oshawa was then very much a one-industry, one-company town (General Motors) but Mr. Robb had been bold enough to purchase a DeSoto. George McLaughlin, brother of the president of General Motors, and a major contributor to the coffers of St. Andrews, let Mr. Robb know that he must get rid of the new car, or face complete withdrawal of his contributions. I was never told the rest of that story, though I understand that, a couple of decades later, even GM employees could park Volkswagens at the plant with impunity.

One Sunday after the morning service, Mr. Robb told me, "You should be coming to the Young People's Group." Because my slow habits made it difficult to get my daily homework done, I felt that I should never go out on week nights. If I had gone to Young People's, would I have related more successfully to teens later on when I actually had to teach them? Another what if!

I remember two successive organists. George Hindley had a different day job and was self-taught as an organist. He gave us a diet of great music in his voluntaries (it was in this way that I learned a movement from Carl Goldberg's *Rustic Wedding Symphony*) and played the hymns with dignity. His successor, a Mr. Taylor, never seemed to have the time right in anything. I don't recall which regime it was when, for years, the choir processed to their places every Sunday singing, *When morning gilds the skies.*[44]

> *When morning gilds the skies my heart awaking cries:*
> *May Jesus Christ be praised!*
> *Alike at work and prayer, to Jesus I repair:*
> *May Jesus Christ be praised!*

At another time, Mr. Robb called me into his manse to ask me to join the church. The major reason seemed to be the chance to take a stand against Hitler and Mussolini. I had by then got a broader, more positive view of what Christianity meant than that, and I was not impressed. Moreover, I had come to observe that Communion was central to church life, and, at that stage, it meant nothing to me except long faces on the elders as they distributed the elements and cold dinners after a prolonged service. So I did not join the church as a teenager. During university, I came to see communion as the celebration of real community in the congregation of Carlton Church in Toronto. I phoned the minister, Jim Finlay, on a

Wednesday night, and he did the ceremony for me alone the following Sunday morning.

In the decades since then, my feeling about communion has differed from those of others. To me, it is most meaningful at a retreat at which some of us have been working to deepen our faith. It is then a celebration of a new relationship with friends and with God. I have no interest in the idea that the elements are a kind of magic potion that somehow makes you a better person.

In the 70's, I attended a retreat of the supervisors of the Guelph Separate School Board. After long discussions of the Gospel, there was a concelebration of mass, led by several local priests. As a non-Catholic, I normally would not have taken the wafer, especially with the meaning that Catholics traditionally have given the ceremony. But I found myself so caught up in what the priests were doing that when one of them whom I knew well approached, I opened my mouth. Afterwards, one of my principals told me that my act of participation had had a powerful meaning for him. I had thought that I was the one being privileged!

CHAPTER 23

# Dr. J. R. P. Slater

In the 30's, my family's favourite preachers, who could usually be heard only by radio, were Harry Emerson Fosdick of New York, Dr. George Pidgeon of Bloor Street Church in Toronto, and Dr. Slater. Dr. Slater's church, Old St. Andrews United Church, (on the corner of Jarvis and Carlton Streets, one block from Jarvis Street Baptist Church where T.T. Shields, the notorious fundamentalist held forth), called him from the Old Land, as they called Scotland, soon after the constitution of the United Church. He became moderator in 1942. After his retirement, Old St. Andrews amalgamated with Westminster-Central on Bloor Street and took the name of St. Andrews.

I didn't always agree with Dr. Slater. We thought in different ways when the war came. But he was an extremely effective preacher. And, as a product of Scotland, he exemplified many of the qualities of that land which I had come to love.

Dr. Slater broadcast from evening services on a station we could receive only sporadically in Oshawa. He would tell us how loyal Scottish immigrants were to the towns they had left. Some would come to him to have their passports signed. He said, "They're not going to Scotland. They're going to Pitlochry, Sterling, or Tobermory." Another time, he was recalling a bit of history, "After Bonnie Prince Charlie was defeated at Colloden, the English put a large price on his head. The Highlanders," he said, "All knew where he was, but not one of them betrayed him."

He used a colourful way of preaching against the dictatorship of Mussolini. "I have often felt that my ideal year would constitute three months in Italy, a visit to Canada, and the rest of it in the Highlands of Scotland! But three months in Italy." He then enlarged on that country's charms.

He could make a life with God vivid. He reminded us that we are never alone. "NEVER ALONE!" And he could make scripture come alive. "O Jerusalem, Jerusalem (he pronounced it "jer-yoo-salem"), how often would I have gathered ... and ye would not."

On prayer petitions: "It's a ticklish business, this asking." I have to remember that Slater was a "modernist", who did not read the Bible literally. But he had not yet drawn the conclusions Spong[45] has, for example, about our relationship to God. In one sermon, he referred to Bach's St. Matthew's Passion. He was talking of Pilate's decision to have Jesus crucified, and he called attention to the anger of the crowd in shouting "Barrabas!" which changed his mind. Of course, this was before historians had claimed that Pilate was actually a brute who would never have acted the gentleman in this scene.

On corporal punishment, he approved of a parent's decision to give his son a real thrashing, "and it did him a wor-r-rld of good."

On Joshua's response to a report that the Canaanites were giants, "he gave them the toe of his boot and out they all went." Even then, I had noted that Joshua had, on God's orders, killed everyone, including women and children and I had begun to disagree with many of Slater's assumptions.

During World War II, while I was still in college, one afternoon I dropped in to get his view on pacifism before going to see Jim Finlay whom I knew better. Dr. Slater slammed Dr. Fosdick for his stand. "And Fosdick, of all people!" he exclaimed. He then recommended another author whom he characterized as "Fosdick gone to school." I had already examined the gospels for its bearing on the subject, and I stuck to my position.

But Dr. Slater had a persuasive way of using everyday language to drive home great truths. Once, fifteen minutes into a broadcast of one of Slater's sermons, Dad said, "This time, Slater's failed." Ten minutes later, Dad completely changed his mind.

CHAPTER 24

# The CCF[46] to 1950

The market crash of 1929 ushered in the Great Depression, which resulted in tremendous suffering. Unlike the welfare system that we can count on today, there was only "relief"—10 cents a day which bought little even with the cost of living that prevailed at that time. Oshawa had the worst unemployment in Ontario, with one third of its citizens out of work. Beggars regularly came to our door.

The churches were constantly being asked for charity and the response was often a matter of life and death. Those who founded the CCF in 1933 argued that there must be a better way of insuring that people don't suffer because of the inefficiencies of the economic system. Drafted by Toronto Professor Frank Underhill, the Regina Manifesto[47] called for economic planning, nationalization of financial institutions, public utilities and natural resources, a national labour code, security for farmers, socialized health services, and greatly increased economic powers for the central government.

The CCF was an amalgamation of the Socialist Party of BC, the Independent Labour Party of Manitoba and the United Farmers of Alberta, Saskatchewan and Ontario. Getting these groups to work together was more successfully done in the 30's than was organizing for electoral success. The idea that the poor would flock to a party with the ideals of the CCF was found to be sadly lacking in reality. Many had not heard of a party that had little money with which to advertise and many others didn't dare oppose the government of the day lest they lose what they had. It was not until the relative prosperity of the Second World War that people felt free to support a new party.

Other factors were at work. The Communist Party, renamed the Labour-Progressive Party (LPP) after the CP was banned, often ran candidates that split the CCF vote. In the 1945 federal election in BC, the CCF won four of the sixteen seats, but, in each of nine others, the margin by which the CCF candidate was defeated was less than the vote the LPP candidate received. From the mid-fifties, this was no longer a problem.

The CCF was not the only new party. In Alberta, the Social Credit Party[48] swept both provincial and federal elections in 1935, defeating several of the best CCF members who had been elected for the United Farmers. And nationally, William Duncan Herridge[49], (no relation to Bert Herridge[50]) who had resigned from the R.B. Bennett[51] cabinet to oppose a facet of business practice, formed the "Reconstruction Party". It elected only Mr. Herridge himself and lasted only one election. But it attracted almost as many votes as the CCF. The CCF won only 7 seats that year, but the calibre of the 7 was outstanding.

CHAPTER 25

# By-election, 1942

In the federal Liberal sweep of 1940, Dr. Manion, the Conservative leader, lost his seat in the riding of Port Arthur. (At this point, they called themselves Liberal-Conservatives. The term Progressive-Conservative wasn't used until 1944.) In due course, Manion resigned as leader and to have someone in place for the rest of the war period, they brought back Arthur Meighan.

Meighan had been Prime Minister from 1919 to 1921, and briefly in 1925. He had acquired the reputation of being an extreme reactionary. He was also a strong militarist. During World War One, while speaking in Winnipeg, he had been heard to say, "England is fighting with her back to the wall and Canada is right behind her." This reminds me of Tony Blair speaking of the USA.

Meighan was a senator in 1941 and, feeling he needed to lead his party from the House of Commons, he accepted the offer of Alan Cockeram, the Tory member for the riding of South York (in Toronto) to step aside in his favour. The Tories seemed unaware that, since the CCF had been founded, we had always done better in South York than in any other Ontario riding. They probably thought we couldn't win a seat in Ontario anyway.

When the by-election was called, the Liberals announced that, as usual, they would not oppose a leader. However, the behaviour of local Liberals was interesting. Taylor Statten, the well-known owner of summer camps in Algonquin Park, and a resident of the conservative Forest Hill section of the riding, publicly called on local Liberals to support Meighan. But Arthur Roebuck[52], the MPP for Bracondale, who five years earlier had been fired from the provincial cabinet by Premier Hepburn for supporting the General Motors strike in Oshawa, took a different line. He bought 15 minutes' time on CFRB to explain why he would be supporting Noseworthy.[53]

I was attending a CCF rally in Massey Hall in early January of 1942, when Ted Jolliffe, our provincial leader, came on stage to announce the decision of the South York riding association, "Senator Meighan will be opposed!" There was great applause. "And they have nominated Joe Noseworthy as our candidate", whereupon Joe walked on stage to more applause.

At one point, an Ottawa newspaper termed Joe an obscure candidate. The writer evidently didn't know that he had been teaching History for many years at Vaughan Road Collegiate and was well known and respected in the community.

The campaign affected children. One evening, two key members of our team were chatting in the home of one of them, and one said in jest that, of course, they would be voting for Meighan. But his 10-year-old son had been listening and took him seriously. He asked, "But what's he done for the people?"

One night, I was distributing copies of a special election edition of the New Commonwealth. This CCF paper had been founded in 1934 by Graham Spry. With no financial backing, it might have folded after a few issues, but for a bit of luck. Herridge, of R. B. Bennett's cabinet, brought out the report of the Royal Commission on Mass Buying and Price Fixing. Bennett was not pleased to have his friends' practices exposed and hesitated about giving it to the press. But Spry quickly printed and sold 25,000 copies as a special issue of the Commonwealth. The revenue from that issue established the paper for some time. On this occasion, it was dark, and a policeman asked me what I was selling. "Election literature, Sir. Would you like one?" I got the impression that he was for us. Joe was elected with a plurality of over 4000 votes.

*Joe Noseworthy*

CHAPTER 26

# Eleanor, Before Marriage

Eleanor and I met in the lobby of the old Conservatory at College and University, as we were registering as two of eight who were taking the Honours Music BA course that began in September, 1937. It turned out that we had been previously associated. Years later, Eleanor found an old concert program on which we had both been named. The Ontario Education Association used to sponsor an Ontario High School Choir which consisted of groups of students from all over the province who assembled during the "Easter Holidays" (Good Friday to a week after Easter) and give a concert in Massey Hall. Evidently, we had both taken part, from our respective schools, in the same year.

Eleanor told me later that, as we met, she had a sudden feeling that I was the man she would marry. But, since she didn't believe in picking one's mate in this way, she resisted for a long time any feelings she might have had that would encourage the idea. I don't recall any outward evidence of this. In the event, she was only one of a number of girls that I dated over the next four-and-a-half years.

*Eleanor Dillon*

One Saturday, we went by streetcar and ferry to Toronto Islands and hiked from one end to the other. This was familiar territory for her, since her family had lived there in the summers during her childhood. One Sunday, Eleanor invited the members of our music course to her family home in Cooksville, now part of Mississauga. Her mother, of course, was a model hostess, and her sisters Marg and Bunty and her brother Rob must all have been there, though I don't remember them then. But the most impressive experience had to be meeting her father.

Ernest Macaulay Dillon once told me that, in his early years as a lawyer, it was a struggle to support his growing family. But, in his later years, his income was "more than adequate." He had an unforgettable personality which impacted most of those he met. On this occasion, he tried to use impeccable logic to knock down some new theories about children's self-expression. This was an early example of a long-standing failing of mine: I think of answers to arguments I have heard only on the way home from a meeting. I disagreed with a lot of his views. But I had to admire the way he expressed them.

Of course, I was conscious of Eleanor all the time we were taking classes together. I knew of some of her special talents. The story of Healey Willan's poetic ventures featured Eleanor as the more vocal of the two students and the author of their verse, (See chapter 11.) None of it would have happened without her initiative. On another occasion, Leo Smith gave a recital (was it on the cello or viol da gamba?) in Victoria College's Wymilwood. One number on the program he announced as having been written by a "composer unknown". (His own modesty, of course.) Afterwards, Eleanor knowingly asked him, that if he ever met the composer, would he tell him how much we enjoyed the music!

We were also part of a music appreciation group which was started by Norrie Frye, continued during his year at Oxford by Marcus Adeney, a cellist in the Toronto Symphony, and led again by Norrie on his return. Norrie, of course, was an ATCM[54] and had many unique views on music. I recall that he found one of Bach's vigorous concerto movements absolutely hair-raising.

But I became sure of my love for Eleanor only in the spring of our year at the College of Education. Ironically, this happened only a few weeks before our enforced separation when I was sent west. We had been to a concert in Massey Hall of the Minneapolis Symphony. We noticed that Dmitri Metropolis stood still on the podium during the playing of *The Queen*. The feature was the *Fifth Symphony* of Shostakovich which subsequently became a favourite of mine. I threw the bomb, (proposed) as it were, on a park bench on our way back to residence.

After that, we had to communicate chiefly by correspondence, while I was in the BCFS[55] or teaching in Lemon Creek. This was an experience in itself. We were really very different people, with different styles of writing and different ways of talking about the things that mattered to us. Sometimes, in my letters, I would ask some rather specific questions which it didn't occur to her to answer. I'm sure that she found my letters just as exasperating at times. But, sixty years later, I have to declare that the sometimes difficult process of getting to know each other has been immensely worthwhile.

I went home for Christmas, 1942, and visited Eleanor at her home. During the next 18 months I was continuously in BC, and this period failed to support the theory that "absence makes the heart grow fonder." However, in June 1944, Eleanor met my train; we paid a visit to the camp near Borden where Eleanor had once worked. And from then on we were "as thick as thieves."

CHAPTER 27

# Marriage

Until June of 1946, I was teaching at Lemon Creek on an income that had been set when I became a conscientious objector, an income that would have made it very difficult to support a wife. And there were one or two things at Eleanor's end that made it difficult to set our wedding for earlier than December, 1947.

Of course, correspondence continued as before. At one point, Eleanor became interested in the thought that, before the war's end, I should leave my current job and go to China for the American Friends Service Committee. It was probably because I was closer to it than she was that I felt I should stay with the work I was doing, and I did.

In June, 1945, Dad retired, sold his house in Oshawa and moved to Niagara Street in St. Catharines. Eleanor's mother was at that point cool about our association and said so in fairly strong language. But Eleanor was making her own decisions, among which were visits to my parents' home and to Muldrew Lake. At Niagara Street I recall a hike we took which involved a visit to the historic Anglican Church in Niagara-on-the-Lake. Why do I remember that we embraced in front of the altar? (No symbolic meaning in this, please!)

On another occasion, after Mother and Dad had moved again, we took the ferry from Toronto to Dalhousie and the inter-urban street-car to Fonthill, from which we walked to Ledcriech. Eleanor, on at least one occasion, went there when I was in the west. As she put it, sometimes she had the feeling that British Columbia was sliding into the Pacific Ocean and wanted the feeling relieved by her future parents-in-law!

*Eleanor's parents, Ernie and Madeleine Dillon*

*Eleanor on bike*

In 1945, shortly after I had returned from the west, she wrote me about a new teaching job—the place—Oshawa! In the 2 1/2 years she taught at OCVI, my old high school, she made friends with several people that my parents and I had known well. They included Dorothy Van Luven who taught me first form Art and Latin, Ada Kelly who had been a close neighbour of ours, and the Kirklands who had a cottage near the Dillons' in Algonquin Park and who subsequently attended our wedding. Eleanor was Irish enough to hit it off with the principal, A. E. O'Neill, in a way that my father never quite managed. In any case, when she handed in her resignation in the fall of 1947, she was able to refer to me as belonging to a family he knew well.

In the fall of 1947, I accepted a job teaching high school in Regina and with our wedding scheduled for Christmas time, looked hard to find us living quarters. During the war, when service people had been away, others had expanded their use of housing, with the result that there was a severe shortage which continued for a few years afterward. I was able to get a basement apartment on Quebec Street, in preference to the hundred others who stood in line, because I had no children and didn't smoke or drink!

In early December, Eleanor's friends organized a breakfast shower where everyone was asked to bring something for a new kitchen. I think she received 27 dish-towels! The wedding took place in the old Cooksville United Church on the Dundas Highway where Eleanor had once been the student organist. Tom Dale, my best man, and I went for a country walk in the afternoon before the wedding which, I believe, was scheduled for 4:00 pm. At about 3:40, we wandered into the church basement. But Eleanor's mother arrived at the door and promptly commanded, "Get these men out of here!" Evidently some vital female preparations remained to be done—I'll never know what!

The organist for the ceremony was Don Kennedy, one of

the five of us who in 1941 had been in the first graduating class for the Music BA course. During the signing of the register, Eleanor's sister, Bunty, played a movement from a sonata for recorder by Loeillet. The bride processed down the aisle not to Wagner's Here Comes the Bride but to Bach's Sleepers Awake and we recessed down the aisle to the Hornpipe from Handel's Water Music.

The dinner at the Queen Elizabeth Lodge was planned along very traditional lines. The speeches were all given by men. The Master of Ceremonies was Eleanor's Uncle Eddy, her father's brother and law partner. I responded to the Toast to the Bride. Her father responded to the Toast to the Bride's mother. My father responded to the Toast to the Groom's mother. And the best man responded to the Toast to the Bridesmaid who was Margaret, Eleanor's sister. As I recall, the speeches were all interesting and well-composed. Eleanor whispered to me at the last minute what I should say. But I had mentally rehearsed exactly what I would say and I stuck to it.

After the dinner, Eleanor's brother, Rob, drove us to the house to change for the honeymoon. In his address, my father had offered the newlyweds advice from his experience. In the course of it, he quoted someone, "In an argument, the one who gives in first gets his way in the end." In the car, we differed about I don't know what and Rob immediately reminded us of my father's advice!

We had many arguments in the following years. But one thing stood out. No matter how strongly we had disagreed, Eleanor never let that affect our relationship. The moment the argument was over, my standing with her was as solid as ever. It was only a few days from Dec. 17th till the time we would have to begin the 48-hour train ride to Regina. My parents had ar-

*Eleanor & Don in Cooksville*

ranged to be away visiting at that time, so that we could use their house in Fonthill for a honeymoon. We took the Toronto Hamilton & Buffalo train from Toronto to Fenwick, then a cab to Fonthill. But we never saw Niagara Falls. We simultaneously came down with flu! I think we did manage to work in a movie, but don't ask me which!

On the train returning to Toronto, a lady was rude to me, I don't remember how. Eleanor felt she should intervene. Afterwards, she explained possessively, "If anyone is going to abuse you, it's going to be me!"

On our way to Regina, we used the 90-minute stop in Winnipeg to visit friends. Then at Portage La Prairie, we were met by relatives on both sides of the family who happened to be mutually acquainted. My cousins were Andrew and Ann Rutherford. Eleanor's relatives were her Great Aunt Wicky and Uncle Horace. The train reached Regina in the early evening. At the apartment were several friends in whose presence I carried the bride over the threshold.

Part of the preparation for the wedding concerned my Board of Education. At that time, the Saskatchewan Department of Education had a rule that, to qualify for the full grant, boards must keep their schools open for at least 200 days in the year. This made sense in the country, where snow would force boards to close for a period in February, making up the time in July. But, in the cities, it meant staying open on odd Mondays and odd Fridays. Typically, few students bothered to show on those days. But teachers had to be on hand.

But in order to buy a marriage license in Ontario, one had to be in the province at least 48 hours before the wedding. That meant missing a school day in Regina. The Board gave me permission to miss the day, but they docked my pay accordingly. At their January meeting, as reported prominently in the Leader-Post, they decided that the institution of marriage should not be discouraged and that the day's pay would be restored. This did not go down well with other teachers who felt they had better reasons than I to miss the day.

CHAPTER 28

# World War II

When the war began, I registered as a conscientious objector. This meant that, if required to serve in Canada's armed services, I would refuse to comply. In practice it meant that I would be doing whatever alternative service was put in place. When I was called to register, the official asked me how long I had been a pacifist. I replied, "Ever since I began to think." That didn't satisfy him. "How long?" he asked. I said, "You can put down ten years." What influenced my thinking?

One early influence was the New York preacher, Harry Emerson Fosdick. I recall one sentence from a radio sermon, "There are worse things than war and war brings all of them." Another influence was my mother. I don't recall details but I know that peace was a constant interest for me. But I believe that United Church ministers that I knew had a lot to do with it. Reverend J. Lavell Smith was an early cottager on Muldrew Lake and an ardent pacifist. His brother, Lloyd, was anything but, and I think it was in my nature to decide that one way was right and that I should stick to it.

In addition, I know that my interest, in the late 30's, in J. S. Woodsworth[56] made a difference. The first CCF leader, sometimes called, "A saint in politics," was a life-long pacifist. During the First World War, he resigned as a Methodist minister over the church's part in recruiting soldiers. And in 1939, he disagreed with his party by opposing Canada's participation in the Second World War. During the war, election night results were sometimes changed by the arrival of the military vote a few days later. In the 1940 federal election, Woodsworth was pronounced defeated on the basis of the civilian vote and it was expected that the service people would also oppose this pacifist. But Woodsworth was known personally by these constituents, and the service vote re-elected him!

In the period between the outbreak of the war and the call-ups, we pacifist students at the University of Toronto (U of T) would meet to consider our strategy. We received tremendous support and advice from Reverend Jim Finlay, who had been called to the ministry of Carlton United Church in 1938. It was natural that he would be criticized by members of his congregation for his stand, and, in the spring of 1940, he called a meeting of the congregation to determine his support. Some friends advised him to compromise, "Suppose there is bad war news on the day of the meeting. You might find yourself out of a job." In the event, the Fall of France happened that day. He stuck to his position and received an overwhelming majority in favour of his staying on. His congregation members didn't all agree with his pacifism but he had their respect.

On the campus, while we were waiting for the authorities to respond to our failure to belong to the COTC (Canadian Officers Training Corp), we took a First Aid course, and donated our blood to the Red Cross. Finally, in June of 1941, those of us who were graduating were required to do two weeks' civilian work at a military camp at Niagara-on-the-Lake. The officer of the COTC who was arranging this went out of his way to be sure that our duties would not conflict with our principles. One day when some of us expressed appreciation for his consideration, he retorted, "Oh that's what the war is about!" We didn't receive that respect from everyone!

I was lucky in being able to finish my teacher training before the Government got round to calling me up. In the spring of 1942, I even did what many of my colleagues were doing. I applied for teaching jobs. I had one interview, with the principal of Kenora High School. He first asked me what my position was with respect to the war. I told him I was a Christian pacifist. "Then you're out as far as I'm concerned! I'm just as good a Christian as you and I'm giving the war all the support I can."

CHAPTER 29

# BC Forest Service (BCFS)— Part One

In June of 1942, several of us who had registered as conscientious objectors were ordered to appear at the Toronto Union Station one night at midnight. From there we were taken west by CNR. For most of us, this was our first trip that way, and we became familiar for the first time with Northern Ontario lakes and muskeg, the prairies, and the mountains. I recall that our train stopped at a section point in the woods of Northern Ontario, allowing us to get some fresh air as we walked up and down the platform. Finally the conductor called out, "Booooooooooard" as he had presumably done many times before. At any rate, he got our immediate attention. None of us wanted to be left behind! We left the train at New Westminster, BC and were then taken by truck to Green Timbers, the headquarters of the BC Forest Service. A few weeks later, we were scattered among several camps, in each of which we spent three to four months. We were always on call for fire fighting, and, at other times, were given work to reduce the likelihood of fires.

Each camp employed a foreman and a cook. The foreman's position allowed him pretty general authority over us, and, of course, there was a big difference among these men. The cooks often came from lumber camps and were used to all sorts of rough living. At Vedder Crossing, the kitchen was at one end of a large tent. The cook had to bake bread, but could never put the dough out to rise before noon, because the Vedder River which was fed by mountain streams supplied us with abundant cold air. Vedder Crossing, the site of the camp called GT#3, was a tiny village about 8 miles south of Chilliwak in the Fraser Valley. Nearby was Cultus Lake, a favourite tourist centre at its north end, with the USA visible on the south shore.

In the BCFS experience, I found that two things took a bit of getting used to. One was doing entirely physical work after university studies. The other was the religious outlook of the other campers. The camps were not filled with pacifists who drew their position from a modern understanding of the Gospel. Almost all of the others were fundamentalists of one kind or another. There were a few Jehovah's Witnesses and other members of small sects. But the great majority was Mennonite. The main difference between me and them was that they were conscientious objectors because of their church's dogma and, if they referred to the Bible, they used certain proof texts, whereas my church was officially in favour of the war and we, the exceptions, had to defend our positions by our own thinking and our own interpretation of Scripture. If it were today, after I had found out the many virtues of the Mennonite people, my attitude might have been different. But, in 1942, I found little occasion to warm up to my fellow-campers. I dare say we got along. But at the religious point—and religion was the main reason we were there—there was little dialogue[57].

One very rainy day, I was in a large cabin with two other lads, one a Jehovah's Witness, the other a very vocal Mennonite. They got into a heated argument about whether being saved was permanent or whether you could backslide and need saving again. Pretty soon I chose to go for a walk in the rain! On another occasion, while we were being moved from one camp to another, a red-headed Jehovah's Witness began lecturing the rest of us on his particular theology. As soon as he realized that he was getting nowhere with us, he turned off his lecture like a tap and from then on, we got to know him and admire him as a person. I had heard it said that some people were better than their creed. Here, it seemed to me, was a concrete example.

From Vedder Crossing, we were sent to deal with our first forest fire, on the side of a mountain. Our job was to dig a fire trail near the front edge of the fire, getting down to the depth of the mineral soil, and then patrolling our trail to prevent the fire from jumping it. We dug many meters of trail and, in our patrolling, often used logs to cross ravines, or swung by fir branches to get down the side of a ravine in a hurry. On the first day, I had made myself a bacon sandwich, and, before eating it, I made a wooden fork and toasted it in the coals of the forest fire across the trail. No sandwich ever tasted better!

I also learned skills from other campers. Once, two of us were told to cut up a large fir log into firewood. The log was two feet in diameter—much too heavy to lift. Also, before our cross-cut saw finished a cut, the wood would "bind" on the saw, keeping it from moving. My colleague showed me how to put another log underneath to pivot the main one up.

Everyday living in the camp had its difficulties. First of all, rain was a problem. We had been issued suits that were supposed to be waterproof, but weren't. When we did our laundry, it was only occasionally that a fire was lit in one of the cabins to allow drying. And our meals deteriorated. To start with, we were served a lot of good things. But as each item of supply ran out, the new order had to be approved by five different government authorities, a process that took time. Meanwhile, we were served what remained of the camp supply.

The BC forest had its own types of vegetation. Once I thought I had found wild raspberries—a delicacy in Ontario. What I picked led me to make a face. They were salmon berries which tasted very bitter. In another area, I encountered a nicer berry. They were

Top: Forest fire in British Columbia
Bottom: Rev. Jim Finlay and Don, posing as foresters

*Top: Forestry camp personnel; Don, middle row, centre*
*Middle: Don, Rev. Jim Finlay, Joe Mottishaw, camp foreman*
*Bottom: Camp shacks near Campbell River*

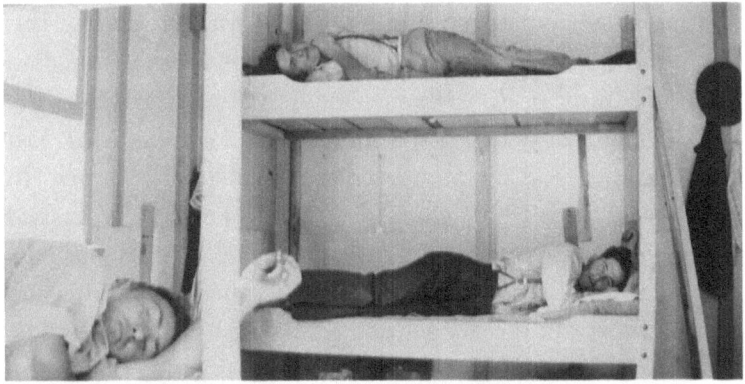

*Top: Road approaching the camp*
*Middle: Camp bunks*
*Bottom: Men on truck, Don, first from right*

shaped like blueberries—obviously a part of the huckleberry family—but red, when ripe. On a hot, sunny day, these berries were very refreshing, though I have not heard of anyone using them for cooking.

In the winter months, we were stationed at Green Timbers, the headquarters camp of the BCFS. This was where plants were developed which would be sent to other parts of the province. The elderly gentleman in charge tended to be fair but the young assistant ordered us about in a surly manner. Before we were again transferred, he was promoted to a job in Victoria. A local workman we got to know was scornful, "He'll be emptying waste-baskets", he said.

That year, I got to go home by train for Christmas. This time, and in the next several trips, I went by the Canadian Pacific Railway (CPR) which had the better scenery. In the Rockies, the tracks climbed a mountain on a spiral track and used the five-mile tunnel under the MacDonald[58] range. In the decade after 1900, when the track followed a V-shaped valley, there was a gigantic snow-slide which literally buried a freight train killing the whole crew by freezing. The tunnel had been built to end the danger of a repetition.

While we were stationed on the BC mainland, there were opportunities to visit Vancouver. At university, I had gotten to know Hugh and Agnes Herbison. Hugh's parents (his father was a retired minister) lived in a small bungalow in West Point Gray, and I was warmly welcomed there, sometimes in the company of Hugh and Agnes, sometimes not. The first time, I was treated to dessert consisting of the most luscious raspberries I have ever tasted—from the back yard. The last time I visited that home, I found that Mr. Herbison had died. Mrs. Herbison's ideas of death were similar to my own. During these visits, I felt that my better side was allowed to come out. This was my home-away-from-home.

Chapter 30

# BC Forest Service— Part Two

I paid a visit once to another camp—G.T. #2 I think it was called—where conditions made for a high degree of happiness. I hitched over from Green Timbers to the camp near the village of Haney. Several of my friends were there, and, on my arrival, one of them remarked, "We've really got the proper set-up here." Strangely, I don't remember what those conditions were except that they had a foreman who went out of his way to establish a good relationship with the campers. At another time, I heard that an independent observer had asked this foreman what he thought of the men in his camp. Thinking he was being asked about the quality of their work, he replied that he had never had better workers. But the questioner persisted, "What do you think of their ideas about war?" "Well," said the foreman, "I sometimes wonder if they're not right."

In February, 1943, some of us were moved to G.T. #4, Campbell River. This meant a truck ride to the Vancouver docks, a ferry ride to Nanaimo, a long bus ride to the village of Campbell River on the Georgia Strait, and a 16-mile truck ride west to the camp. Here, there had been a thaw before our arrival and the ground between the tents was a lake, reminding me of some of the farmyards I had known in my childhood.

I forget what kind of work we did at G.T. #4, except that in one week we were put at planting baby fir trees. By the process we were taught, a tree had to be planted about every 7 seconds. My physical coordination was not of the best. I failed to keep up, and I was then made camp night-watchman till the planting was done. I found myself sitting in the kitchen peeling potatoes. I mostly kept awake and but I didn't always. One

*Staff of* The Beacon, *Wes Brown, editor, 1st row centre*

night, someone had set an alarm-clock, and when it sounded at about 2:30 am, I jumped.

One of the campers at G. T. #4 was Wes Brown of Toronto. Wes organized a mimeographed newsletter called *The Beacon*[59] which was circulated to all the camps. I recall being one of a dozen or so people who walked round a long table at G. T. #4, to collate the thing. Wes was very careful not to sound critical of our employers. Nevertheless, an official from Victoria did an inspection of the camp in which he assumed that we conscientious objectors were like the occupants of the camps in the previous decade. At that time, the men had been on unemployment relief, and apparently some were troublemakers. Wes was hauled onto the carpet and told that he was in the doghouse. He subsequently made up a song which he called the Doghouse Blues.

G.T. #6, to which we were moved in May, was about a mile from the town of Port Alberni at the head of the Alberni Canal, a salt-water fjord leading west to the Pacific Ocean. It was there that we had a visit from Reverend Jim Finlay who came to encourage the pacifists among us. His son Jack was in another camp. We arranged for him to preach in the local United Church and he chose to preach on God's Other Children—those who were racially different from us. One of our members was Keith Woollard, a theology student who, many years later, occupied the position of director of religious broadcasting for the United Church. Keith led us in a study of a Quaker book. He also tried to organize a camper's council but failed when the fundamentalists wouldn't support it. Paul's verse, "The powers that be are ordained of God[60]" tended to undergird their thinking on such matters.

During our stay at this camp, the cook walked out without notice. As a result, the foreman, a rather nice guy named Joe Mottishaw, took me to the kitchen and taught me some rudimentary procedures, with the result that I was camp cook for ten days, until a new cook could be engaged. Well, I tried. My first lot of bread fell in the oven and was almost inedible. My last lot was hungrily eaten. I remember going to a nearby field to pick mint for a roast of lamb. I think I might have continued in this role if BCFS rules had allowed.

In the woods, I usually scaled stumps. The work for most of the campers involved felling snags, dead trees that constituted a fire hazard. My job amounted to measuring the work of my fellow campers. When a tree had been felled, the cutters marked the stump with their team number and an arrow identifying the next snag to be felled. I followed with tape and a book. I measured and recorded the diameter of the stump, then set out to find the next stump—not always an easy task in dense bush. My efforts didn't make me popular. I tried to be accurate. But I acquired the nickname, Gippo.

The land involved in the activities of GT#6 included a branch of the CPR railway that ran from Nanaimo to Port Alberni. Routed along that line and into the Alberni Canal was the trans-pacific cable, a vitally important means of communication in the days before electronic devices had become common. One day, a dead tree had to be felled that might have severed the cable if it fell the wrong way. So officials from Victoria supervised that operation and the campers who carefully carried it out felt they had earned praise where it counted.

Near that point, I once encountered a section man whose job was to keep the CPR track in good repair. I got an earful about the sins of the engineers who drove their trains faster than was allowed for the given stretch of track. As a result, he would get blamed for the damage that resulted. He was probably blaming the wrong party, as I'm sure that engineers were often just carrying out orders. The incident made me understand why there were so many unions among railway workers.

On civic holiday week-end, three of us set off to climb Mt. Arrowsmith[61]. Townspeople claimed that they walked to the top regularly. We found it was not that easy. On the Saturday, the camp truck took us to a point near the beginning of the climb. We spent that night on a 45-degree slope. Once I laid an orange on the ground, only to have it roll rapidly out of my reach. After trying unsuccessfully to climb one side of the mountain, we came round to a more favorable vista. As we walked up a small glacier that was visible from great distances, we saw a mountain goat walking easily up a vertical slope. Then we realized that the 200-odd foot climb to the peak would have required equipment that we didn't have, and we didn't go higher.

That night we slept on a ledge about six feet wide with our feet toward the edge which was bounded with a natural hedge about 4 inches high. When the sun set, we could see the lights of the Lions Gate bridge north of Vancouver; in the morning we watched the sun rise behind the coastal mountains. This is the sort of thing that makes mountain climbing worth-while.

The other tourist attraction of the area was the steamer that plied up and down the Alberni Canal. Members of this camp booked themselves onto it for Labour Day. But for me, that was not to be. Just before that time, I departed for Lemon Creek.

CHAPTER 31

# War-Time Supporters

I've mentioned Jim Finlay. I'll do so again, because I really believe he has been the greatest influence in the life I have tried to lead. One group of the people he called, "God's Other Children" was a family of Japanese-Canadians named Kitigawa. Ed Kitigawa was a Canadian citizen, bank manager and United Church elder in Vancouver who was saved from having his family torn apart in the evacuation by an invitation from Jim. The invitation was for his family of six to share the Carleton Street manse in Toronto with the Finlay family until he could find independent accommodation and work. Prejudice was strong at that stage and the sharing lasted seven months! While Jim preached racial tolerance, he also practised it!

*Rev. Jim Finlay*

During the early weeks of World War II, a statement was signed and publicized by 75 United Church ministers and theology students including Jim Finlay and Jim Norquay who later became my brother-in-law. It was called a Peace Manifesto and declared that war was contrary to the mind of Christ. The statement was drafted by Reverend Edis Fairburn.

Edis Fairbairn was then minister of Bracebridge United Church. Soon afterward, that church relieved him of his position because of his stand and he moved west to the three-point Windermere charge near Lake Rosseau. Soon after we were sent west as conscientious objectors, Edis began corresponding with us pacifists. He was sometimes accused of having an acerbic tongue. But I found him a wonderful man to write to. He had had an interesting life. As a university student, he took up Esperanto[62], an early attempt at forming an international language, which at that time had three million practitioners around the world—practitioners, not merely supporters, because these people used the language to communicate with people of different cultures. Once, his college principal worried that he was spending too much time studying Esperanto. He replied, "I no longer study it. I speak it!"

Before proceeding to ordination in the Methodist Church in England, Edis spent a year as an apprentice to a cabinet maker. As a result, he had a life-long hobby in carpentry. He once told me proudly of his non-slip, non-spill collection plates! He did a crucifix as a gift to Jim Finlay. He once did a gorgeous chess set for an American customer. And he made a coffee table for me to use as a wedding present. He apologized that, due to war-time shortages, he had had to use cherry wood instead of mahogany. But the table was greatly cherished as our family grew up. He had preached in Bermuda before coming to Canada.

I believe our correspondence was largely theological, though the details have faded in the memory. But I'm sure my thinking was influenced for a long time. After the war, I used a Muskoka Lake steamer to visit him, and, among other things, saw the room where he kept his power tools and pursued his hobby.

Shortly after I reached Vedder Crossing, I saw a letter-to-the- editor in a Toronto paper from a Mrs. Leavens at Cultus Lake. I got in touch and visited her little cabin on the side of a mountain. She kept goats and filled me with the outlook of a goat-herd. "Goats," she told me, "have a reputation of being willing to eat everything. Well, you know how a mother will sometimes start eating an apple and offer a child the other side of it? A child will accept that but my goats won't." I don't believe Mrs. Leavens was a pacifist but she had an interesting and earthy view of society.

The pacifist publication that was begun by Jim Finlay during the War was called Reconciliation, the organ of the Fellowship of Reconciliation (the FOR). Interestingly, it took its inspiration from the American parent, Fellowship, which was edited by Reverend A. J. Muste of New York. One day the very conservative superintendent of the Lemon Creek Centre, Mr. Burns, heard of the FOR and began talking about it at the dinner table. He called it, "An organization that criticizes our boys for fighting." That was never the emphasis. Indeed, it maintained a respect for those who could not share our view of war. No, the FOR preached good will to those people among us whose national origin was that of the enemy. During the war, in a city in California, I heard that a young Japanese-American was yelled at by a woman who cried, "You killed my son!" She didn't know that the young man had served in the American army. The FOR sought to reconcile these alien minorities with a prejudiced population, to treat them as we would ourselves. But for Mr. Burns that was not an easy concept.

CHAPTER 32

# Train Journeys

In the 40's, the trains made the trip from Vancouver to Toronto in three-and-a-half days. A lot of scenery was visible on that journey. My more recent experiences have shown me that one doesn't really experience mountains from a plane. As one who had a soft spot for the sight of mountain peaks, the train gave me great satisfaction as we passed through the Rockies. In June, 1942, it was the Canadian National Railway that took the Jasper route in the North. In December of that year, when I went from New Westminster by CPR, the mountains were those of the Kicking Horse Pass, with the spiral tunnels and the five-mile tunnel on the way. Once I took the Kettle Valley Line from Nelson to Medicine Hat, where I got the main line train. During the time between trains, I took a walk and found that the foothills of the Rockies were visible in the distance. Eleanor liked the description in one of my letters, "They looked like a set of badly pitched tents."

Once I went from Lemon Creek by bus to Nakusp where I got the paddle-wheel steamer that used to ply the Arrow Lakes. On deck, I had an interesting discussion with a politician. At Arrowhead, I took the "puddle-jumping" train to Revelstoke, where I boarded the transcontinental.

Section points were reached every three hours or so, on the transcontinental. They allowed the train to be serviced, and they allowed passengers some relief from sitting. Some passengers just spent the time in a station restaurant. Others, like me, often took advantage of the chance to exercise. In this, we trusted the railway officials to stick to schedule. If we had 15 minutes to walk, we wanted to be sure that we wouldn't be left behind. Trains in wartime were notoriously late, and the temptation to make up time by shaving it from these stops was always present. Passengers sometimes WERE left behind, even though their belongings were scattered around their seats. The nearest I came to this was that I once had to get on a moving train.

I sometimes got into interesting conversations with other passengers. One was an instructor at a Roman Catholic Seminary in Seattle, who talked about his church being the only real church, a stance Catholics no longer seem to take. But on one point, he and the son of a United Church minister were agreed. I had contended that Christian precepts applied to the whole of life. They both took the position that there were areas of life to which religion is entirely irrelevant. How would our church members divide on that point today?

Some of my train experiences were just plain fun. At a 7:00 am section point stop at Port Arthur (now Thunder Bay), I decided to exercise on the station platform. As I got near the engine, I was startled to find boys standing around with hands in their pockets singing in four parts, and discovered that there was a choir on board. Walking through the train after we were again on our way, I met the priests who were shepherding these boys. They came from the Catholic school in Edmonton called St. John's which provided both elementary and secondary education. In June, with classes finished, the choir (with unchanged voices doing soprano and alto, changed voices doing tenor and bass) rehearsed the program consisting of folk songs in French and Sacred songs in Latin that they were taking on tour. The Dominican order had arranged for them to tour Quebec, starting with an appearance at Notre Dame Cathedral in Montreal on the following Sunday morning.

At the section points across Northern Ontario, the choir formed up on the platform and gave us a sample of their repertory. I told the conductor that the CPR should provide this kind of service regularly! We were on the second section of our train. To get the choir to Montreal on time, this train would have to overtake the first section during the 50-minute section stop in Sudbury. Of course, I was on the way to Toronto so I never heard whether the choir was on time!

In those times, we young people who couldn't afford sleepers made a point of getting into an "air-conditioned" coach, the chief advantage being that the seats could be reclined, allowing for sleep. On one such journey, I thought I'd been getting a lot of sleep. But when I got home, I was so tired that I slept the clock round!

In the summer of 1944, a national convention of the CCF was scheduled to be held in Montreal. I had planned to attend as an observer. But before it could be held, a provincial election was called in Quebec. So I went along anyway, sleeping in a French-Canadian home and putting up signs through the day. I found that, although my hosts supported the CCF, they were not tolerant of the Japanese-Canadians, and I think they were glad to be rid of me.

From Montreal, I took the CPR to North Bay where I was able to board a CNR train to Gravenhurst. When I got on the CPR, at around 10 pm, there appeared to be no seats available. But four burly men who seemed to be filling their seats, insisted on squeezing me in. It turned out that these were French-Canadian lumberjacks. One of them was a singer and entertained me all night with lively lumberjack folk songs. Such an experience was worth a thousand records.

CHAPTER 33

# Lemon Creek

In recent years, a Japanese student at OISE in Toronto, who did a treatise on the Japanese-Canadian experience during World War II, came on the following letter:

*Camp Q 3, B.C.F.S.,*
*Campbell River, B.C.*
*March 28th, 1943*

*Miss H. Hyodo*
*Education Department*
*New Denver, B.C.*

*Dear Miss Hyodo:*

*I am a conscientious objector whose Christian convictions forbade my entering the armed forces of this my country. Therefore, I am now serving, as an Alternative Service Worker, with the B.C. Forest Service. This work I recognized to be of national importance.*

*However, I understand that you are in desperate need of qualified assistance in your work in connection with the education of Canadian-Japanese children who have been evacuated from the Pacific Coast area. I feel that your work is of just as great national importance as that in which I am now engaged, but that it is infinitely more difficult to secure assistance in your case. I feel also that I could render better service in that capacity.*

*May I state that before being called to my present work, I obtained a Bachelor of Arts degree from the University of Toronto, and proceeded to the Ontario College of Education, where I received certificates as a High School Assistant, and a Specialist in Music. At various times in the past, I have also participated in leadership in connection with boys' summer camps.*

*Therefore, I wish to apply, pending the permission of the proper authorities, to be transferred to work in connection with the education of the Canadian-Japanese in Inland British Columbia.*

*Yours Faithfully,
Donald M. Ewing*

When the Japanese immigrated to British Columbia in the late 19th century or the first third of the 20th, they realized that, to survive, they would need to work hard and be prepared to work long hours. As a result, many of them were quite successful economically. This led to jealousy among white people who were unwilling to work that hard. As the Japanese tended to keep to themselves, and as they established Japanese language schools which operated after the regular schools were dismissed, many false rumors were circulated at their expense. When the Japanese bombed Pearl Harbour, the Canadian Government decided to move all people of Japanese origin away from the Pacific coast. There was no distinction made between citizens and foreign nationals or those of other Asian descent, in many cases. All of them were herded into the Hastings Street Exhibition building, until accommodation for them was ready in the Interior. For this purpose, centers were created by construction of tar-paper shacks, into which were crowded populations of 1500 to 3000. Some of the centers were located in abandoned mining ghost towns.

The greatest injustice had to do with the disposal of the Japanese property. The government assured the Japanese that anything they had to leave behind would be kept in safety for them until after the war. But they were hardly out of sight before the government agency, the BC Securities Commission (BCSC) auctioned it off to the lowest bidders, returning to the owners a fraction of its value. Thus a $60,000 fishing boat was sold for $5,000, and a 100-acre berry farm in the Fraser

*Lemon Creek High School, January 1946*

Valley went for a few hundred. One missionary, suspecting what would happen, filled every square foot of the basement of his Vancouver home with furniture that he kept for Japanese friends till they could be returned.

The Japanese in the camps were constantly being urged to find work farther East. So, although the BCSC provided elementary schools of a kind, they did nothing for secondary education, arguing that, with this convenience, young people would not make the effort to relocate. To fill this need, three denominations set up high schools, Lemon Creek being one assignment of the United Church. And the Women's Missionary Society, my employer for three years, managed to get permission for me and two others to be released from the Forest Service to become teachers in these schools.

Lemon Creek lay in an open plain in the Slocan valley, seven miles South of Slocan City, 26 miles North of Nelson. Our teaching conditions were not ideal. In our first year, we used the elementary school building at night and on Saturday mornings. Since this building had no electricity, we had to teach with Coleman gas lanterns. It was not bad when the lanterns worked. When they faded out, classes sometimes had to be cancelled. In our second year, a two-and-a-half room building was erected, permitting us to teach in the day-time.

That first year, we had to adjust to conditions as we found them. The more enterprising girls and boys had taken correspondence courses in the year before we arrived. But they tended to concentrate on their favourite subjects, rather than following any complete course of study. Thus we found, for example, that some had completed grade XII Math, but lacked grade IX English! Making a time-table for 69 students was rather a nightmare.

I could have wished for better circumstances for my first year of teaching. Some Japanese students, for instance, those quartered in New Denver, seemed to accept their lot very meekly. Not so those in Lemon Creek. For them, thoughts about the injustices done to the Japanese were never far from the surface, and we, as white people, were classed with the BCSC. I committed a faux pas on the first day of school. I asked them to sing *O Canada*!

Another condition was the inexperience of our principal. Gertrude Hamilton, as a missionary to Japan who had to leave that country before the war began, had run a school for girls. But she had never dealt with boys. However, she must have learned. One Hallowe'en, some of the boys knocked over some of the neat wood piles that were kept behind the houses. Mr. Burns, the superintendent, came around to investigate, but by the time he arrived, parents were already helping Miss Hamilton supervise a group of boys who were putting things right.

From Vancouver, the trip to Lemon Creek involved the old Kettle Valley line of the CPR to Nelson. Then we took the daily bus that followed our valley and proceeded to Nakusp[63] on the Arrow Lakes. At Christmas, I went to Penticton to visit a friend who had to wait to meet my train until 2:30 am—during the war, trains could be hours late. Then I went on to

Vancouver to visit others. On that trip, I had entrusted my baggage to a stout paper shopping bag. All was well till I got caught in a heavy shower on my way to the Vancouver railway station. This weakened the bag. On arriving at Nelson, I decided to use the passenger-freight train that went up our valley once a week. There was no station at Lemon Creek, but I persuaded the conductor to slow down, so that I could jump into a snow bank. Alas, my shopping-bag chose that moment to disintegrate, and my tooth-brush went into one part of the snow bank, my pajamas into another!

That first year, I was boarded in the farm house and prefab cabin that were used by the BCSC officials. These included Mr. Burns, the superintendent, his wife, the mild-mannered RCMP officer, the assistant superintendent who was a devoted navy man who was invalided to this paper job, and Helena Gutteridge, the social welfare worker, a lady veteran of the CCF and a former alderwoman in Vancouver. I kept quiet at table most of the time. But there were arguments that I didn't win!

Lemon Creek's 1800 people lived on streets named alphabetically after trees—Cedar, Dogwood, Elm, Fir, Gilead, Holly and Juniper—and avenues named for flowers—Rose, Spirea, and Tulip. A large majority of the Japanese people were Buddhists, though a significant minority belonged to the United Church, led by our "little minister", Reverend Tak Komiyama. Tak alternated between English and Japanese language services. His mother was very domineering. Tak never married until after she died.

About once every two weeks, someone in Lemon Creek left for employment somewhere east of BC. The farewells were usually emotional. A large crowd would assemble at the highway to wait

*Staff of Lemon Creek High School & Church, Don Ewing back row, 2nd from left*

for the daily bus. Since the bus drivers usually operated on the principle enunciated by one of them that, "Nelson will be still there when I get there," long waits were not unusual. The favourite hymn from those occasions was, *"God be with us till we meet again[64]."*

> *God be with you till we meet again;*
> *By His counsels guide, uphold you,*
> *With His sheep securely fold you;*
> *God be with you till we meet again.*

Refrain

> *Till we meet, till we meet,*
> *Till we meet at Jesus' feet;*
> *Till we meet, till we meet,*
> *God be with you till we meet again.*

In our second year, our staff was joined by another conscientious objector, Joe Grant from Toronto. He and I occupied two rooms at one end of the high school building. The ladies, Gertrude Hamilton and Helen Hurd, who ran the Church Kindergarten with help from a group of high school girls, lived across the street. Joe managed to get closer to the students than I. In that second year, the students tried to boycott plans we had for their extra-curricular activities. One night Joe met some of the more vocal students on the street, and won them round.

I never got to teach music in Lemon Creek. I was needed for the subjects that were regarded as essential. The Nisei or second generation Japanese, were keen to be thought of as proper Canadians and they associated that with the promotion of "popular" music. A group of them, who claimed to be all of the "talent" of the community, learned and performed some numbers from the current hit parade. I was pigeonholed as a "classical" fellow, and therefore no one with anything to say to them about music. When they heard that Joe Grant was coming to be their teacher, they asked me, "Is he classical or popular?" When I told Joe, he replied that he was sorry he'd have to disappoint them.

When Lemon Creek High School opened, a number of students had been taking correspondence courses. These were organized into units called "papers". In easing into the work, we at first taught from papers, and then tried to move into our own curriculum. But, even in our second year, students would ask, as one boy did, "What paper are we on?" At the Coast, Japanese students did well by using a somewhat limited vocabulary. Once I forgot how true this was, and set a grade XI Social Studies exam, sticking to material covered, but referring to it with different language. The students were floored, getting average marks of around 25%, so that I had to re-do the exam.

The Lemon Creek students were a tougher crowd than those who peopled other centers such as the one in New Denver. On one occasion, Gwen Suttie, the New Denver principal, addressed our school on etiquette. For an example, she referred to the situation when a boy is entering a store. A girl who got there first will wait for the boy to open the door for her. One of our boys blurted out, "But they don't!" Gwen had to catch her breath. Then she responded, "We're talking about etiquette. Let's practise it." The boy came up after the meeting to apologize.

In Joe Grant's first year, the staff presented a plan to elect a student council. Thinking they should set this up themselves, the students all declined nomination. This went on for about two weeks. Then one evening, Joe met a gang of them in the street and managed to talk sense into them, after which a council was successfully elected.

Before I got to Lemon Creek, I had never tried to ride a bicycle. Mother always thought roads were too dangerous for bikes and I was never given one. But Joe Grant brought his bike to LC and let me practise on his. A grade 12 girl once handed in an English composition which described my crude efforts to ride in a nearby field!

The BC Securities Commission, which ran the seven cen-

*Lemon Creek High School Christmas Dinner, Dec. 21, 1945*

tres, used inadequately trained personnel for education and health. For the public schools they pressed into service students who had completed grade XII. For health, a lad who had had two years of medicine became Lemon Creek's first aid person. His brother, Dr. Shimotakahara, who happened to be the only doctor in the centres, became the supervising medical officer. Shimo, as he was known, had other talents, including that of lay preacher. One Sunday, he was the guest preacher at the Japanese language service at our United Church. I understand that he kept those folk on the edge of their chairs for nearly two hours!

Howard Green, the long-time Conservative MP for Vancouver South, grew up in Kaslo and his family were among those who advocated during the war that all people of Japanese origin, including those who had been born here, should be "sent back" when the war was over, and they keenly resented the placing of a thousand Japanese-Canadians in their neighbourhood. Howard's father was a chronic invalid who frequently called on the local white doctor. But on one occasion, when Mr. Green needed help, the white doctor was out-of-town, and they had to call on Dr. Shimotakahara. They liked Shimo so well that they wouldn't have the other man back. And the family prejudice melted right there.

Some of us visited back and forth with our opposite numbers in New Denver. This beautiful village, at the far end of Slocan Lake, was another centre in which the United Church had jurisdiction. Returned missionaries, Gwen Suttie, the school principal, and Ella Lediard were great to have as friends as were volunteers Helen Lawson, from Hamilton, and CO John Stan Rowe[65]. My own associates were probably just as great. But it was good to get a perspective on one's work from a little distance. On one of these visits, in the fall, several of us hiked up a gradual mountain slope to the east of New Denver. I especially remember the pure, cold, mountain streams that we frequently stepped over and often used for drinking.

One fall, I went to a teachers' convention in the city of Trail. One of the main speakers was the president of the company that controlled the local industry, a smelter. He told about a judge who exonerated a young lad who was accused of a crime, only to have the boy steal his watch. In other words, his message was that the young people of the day couldn't be trusted —and this was 60 years ago! I was billeted with a Mrs. McLeod. When she welcomed me, I wondered about her strange accent. Had a Mr. McLeod married an eastern European? In conversation, I discovered that her native tongue was Gaelic!

Thirty-five years later, Eleanor and I attended a reunion in Toronto of people who had either lived at Lemon Creek or were married to someone who had been there. These people had done well for themselves. And, as each one came up to say, "Remember me, Mr. Ewing?" they were falling over themselves in gratitude for what we had done for them in the 1940's.

*Don with high school class*

# Part 2—

# The Middle Years

CHAPTER 34

# Teaching in Lemon Creek, Sault Ste Marie and Regina

I put in 39 years as a teacher. How much of it can be called a success, and how much was achieved?

A high school principal once said, "If you haven't got discipline (over the kids), you've got nothing." Most educational authorities seem to agree with that. And that is the basis of most judgments of teachers' performance. Disciplinary weakness was the basis of five of my moves. Then why did I stick it out?

For one thing, the setting wasn't always the same. I couldn't seem to maintain effective discipline when I was alone with the students in the classroom. I could do effective teaching when another teacher was present. I was good one-on-one with students. And I could do effective supervising where I could share musical expertise with teachers. That may be why I got so many recommendations from Dr. Fenwick. G. Roy Fenwick[66] was Director of Music for the Ontario Department of Education for about 25 years. He probably did more in strengthening the teaching of music across Ontario than any other individual. He retained the notion that I could be an asset in that work.

Secondly, a lot of my work was done through extracurricular activities, a setting where it was usually easier to be in control because, since the students had chosen to be there, their interest was higher. This was not true in Lemon Creek where I was hired, not as a music teacher, but as someone who could do what were considered the "basic" subjects. Everywhere else I had a means of communicating with students and their parents in a way that didn't depend on classroom performance.

Thirdly, I've always enjoyed lesson-planning and organizing

material. But the discipline thing got to me after a while. I've often re-lived, mentally, situations I've botched, with what I thought would have been better handling. And I still dream occasionally that I'm back at high school teaching, and that I've arrived on the first day of school, not knowing which room I am to use, ignorant of the time-table, and without any lesson preparation done!

In 1946, the Sault Ste. Marie Board appointed me to a new Music Department headed by a somewhat old-fashioned teacher and violinist named David Warner-Smith. The work at the Collegiate and of the public schools was divided between David and me, while the third member, a rather resourceful contemporary of mine named McGregor, did music at the Technical High School. I used to visit him and his wife a lot and hear some fantastic stories from his Italian landlord.

A competitive festival (Rotary or Kiwanis) had long been established in the city. Typically, three-part choirs were entered from all the public schools. Warner-Smith did not approve of choir competitions. But, since the Festival needed the revenue that came from the appearance of these choirs, we agreed to have the choirs perform non-competitively. I had noticed that one school had strong first soprano and alto sections, while another had a strong middle section, and I arranged to have the two choirs sing together. But, the morning after the combined choir had performed, when I visited one of these schools and spoke to the principal and vice-principal, the atmosphere was so thick you could cut it with a knife. I had interfered with the honour of their school by combining choirs!

At mid-year, Warner-Smith relieved me of high school duties and gave me another group of public schools to visit. One of these had a rather straight-laced principal named Ashton Upper (the kids nick-named him "Ashcan Upper"!), who was very finicky about what time I arrived at his school. I'm sure I learned from my mistakes that year, though I don't recall taking Warner-Smith's advice, "When teachers are not doing what you want them to do," he once told me, "raise hell"!

Provincial inspectors made annual visits to the High Schools. One of the older women on the collegiate staff had a method of finding out just when they would be coming, so that her colleagues could prepare for the event. The inspectors always stayed at the same hotel, and this teacher had a boy in her class whose father worked at the hotel and had access to the hotel register. Naturally, the teachers came to expect the annual warning.

In 1947, Regina Central Collegiate was located in the more fashionable part of the city. I taught Music and Social Studies. The music classes consisted of the singing of semi-popular songs, accompanied by a woman who had been hired for the purpose. She used a transposing piano. The middle pedal served as a clutch to a lever under the keyboard for shifting the said keyboard to right or to left, activating different hammers. The result was that the singers could use easier keys without the accompanist having to transpose. The problem was that this piano didn't hold its tune well. The player also had to leave it at A440[67] if mistakes were to be avoided. At one of our concerts, a boys' choir was given an introduction from this piano that was so low that the number had to be abandoned. The accompanist forgot to check the adjustment.

At Regina Central, I followed a very weak teacher who, in turn, followed a legend. R.J. Staples (this is how he spelled it), according to my Aunt Mary, was born in or near Cobourg, Ontario. His parents couldn't agree on a first name and used initials instead. In Regina, he was famous for his initiatives and for his shows. I inherited a number of instruments including a bass Saxophone which was kept in a trunk! R.J. also devised a contraption that would ride over RCA records (78 speed in those days!) and indicate numerically just where you were in the music. Then he published a book on music appreciation in which he commented with references to these numbers. Alas, for him, RCA made major changes soon after that, making the references unworkable.

I probably spent more effort on extra-curricular activities

than in classroom work. I had an orchestra where the strings usually got drowned out by the winds. There was a girls' choir and a boys' octet which sometimes got expanded into a boys' chorus for special purposes. The octet began as a quartet. One day, there was a misunderstanding as to which of two baritones I would include. So I just added three more to make it an octet. One Sunday, Eleanor invited the octet to our basement apartment for dinner and a sing around our kitchen piano. Seeing the initials engraved on Eleanor's silver, one of the boys asked which hotel they had come from!

I made good use of the boys in the concerts I staged. One of these began with an overture to a Gilbert and Sullivan opera and finished with selections from *Oklahoma*. That may have been the occasion in which we played around with the national anthem. In Ontario, we used to start concerts with *The King*. In the West, I learned, they began with *O Canada* and finished with *The King*. On this occasion, I ventured to follow the Ontario custom, and started with *The King*. When the last rousing choir number was finished, I just walked off the stage. But the audience wasn't satisfied. My student accompanist was nudged and they finished by singing *God Save the King* again, without me!

Another time, we actually produced the Gilbert and Sullivan operetta, *Trial by Jury*. About a month before the performance when we were still practising one song at a time, I called in sick. But the message wasn't delivered to the students until the noon-hour when they were to practise. On receiving my news, the students headed down the stairs from the auditorium. But they were met on the stairs by the soprano soloist, who said "About turn!" They went back and she took them through the whole operetta for the first time!

The Rotary Competitive Music Festival was one of a chain of such events across Canada that was served by adjudicators from England. I encountered one of them, a Mr. Heath-Gracie, when I entered my girls' choir one year. The test piece, *To Spring*, by Healey Willan, took a lot of work, and, to enhance interest, I chose as a second number a song from an operetta by Jerome Kern. Mr. Heath-Gracie gave us the highest mark for our treatment of the Willan. Then he marked us down for the other choice. He threw my music on the floor, declaring, "That sort of trash should never be heard in an institution of cultiah!" He didn't win friends with my girls that day!

Each year school council elections featured a major parade. In spite of restrictions, the floats were very elaborate, and many students stayed up till 5:00 in the morning getting theirs ready. The parade happened on a Friday morning, followed by the vote. By Friday afternoon, a lot of students couldn't stay awake. One teacher told his class, "Do ten minutes' work and then you can put your heads down." Later the principal dropped by. The teacher whispered," What do you think of my sleeping beauties?"

A Math and a Science teacher had adjoining rooms. One day the science teacher decided his class needed a dressing down. As he began, his voice became clearly audible in the next room. The math teacher stopped teaching, letting his class have the full benefit of what was coming from next door. At last he said, "And that goes for you too!"

CHAPTER 35

# Teaching in Ottawa and Goderich

The Ottawa High School of Commerce and Glebe Collegiate are two ends of the same building. The auditorium in the middle is shared, with assemblies for one school in the morning, in the afternoon for the other. In the 50's, a pipe organ had been built in the auditorium, so that a downtown church organist could give monthly recitals for each school. In my day, the organist who had been engaged knew little about music appreciation for teenagers. He would play some of the great organ classics, rather than shorter numbers with more obvious appeal. And he never repeated music from recital to recital, which would have allowed him to use the tool of familiarity. Students would applaud loudly, knowing that, the more encores he gave, the less class-time they would have.

I was employed to teach band instruments in the classroom, to rehearse a band, and to teach social studies. A lady next door taught strings and trained a girls' choir. My predecessor had left to develop a band at Glebe.

The principal, Blake Spears, operated very differently from Mr. Hunt in Regina. The latter had staff meetings that followed parliamentary procedure and usually took about 1½ hours. Spears' meetings consisted of a series of announcements. They began promptly at 4.00 pm, and if you were 12 minutes late, you had probably missed the meeting entirely.

At that time, the vice-principal was promoting nuclear air-raid shelters. The theory seemed to be that you could escape death by entering a well-supplied basement and emerging, after two weeks, to a world that was back to normal. How naive could you get?

I remember a tall English teacher named Ted Nicholson. He was noted for his stamina for spending endless hours helping students get ready for the school's annual Variety Night. I can still picture him violently signaling from back stage for the next participants to come forward.

Ted also had an identical twin in the army and was frequently mistaken for him. Once the army brother (who was not in uniform that day) knocked on Ted's classroom door. After they had consulted, Ted handed his brother the book from which he was teaching, indicating where he had got to in the book. The brother went in and carried on the lesson. Then Ted knocked; the exchange was made again, and this hoax was continued till the students twigged what was going on.

I recall a character in the form of a student who haunted the music department named, Herve (Champ) Champaign. If you gave him time, he would tell you how superior jazz musicians were to classical musicians. He would be at the piano during after-school dances.

A sizable minority of the students were French, although you often couldn't tell that from their names—names such as Joan Morgan.

Usually, at assemblies, my band would play accompaniments to hymns whose words were projected onto a screen. That gave the members good practice, but it exposed any weaknesses in the band to the whole school. My band was never in a class with bands like that of the Technical School, though I was given credit for my entries in the Festival competition.

Perhaps the most memorable event of my tenure was the visit of Lord Alexander[68] to the School of Commerce commencement in 1951. The Governor-General had sent his daughter to the school and he was invited to be the speaker, which, of course, he did with great aplomb. All went well, except that I had misunderstood the agenda. I had thought that the band's feature number was to be played when the curtains opened, rather than before the curtains opened. We had practised an arrangement of the Barcarole from the Tales of Hoffman. But, in the event, we didn't get to play it. As you can imagine, my mistake didn't help my standing with the band.

In the fall, the school was dismissed early on Football Fridays. To make this possible, the periods were all shortened on Friday mornings and one period was left out, a different one each week. Logically, the students would work harder in the 20-minute periods than in the 40's. In practice, the excitement of the coming game made them higher than kites from early morning. Good, short videos might have filled the bill, had they been available then.

In one of these years (1950-53), Eleanor trained a junior choir at Glebe collegiate. In an entry in the Festival, her choir won their class with her interpretation of the English Song, *Cherry Ripe*.

Two decades afterward, two of my Commerce students turned up in Guelph and seemed to have fond memories of my teaching. Perhaps it wasn't all bad!

The town of Goderich is on Lake Huron. Perhaps because it was at the end of two train routes and one bus route, it was considered one of the worst locations for gossip. I went there in 1953 as music teacher of the District High School and Supervisor of Music in the Public School. At the same time, Eleanor had become organist and choir director of North St, the larger of the two United Churches. The long-distance phone calls leading up to these appointments put us in a phone charge bracket that I hadn't imagined we would ever see—$26.00!

I found that I was training at least a quarter of the 400-odd entries to the annual Huron County competitive Festival. Besides the various choruses, there were the vocal solos—7 boys, 7-9 (in age); 7 girls, 7-9; 7 boys, 10-12; 7 girls, 10-12; duets; trios; double trios; junior choruses; intermediate choruses; senior choruses—you may get the picture.

The first year, the adjudicator was Cyril Hampshire, supervisor of music for the Hamilton Public Schools. His favourite advice for dealing with a piece of music was, "Do something with it". Pupils and teachers who treated music as something to be interpreted, not just reeled off with correct notes, received his praise, and a lot of that reflected glory came my way. After one competition, I was asked to conduct the various choirs in the piece they had all performed.

The next year, the adjudicator was a Mr. Rose, a vocal teacher in London with whom I studied for a few months. I recall the praise he gave to my 22-voice high school group who sang Hugh Roberton's setting of *Go Lovely Rose*. At one point the music breaks into eight parts, and I so positioned the singers that there weren't more than two singers on any one part standing together. The resulting blend was not lost on Mr. Rose. I had been inspired by my recording of the piece by Roberton's own Glasgow Orpheus Choir.

I don't think that group of kids enjoyed me. I recall an occasion in Ottawa when a colleague heaped what seemed like extravagant praise on his home-room class for the way they had conducted themselves on one occasion. I probably neglected that practice of praising when it could have done some good. Some of these singers I trained to take part in the Provincial High School Choir that was organized one Easter. I had the group over to the house on Good Friday to practise. I think I had imagined that they could practise all day. But by noon they had had it.

That year, the provincial conductor was Don Wright, who was famous for his approach to the changing boy's voice. The main idea was to get boys to use their lower range before the change set in, since they would still have that range after they had lost their higher notes. This also negated the older practice of telling boys not to sing during the changing period. Of course, they were not told to stop yelling during sports! And, many of those boys never got back to singing, assuming they were not musical.

Because I promoted the Don Wright approach, I found that the music director at the Anglican Church was much perturbed, since he needed to have his boy sopranos continue to produce the top notes—some of the same boys that I was classifying as alto-tenors. I forget how the matter was resolved. But I had never told the boys they should quit singing soprano.

In addition to participating in the spring festival, I put on at least one concert for the public school. I invited the provincial supervisor, Dr. Fenwick to grace the occasion. (Or Dr. Friendly as Esther used to call him after some of his broadcasts.) When it was his time to speak, Dr. Fenwick said, "I really shouldn't have come, because I am a very busy man. But I wanted to drop by on my way from Renfrew to Pembroke!" My stock rose in the community following that speech.

About a month before we left Goderich, the historic County Court House burned to the ground. The fire had begun just after the High School's Variety Concert had got under way. One section of the school was being used for the students whose act hadn't yet been reached. News of the fire reached them first, and some students were about to head for the auditorium to let the parents know of it. But the teachers in charge had the presence of mind to prevent this from happening, knowing that that would have spelled a very premature finish to the carefully prepared concert. As it was, when the parents came out, many openly wept, such was the attachment they felt for their court house.

One thing I recall from preparation for that concert. Someone had done a parody of a famous poem to work in local references. I found that the rhythm of the parody didn't scan and said so. I was told that this didn't matter when it was all for fun. I had to remind them that the fun would be spoiled if the rhythm wasn't right.

My predecessor, Alex Clark, a son-in-law of Mr. Scott the high school principal, had moved to London. On my first day in the public school, I helped a grade 3 class by singing an octave lower than they would be singing. Having done only high school work for some years, I had not recently developed my falsetto voice. But, on my way home for lunch, a chubby boy from that class told me cheerfully, "You haven't got as nice a voice as Mr. Clark has!"

CHAPTER 36

# Teaching in Burlington

In 1955, I became supervisor of music for the Public School Board of the little town of 9000 that carried the name of Burlington. There were three schools: Central, East Burlington (later renamed Lakeshore) and John A. Lockhart, named after a long-time principal of Burlington Central Collegiate and treasurer of Trinity United Church. A year later, the newly built Wellington Square Public School was added to my circuit. In 1958, when Burlington annexed two townships to multiply its population several times, I remained with the four schools until a general reorganization of 1961.

One feature I shall always remember is the groups of boys of changing and changed voices that I rehearsed at recesses in each school. Spirituals and sea shanties made up most of the songs I used. A group I had in Wellington Square was special. There were 18 boys in grades 7 and 8. Unlike most boys who tend to lose their upper range before they have confidence with a their new range, one boy had a range while in grade 7 from G above the treble clef to second space C in the bass clef.

I once took this group to sing for the Masons[69]. The boys were specially entertained by their aprons. Another time, I heard indirectly that the boys met frequently in each other's homes. And what did they do but sing the same songs I had taught them! Of course, they never told me about that.

At Christmas, each school would have an in-school concert featuring every class. One year in Central School, I organized so elaborate a day of carols that my very supportive principal, N. Stevenson, decided that I had stolen rehearsal time that properly belonged to other subjects and made sure that that kind of thing, though successful, was not repeated!

For spring concerts, I finally followed a pattern that had been set by Stewart Buchanan, who supervised five schools to

*Staff of Wellington Square Public School*

the east of mine and who eventually became the director of music for the entire Board of Education. The pattern involved a massed choir, representative of a group of schools, which performed in the Burlington arena in the latter part of May. One part of Stu's pattern that I never used involved square dancing, an activity that I've always found more fun to do than to watch.

I tended to fill up my programs with special groups. One year I had a boys' chorus of about eighty from the four schools which did a group including the folk song, *The Eddystone Light*. There was a punch line, in which the keeper's mermaid wife called out, "The Devil wi' the keeper of the Eddystone Light" that I assigned to a grade 8 girl in one of the back rows of the massed choir. Most of the audience hardly knew what was happening.

There would be songs done by each of grades 6, 7 and 8, and songs done by all members of each school. And the great majority of songs came from our rich heritage of folk songs.

One year, I featured a child prodigy on the piano from grade three. Another year, two sisters played who had mastered the accordion, an instrument for which I have always felt an arena was an eminently appropriate place!

In 1959, the national anthem was still God Save the Queen. Typically, this song dragged. But that year, I managed a four-part arrangement of all three verses that really moved!

My favourite choir marshal—of the hundreds of kids who took part—was Larry Davis, later one of Esther's teachers. He seemed to have what it took to manage a crowd of excited youngsters. This was just another reminder that these events are necessarily the result of great team-work.

Wellington Square School was the scene of my re-uniting with Don Farquharson, with whom I had shared the Campus Co-op Residence 15 or more years previously. Louise, his daughter, was among some singers who entertained the school's Home and School Club on the night in question.

It was also at Wellington Square that the principal, Marshall Mayes, staged a local victory over the School board. He had been after them to create off-street parking for the staff, since parking was not permitted on the street. Then one day he could wait no longer. He told the teachers all to park on the street the next morning. Then he arranged that the police would give them all tickets after they had done so. When the tickets were all in view, Marshall collected them and took them all to the board office. The bulldozers were on hand that afternoon!

It was also Marshall Mayes who reacted typically to what I did with one song. While the *Maple Leaf For Ever*[70] originally contained the line, "The Thistle, Shamrock, Rose Entwined," some of us wanted to be more inclusive of those who made up the population of Canada. So I taught the line to read, "The Lily, Shamrock, Thistle, Rose". Marshall, a long-time Conservative supporter remarked, "That's not the way I learned it!" He probably learned it like this:

*In days of yore, from Britain's shore,*
*Wolfe, the dauntless hero came,*
*and planted firm Britannia's flag,*
*On Canada's fair domain.*
*Here may it wave, our boast, our pride,*
*and joined in love together,*
*the thistle, shamrock, rose entwined,*
*The Maple Leaf forever!*

*Chorus:*

*The Maple Leaf, our emblem dear,*
*The Maple Leaf forever!*
*God save our Queen, and Heaven bless,*
*The Maple Leaf forever!*

In 1961, after the city's Board of Education had appointed what became known as "the three wise men," that is, the Director of Education, the Superintendent of Public Schools, and the Inspector, it was decided to down-size music and other arts. Accordingly, Stu Buchanan got the top appointment, one supervisor became his assistant, another got a job elsewhere, and I was demoted to do the very exacting job of teaching music at the grade 7 and 8 level in Glenview and Laurie Smith Schools. I was no longer a supervisor of other teachers. Three years later, my experience there led me to find my job in Guelph where I became the music supervisor in a setting where I was free to plan and create the role in my own way.

CHAPTER 37

# Summer Courses

I've mentioned that the BA Music course at University provided a good liberal education, but little practical preparation for teaching school music. In my case, the gaps were filled by a number of summer courses. At the College of Education, I was awarded a Specialist Certificate in Vocal Music in secondary schools. To add the equivalent certificate in Instrumental Music took three summers.

The first of these summer courses must have taken place in 1949. Dr. Roy Fenwick was the principal, with Martin Chenhall directing the instrumental section. Every summer, Dr. Fenwick directed a choir to which virtually all students belonged. I remember that one number we practised, *My Father's Green Pastures,* assumed a Christian background in most students, as you could do in those times.

In the instrumental work, we used instruments belonging to Toronto High Schools, and part of our training was necessarily focused on the care of instruments. Sometimes, summer school teachers could at first be as hard on the instruments as high school students in this regard.

In the string classes, most of us had violins and were constantly reminded to let our bow sail freely across the strings. In the clarinet class, beginners frequently produced squeaks. Once Dr. Fenwick dropped in and commented that he had enjoyed 'the descant part'! When we tried playing oboes, Chenhall would compare us to Sandy McPherson, the bagpiper[71], because of the tone we typically produced.

In the daily orchestra classes, Mr. Chenhall gave us regular school orchestra repertory and challenged us, as beginners, to play one note in every bar to at least keep our place in the music. Being indifferent sight-readers, many students found the challenge too much.

One day I had the opportunity of going to North Toronto Collegiate to observe the instrumental program led by Jack Dow and a string specialist. For a long time, this program served as the show-room for instrumental music in the schools of Ontario. Later, I attended a concert in Eaton Auditorium by the North Toronto Orchestra, featuring Schubert's Unfinished Symphony. Nancy Charles of Muldrew Lake, (later Smale) was the first desk cellist in that concert.

Another summer, I got my Certificate as Supervisor of Vocal Music in Elementary Schools, the most useful of all my summer courses which were designed specifically for teachers.

We took Orff courses in the 1960's. One afternoon, in Burlington, when Eleanor was having an afternoon sleep with the radio going (how does she do that?) she suddenly found the rhythms too vigorous to ignore. It was Carl Orff's opera, Carmina Burana.

Carl Orff was a German composer who gave much of his life to developing an approach to elementary music education which he called Music for Children, or Schulwerk[72]. He used the human body as a rhythmic instrument and taught children first of all to sing the interval of the descending minor third. First he taught them songs that had only two notes and gradually adding one note and then two, he worked them up to singing songs with five notes or the pentatonic scale[73]. Since one can sing most Asian music as well as western folksongs using that scale, his approach depended heavily on these songs.

Orff found that the ear would accept just about any combination of notes within the pentatonic scale, and taught children to improvise within these limits. He designed tuned percussion instruments, including xylophones of different sizes whose notes were removable to make them easy for beginners to play. From the child's point of view, however, notes were added, not subtracted!

In the course, we made a lot of music in different ways. Every afternoon, we had a movement class designed to train the body as an instrument. We were taught to tense only those muscles that were immediately needed, and to be endlessly creative in the movements we made. At one point, our instructor told us, "Just think where you aren't!"

Many students used this training for private Orff classes. Many children failed to persevere with learning instruments like piano or violin because of the reliance on small motor skills. After a few weeks, the beginner would lose interest because his/her fingers had yet to manage the notes with any facility. A year's preparation in Orff classes which relied on gross motor skills often meant that the student could turn successfully to piano or orchestral instruments. And of course, the Orff experience was itself a joyful one.

For a time, Eleanor and I conducted Orff classes in our Burlington basement. For me, however, the big gain was the inclusion of Orff activities in my school curriculum. In Guelph and the Wellington county area schools, I gradually accumulated a set of Orff instruments for each floor of each school. Copying a design developed by Keith Bissell[74] in the Scarborough schools, we had carts made which housed xylophones, glockenspiels, hand drums, and, sometimes, metalophones, with a drawer to keep mallets, triangles, cymbals, maracas, and other noise-makers.

As a result of the Orff influence, I used physical movement with greater frequency. I also discovered that if I had the children move to the rhythm of the song, it helped them learn the notes in half the time. It was more fun, too. Another current influence in school music came from Zoltán Kodály (pronounced ko-dye) a well-known Hungarian composer[75]. Kodály's approach, based on Hungarian folk-songs, stressed knowledge of the scale with constant use of the tonic sol-fa and of hand signs. Being an eclectic, I used as much of his methods as I could fit in as well.

CHAPTER 38

# Life in Sault Ste. Marie

On a hot day in late June of 1946, I took the CPR train to the Sault, to find a room for the fall. About half way there I heard a loud bump and the train came to a halt. I found out afterwards that we had hit a sun kink. Rails are, of course, laid down with gaps to allow for expansion of the metal in heat. On this occasion the expansion was so intense that he rails got pushed together and caused one of them to bend. The engine and the first coaches managed to jump the kink. But the rear cars, including mine, were derailed.

However, during the hour or more which we had to wait to be rescued, I discovered a profusion of wild raspberries by the tracks!

I found a room in a boarding house kept by an eccentric lady who was very strict about people not leaving a ring around the tub. And she believed that she could be a perfectly good Christian without leaving her house on Sundays.

I managed to get involved as the pianist for the Church of All Nations (a United Church). Reverend Mr. Stymiest had succeeded a much more successful minister and moved about in his shadow. Many of the members were CCF activists who nevertheless spoke of having cooperated successfully with the Communists in the past. I listened to those stories in silence. In my experience, when Communists made friends, they usually managed to dominate the relationship. But there were good folk in that church and I never regretted joining them.

It was a popular sport, in that border town, to beat the customs. Often a product would sell for less in Sault, Michigan, and people would brag about how they deceived the border officials. One fellow teacher at the Collegiate told me of how he had worn running shoes when heading for the States, bought new leather shoes across the border and on returning, hid his running shoes under his coat. This was a wide-spread practice.

There was no bridge over the St. Mary's River at that time. Ferries ran every half hour until about 11:00 pm. I took in a game which used to be played every year in January. The basketball team of the Sault Ontario Collegiate almost always lost to the Technical High School of Sault, Michigan. That year, the game which was played on the American side, was a cliff-hanger with the lead changing hands over and over again. The score was still almost tied as the time approached for people to run for the last ferry. But the referee came out and said, "I have to announce that there will be a late ferry at midnight." The Canadians won by about 49 to 46. I don't normally cheer at games but that night I totally lost my voice!

In 1943, the CCF had amazed everyone by winning 34 of the 90 seats in the Ontario Legislature. Two years later, however, only eight of those survived in a run-off election. Sault Ste. Marie was one. The member had evidently received strong support among the employees of Algoma Steel, but very little at the paper factory. I got to know one paper-worker named Callahan who belonged to the CCF. He would tell me how conventions of his union would be booze, booze, and booze from start to finish while CCF conventions would be relatively civilized. I was once at his house when a gallon of maple syrup had arrived. I was tempted to be greedy but didn't want to appear so. "Oh, have some," he said.

That winter, the weather was very different from elsewhere. The news was full of blizzards and deep snow-drifts in England, in Saskatchewan, and in Toronto. But, in the Sault, we had about one inch of snow. When spring came, I had wanted to go on the Algoma Central Railway to Hearst and back through what I had heard was some of Ontario's most picturesque scenery. But it was not to be—perhaps in the next life!

CHAPTER 39

# Life in Regina

Weather was always an appropriate topic in Regina. I have three observations. When I first got off the train there, a strong wind was blowing, and it felt, not like a city in the middle of a land mass, but like a sea-port. In the winter, you get the same, only more so. One Sunday afternoon in January, Norah McCullough was flying in from Regina, and feeling the need of exercise, I proposed to walk out and meet her. It was scarcely more than a mile from the airport to the nearest city buildings. But I was dissuaded. The temperature was about minus 39 (at which Fahrenheit and Celsius are almost the same) and, unimpeded by the buildings, the wind I was told, could be deadly. During six weeks of our last winter there, the temperature never rose above 30 below (F), and one morning, when the reading was minus 52, there was an ice fog which prevented me from seeing even a short block away. Of course, these temperatures would have produced more complaints in Ontario where high humidity is added to the equation.

Our first landlord was Mr. Vasilash, a carpenter of Romanian origin who had some extraordinary ideas about what being Canadian meant. A carpenter by trade, he was very proud of the two houses on Quebec Street he had built. He lived in the upper floors of one and rented the basement to us. We entered through a kitchen, 9 feet by 12. The bathroom, 9 x 5, went off to the left. Ahead was the living room, 9 x 9, and, to the left of it was the bedroom, 9 x 9.

Relations with our neighbours upstairs were cordial at first. At one point, Mrs. Vasilash bought a pressure cooker and was delighted when Eleanor had showed her how it worked. She finally exclaimed, "The pressure, she cook!" But after a few weeks, relations turned sour. Mr. Vasilash complained that we had too much furniture and there'll be bugs! How did he know? One day, Eleanor left a jar on the floor, just inside the main door and, on returning, found the jar back against the wall! And she had written her father about our situation and had left his reply in the living room. She was sure she found it in a different place on her return.

The place was certainly full, including the furniture people had given us, and I recall that we had to enter the bathtub cornerwise because the remaining floor space was covered with boxes of books. Having only so much money at the beginning, we decided that we would rather have a quality mattress and quality springs than a full bed that was less comfortable. And, when we had brought apple-boxes from a fruit store, Mr. Vasilash cut them to size for the springs. But the arrangement was plainly a very temporary one in his mind, because he kept asking us when we were going to get the rest. And, because she wanted all the light the kitchen window would allow, Eleanor didn't put curtains across it. One day a Romanian friend of Mr. Vasilash was walking by and asked whom he had in the apartment. "A school teacher," he replied. "Doesn't look like a school teacher when there are no curtains in that window!"

We found out why our landlord had got nasty. He had a chance to sell his other house, and he thought that if he made life unpleasant for us that we would leave, allowing him to move his tenants from the other house and thus make his sale. But summer found us still there and we came east for the holiday. On my return for the new term, Mr. Vasilash greeted me with the pronouncement, "We've decided you can stay for another year. But you must put curtains on the kitchen window and get a proper bed like ordinary people!" Naturally when he put it like that, we complied.

The apartment in which we spent our third year was not a great deal better. The landlord had bought a three-story house and divided it into four flats—ours on the main floor, two smaller ones on the second, and a tiny one in the attic. No thought had been given to equalizing the heating, which, in winter, varied from 75 degrees F in the basement to 60 degrees F on the third floor. Worse than that—the electrical wiring had never been redone for the apartments. We all had to have half power stoves, and there could not be more than two of them going at once. It was not uncommon for us to be starting preparations for a meal, only to have a knock at our door with the request that we wait till our neighbour had cooked because company had arrived unexpectedly. Our landlord would go into a week-end with a bag of fuses, hoping they would last.

But, for all the inadequacies of our living arrangements, we enjoyed Regina whose people we found both friendly and outgoing. We frequently gathered at the home of David Smith, the Director of Adult Education in the Government. There we found Norah McCullough, secretary of the Saskatchewan Arts Board, other workers in adult education, and people with the same frame of mind. (Some of these had witnessed our first arrival in Regina.) But we did have friends with whom we didn't necessarily talk politics.

I belonged to the 85-voice Regina Male Voice Choir, directed by Lionel Allen, which represented most walks of life in the city. I vividly recall Wednesday night rehearsals in the Labour Temple, which the men would fill with smoke at intermission. But the accompanist, who was organist at the Catholic Cathedral, was outstanding. And we performed some great stuff.

We joined a local film club, where we shared some great films with many of our friends. Was it there that I took in one about a Jewish doctor in Nazi Germany named Dr. Mamlok? Some of the films were produced by the National Film Board and told us intimate things about nature.

Tommy Douglas[76] was not only the provincial premier, but one who played his part in the needs of the community. It was said that CCF support in a residential area was high because of people's admiration for his wife, Irma. On one occasion, when the riding needed an auctioneer, Tommy found one among the rural members of his caucus. At another time, I was on a committee to line up topics of discussion for local members. Douglas had started a series of Sunday broadcasts on a local private station. Calling the broadcasts Fireside Chats, after the series by Franklin D. Roosevelt, Douglas' series were non-political and nostalgic. This bothered some members of the CCF who thought Tommy should be taking the opportunity to proselytize. Anyway, I included in my list, The Premier's Fireside Chats: Are they in line with CCF Policy?" As a member of the riding association, Tommy received a copy. And he lost no time in putting me in my place. His letter as good as said that his broadcasts were none of the CCF's business. I suppose there are times when every politician has to be brutal!

Then there was the bassoon. The Regina Symphony didn't have proper bassoons, and someone informed me that W. Knight Wilson, the violin teacher who conducted the orchestra had an old bassoon in his studio. He loaned it to me, and I took it downtown for repairs. The joints were made, not of cork, but of string and the string had come unraveled. The repairs set me back $35, a lot of money in 1948. I then took it to the summer school in instrumental music in Toronto. My first disappointment was the refusal of the 1st bassoonist of the Toronto Symphony to give me lessons. This was a mere French System bassoon, not the approved Hoeckel system. However, I bought a case for my instrument for $2 and my father-in-law used his power tools to rearrange the partitions to make the instrument fit. And I used the thing in the summer course. One morning, Martin Chenhall, the principal, asked us to name a tempo that was slower than Largo. When the class had failed to suggest an answer, I suggested Molto Largo. Said he, "It'll be molto bassoon, in a minute." We had fun.

In the fall, I joined the Regina Symphony, being careful to play every half note. In that way, I lasted one concert, which included the Strauss overture to Die Fledermaus. Afterward, the tenor and baritone saxophone players who supplied the bassoon parts and who were long-established players complained that my instrument was out of tune with them. So Mr. Wilson told me, "I think we'll drop it."

The first desk cellist heard that Eleanor had a cello and tried to persuade her to come and play with him. But she couldn't see herself fitting the role, and declined.

When I was leaving Regina in 1950, I wondered what to do with the bassoon. It really wasn't mine, but, as I had spent what I had in repairs, and, as it had proved useless in Mr. Knight's setting, I probably could have got away with keeping it. But I did the honest thing and returned it!

For a church, we attended Carmichael United, now no longer listed in Regina. The minister, Reverend Homer Lane, was an effective preacher. I recall that, among other features, he would pause after a long sentence to let the listener catch up with his thoughts (That's one of the things I like about our present pastor, Reverend Diane Clark). His children's stories were also special.

Homer Lane was sometimes mistaken for Tommy Douglas. Once at a church camp, someone saw Homer heading for the chapel for the regular worship, and spread the rumour that Tommy was speaking. Homer had a good turn-out that day!

While in Regina, we overlapped with Coster and Mary Scovil. Coster had become principal of St. Chad's, the theological school for the Church of England which had a reputation for being a bit more flexible in its intake process and whose graduates would often find themselves in rural parishes. Coster insisted on giving the students practical programs, such as a motor mechanics course lest their cars break down far from help across the prairie. I understand the students wondered what it had to do with theology!

Mac Hone was the Art teacher who shared a classroom with me at Regina Central Collegiate. We still have his representation of a Greek Orthodox Church in our hall. We left Regina when Esther was barely a month old. But we received a card from Mac, covered with drawings of recorders in the appropriate numbers, with the message, "Now you are a trio where you were a duet. Advance congratulations on the Ewing Octet!"

We once visited the Hones in their suburban house where water had to be fetched from a public tap. How they managed in winter, I never asked.

CHAPTER 40

# Life in Ottawa

Esther was born a month before we left Regina. Years later, when she had started piano lessons, she was given a ditty to apply a rhythm to a scale she was practising, "I was born in Re-gin-a-Sas-katchew-an." In Regina, my mother came out to help. As she was bathing her, she remarked how long her back was.

As we took the train to the east, we got a good view of the, rather historic, Winnipeg flood of 1950[77].

We were in our Bay Street apartment for only a few months. But it seems that a lot happened in that time. As I recall, the main door gave onto our general purpose room which had a view of the street. To the left of this door, a hallway led past a bedroom on the right, and the kitchen, also on the right, which paralleled the bathroom at the end to the hall. We may have had room in the kitchen for eating breakfasts. But meals with company had to be carted to the room at the front.

Gordon Jocelyn came round a lot then. Joy was in Toronto then. Gordon had a room for himself but hadn't gotten quarters big enough to bring his family yet since, after the war, affordable housing was scarce. One night, during dinner, Gordon went to the kitchen and returned saying, "I've just done a complete job on your coffee-maker." Our Pyrex had been standing on the gas stove keeping warm over a low flame. And Gordon couldn't find the light switch.

It was to the Bay Street apartment that Bill Dale, then a curator at the national Gallery, used to come, in the days preceding the arrival of 'my friend, Jane Laidlaw'. Until that time, we three found a unique way of making music. At that time, Bill had acquired some skill on the viola, while Eleanor had been working on the cello and I, on the clarinet. Since there was no known music scored for that combination, I had to arrange everything specially, even with Christmas Carols! A famous New York jazz group of the time called itself, The Chamber Music Society of Lower Basin Street so we called ourselves The Chamber Music Society of Lower Bay Street.

Jane's arrival was on the night of Swan Lake. The Royal Ballet was making only one appearance in Ottawa. As the Trembles, the arrogant ticket agents, wouldn't allow mail orders, tickets were available only at the box office of the Bank Street theatre one day starting at 10 o'clock. So groups of friends organized relays for holding our places in the line. I arrived at 7:00 am when there were 50 ahead of me! By the time I had to be relieved to depart for school, there were hundreds, and by 9:30 when the police intervened to require the box office to open early, the line was completely around a long block.

It was a snowy morning in December, and there was great camaraderie among those waiting in line; thermoses of coffee were passed up and down, and many had brought portable stools. Eleanor found that Esther in her buggy was happily quiet as long as she was outside. But when the line moved inside, she immediately began to complain. At this point, one of the men in line seeing her problem loudly urged that she be moved forward.

It was on the night of the performance that we first met Jane. Eleanor had always enjoyed hosting a party to mark special events and so we had quite a party. But who all were present that night besides Bill and Jane, I don't recall.

One set of neighbours that became long-time friends were the Milners. Bruce, their first boy, was a little older than Esther but needed just as much supervision. We did a lot of mutual baby-sitting at a time when extra pennies were a bit hard to come by in both families.

Another neighbour, who was Irish, wondered why we had chosen to call our daughter Esther which had religious and political associations. But we wondered back when their baby arrived and was called Michael Sean.

We were living on Bay Street when the Census takers arrived. Eleanor patiently answered their questions, including the query about languages spoken. "And is the baby bilingual, too?" Said Eleanor, "Well, she says sounds as much like French as English so I might as well say yes."

In the spring of 1951, we bought 30 Pansy Ave., and moved in. 30 Pansy was a two-story brick house on a one-block street in Ottawa South, a little south of the Rideau Canal and not far West of Dow's Lake. It took us about 7 minutes to get to the southern terminus of the Bank Street car line, a means of getting about of which we car-less people made frequent use. We were able to afford the down payment on the house because of a low-interest loan from my Aunt Muriel, who was at that time living very modestly in British Columbia. Without this loan, I could not have qualified for a mortgage—or bought a house at all at this time.

For over a year, Bob Norgate[78] boarded with us. Bob was an artist who had been hired to teach Art at Fisher-Park High School where Gordon Jocelyn taught. Bob was there under a misunderstanding, since the principal had wanted commercial art and Bob had no interest in doing this. So he was out of a job at the end of the year. He opened a local studio which didn't last and went back to Toronto where his large family completely disowned him because he was not working at what they thought was marketable. He died very young, unfortunately.

While with us, Bob did a small sculpture of Eleanor playing the cello which Eleanor later got cast in bronze. He also produced in charcoal a large mural on a religious theme. He kept bringing down sections of this work from his room, a few at a time, to show us, spread out on the floor. One week-end, Bob was away and it was not clear as to whether he might return by the Sunday night. My father was visiting at the time, and would have slept on our sofa in the living-room, but that we thought Bob's return sufficiently problematic that he might as well use Bob's room. At about 10 o'clock, the door-bell rang—I forget who was there, but it wasn't Bob. But Dad appeared on the stairs, complete with his bedding, thinking the move to the sofa was called for. He would never have been caught in another's bed!

We had no piano at Bay Street but a family of musicians whom sister-in-law, Marg, had known during the war were getting a new one. The Benders wanted their old one to go to a home where it would be appreciated. When we told them we'd love it but just couldn't pay for it in the foreseeable future, we thought that that had settled the matter for a time. But we rented the house that summer, and, almost as soon as we reached the cottage our tenants sent us a message, "Your piano has arrived." Thus we acquired an old Heintzman grand with 19th century legs.

30 Pansy was also the scene of the engagement of Bill Dale and Jane Laidlaw. One evening, they disappeared into the kitchen briefly, and when they re-appeared in the living-room, Jane held out her hand to show us her ring, and remarked, "The pause that refreshes." The wedding was in Deer Park United Church in Toronto where Jane's father, the registrar of the University of Toronto, was a member. Soon after Michael, the Dales' first-born, arrived on Valentine's Day, 1953, Esther's first act was to fetch her favourite afghan to cover the baby.

And it was at 30 Pansy Avenue that Suzanne Butler and Eleanor were reunited. As children in Port Credit, Ontario, they had been in Sunday school together. But then the Butlers had moved to Vancouver and were out of touch with the Dillons for some years. One day, in Ottawa, Eleanor was wrapping garbage in a piece of newspaper, something we did in those days, and noticed an ad for a meeting that was sponsored by the National Association of Canadian Clubs of whom the secretary was one, Suzanne Butler[79]. A phone

*The old Heintzman in Burlington*

call assured Eleanor that it was indeed THAT Suzanne Butler. From then on, Suzanne became the friend who dropped around with great frequency. It was there that these two spent hours revising the first draft of Suzanne's first published novel, *My Pride, My Folly*. Eleanor would suggest how a certain sentence should read and Suzanne would respond, "But that's not what I mean!" The book was published by Little, Brown a year or so later.

At that time, Suzanne was living with a civil servant named Sally Morton, who was keeping company with Allister Crandall whom she later married. The house happened to be near the Rideau River and across the street from the Russian Embassy. Someone in Allister's office who had a gripe noticed that his car was frequently parked opposite the Russian Embassy and reported him to the RCMP. I believed Sally must have saved him from embarrassment by owning up to the relationship.

Allister conducted the Ottawa Choral Society. I remember hearing him conduct a performance of *Messiah*. Eleanor and I also attended a performance, in St. Andrews Presbyterian Church (the church MacKenzie King[80] attended) of Bach's *St. Matthew's Passion*. It was done by a choir of just 40 singers from a loft half way up one of the walls. We tended to prefer the intimacy of this performance to the cast of thousands whom Sir Ernest MacMillan had involved.

One day, Bill Dale and I went up to the attic room of our home to construct something that would help store bathroom equipment. We became poetic. To my quote of Alfred Lord Tennyson,

> *How dull it is to pause, to make an end,*
> *To rust unburnish'd, not to shine in use!*
> *As tho' to breathe were life.*[81]

Bill responded with Shakespeare,

> *There is a divinity that shapes our ends,*
> *Rough hew them how we will*[82].

About 1990, at a meeting of Hamilton Conference, I got speaking to a St. Catharines minister named Ron Wallace. Comparing notes, we realized that we had both lived in Ottawa, and I mentioned that we had lived on a street with a funny name. He asked the name, and then asked for the number. When I said 30 Pansy Avenue, he replied, "Yes, we bought that house from you in 1953 and your name is Ewing!" He had been a teenager then.

Before we left Ottawa, Esther had become old enough for clever sayings. At Christmas, 1952, someone gave Eleanor some wide, green slippers. Esther had to be the first to try them on. And, when Morrey was quite small, he fussed a lot, and his sister had a suggestion, "Mommy, let's put him back in your tummy!

CHAPTER 41

# Life in Goderich

In the summer of 1953, Eleanor traveled to Goderich to find accommodation. I was surprised that she was able to rent a good-sized house. A recent mayor named Mooney had passed away and his widow moved into an apartment, making her comfortable house on tree-lined North Street available for rent.

I recall 7½ rooms with 1½ bathrooms. From the front door, a hallway ran to the back, with two bedrooms opening on the left, doors on the right leading to front and centre living-rooms, and the kitchen at the back. Through kitchen and pantry, to the right, one accessed the dining-room. On the left of the kitchen, stairs led up and down, and a two-piece bathroom opened on the far left. Upstairs was a bedroom and full bath, with a small sitting-room between. The front 3/4's of the upstairs was floored but unheated and served as a gigantic storage chamber.

The house was steam-heated. That meant that the furnace drove the temperature of a huge water-tank in the basement. The water level had always to be kept right. If it were too low, one risked destruction of the heating-coils. If too high, the water could overflow. You read the level by means of a gauge where the bubble needed to be always visible. If it wasn't visible, one was never sure whether the level was too high or too low. To add to the water, one turned on a tap with a tiny spout. It took a lot of patience to stand in front of it till the job was done.

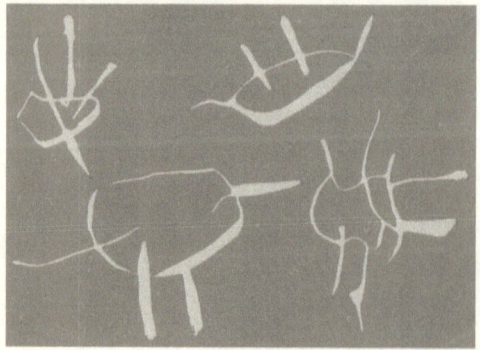

*Family drawing by Esther at age 3, from which Eleanor made Christmas cards*

One day, I was sure I needed more water, and I turned on the tap. The phone rang, and I was alone in the house. You guessed it—I had a major flood to contend with. And had the basement floor been constructed so that the drain was at the lowest point? No such luck! The only drain was through the laundry tubs, and all the surplus water had to be shoveled up into those tubs. However, when the furnace worked, the house was very comfortable.

Dr. Graham lived on a corner lot next door. Since many of his patients failed to get his prescriptions filled because dollars were too few, he put us all on tonics. For most of us, the colour was pink. But, for pregnant women, the colour was green. So local busybodies would stand near his door to see what colour of tonic each woman took out!

In the summer of 1953, our family spent two weeks or a bit longer at 75 South Drive in St. Catharines, a house into which my parents had moved the previous year. I forget why my parents were away. But I know that I took a couple of low-paying jobs while we were there. I served gas at an Esso station at $35 a week; how much the fruit-farmer paid me to thin peaches, I don't recall. But I was called in from the orchard one morning to answer a family emergency. Eleanor had taken the children—Morrey in a carriage, Esther, a 3-year-old, by her side—down-town for some shopping. In a hardware store, Esther left her mother to explore, and when she realized she didn't know exactly where her mother was, she thought she would set out for 75 South Drive. The back door of the store was open, and from there she looked for the viaduct over the old canal. Instead, she found the St. Paul Street Bridge leading to the west end of the city. Eleanor was understandably frantic, and in addition to summoning me, called the police. Finally,

*Esther*

a lady in the west end phoned the police when she found her children playing with a strange child who didn't know her way home. A few days later, Esther and I were taking a bus to Toronto, and, as the bus passed through the West end, Esther cried out, "That's where I was lost!"

The train journey from St Catharines to Goderich was then an interesting trip. For reasons I don't remember, I went one day with my mother and Morrey, while Eleanor and Esther followed a day or two later. A blistering heat-wave was in progress. We left St. Catharines late in the afternoon on a local train. From Hamilton to Brantford, we rode the Montreal-to-Chicago express, which used to back out of Hamilton before continuing west. Then we got a puddle-jumping, two-coach train to, I think, Tavistock where we boarded the Toronto to Goderich train for the rest of the trip.

We reached Goderich about midnight and stayed the night in the Bedford Hotel. We asked the management to store one of Morrey's bottles in their fridge. They seemed strangely reluctant. We had forgotten that this was still a temperance zone. To have stored a bottle, the manager risked jail at least!

After the movers had gone, the heat wave came to an end. I recall that Eleanor and I especially enjoyed leaving the children with my Mother while we had a refreshing stroll in the north-west breeze off Lake Huron.

In June, there had been a lot of long-distance phoning to get me appointed to the joint position of High School music teacher and Public School music supervisor, and to get Eleanor appointed organist and choir mistress of North Street United Church. I wondered if we would ever recoup the phone bill, which came to about $25.

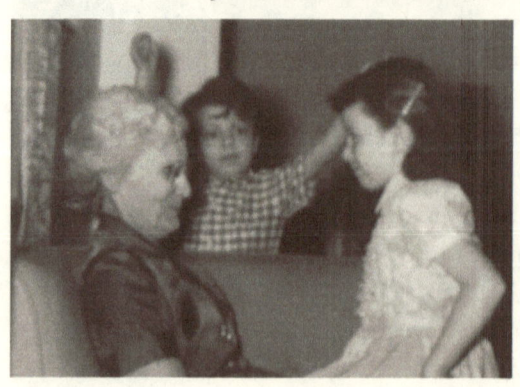
*Morrey and Esther with Grandma*

Eleanor had to sign an extra statement for her church job. Her predecessor was a great success musically. But he had been caught cohabiting with his wife before marriage. So Eleanor had to sign away her job in the event of a moral lapse!

I believe that Eleanor did an outstanding job at the church. I remember the enthusiasm with which we men processed at our first Christmas, singing *Masters in this Hall*. And the junior choir was a going concern. Annually, the Women's Association put on a dinner for these children. For this occasion, Eleanor laid down certain behavioural rules. One was that the children were not to start eating until the president began. The president was a bit garrulous, and seeing the situation, one of the women came to her and told her, "Pick up your fork!"

There was a local men's choir called The Harbouraires. In the Festival of 1954, after they had been heard by the adjudicator, Cyril Hampshire, he remarked, "What basses!" Since several of the best of these basses were also in the North Street choir, Eleanor went up afterward and said with a twinkle in her eye, "You can't have them!"

My only connection with the Harbouraires had to do with one of the Sunday night rehearsals when I was asked to substitute for the accompanist. The leader, George Buchanan, a bass in the North Street choir and assistant manager of the post office, was very insistent about correct rhythm. The choir rehearsed in a common room of a hangar at the local airport. It was the time of Hurricane Hazel which produced floods in central Ontario and heavy rains farther out. There was a leak in the hangar roof and there was an inch of water on the concrete floor. The men practised standing up. They were doing a complicated number about Daniel and the lions' den, which I remembered doing with the Regina Male Voice Choir. But the first tenors couldn't seem to feel the beat. So forgetting the water, George stamped out the beat, causing the men to go home with wet trousers!

Catering was an essential activity of the church women. They would compete consciously with the Presbyterian women for some of the key community events. One day, the North Street women were working all day to prepare for a turkey supper. Every turkey had to be stuffed. When they were almost finished, one of the women realized that a band-aid that had been on her finger at the start of the day was now missing. All the turkeys had to be re-done until the offending band-aid appeared. If it had been known that such a thing had been found in a North Street turkey, they'd never have heard the last of it!

In the end, small-town politics in a church setting cost Eleanor her job. In her first year, Eleanor would counter complaints that she sometimes had the choir do a hymn as an anthem. When someone sang out of tune, she would let them know, and, in other ways, she refused to pander to the wishes of individual singers who would prefer to be treated as prima donnas. About three of these quit, one by one. Eleanor was able to replace them with better singers, and her choir probably ended the year in the best shape it had been in for a long time. Unfortunately, the quitters had social standing where the new members didn't. Accordingly, in October, Eleanor was summoned to a meeting of the Music Committee and accused of alienating the affections of certain choir members, who were not named. Of course, her resignation was requested. Later the church board was astounded to be told that she had resigned. But the damage had been done.

In that church, the Music Committee was strictly a hiring and firing committee. It never functioned as a support group for the incumbent. The record of that congregation could be seen in the number of appointees they had had as organists and the number of ministers called in the two preceding decades.

One institution inspired much local pride. Before my time, one of two public schools had been closed while a large addition was made to the other. The one that closed was taken over by a long-time resident named Mr. Neal, who had accumulated a lot of historical objects in his house. He transferred his collection to the school and opened the Huron Country

Museum.

I remember different rooms that were given over to showing the historical development of certain machines, like the fire engine. Typically, he did not put up signs, "Do not touch." Rather he would say, "Try it and see if it works." He had reconstructed the country's earliest jail cell and the visitor was invited to sit in it and get the feel of it.

In the spring of 1953, the historic County Court House burned to the ground. Much of it was destroyed but in one corner they were able to salvage some lumber. As the demolition crew freed up individual planks, Mr. Neil was there to receive them and proceeded to build an addition to the museum using the planks. The addition displayed the Model-T Ford in which he had crossed Canada in the 1920's. This car was very special because in addition to regular wheels, it also had railway wheels. Since Northern Ontario didn't have a highway then, he had to use the railway tracks. He didn't tell us how he knew when the trains were coming!

In Goderich, Morrey, who was then a little over a year old, learned to walk. Afterward he figured out a trick for escaping the hand of the adult who was leading him. He realized that he was short enough that if he bent down, the adult couldn't reach him without stooping. He then ran beyond reach. This trick was especially useful in stores where he could escape and then explore other parts of this fascinating environment. We'd catch him eventually, of course, but not until he'd had some fun!

This desire to explore was more pronounced in his sister. One day in church, Esther had been left back in a pew in the company, I think, of Mrs. Howard, our favourite sitter. That, of course, meant

*Don with Morrey*

that she was down in the congregation while her mummy was at the organ and her daddy was in the choir. No one should really have been surprised when she escaped and headed for the organ during a serious part of the service.

Another day, Esther was missing until a neighbour noticed her down on the beach. In those days, you could rent bathing suits and it seemed that Esther had persuaded the rental lady that her mother was just coming and had sent her ahead to get dressed in her suit. When found, Esther was in a strange bathing suit about to enter the water, showing no fear of the water despite not yet being able to swim.

This interest in exploring came naturally in both children. From my curiosity about the car-barns in Winnipeg, to my walking along all roads near Oshawa in my teens, to my trying all alternative routes I could find between Burlington and Guelph during my commuting years, I always wanted to know what was just beyond my vision.

Those were still the days of fountain pens. Pens that needed to be filled, if they wrote well, were treasured and were often the subjects of special gifts. I don't remember where mine had come from but it was a special possession. One day in Goderich when Eleanor had a woman in for cleaning whom she didn't entirely trust, and finding my pen on the mantelpiece, she hid it—with the best possible motives. But afterward she was never able to find where she had hidden it!

Someone once remarked that, being at the end of a railway line, Goderich was an ideal location for gossipers. In particular, there were two women, both members of North Street Church, who were good at it. They had developed the skill to the point where it gave them power over people's lives. But Eleanor learned a trick to counter the process. Often the gossiper would make a statement, tempting the listener to add information. Eleanor's answer became, "Is that so? Do tell me more!"

Our minister in Goderich was Howard Dickinson. I remember his christening Morrey. I'm afraid I don't recall the subject of any of his sermons. But I do recall the Sunday when the North Street service was broadcast on the CBC, an occasion for which Eleanor prepared the choir in a special way. I recall that Howard and Isabel would take turns in selecting new cars. His view was that he didn't believe in acquiring "a ton of steel that we don't need." Isabel was a good friend. A married daughter was killed in an out-of-town accident while we were there.

Special friends of ours in Goderich were the Holmes. Dave taught at the collegiate. Both were great supporters of the work Eleanor did at the church. Dave insisted on valuing my successes in the town's music. On the day his principal told me that I wouldn't be kept on at the collegiate, he came over to reassure us both that my work was just fine. These two had the name of Holmes before marriage, a fact that led to endless confusion in the Department of National Revenue.

From Goderich the Holmes eventually moved to St. Thomas. I remember hearing that Jesse won a law suit for $300,000 against a doctor who had made a crucial misdiagnosis. I believe I heard that, having made her point, she accepted legal expenses and forgave the rest.

While we were in Goderich, a Baptist minister was, with great difficulty, eking out a living on a most inadequate salary. He had only one arm, though what he could do with that arm, many are unable to do with two. His wife was an artist, and when her husband received a call to a larger church in Brockville, she tried to sell her paintings, so they could discharge any local debts they had. One of these paintings dealt with the fire at the County Court House. She tried to sell this to Mr. Neal, the curator of the Museum. But he didn't appreciate art. What he would have liked was a cheap picture of a blaze that he could hang at the museum entrance with the caption, "Leave your fire here."

CHAPTER 42

# Dad and Mother, 1945-1983

*Morrey with his Grandfather Ewing*

In June, 1945, Dad retired from the Oshawa Collegiate and Vocational Institute (OCVI), sold the house at 602 N. Simcoe Street, and moved to a bungalow with an acre of peach trees on what was then the Niagara Street Highway at the northeast corner of St. Catharines.

Dad's chronic migraines had been getting worse, and Mother schemed to make it financially possible for him to retire at age 60. It surprised her that they were able to live as comfortably as they did for the next 18 years. Indeed, they did so well that, not only were they able to spend six weeks in Florida for each of many years. But, if Dad had $100 or so left at the end of a month, he would slip it over to his son on the basis that my expenses were never ending.

Knowing nothing about growing peaches when he began, Dad crossed the road to the government experimental farm, read up on the best advice, and carried it out meticulously. Even though he had never grown anything but grass all his life, he had the best peaches on that road that year and the next. A man with a truck came by every morning and bought all the peaches he had ready and paid him a good price.

*Esther & Morrey with their Grandmother Ewing*

A specialist had provided Dad with a kind of pill that would stave off his headaches. But, as long as he was teaching, it had little effect. With the out-door work, the pills worked.

Thoroughness had always been one of Dad's characteristics. But one time it didn't pay. Finding the odd mouse in the bungalow, Dad took two measures. He scattered mouse-seed, and finding a little hole in the cellar wall, he plugged it. The mouse-seed caused the creatures to crawl away and die. But, since Dad had closed their exit, he found one carcass in the motor of the fridge and another in his bed-room slipper. I'll not describe the stink!

*75 South Dr., St. Catharines*

After two seasons, Dad got the feeling that he'd like to expand his agricultural operations. So he sold the Niagara Street bungalow and bought Ledcriech, a two-story house on four acres of land in Fonthill, half way to Welland. Aesthetically, it was a good move. Economically, it wasn't. The peach trees were downhill and Mother estimated that in the first season, they carted two tons of that fruit uphill. And the market was much more difficult and not nearly as lucrative. In addition, they sowed beans in the side field—backbreaking work, even had they been younger. To make up for the poor peach market, they had the upstairs of the house made into an apartment. They had no trouble renting it, but the tenant was an Englishman who was used to giving orders, and he never hesitated to give them to his landlord!

Aunt Muriel was a part of this ménage for a time. In the running of the Brechin store, she had been a full partner with Uncle Don. But when Uncle Don moved to Keswick during the war and teamed up with the Rutherfords, there was no place for Aunt Muriel. So she came to Fonthill. But the dynamic wasn't right. Aunt Muriel found herself filling the role Mother usually expected to fill. Anyway, after a time, Aunt Muriel moved to Brit-

*Don, Charles, Eleanor, Isabel & Morrey*

181

ish Columbia, where she stayed for over 20 years.

There were compensations for the practical difficulties of life at Ledcriech. They made some great friendships in the village. In the local United Church, Dad taught a Bible Class, giving it the best that he knew. And it was in the car of one set of friends that they drove repeatedly to Florida, between New Years and Easter. One year, on their way back, they followed a route which lay through one of the more primitive villages in Tennessee. They mentioned that, at the sight of some of the characters that appeared, they decided not to open their windows.

It may have been the same year that they got shown over the White House. On the way out, Vice-President Nixon was shaking hands. He would ask where people were from and smile suitably. When they said they were from Canada, the smile froze!

My parents used the same Florida cottage every year. The landlady would write each fall to ask if they wanted it again, they would reply in the affirmative, and around New Year's, they would be off to Pass-a-Grille on the Gulf shore, now part of St. Petersburg. A lot of the time they played shuffle-board, a game I have never learned. They seemed to spend more time with other Canadians than with the permanent residents of Pass-a-Grille.

One day when I was visiting Ledcriech, the Jack Nixons, cousins of cousins, paid a visit. I recall how well the three children managed to be part of the social group. I am making it sound as though this story concerned Dad most of all. But Mother was a part of it all, and was often the one who informed me of what had been happening.

In 1952, after about five strenuous years at Ledcriech, my parents moved to 75 South Drive in St. Catharines. I believe they really pulled their weight as members of First United Church of that city. One day I remember going for a walk with Dad in some light rain. For him this was deliberate. He wanted to go overseas again, and was getting himself accustomed to the weather he would likely encounter when he went.

In 1958, Aunt Mary retired from her work in Japan, and took an apartment on Welland Avenue in St Catharines. That way, she was close, but not an integral part of the Ewing household. When Dad died, she moved in to look after Mother.

In 1960, Mom and Dad visited Britain, traveling by air. That was before jets were used, and the flight was a very tiring ten-hour trip. I believe that, before Dad's last illness, they had decided that this would be their last time overseas. Around this time, I also recall people at Muldrew being amazed when Dad and Mother paddled to Memorial Pines unaided.

In the fall of 1962, Dad was operated on for cancer of the colon. A Toronto specialist, Dr. Murray, had been searching for a cure for cancer and he was confident that this operation would be successful. As a matter of fact, within two weeks Dad was up and around and feeling fine. They went to Florida again in the winter. And early in the summer they were at Muldrew. But then the disease returned and Dad was again in a Toronto hospital, where it was found that the cancer was in the liver, where it was inoperable. Dr. Murray came to see Dad, expecting to commiserate with him. But Dad had already faced the situation, and it was he who sympathized with Dr. Murray in his disappointment over his failed operation the year before.

Dad spent his last days in a Catholic Hospital in St. Catharines. Because he was in considerable pain, he didn't want the experience unnecessarily prolonged. But he did find time to be considerate of the nurses, saving them trips when possible. Before he was gone, they made sure that we knew that they had loved him.

A day or two before Dad's expected passing, several of us were at 75, discussing immediate plans. I had long believed in cremation in preference to burial, and also felt that, if the casket were to be in the funeral home, it should be closed, as a recent photo would prove a more accurate reminder than the best the embalmers could do. But I found that this was not a time for arguments, and when Mother declared that Dad's friends would be hurt if they couldn't see his likeness, I gave way and her wishes were granted. A decade later, we used cremation as a matter of course when she and Aunt Muriel died.

Dad's funeral was held in First Church, with interment in Oshawa. Hugh Dale drove from Guelph to be a pall bearer. In his homily, Reverend Mr. Ward told of the first service he had taken as minister of First Church. In doubt as to whether what he offered would be right for this congregation, he was completely reassured when an elder (Dad) patted him on the shoulder and told him everything would be fine.

After we had been to the Oshawa cemetery, we gathered in Dorothy Van Luven's home for a social time. It was there that, when they arrived, Bill Stevens' parents brought the news of President Kennedy's assassination.

In the 1950's, Laura Haines, a Nixon relative of our McLeod cousins, lost her memory and behaved in what my mother described as an unseemly way. Somehow she got away from her care-givers and walked down the street without her clothes on. My mother, horrified, declared at that time that she hoped that SHE wouldn't outlive her mental capacities.

As long as Dad was alive, he leaned on her because of his chronic ailments. When Aunt Mary joined her at 75 South Drive, the shoe was on the other foot. Mother became the one receiving most of the care. But one's tendency to remember a person more vividly by their last years has made it harder to recall the Isabel Ewing that I knew and loved. Of course, we made many trips to St. Catharines, and she and Aunt Mary came often to Burlington. They continued the habit Mom and Dad had formed of spending the winter in Florida. Then, in 1970, Aunt Mary went to see Aunt Muriel in BC.

For years, our family had been urging Aunt Muriel to come back east where we could see her more often. She had been determined to remain independent, even though her circumstances weren't of the best. But in 1970 while she was walking with Aunt Mary on a Vancouver street, her purse was snatched and she was knocked to the ground and her arm broken. This time she agreed to come to St. Catharines after recovering and in January the three of them left for Florida. By then we had moved to Guelph, and, since the trip to St. Catharines was far enough that we just didn't feel we could do it often enough, I got power of attorney for Mother's affairs before they left. In their absence and with their agreement, I was able to sell 75 South Drive, buy a house within a block of ours in Guelph and get their effects moved, so that they could move right in when they returned.

I don't want to dwell on Mother's difficulties in her last years but one story is particularly fun. One day as the Ron Williams' family was arriving at the cottage, Mother wanted to provide the children with something to drink, but mixed the canisters and used flour instead of powdered milk to mix it with. Glynis recalls that their mother made them drink it up!

Mother kept declaring that she wanted to make one more trip overseas, but Aunt Mary was sure this would not be a success. Esther remembers that if I began to play a familiar hymn on the piano, Mother would sing all the verses from memory. Soon after moving into her Guelph house, she went out for a walk and couldn't remember how to get back. When a stranger asked her where she lived, she gave her St. Catharines address! In her final weeks, she no longer knew even me, and, when I took her for a drive, she asked, "Why is that young man taking me out?"

Mother died while her sisters were in Florida. Her body was cremated and a memorial service was held at Harcourt Church when they returned. The minister at that time was Reverend Donald McLean, whose brother-in-law, Reverend Norman McKenzie, remembered learning his Greek from my father in Oshawa.

CHAPTER 43

# The United Church 1946-1955

Some time in the winter of 1946-47, I visited Central United Church in the Sault. I remember only the minister's first name, because he and the minister of another Sault church, Saint Andrews, were sometimes dubbed Alex the first and Alex the second. Alex the first talked about stewardship that day and was bemoaning the fact that average United Church givings, nation-wide, were just 4 cents a Sunday—one postage stamp (the price of stamps at that time). Then he admitted that Central's givings were slightly better—8 cents a Sunday—two postage stamps.

The next few years saw major campaigns across the country to change that situation. The Wells organization was popular with church planners because of their spectacular results. However, they used methods that alienated many members, and made many resolve that they would never use Wells again. So the church developed its own organization which was effective, without publishing the amounts everyone gave.

In many cases the campaigns were targeted around new buildings. It was a period of new development which led to new churches which began worshipping in schools, but dreamed of being able to have their own building.

This was also a time when more women were entering the ministry. The Church had ordained their first woman in 1936. But it was some time before married women were allowed to serve. This affected Lois Wilson[83] who in 1980 became the first woman moderator. Her ordination had been considerably delayed, although her husband was a minister.

CHAPTER 44

# The CCF-NDP, 1950-1980

The party's fortunes have usually been different in Saskatchewan and in the rest of Canada. I remember Professor Carlyle King telling about the CCYM or youth branch of the CCF. In various provinces, the Communists would ply their skills at boring from within, until they effectively controlled the CCYM of a province. Then the party would dissolve the organization. After the smoke had cleared, a new organization would be put together. Said Dr. King, "That never happened in Saskatchewan."

The CCF, of course, was founded in Regina in 1933 and won power in Saskatchewan eleven years later. The Liberal Government had quietly kept their supporters in line by threatening to cut people off welfare if they didn't vote Liberal. When the war began, however, most of those people had jobs and felt much freer to vote as they pleased. This facilitated the CCF sweep in 1944.

When the CCF came to power, the province was as close to bankruptcy as a province can get. So, before carrying out the party's radical program, provincial treasurer Clarence Fines had to make the province solvent. Nevertheless, in the first term, Tommy Douglas' Government legislated a solution to the farmers' acute shortage of seed grain, and introduced Hospital Insurance and Government auto insurance. In the election of 1948, money poured into opposition coffers from the private insurance companies. They were nearly successful. The CCF majority dropped from one that was overwhelming to a ratio of just 3 to 2. However, by 1952, the people had come to accept this government and the CCF was returned by 42 seats to 11 for the Liberals. In 1956, they withstood a major challenge from Social Credit, and, in 1960, Tommy sold the idea of Medicare for a fifth majority.

Douglas was sometimes criticized for not bringing in Medicare till he had been premier for 17 years. It had been included in the party's platform in 1944. Evidently Tommy thought that circumstances were more propitious for it in 1959. However, by that time, a number of doctors had arrived who had opposed the National Health Plan in Britain. These spearheaded a campaign in Saskatchewan to make people afraid that, if Medicare were introduced, few doctors would be willing to serve. As a result, in 1964, after Tommy had left to become national leader, the CCF, under Woodrow Lloyd, lost power to the Liberals under Ross Thatcher, a former CCF MP. Thatcher won again in seats in 1967, though the CCF (then the NDP) got a larger popular vote. But, by 1971, Alan Blakeney[84] had become leader and won a large majority on a platform that included an increased respect for the integrity of the northern forests. When Thatcher went over to congratulate Blakeney, NDP supporters sang generously, *For he's a jolly good fellow.* Shortly afterward, Thatcher died of heart failure.

Blakeney remained premier for eleven years. One of his talents had to do with getting the cooperation of the civil service. Typically, he would tell them, "We have just passed a certain law. I want you to think tonight about the best way to carry out the legislation, and surprise me in the morning."

After the 1934 election in Saskatchewan, the CCF became one of the two stronger parties in the province, and they have never lost that position. The party attained that position intermittently in British Columbia and for much shorter periods in Ontario and Nova Scotia. The history of the party in most of Canada—always in the federal field, usually in the provincial—has been a situation where there was another choice for those who were dissatisfied with the government of the day.

Everywhere outside of Saskatchewan, the 50's were a period of difficulty for the party. In Ontario, the successes of the 40's (34 seats in 1943, 8 in 1945, 21 in 1948) were succeeded by 2 in 1951 (Oshawa and Timmins) and 3 in 1955, when the new leader, Donald C. McDonald[85] won back the riding of York

South which Ted Jolliffe had won twice and lost twice. Donald kept that seat until 1982! But rebuilding the party was slow business—5 seats in 1959, 7 in 1963 (when Stephen Lewis[86] first took Scarborough West) and 20 in 1967.

The party has also done well in by-elections—when canvass resources could be concentrated. In the 60's, three stand out. In 1964, Waterloo South federal (now Cambridge) elected Max Saltzman, a dry cleaner. Tommy Douglas had repeated, "Let Galt speak for Canada when it came to bringing in Medicare." It was part of the pressure that induced Pearson to bring in a national health plan a couple of years later.

In 1966, James Renwick took Toronto Riverdale, a riding the CCF had won back in the 40's. The Liberal candidate was a well-known recent evangelist. But Stephen Lewis brought his organizational skills to bear with good results. On election morning before rush hour, hundreds of tiny sandwich boards were put on the side-walks of the main intersections. They said, "Vote Renwick today." At 9:00 am the police made the party remove them. But by then, the impact had been made!

Then, in 1969, Middlesex South, including part of London and the town of Strathroy, a native settlement, and a rural area, became available. This time, Morrey was able to spend two weeks campaigning while staying with Eleanor's cousins, the Bigelows. We elected Archdeacon Ken Bolton. Afterwards, Jane Bigelow[87] was elected, first a controller and then as Mayor of London.

In 1968, McDonald was seriously challenged for the leadership. Jim Renwick didn't win. But his campaign undoubtedly contributed to the success of Stephen Lewis' campaign two years later. At that time, McDonald retired in favour of Walter Pitman[88]. Seven of Wellington South's eight delegates, including Morrey and me, supported Pitman. But Lewis had garnered the early support of the motors unions, which sent large contingents of delegates to the convention, and he won handily over Pitman.

One issue that divided some of the delegates at the 1970

convention was whether provincial grants to separate schools should be extended to the high school grades (at that time, partial funding went to grades 9 and 10; none beyond grade 10.). Premier Davis got votes in the 1971 election by refusing extended aid, though he changed his mind 13 years later. The NDP was on the other side, though we were by no means unanimous about it.

When the resolution to favour extended aid came to the floor, Stephen Lewis and Walter Pitman both went to the microphones to support the resolution. Morrey did too and, as he found himself at a mike between the other two, he remarked on the fact. He was at that time in grade 13 and student president of Centennial Collegiate in Guelph, and his argument was based on observations of actual Catholic students. He had a little too much to say. The chairperson, his cousin, Jane Bigelow had to call time. With lots of others wishing to speak, and limited time allotment for the resolution, the 3-minute rule had to be strictly observed.

As leader, Stephen Lewis came across at first as rather strident, and the 1971 election saw us lose elected members, including Pitman and Bolton, and saw Stephen himself surviving in Scarborough by a narrow margin. But, by 1975, Stephen had become relaxed with voters. He shared a free-time telecast with the famous Gordon Sinclair[89] to good effect. And he made the most of three TV debates in each of which a different two leaders were to debate. In the first, he refused to appear because the CTV network had mistreated their employees and Liberal Robert Nixon had to debate with himself. In the second, Premier Davis and Nixon performed at such a childish level that Lewis gained by comparison. In the third, Lewis effectively took on the Premier. When the votes had been counted, the Davis Government had been reduced to minority status, while the NDP had won the official opposition with 38 seats. This result compared well with that of 1934.

In 1945 in British Columbia, a coalition government weakened the CCF opposition, and the coalition was returned in

'49. They then instituted the Single Transferable Vote, whereby a candidate would win a seat on the first ballot only by winning a majority of first choice votes. Otherwise, the voters' second choices were distributed till a candidate won a majority. In the 1952 election, the CCF under Harold Winch got 21 seats among first choices to 19 for the newly minted Social Credit party. But many of those who voted CCF as their first choice gave Social Credit their second choices and Social Credit, under W. A. C. Bennett was able to form a minority government.

For the next 20 years, a right-wing Bennett Government held sway. After winning majority status, they had returned to the old voting system, and former Liberals and Conservatives kept them in power. A long-time Minister of Highways, Reverend Phil Gagliardi, had a lot of modern highways built, while getting a record number of speeding tickets!

In September, 1972, Dave Barrett[90] scored an upset win for the NDP. Dave had first won a seat in the Legislature, after he was fired from a government job, and captured Dewdney against his former boss. While a law against the publication of public opinion polls during election campaigns was in force, a Vancouver merchant sold Bennett-burgers and Barrett-burgers and kept track. As Premier, Barrett brought in a number of forward-looking measures, including Government Auto Insurance. When the Socreds (Social Credit Party[91] Members) were voted back in, in 1975, they promised to privatize this insurance. Instead they raised premiums and made it pay. But young Bill Bennett was even more right-wing than his father. And, until 1991, he managed to keep the socialist hordes at bay.

In Manitoba, the CCF made the mistake in 1941 of taking part—for a year—in an all-party coalition. Following the next election, the CCF, and then the NDP, remained a distant third until 1969. In that year, the unpopular Weir Tories were seeking re-election. The Liberals held a leadership convention and chose an ineffectual party hack. The NDP scheduled their convention for the last week in June. When the election was called for that time their convention had to be moved to the beginning of June. Eddy Schreyer ran for the leadership and got TV coverage, both for his speech accepting the nomination and for his acceptance speech after winning the nomination. In the election, the NDP surprised most people by finishing one seat short of a majority. A French-Canadian Liberal from St. Boniface crossed the floor to give the NDP a majority. But Schreyer had few outstanding members from which to choose his cabinet. Many of the MLA's had run to carry the party's colours, not expecting to win. Nevertheless, Manitobans got Government auto insurance and a lot of other social legislation.

Schreyer ruled for 8 years, before being trounced by the Lyon Conservatives in 1977. Two policies of the party helped win the election of 1981. One was a rule that riding associations couldn't nominate until their membership attained a certain percentage of the vote in the previous election. The other was the search for candidates who could grace a cabinet. They planned a return to power and managed it resoundingly in '81.

Federally, the CCF in the 50's was a western party. Suffering badly from the Saint Laurent sweep of 1949, they made a modest comeback in 1953 with 23 seats. But in the Diefenbaker sweep of 1958, they were down to 8 seats, with both leaders M.J. Coldwell and Stanley Knowles defeated. Then the New Party was fashioned out of the CCF and the Canadian Labour Congress. While it was getting organized, Walter Pitman, then professor of History at Trent University, won a by-election in Peterborough. Members' hopes ran high when the convention assembled in Ottawa. Both candidates for leader were from Saskatchewan: Hazen Argue, the only CCF survivor from that province in 1958 and house leader from then till the convention, and Tommy Douglas. The name, New Democratic Party was the result of a convention vote. After losing the leadership, Hazen Argue defected to the Liberals.

In 1956, a significant change of policy occurred in the NDP. The Regina Manifesto of 1933 had called for the nationalization of the major means of production and distribution. The Winnipeg Declaration of 1956[92] cancelled most of that program, proposing instead that the corporations should continue to manage their business, but that they should be subject to rules governing their relationship to the state and society generally. A similar change took place in almost every social democratic party in the world. But there were people in the CCF who were greatly dissatisfied with this change.

In the 60's, Professor Mel Watkins[93] headed a royal commission on the economy. Among other things, he recommended that corporations be charged their full share of taxation. "A buck is a buck," he said, "where tax rates are concerned." Mel soon realized that the NDP was the only party prepared to support his ideas and he took a membership. Sometime in the next year or so, he became dissatisfied with the party's economic policies. Since passing the Winnipeg Declaration of 1956, the NDP had not advocated wholesale nationalization of key corporations. But Watkins wanted nationalization restored to make the party really socialist.

At the 1969 federal convention in Winnipeg, Mel was accused of waffling, and he replied, "I'd rather waffle to the left than to the right." From then on, members who shared his views were dubbed members of the Waffle.

At first, Ed Broadbent and others supported the Waffle. But, as the movement took shape, it lost its appeal to such people. During the three years of the Waffle's presence, meetings of the party tended to divide into two camps, with little friendly intercourse between their adherents. Waffle supporters were intolerant of others whom they called anti-socialist. They would shout slogans and finish every speech with "Yours for an Independent Socialist Canada." As a result, many activists tired of the conflict and preferred to stay away from meetings.

The federal leadership convention in Ottawa in April, 1971 became a major focus for Waffle activity. They organized strong support for the candidacy of Jim Laxer[94], especially among university students. A large body of delegates arrived in Ottawa, committed to his support. That support was caucused every night, so that they would be in no doubt how they were to vote during the day. They contested every executive election, every constitutional election and every policy resolution and lost every time. The final caucus resulted in a resolve to continue the fight, day in, day out, throughout the year.

A principle was involved here. Ordinarily, democratic control of policy in the NDP involves the period leading up to a convention, when resolutions come from the ridings and are debated and voted on in that context. The rest of the time, members of this party of volunteers need to use gatherings as a time to celebrate their points of agreement. Most of our members are busy people. Indeed, I once half seriously defined an NDP member as someone who was president of something else. Such people don't need to be lectured for their failure to qualify as socialists because of a technicality.

In the spring of 1972, a three-man committee was named to try to resolve the internal argument. As a result of its deliberations, it called for the dissolution of the Waffle as a part of the NDP. This was taken to the Provincial Council meeting in June which was held in Orillia. In Guelph, some Waffle supporters managed, at a poorly attended meeting, to get one of their adherents elected as an alternate to Council. Doris Bannon was the regular delegate. A guest at this Guelph meeting, Ms Kelly, wife of Mel Watkins, tried to manipulate proceedings as the price of her continued membership in the party.

Three days before the Council meeting, a well-attended meeting in the Guelph Public Library considered the fate of the Waffle. Eugene Benson moved a motion about freedom of discussion in the NDP, which was, for him, the real the issue. The meeting ended with confusion in a lot of minds.

The Orillia meeting was the best attended meeting of Provincial Council in the history of the party. The Waffle had made some stinging attacks on the leaders of some of the union affiliates, and the unions were having none of it. They took advantage of most of their delegate entitlements to attend the meeting. The motion to dissolve the Waffle party passed by approximately 212 votes in favor to 85 against.

Following this meeting, there were contentions, both in the party and in the press, that Waffle members had been expelled from the party. In fact, the only people who left the party did so on their own accord. In the years following, some of the former Waffle supporters got together as a Left Caucus. One couldn't object to this. But after 1972, party factions didn't tear each other apart as had happened in the Waffle era.

That Ottawa Convention in 1971 showed something else. The Ontario Conservative Convention that had chosen William Davis[95] as leader and Premier experimented with the use of voting machines. But the machines broke down and Davis had to give his acceptance speech on TV at 3:00 in the morning! The NDP convention, by contrast, counted ballots by hand (Morrey supplying one of the hands) and ran through four ballots in about two-and-a-half hours.

It was also about this time that the NDP stand on a matter of principle was not strongly supported in the country. A tiny separatist group, the FLQ[96], in Quebec, kidnapped and later murdered a Quebec cabinet minister and a British diplomat Assuming that this criminal act was part of a revolution against the state, the Federal Trudeau[97] Government put the War Measures Act[98] into force, and arbitrarily arrested hundreds of citizens, denying them counsel or even communication with their families. Their crime? Supporting the democratic Parti Quebecois which later came to power in that province.

16 of the 20 members of the NDP caucus stood alone in condemning the government measures. For his pains, David Lewis received thousands of anti-Semitic communications, many from union members.

But, by 1972, as the new federal leader, David Lewis was on another war path, this time against corporations that didn't pay their share of taxes. Dubbing them "Corporate Welfare

Bums", he gave details of case after case of corporate rip-offs. (The plane that carried him across the country was nicknamed, "Bum Air"!) This time, he won more approval. In the election of 1972, Trudeau was forced into minority status with the NDP holding the balance of power. Several policy decisions were brought in, including the National Energy bill, according to which Canadian consumers could buy Canadian oil at not more than the export price. The trouble with minority governments is that they usually find an excuse to call an early election—one they can win. And so, in 1974, the NDP lost the balance of power and David Lewis lost his seat.

One of Trudeau's 1974 promises was that he wouldn't bring in wage controls, when the Right was blaming wages for inflation. But, with a new majority, he felt free to break his promise. Hundreds of union members sacrificed a day's pay to go to Ottawa to protest. But, by 1979 when they could have supported the only party that opposed wage controls, they seemed to have forgotten their concern and widely ignored the NDP.

CHAPTER 45

# The CCF-NDP, Locally

In Ottawa, I was treasurer—not a very efficient one, I'm afraid—of the CCF in the Ottawa district. Several ridings were grouped together on the understanding that, at the time, none were winnable. Donald MacDonald, who later became the Ontario leader, was national treasurer and used frequently to phone me to tell of civil servants who were willing, confidentially, to become members of the Sixty Club, as people were then called who would give the party $60 a year, a large sum at that time.

I remember a meeting to hear Michael Foot, a British Labour MP, who became party leader during the 80's. Bert Herridge, the Kootenay West MP, was present and was at pains to inform me if I didn't already know that, "Foot is one of the rebels, prominent in Labour's left wing." But, from his address, it was difficult to distinguish between his views and those of his leader.

Once I visited the Unitarian Church on Elgin Street and noticed the presence of Donald MacDonald and several other CCF friends.

There have been only two occasions when I voted for candidates who were not CCF or NDP candidates. In both cases, the party was too weak at the time to be able to field a candidate. The first was in the 1940 federal election when, as a student, I was living in Toronto Spadina. My vote went to Stewart Smith, the Communist (or Labour-Progressive as they called themselves at this stage). The other occasion was the provincial election of 1955 when I supported the Liberal as the lesser of two evils in Huron, which included Goderich. In 1959 and 1963, I was able to support our candidates in Burlington (or Halton West), but without any hope of winning.

Enter Ted McDonald, a high school teacher who had had

a term as the very effective president of the South York riding. Ted set about getting the Burlington NDP members organized, starting in 1966. After he had received the provincial nomination, he appeared one day at our door. Morrey was immediately enthused. He told Ted, "You win!" We worked hard, with the result that, in the election of 1967 when the party elected 20 members provincially, Ted got 28% of the vote in Halton West. The sitting member was George Kerr, who became Minister of the Environment, and whose children told their schoolmates, "Our Daddy is responsible for all the pollution in Northern Ontario!"

Ted ran again the following year in the federal election. It was Trudeau's first election and NDP candidates did not do well in Ontario. Dr. Howe, our one MP in Hamilton, and an effective campaigner for affordable drugs, was defeated. Ted's view of Trudeau was once expressed in terse language, "It's the same old gang with a sex symbol."

Top: Doris Bannon
Bottom: Carl Hamilton

I was elected president of the Halton West riding association during our last year in Burlington. One of my two opponents couldn't be present at the nomination and sent a speech via a tape recorder, a move that did not impress the members.

I might have had a year to rest from my political labour after moving to Guelph in 1969—but for Doris Bannon. Doris, an executive of Canadian General Electric, had known Eleanor from the Neighbourhood Workers' camp in Bolton. Somehow, she knew of our activity in the NDP. She chaired the nominating committee of the Wellington South organization and, in the fall of 1969, almost as soon as we arrived, she persuaded both Morrey and me to stand for the executive.

For almost a decade, Doris had been THE moving spirit in the local NDP. Her biggest find was Professor John Harney who was the federal candidate in the elections of 1962, 1963 and 1965. Together, they built the organization, and in 1965, John came within hundreds of beating Alf Hales, the perennial Conservative, leaving the Liberal candidate, Don McFadgen in third place. After that, John became provincial secretary, contesting the 1968 election in Scarborough West.

Often when I drive by a stone bungalow on the corner of Waterloo and McGee, one block east of Edinburgh, I remember Philip Lanthier who lived there. Phil was our federal candidate in the 1968 (Trudeaumania) election. We didn't move to Guelph till the following year, but he was definitely around for a few years more. A professor of English at U of G, he lost his position for taking too long to complete his PHD—the "Publish or Perish" syndrome, although I seem to remember something about his mentor, Marshall McLuhan, holding him up by being ill, but also about Phil being accused of spending too much time on community projects. In any case, he eventually moved to teach in a community college in Sherbrooke, Quebec. Since then, I have heard nothing about Phil. But I remember trying to cheer him up by reporting a by-election victory, and hearing his scornful response, "BY-Elections!"

Our provincial candidate in three provincial elections—in 1972, 1975, and 1977—was Carl Hamilton. Federal secretary when the CCF was becoming the NDP, Carl had subsequently studied law and begun to practise it in Guelph. In the 1969 election, I sent out about 50 canvassers for a municipal slate that called itself, "Action Guelph". None were elected, but Carl was the runner-up and, when a vacancy occurred the following year, was appointed to fill it on the Guelph City Council. He was re-elected every time until his retirement in the mid-nineties.

Carl's main opponent at the provincial level was Harry Worton, Liberal MPP from 1955 to 1985, and a real fixture in the job. Carl once told of an all-candidates meeting, held in the Ponsonby School before about 100 farmers. Carl carefully explained what the NDP would do for farmers. Then it was Harry's turn. "You know, I didn't have the educational opportunities that Carl had," he said. "But I'll tell you one thing, if I'm elected, I'll do my best." Harry got 90% of the votes in that poll!

On our executive, there has always been a character, someone who makes life interesting, but often creates problems for the group. Saul Berman turned up around 1970, claiming to have originally recruited David Lewis in Montreal! As we searched for a candidate for the federal election of 1972, Saul had the craziest ideas—people with public profiles—but little interest in what we were about. One day during the campaign, Saul had a knock-down argument with the campaign managers. In this argument, he loudly raised his voice. The next moment, he collapsed, and died in hospital two hours later.

Our candidate that time was a retiree. Margaret McCready had been Dean of MacDonald College at the University of Guelph. On her retirement, she had spent three years in Ghana, setting up a home economics department for their university. When we realized that she was back in Canada, she had settled in her mother's house in Toronto. But she was a long-time NDP member, and she accepted our challenge. During the campaign, she boarded with us at 44 Dean Ave. She was a gracious guest, sometimes appearing with fresh mushrooms.

At one point in the campaign, someone shot at the NDP candidate in Kitchener, missing him by inches. Thinking that the event might have political significance, our police put a cordon around our house and asked anyone approaching the house what their business was. This included the teacher who picked Eleanor up each day to teach in Elora. Eventually, the police realized that exposure was the name of the game in a campaign and left us alone.

One day, Margaret addressed a group of union leaders. She said, "I've been out of the country for three years and am a little out of touch. I want you to tell me what I should be standing for." For a minute, this took my breath away. I was afraid that she was sounding wishy-washy. But her approach was appreciated. They thought her a rarity—a politician who listened to her electors.

It was in the fall of 1970 that Stephen Lewis defeated Walter Pitman as Ontario leader. Stephen's strength was that he had won over the United Auto Workers, and was able to have busloads of their delegates arrive at the convention. In Wellington South, we were entitled to send eight delegates, and seven were for Walter, including Morrey and me. At another meeting, Stephen remarked that he couldn't see any generation gap between us.

Around this time, I was elected president of the Wellington South NDP. I kept the job for enough years that it became difficult to find someone else to take it on. Actually, I remember more vividly my efforts to build the membership. When I began, there were about 190 members. By the late 80's, we had exceeded 600 and had earned three delegates to Provincial Council. But I may not have demanded enough of these members. Many were hard to reach between membership renewals. After the Bob Rae Government was elected, it became more difficult to hold them all. Some had joined on one issue and when they didn't like the way the Government was handling that issue, they were gone.

On two occasions, I found myself in conflict with important members of the riding. In 1982, three men were running for provincial leader, and each had people working for him locally. By far the most popular was Bob Rae. Our riding was assigned 20 delegate places, and I not only lined up potential delegates who would vote for Rae but circulated a list of them at the meeting to select delegates. But the president at the time, abruptly resigned in protest. As it turned out, he was comparing my practice to the custom at provincial conventions to circulate official slates of candidates for executive. I could never see the point of comparison. My list was not being handed down from the president or secretary. It was merely a case of informing the members of whom they could vote for to support Rae. The president was supporting another candidate, and he could have followed the same procedure. I thought too highly of this president to believe his action was sour grapes, since he didn't get many supporters of his candidate elected. Perhaps we were both stubborn. Four years later, the issue of extended support for separate schools was politically divisive. Up to this point, full funding reached only to grade 8, with limited funding in grades 9 and 10. Catholics had campaigned for years to have full funding extended to grade 13. Liberals and the NDP had agreed with them, though each had dissenting minorities. But in 1984, the Davis Tories reversed their stand, and so the election of 1985 saw all parties on one side, and the Ontario Secondary Teachers Association asked their members not to vote.

At the 1986 NDP Convention, opponents of extended aid tried to reverse the party's policy. Local separate school teachers heard of this and wanted to campaign from within the party, and I was approached for membership forms that would enable them to stand as delegates to the convention where they could support the long-time party stance.

In agreeing to this request, I miscalculated in two ways. I didn't anticipate that they would take over the delegate-selection meeting. They were a small minority of the riding's membership. But they were a disciplined minority. Normally, delegates are selected by a small minority of the members. But the new separate school members all came and they captured nearly all the places.

My second miscalculation was that I hadn't realized the extent to which these Catholics could use the party without committing themselves to supporting it after the convention. Naturally, the other members of the NDP were angry at the outcome, and just as naturally, they blamed me for letting it happen. It was no answer to have said that the members should have turned out in sufficient numbers to defeat the Catholic teachers. We were taken advantage of, and a nasty taste remained in the riding after the event. In the 1988 Federal campaign, the former riding president was campaign manager while I was canvass organizer. One day I remarked that I was enjoying how harmoniously we were working together again.

CHAPTER 46

# Life in Burlington—Part One

We rented a red-brick house on Caroline Street west of Brant, for the first six months. From there I walked to my three schools. Our favourite baby-sitter was Mrs. Jarvis who had a broad Scotch accent. We began attending Trinity United Church, where the minister was already preaching his last sermons, and Keith MacMillan was expected in January, 1956. We made the acquaintance of some of the Trinity people that we later came to know well, at the annual church picnic held at a park north of the town in early September. In particular, I can picture Laura Barr coming down the road holding her daughter Pat by the hand. She had heard that Eleanor took piano pupils, and wanted to sign Pat up with her. I think Eleanor must have agreed to the proposition, though I remember more vividly successive Barr girls in Eleanor's choirs.

At that time, the population of Burlington was about 9,000. In 1957, when Burlington annexed Nelson Township to the east and part of East Flamboro to the West, the population jumped to more than 30,000. Today, it is well over 150,000.

In March, 1956, Eleanor came in from a ride with a realtor to announce that she had found a house, four miles out in Nelson Township! Our address, to start with, was "21 Spruce Street" numbered from the nearest creek. Then, for a time, it was "Group Box B". Then after the new town had re-numbered everything, using a new thousand for each new concession from the west, and the same arrangement north-west from Lake Ontario, we became 4379 Spruce Avenue.

4379 was a large frame bungalow just two blocks from the Lakeshore highway No. 2. As you entered the front door, the large living-room opened on your right, with dining-room and kitchen behind it. On your left lay the three bedrooms, with coat closet immediately ahead and bathroom at the end of the hall. The basement ran the whole length of the house.

This house and others near it were part of a new survey which replaced vineyards. Some cedar rails with grape vines could be seen in a nearby field. The developers did not save the rich topsoil in which the grapes had grown. I had to try to develop a front lawn on very sandy ground. In the back, the septic system that preceded sewers had the effect of fertilizing the lawn, which required twice the effort in cutting that I needed in the front. We planted a row of Lombardy poplars as a wind-break between us and the park behind. They didn't thrive in the soil they were planted in, and about half of them were dead before we moved away after 13 years.

The day before we moved in, Doris Dillon, Eleanor's brother Bob's wife, came over and helped Eleanor clean the house so that we started with good standards of housekeeping. Every year, I devoted a Saturday to cleaning the cellar. I would move all contents to one end while I cleaned the other, then reversed the process, finally giving all contents a legitimate place. When Eleanor came in, she would declare my job "a scene of loveliness and delight." This, of course, made it all worth doing!

It was two and a half years before we got our first car. Meanwhile, we went to Burlington and back on the Grey Coach bus which passed along the highway every hour. Or we accepted rides from neighbours. For quite a time, I would connect each morning with a business man.

One of our first purchases was an electric range you could set up for cooking according to previously determined timing. One Sunday, I carefully set it to do our dinner, and then got on the bus with the children. We were half way to church before I remembered that I had left the food on the counter!

One evening, when I answered the phone, a voice said, "My name is Sam Ferguson." As I already had met Sam at the church, this sounded formal. But he proceeded to ask if I would consider taking over the junior choir at Trinity. I immediately referred him to Eleanor and thus for her began a wonderful ten years of music.

At the beginning, Eleanor found that there were over sixty somewhat unruly kids in the choir and there were some limitations because they only had a certain number of choir gowns. So she restricted the Junior Choir to those who had passed grade three at school; and the younger ones—those who could not yet read words—were called the Training Choir. Once she got the divisions established, she would tell the training choir members, as an incentive, that as soon as they could sing in tune and read words, they could graduate. This helped them concentrate their efforts immensely. Later, she used former Junior Choir singers to form an SAB Youth Choir. In Trinity Church, the Junior Choir was the regular choir for the early 9:30 am service, with an anthem to perform every second week. The Training Choir appeared about once a month. I recall that they once rendered a tune for *Jesus bids us shine*[99] that was much more interesting than the traditional one.

That of course was one of the ways that Eleanor kept interest high; she chose music she could be enthusiastic about and in which she could insist on high standards. She used to invite Mrs. McKeen, who was the church secretary, to come in to the rehearsals and stand at the back of the rehearsal hall and tell her whether the words were clear. The kids worked very hard to make sure that her answer was positive.

At Christmas and in the spring, there had to be concerts. After one of these, there was a fair amount of money in the proceeds (about $200). In the past this money had been used to buy ice cream for the kids but Eleanor thought the money should be used for a musical purpose. She persuaded the Women's Association to match the funds raised to put towards a singing scholarship. Thus was born the Singing Scholarship Program. A competition would be held and the winner was to receive two years of singing lessons. There were some conditions. The winner and his/her parents would have to agree that during the two year term, the recipient would also study piano as well as continuing to sing in the choir. At the end of each year, the singing teacher would be asked for a letter of recommendation that the student continue in the scholarship program, based on the singer's efforts and progress.

That spring, the first of many competitions was held with George Verey, organist of the Hamilton Anglican Cathedral, as adjudicator. The first recipient was a boy soprano named Randy Chisolm. His win took the form of two years of lessons with George Verey who led the Cathedral Boys' Choir and taught young male students. However he did not teach girls and the next year, the winner was Nancy Clark. Eleanor called up Dr. Ettore Mazzolini, then Principal of the Royal Conservatory in Toronto to find out who their best teacher was of adolescent girls. He suggested Helen Simmie.

From then on, the girls who won were driven to Toronto every week by parents to study with Helen Simmie of the Royal Conservatory. The first year, there was one scholarship, the second year two, as the Women's Association added to the fund. And Eleanor worked hard to raise funds for this. One year, rather than simply selling tickets to the choir concert, she had official-looking certificates printed up and sold "shares in the musical future" of the children of the church.

In 1962, Esther entered. The set piece that everyone sang was, *My Faith it is an Oaken Staff*[100] sung to a traditional Swiss tune:

> *My faith, it is an oaken staff,*
> *The traveler's well loved aid;*
> *My faith, it is a weapon stout,*
> *The soldier's trusty blade,*
> *I'll travel on, and still be stirred,*
> *By silent thought or social word;*
> *By all my perils undeterred,*
> *A soldier pilgrim staid.*
>
> *I have a Guide, and in His steps*
> *When travelers have trod,*
> *Whether beneath was flinty rock*

*Or yielding grassy sod,*
*They cared not, with force unspent,*
*Unmoved by pain, they onward went,*
*Unstayed by pleasures, still they bent*
*Their zealous course to God.*

*My faith, it is an oaken staff,*
*O let me on it lean!*
*My faith, it is a trusty sword,*
*May falsehood find it keen!*
*Thy Spirit, Lord, to me impart,*
*O make me what Thou ever art,*
*Of patient and courageous heart,*
*As all true saints have been.*

The winners were always announced at the year-end choir banquet which the Women's Association served and which included the parents. George Verey, as adjudicator got up, as usual, to announce the winning scholarship recipients. He announced Eleanor James whose voice was already showing the promise of what would become an opera career. He then went on to tell of the other recipient, whom, he remarked had two strikes against her and needed to be especially good to be chosen. It was Esther. Subsequent winners included Jeannie Barr and Nancy McCollom. For many years there was a lot of shared driving for these lessons in Toronto.

A highlight of Eleanor's musical leadership was the performance in 1965 of *Let there be Joy*. Eleanor had been reading a Book of Prayers from the Gaelic by Alexander Carmichael. She chose some of the more expressive words and commissioned the music from Keith Bissell, the supervisor of music for the Scarborough Board of Education, and a leading proponent of the Orff Method. The work was scored for SAB Choir, soprano and tenor soloists with organ, flute, cello, alto xylophones and alto glockenspiels. It was dedicated to Eleanor's grandparents who had attended Trinity Church in the early part of the 20th century. Eleanor's mother, Madeleine Dillon, paid for the commission.

In the performance, Esther and Randy Chisholm did the vocal solos. The cellist was a boy from Hamilton who was a direct descendant of Anton Dvorak. I conducted it. On the last page, the soprano soloist was supposed to sing a high A. Esther had been fighting laryngitis and, at the last rehearsal, sang a different note which the composer had allowed. But, in the performance, she managed the A, loud and clear.

Because *Let there be Joy* was only ten minutes long, a lot of other music was performed, including *Singet dem Herren ein neues Lied, (Oh Sing to God the Lord)* a cantata by Buxtehude[101] which was sung in English. The audience which filled Trinity Church appreciated the latter more than the former, which used a lot of modern harmonies. The Bissell piece was the kind of music that required repetition to be appreciated in those days although today, his music would more likely be considered mainstream to audience's ears which have adjusted to much more dissonance. Performances in Guelph and Elora during the 70's were a bit more successful in that way.

The audience for this concert, besides Keith Bissell, included many of his composer colleagues, his wide network of school educator colleagues and choral directors from across Southern Ontario as well as the many Dillon relatives and friends of our family to whom Eleanor had sold tickets. The church was packed. Gordon Douglas, the organist throughout our 14 years in Burlington, performed Bach's *Toccata and Fugue in D Minor*. He remarked afterward, "If I'd known there would be this big an audience, I'd have practised!"

Gordon Douglas was an interesting mixture. As an organist, he was competent as operator of the Casavant[102] organ that gave us a great sound in Trinity Church and an even better sound after it had been moved to the new Wellington Square sanctuary with some renovation and re-voicing. Gordon trained several organists of the Burlington area, including Eric Hopkins who spent almost his whole career as director of music at Port Nelson Church. I studied with Gordon from 1960 to 1963, passing my grade nine Royal Conservatory piano exam during that time. I recall that, in trying to train me to handle an instrument where the finger action was very different from that of the piano, he remarked, "Don't use weight. It doesn't do anything." My practice time was between 4:00 pm and 5:00 pm. But, in the fall of 1963, I took that time to drive daily to St. Catharines where Dad was ending his days. After he died, I never got back to organ practice.

As a choir leader—he always led the Senior Choir—Gordon was not outstanding. Rehearsing, for him, was just a matter of running through the anthems. He rarely made demands of the singers. And, as the strategic head of the church's music, he often acted in a way that fell short of giving Eleanor the support she needed. She would say, "I just wish he'd come down on the side of music."

Another highlight of Eleanor's church choir accomplishments came about because of Eleanor's involvement on the National Board of Women of the United Church. The United Church Women (the successor organization to the Women's Association) created a Sunday School curriculum based on Trinidad and Brazil. Eleanor undertook to have her Youth Choir create a recording of songs that could accompany the other curriculum materials. She and I researched and discovered a portfolio of songs. I created SAB arrangements and Eleanor rehearsed the choir. The Berkeley Studio came from Toronto and recorded the full-choir arrangements in Trinity Church. The technology now, of course, is far more sophisticated but at the time, the kids had to be told not to take breaths that were too noisy for fear of causing extraneous noise on the recording. About a month later, Eleanor drove in to Toronto with Esther, Eleanor James and Don Storey to do a recording session at the Berkeley Studios where they laid down the tracks of the soprano, alto and bass so that Sunday School groups could learn the individual parts. One side of the finished recording featured the full choir performances of the music and the other side the parts to aid Sunday school teachers in teaching.

For several years, we took part in a square dance club. Once a month, we joined 30 to 40 other couples in a large gym, and were put through our paces by a first rate caller and fiddler. It was always most successful if the caller had full attention and managed to keep under control self-styled teachers of whom there was usually at least one in every square.

I was, for most of our years in Burlington, a member of the church session. About forty of the more than ninety members would meet each month to govern the spiritual affairs of the congregation. Keith McMillan was a fairly good chairman, though I recall one meeting when I strongly disagreed with his ruling. I learned the rules of order from NDP Conventions, and, while the church didn't follow the same book of rules, some procedures were basic—like putting an amended motion to a vote. Jack Lee wrote minutes with a professional style, using phrases like, "pursuant to notice". I always enjoyed my elders' visits, including those involving the occasional self-proclaimed atheists.

In the late 50's, it became obvious that Trinity Church needed a new roof, a new furnace and other major repairs. These were put out to tender and from the high prices the companies mentioned, we concluded that they didn't really want the job. So the search began for a site for a new church. It was found that the geographic centre of the members' homes happened to be the site of Saint John's Roman Catholic Church. We were obviously not going to get that! However, in a nearby block, there was a lot of vacant space where there was a group of houses with really long back-yards. Various realtors had, in the past, tried to assemble the land, only to have the owners raise the price when they heard of it. Somehow Trinity leaders managed to work in sufficient secrecy to avoid that result. In addition, a couple of properties were purchased to give access to the new building. And Wellington Square United Church was born.

CHAPTER 47

# Burlington Part Two—Esther and Morrey as Children

In the 14 years in which we lived in Burlington, Esther and Morrey grew from ages 5 and 2½ to ages 19 and 16½. That alone makes the period special. It was the time when we were all together.

Esther attended the first half of kindergarten at Central School. Then she did the second half of kindergarten and Grade 1 and the first half of Grade 2 at Strathcona School on Walker's Line, far enough from home that she needed the school bus. However, the bus that would have brought her home was always extremely noisy, and, rather than putting up with it, she often quietly got on another bus and went home with a friend. Which friend she went home with, we were never sure, for the friend varied from day to day! When W. E. Breckon School opened and she began the second half of Grade 2, it became much easier to keep track of her.

Morrey's biggest problem was being subject to allergies. One day he was taken to Toronto and put through all-day tests. They found that

*Esther at five, with brother and doll!*

*Morrey*

*Esther*

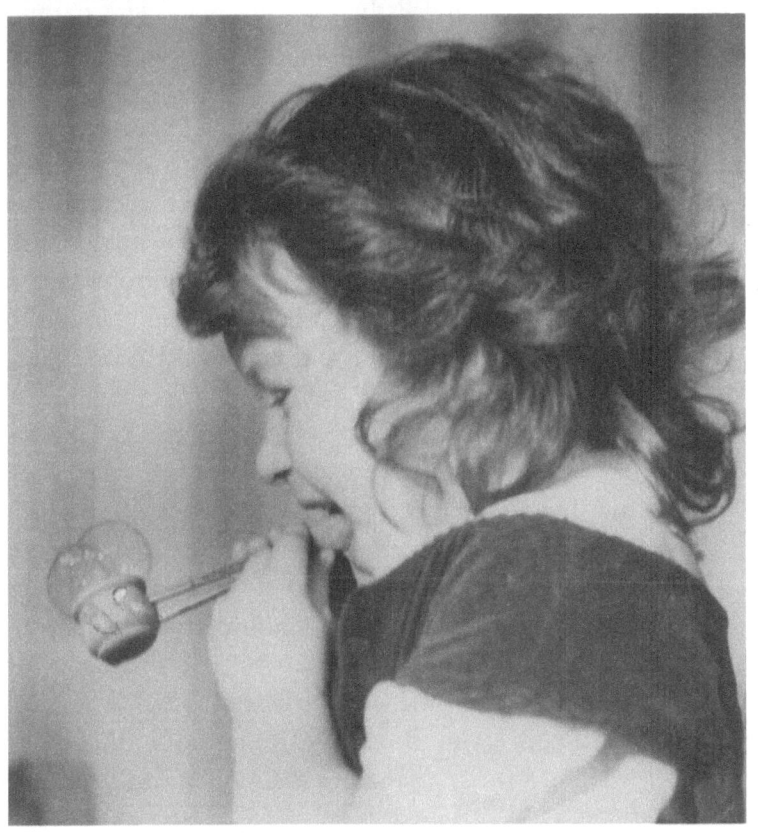

he was allergic to more than 20 stimuli. In addition, he was susceptible to attacks of asthma. More than once, he had to be taken to a Hamilton hospital and laid under an oxygen tent, to restore normal breathing.

One day, Morrey went playing with a neighbour who happened to have access to his father's golf clubs. He appeared at the side door in tears and with blood running down his temple. But before he would let us treat the wound, he insisted on filling us in on the whole story of the accident.

For several years, Morrey had a paper route with the Hamilton Spectator. Customers appreciated the fact that, when the paper didn't publish on a holiday, Morrey would charge appropriately less for the week concerned. Most deliverers would pocket the difference, hoping the customers would forget that the holiday had occurred. One wintry day, there was deep snow. Morrey was sick and Esther took his place with the papers. I had been out and, on returning, was assured by Morrey that his sister was trudging faithfully on.

Between March of 1956 and November of 1958, when we had yet to acquire our own car, we made good use of Gray Coach Lines. One day I had some errands in the middle of town, including one that involved Esther. As we waited for the bus to return, Esther declined an offer of candy from a lady. When we were alone, I commended her for remembering the rule never to take candy from strangers. "Oh, it wasn't that, Daddy," she said. "It would have been bad for my teeth!"

On Sunday mornings, Eleanor had to be at Trinity Church early for her Junior Choir and regularly used, first taxis, and, later, the car. The children and I would follow on a later bus.

For some years, we shopped at a grocery store on the corner of New Street and the Guelph Line, the big attraction being that you could pay at the end of the month! Once we left the children in the car parked on a slope while we shopped. We had left the car in gear. While we were in the store, Morrey put his foot on the clutch and the car began to head for the street. Esther reached her foot over and put her foot on the break and a fellow shopper, seeing what had happened, reached in and pulled on the parking brake.

Some of the store staff were memorable. A very short worker named Nick responded to the sound of a collision outside by remarking, "That's been waiting to happen all day!" One of the cashiers had a delightful English accent. I would rack my brains to think of ways to make her talk!

Diana Goodwin, a good friend of Esther's, although older, joined us for lunch at our kitchen one day. The conversation turned on the meaning of names. Diana mentioned that her name meant 'moon', while Esther added that of course, her name meant 'star'. Not to be outdone, Morrey quickly piped up, "And Morrey means 'little dipper'!"

Once when Morrey was 12 or 13, his mother announced that on a certain evening we would take him and Esther to a Saturday night performance of Carl Orff's opera, *Die Klüge* or *The King and the Wise Woman* being presented in the University of Toronto's MacMillan Theatre. Morrey immediately objected on the grounds that he would be missing the NHL telecast. But Eleanor replied with words that she was to use often with the kids, "Morrey, it's part of your education."

But this was no mere opera. The action was represented and interpreted on multiple screens. When the king was angry, we saw a famous painting of Henry VIII with a scowl. When the King was pleased, we saw Henry VIII laughing. Arguments among the characters became political cartoons by the Toronto Star's MacPherson. At one point, the House of Commons was seen to turn upside down. Toward the end of the story, a peasant has his suit to the king turned down, and he trudges dejectedly home in the snow. The orchestra score calls for accompaniment lasting ten minutes. But on the screen, the time was consumed as the peasant gradually departed through the snow, and we could watch from the time his body hid the camera to the point where the peasant became only a speck on the horizon.

Morrey was delighted with the show and said so. Next day, I

wrote the conductor, Ettore Mazzoleni, telling him of Morrey's feelings. He replied that he had a season ticket in Maple Leaf Gardens and regretted missing that game as much as Morrey!

Once—just once—Morrey persuaded me to accompany him to Maple Leaf Gardens. I believe the Leafs were playing the Bruins and that the Bruins won. But defeat for the home team couldn't dampen Morrey's enthusiasm for the real thing!

Three moments show the way he was impressed with new realities as revealed on TV and wanted others to share the experience. During a play-off hockey game, I heard him announce a Maple leaf goal. "Ellis!" The assassination of Martin Luther King evidently needed emphasis. "King is dead!" In the 1969 provincial election in Manitoba, the NDP under the leadership of Edward Schreyer rose from third place to win power. As results were coming in, we heard Morrey intone: "NDP 22, Tories 16"!

As our kids became teens, there was the usual comment after one of our edicts, "But so-and-so's parents let him do it." One way in which Eleanor and I disagreed in parenting had to do with what we found them doing in the evening when we got home. If they were watching a TV show when we suspected that they should have been doing school work, Eleanor would lower the boom at once. But I sometimes noticed that the show in question had just five minutes to run and to wait for its end before cutting off the TV avoided needless conflict. I'm sure that as parents, Esther and Morrey have both refined the method even further.

## CHAPTER 48

# Books That Were Read Aloud

Morrey has asked me to write about the golden hours during which I read to both children. The problem is that, while I remember the times, the details escape me. Esther has given me a list of books she thinks I read to them. While a number of these were undoubtedly included, I'm sure many others were books that they read to themselves in succeeding years. If my efforts developed the enthusiasm that lead to their learning to read earlier than they otherwise would have done, it was all worth-while. In fact, while reading aloud was something that both kids were encouraged to do, it was Esther who sat down and taught Morrey how to read, which activity he still remembers.

I well remember being read to by my parents. I forget whether it was when I was recovering from mumps or whooping-cough—and was suitably quarantined for the time—that Mother read me J. M. Barrie's *The Little Minister*. I couldn't wait for her to get to the next chapter. I can "hear" Dad's voice as he emphasized a special development in a story, but don't remember exactly which of many books he was reading to me.

With my children, I'm sure I started with books that were mostly pictures. Early books we read included a story about a Chinese boy called *The Tale of Tai* by Evelyn Young. There was a picture of "the back view of Tai." And I remember how much we enjoyed *The Five Chinese Brothers*. A.A. Milne was an early author—stories of Pooh and Christopher Robin. And I remember us singing songs from the poems, especially, *They're Changing Guard in Buckingham Palace*.

The fact that Esther and Morrey treasure these memories probably means that our grandchildren have had similar ones. In any case, I shall append Esther's list, because a lot of it is relevant.

| AUTHOR | TITLE |
|---|---|
| Alcott, Louisa May | *Little Women* |
| | *Little Men* |
| Austin, Jane | *Pride and Prejudice* |
| Berna, Paul | *A Hundred Million Francs* |
| Blackmore | *Lorna Doon* |
| Bronte, Charlotte | *Jane Eyre* |
| Bronte, Emily | *Wuthering Heights* |
| Buchan, John | *The Three Hostages* |
| | *The Thirty-Nine Steps* |
| | *The Island of Sheep* |
| | *Witchwood* |
| | *Greenmantle* |
| | *Prester John* |
| | *Mr. Standfast* |
| Collins, Wilkie | *Moonstone* |
| Christie, Agatha | *Murder on the Orient Express* |
| Dickens, Charles | *Oliver Twist* |
| | *David Copperfield* |
| | *A Tale of Two Cities* |
| Dumas, Alexandre | *The Count of Monte Christo* |
| | *The Three Musketeers* |
| | *Twenty Years After* |
| Edwards, Monica | *The White Riders* |
| | *Storm Ahead* |
| Falkner, L. Meade | *Moonfleet* |
| Frye, Rosalie K. | *Child of the Western Isles* |
| | *Deep in the Forest* |
| Heyer, Georgette | *The Talisman Ring* |
| | *The Black Sheep* |

*Don reading to Esther, Morrey and cousins*

| | |
|---|---|
| Kipling, Rudyard | The Just So Stories |
| | The First Jungle Book |
| | The Second Jungle Book |
| Lewis, C. S. | The Magician's Nephew |
| | The Lion, the Witch and the Wardrobe |
| | The Horse and His Boy |
| | The Voyage of the Dawn Treader |
| | The Silver Chair |
| | The Last Battle |
| Marryat, Frederick | Children of the New Forest |
| Maxwell, Gavin | Ring of Bright Water |
| Mowat, Farley | Never Cry Wolf |
| | The Black Joke |
| | Gray Seas Under |
| Neill, Robert | Mist Over Pendle |
| | Moon in Scorpio |
| Nesbitt, Elizabeth | The Railway Children |
| Norton, Mary | The Borrowers |

| | |
|---|---|
| Sayers, Dorothy | *Murder Must Advertise* |
| | *The Nine Taylors* |
| Scott, Sir Walter | *Ivanhoe* |
| | *Rob Roy* |
| | *The Heart of Midlothian* |
| Serailler, Ian | *The Silver Sword* |
| Shaw, George Bernard | *Arms and the Man* |
| Spyri, Johanna | *Heidi* |
| Stevenson, R. L. | *Kidnapped* |
| | *Catriona* |
| | *Treasure Island* |
| | *The Bottle Imp* |
| Streatfield, Noel | *Ballet Shoes* |
| Tey, Josephine | *The Daughter of Time* |
| | *Brat Farrar* |
| Tracy, Honor | *The Straight and Narrow Path* |
| Twain, Mark | *The Adventures of Tom Sawyer* |
| | *The Adventures of Huckleberry Finn* |
| Ullman, James R. | *The White Tower* |
| Wyss, Johan David | *Swiss Family Robinson* |
| Welch, Ronald | *The Gauntlet* |

CHAPTER 49

# Burlington (3)

It was Mother who made the contact. In 1920, we had had as near neighbours in Toronto Dr. Aitken, whom Dad had got to know before World War I at the College of Education. His daughter, Frances, about my age, later grew up, married Harold Tovee and settled in Burlington. Eleanor continued what Mother had begun, and our families had a long and fruitful relationship.

A related thread was that Dr. Aitken's second wife was Alice Pidgeon of Muldrew Lake.

The Tovees lived in the neighbourhood of Port Nelson United Church, to which Fran belonged. Harold maintained a life-long interest in model trains. This was practised in a Hamilton club. I am sure that his influence had something to do with the annual pilgrimage today of Morrey and family to the model train centre south of Guelph. Harold's death from cancer was not diagnosed until after he was hospitalized. One Christmas, he was put in hospital after failure to recover from flu and died about three weeks later. In later years, one of his boys was assigned to hospital and objected loudly, "When you go to hospital," he said, "You die."

In the dead of one winter, the Ewings' furnace suddenly failed and replacing it took two days. During that time, we all slept at Tovees'. I recall how dreadful the unheated house (4379) felt in winter.

In all the Burlington years that I can remember, Eleanor invited a host of friends to an annual Christmas Carol party. Mother once remarked on how Eleanor simply danced with delight as each person arrived. This was before arthritis led Eleanor to give up playing the piano (she had an ATCM too) and we took turns accompanying the singing. At one of these occasions, groups were asked to make up new words to *The*

*Twelve Days of Christmas.* For his group, Ron Williams finished each line with the words, "And a reindeer." Somehow, people never stopped laughing each time he said it.

Eleanor usually had a party after one of the concerts that her Junior Choir put on. She usually tried to get her parents in Cooksville to be part of the audience. After one of these parties, her father made a remark about why she thought it necessary to invite the whole town in afterward. But, for Eleanor, the party was a necessary expression of her gratitude to those who made the concert possible. It is yet!

It was sometimes doubtful if the annual Church Christmas Concert would have an audience. The Gray Cup was often held the same week-end the concert had to be held. One year, the Cup was scheduled for a Saturday, the concert for the Sunday afternoon. Before the game could be finished, it was called for fog and the remainder scheduled for 1.30 on Sunday. People's hearts were in their mouths until the game was finished in just 20 minutes, and the concert could go on at 3.00 pm as planned.

Some time in the early 60's, the Government decided to build a service road on the south side of the Queen Elizabeth Highway, where Appleby United Church stood. That venerable congregation sought a new site and finally settled on a vacant lot just two doors east of us. We used to say that we didn't drive past Appleby to go to Wellington Square; we drove the other way!

But, in 1958, Appleby lacked a music leader, and Reverend Earl W. Brearley came calling. I did that job for one year. For a time, the choir practised in our living-room. When we moved into the sanctuary, problems were evident from the start. The acoustics of the building were not right. When we sang from the altar, it was difficult to hear in the congregation. Members of the congregation felt when taking part in the hymn-singing that they were doing solos. I won't blame my failure entirely on the acoustics. But after one year, I was asked to resign. Before that happened, I proposed to the Board that we experiment with locating the choir in the gallery, where wood panelling on three sides and proximity to the wooden ceiling would have allowed the sound to be amplified. The suggestion was turned down because, in their view, there would be no point in experimenting with an arrangement that could never be permanent!

I have since learned that Appleby dates back to the days of Egerton Ryerson who often went out as a visiting preacher. The first church services were held in the home of Isaac Van Norman. In the absence of communication, no one knew when Ryerson might be visiting. The story went that when he did, one of the women blew her conch shell[103] and the farmers came running!

Between 1956 and 1969 during which we lived in 4379 Spruce, we made frequent trips to the Dillon home, a half hour's drive away. To get there, I preferred to go up the Appleby Line and east by the Queen Elizabeth highway. That was what took the half hour. But, coming home, usually after dark, Eleanor preferred the slower route via highway #2 because she said that the houses with their lights were friendlier. This was to be just one of many occasions when we disagreed (usually in a friendly way!) about routes.

At age 6, Esther won a CBC radio contest involving a crayon illustration of the song by Alan Mills[104], *I Know an Old Woman who Swallowed a Fly*. The contest was announced on Alan Mills' show on CBC radio, Folk Songs for Young Folks. There were to be prizes for different age groups. Eleanor got big sheets of newsprint paper and had Esther creating a lot of versions and then she sent in the best ones. When the winners were announced on radio, Esther's name was one of the winners for her age group. She received a recording of the song and a copy of the Alan Mills Song Book, personally autographed by him. Esther was doubly excited by the fact that her Aunt Bunty called to congratulate her all the way from Montreal!

It was at Eleanor's parents' large house where Esther continued her very original method of decorating paneled walls.

Over dinner, the contest result had been discussed and her grandfather asked her when she was going to make a picture for his wall. Early the next morning, she got busy and drew him a picture on the paneled wall beside the bed where she had been sleeping! It just shows that you have to be careful what you say to children as we can never be sure how they will interpret your remarks. Eleanor was very cross with Esther but her grandfather refused to let her be scolded. "She was just doing what I asked her to do!" he exclaimed. He asked her to repeat her creation on some paper which he gave her and they had it framed and hung it proudly on their wall for many years. There was a story that Eleanor's mother told that a guest came to their home and upon seeing the work proclaimed, "Oh, Mrs. Dillon. You have a wonderful piece of modern art!"

Another time as we were driving to Cooksville for a visit, Eleanor commented to Esther that no doubt she would be very excited to see her Grandpa again. She asked, "Is he 'cited too?"

At this time, the Dillon relatives lived within easy range. Robert and family lived across a creek behind his father's house. Bunty's family had a house in Clarkson. And the Norquays lived in the Dillon house for a year while Jim was studying in Toronto. So many birthdays and holidays saw the whole clan celebrating together.

Once the grandchildren had grown to a certain age where they could eat independently, Mother and Dad organized a formal dinner for the ten grandchildren. Not only did the kids dress in their finest, but there was a program including toasts. Mother put out all her best linen, china and crystal and cooked a couple of geese or ducks or turkeys and created a wonderful meal. There were always wonderful party favours. Esther remembers that she received her very first pair of stockings with a matching garter belt the year she turned twelve.

Dad carved the birds. The kids always rose to the occasion and currently some of them speak about what wonderful memories they have from these dinners. To be effectively "scarce", the parents ate at a restaurant or at Bunty and Lloyd's or at Rob and Doris' houses nearby and returned at 9:00 pm for the opening of gifts.

Another time most of us gathered was at Thanksgiving by which time the last of the apples in the orchard—the Northern Spies, the Russets and others—had ripened. Those who came divided into pickers, sorters and carters of the sorted apples to the root house on the side of a hill. As we departed, each family would load a share of the apples in their cars, as they could use them. Subsequently, Dad would put the No. 3 apples (apples with blemishes or slight bruises) through his cider press and Mother would gather the cider in gallon jars which she would distribute to needy folk in the area.

These activities took place in the large house which Dad had had built in the early 1950's and to which he moved from the house, a little to the west, which the family had occupied since the area was essentially rural in character. The orchard belonged successively with both houses, although Dad lost a row of trees every time the Queen Elizabeth highway was widened.

In June, 1967, the family gathered in a Port Credit diningroom where Dad read us the story of how he and Mother had got married. Three weeks later, he passed away—just before the country began celebrating our centennial year.

CHAPTER 50

# Overseas—1968 (1)

I had not crossed the Atlantic since 1922. Eleanor and the children had never been over. Our friends, the Perreards, were well established in Geneva, but while we had communicated with the Ewing and Richardson cousins when people died or were married, we couldn't say we knew them well.

In 1968, the Ontario Men's Public School Teachers Association was offering a special deal on flights to Britain, allowing customers eight weeks before returning. At the time my membership was with OECTA, the Catholic union. But I was able to pay $25 for an OMPSTA membership and take advantage of the special rate.

Esther, just turned 18, was keen to improve her French, and Suzanne Perreard arranged for her to be an au pair (nanny) for the Baland family who were cousins of Suzanne's husband, Victor Perreard. So, when we reached Heathrow, Esther immediately changed for Geneva.

Our long-standing Oakville friend, Betty Looseley, had a cousin, George Williams; she arranged for us to stay with him and his wife, Frances in Hayes, Middlesex. Our taxi-driver had to stop and ask directions, and then had to stop and put all our baggage on the side-walk while he changed a tire. However, it was a gorgeous day and we were not inconvenienced.

The Williams were the soul of hospitality, serving us a scrumptious dinner the first night, and supplying us with excellent advice during the week we stayed with them. A little touch—George kept in his umbrella stand at the front door a cane which, if you shook it, revealed a sharp knife blade.

The second morning, we took bus and tube into the heart of London. It was the last day of a heat-wave, and, we asked for a jug of water in the restaurant on the top floor of a department store at Piccadilly Circus. From the reaction of the waiter, this proved to be a most unusual request.

We had hoped to outfit everyone in this department store. But, to fit Morrey, who at age 15 was already well on his way to his ultimate height of 6'4", we had to find the Tall Men's Shop on Regent Street.

We finished that day with a 9.00 pm dinner in Soho with Ian and Molly Richardson, his sister, Helen, and Helen's husband, Finlay Rea. We found things in common with all of them—Morrey had a great conversation with Finlay—and decided we were going to enjoy our cousins in a big way.

Getting back to Hayes by public transportation after 11.30 pm proved a bit daunting. The London Underground employees were on a slow-down in sympathy with a national railway strike, and while the tube took us to the end of their line, we found that no more buses were going from there that night. But, while I was clumsily trying to use an English phone—I never figured out when to pull "leaver B"—Eleanor was able to hail a taxi.

That week, we visited Windsor Castle with Frances though we were a bit restricted in the parts we could see since Her Majesty was in residence. I was able to speak with a clockmaker who talked of the danger of an ancient skill in his line being lost because people were reluctant to become apprentices any more. And, in the city, we took in a play which I think was *The Importance of Being Ernest*.

We visited Westminster Abbey. Over time, I had heard that, for many distinguished citizens, the ultimate honour was to be buried in Westminster Abbey. One didn't ask where all those bodies had to go. Now we were shown the seemingly endless crypt. I was also shown the monuments to nobility from countless centuries. I found this depressing until suddenly the organ was heard playing *Repton*[105], one of my favourite hymn tunes.

> *Dear Lord and Father of mankind*
> *Forgive our foolish ways;*
> *Reclothe us in our rightful mind,*

> *In purer lives Thy service find,*
> *In deeper reverence, praise.*
> *In deeper reverence, praise.*

That was my feeling about all the cathedrals, abbeys and other big churches. I found their interiors gloomy and depressing. But when the organ music or singing began, suddenly the experience was glorious.

At the end of that week, we picked up the rented car that we were to use for the next four weeks, putting in 2300 miles in that time. The car rental company allowed us only one key, a fact that was particularly disconcerting one day in Scotland when Morrey managed to drop it down a sewer—fortunately a shallow one and we were able to fish it out! The rental cost just 66 pounds for an automatic transmission chosen so that Eleanor could also drive, though she never used the privilege. Morrey and I picked up the car on the Albert Embankment, and I had to get used to driving on the left in some very heavy traffic that we encountered on the way to Hayes where we picked up Eleanor and headed for Oxford.

Shortly after World War II, Margaret Dale, the youngest member of the family that brought the Ewings to Muldrew Lake, had taken a ship to England where she had been invited to visit an aunt. The aunt passed away while she was in mid-Atlantic, but she determined to have a holiday anyway. In the course of it she met and married Philip Devereux, and stayed permanently in England. In 1968, they and their family were living just outside of Oxford, in Buckingham. I loved addresses in England. Their address was Third Acre Rise, Whispering Way, Oxford.

The main event of our visit to the Devereux household was Oxford's version of *Son et Lumiere* where the history of Oxford was related through speakers at a stadium while various buildings or parts thereof were appropriately lighted. For instance, while a famous author typed his script, a tiny window on a high story was lighted, and when naughtiness was suspected, a flood light illumined a garden—the part that was visible. Of course, because the sun sets really late in that latitude in July, the show could not begin till 10.00 pm.

Since Tom and Grace Dale were visiting Edinburgh and we were going there soon, Maggie asked us to deliver a bag to them. So we took it north in our car.

I couldn't help noticing the many English lawns that were green although they had been cut short. Usually, the wet climate prevents them from getting brown. Native Britons kept apologising for the national climate. But, in five weeks, we experienced only two wet days, plus a cloud-burst in Stratford.

In Stratford-on-Avon, we were fortunate in getting tickets for an excellent performance of *As You Like It*, though we were not able to get seats. We took turns leaning against the back seats and leaning against the back wall. But the performance was worth it. Then when we came out, there was a violent thunderstorm. We got to our B & B in Warwick. But, the next day, we had to drive through several inches of water in order to get through a village.

I thought it a little strange that my B & B hostess in Warwick offered me at breakfast a choice of grapefruit or cereal. But most of our accommodation suited us well. I carried a list of places, and tried always to phone a reservation first thing in the morning.

North of Warwick, we came to Coventry. This was one of the great examples of creativity growing out of tragedy. Nearly the entire old cathedral had been destroyed by German bombs during World War II. But the people had rebuilt the cathedral in a way that showed that their faith was modern and encompassed the best that architecture could do. A new tapestry, representing Christ, hangs over the altar. And outside, on the site of the old building, memorials with elements of the cathedral's history had been tastefully placed within low walls.

From Coventry we went up the M1 in the direction of York[106]. When we arrived in York, we walked on the wall and sampled the shops. I regretted later that I hadn't carried a pocket tape-recorder with which to record the interesting accents that we encountered. At the minster, we held our noses away from the stink of centuries that was coming up from the site of major reconstruction in the basement. Then we passed a familiar sign which we'd frequently seen around Britain. It was entitled, Friends of the Cathedral[107].

Morrey and I climbed the tower, and it was then that I realized that I was more out of condition than I had realized. I had had fond notions of climbing Mount Nevis when I got to Scotland. Now I had to pause for breath as I mounted the cathedral steps.

Such steps, although made of stone, do eventually wear down and have curved indents in the steps where centuries of worshippers had stepped. In one cathedral, it had been decided that, for safety's sake, the steps should be replaced. Since that work is tremendously expensive, and the sexton had set out to save money by turning the steps over. But he had found that someone had had the same idea centuries earlier, the underside being just as round as the top!

Harbottle, in the hills of Northumberland, is a charming village. So was the house where we found my other first cousin, Bernard Richardson, and his lively wife, Helen. Bernard had found it possible to practise medicine in a rural setting because of the National Health Service funding. Eleanor immediately found common ground with Helen through their shared interest in crafts.

Alas, it was that week-end that I discovered a new allergy. Bernard took us for a walk in the heather, and I began to sneeze. Later he declared that I needed sea air, and we headed for Seahouses and its beach. But I still couldn't keep myself in Kleenex. I hope I sounded grateful for the wonderful hospitality we received.

From Harbottle we headed for Scotland. In Roxborough, in the border country, I learned something about the rules of the road in Britain. In Ontario, one can turn right on a red light if one first yields to any traffic from the left. So I reasoned that, in Britain, one could turn left on a red light if one yielded to traffic from the right. Not so. Fortunately, the policeman saw the Visitor to Britain sign on the back windshield and patiently explained the law without giving me a ticket.

Tom Dale was doing some research on Sir Walter Scott, and he, Grace and Sibby were using an apartment in western Edinburgh. In the few days we were in that city, we had a number of meals there, though we finally had a chance to take them out to a restaurant. We chose a Chinese place, and rather startled the waiter with the way we ordered. It has been our custom in such places to order a few dishes that we would share but have a bowl of rice apiece in which case we usually started with empty plates, something our waiter had a lot of trouble understanding.

Tom and I climbed Arthur's seat[108]. We took in a concert by the North Synfonia. And, one, rather weepy day, I visited a laundromat. I discovered that many people who have washing machines at home nevertheless used laundromats to catch up on the local gossip!

At the B & B where we slept, I first experienced electrified towel-racks, a great convenience for tourists wishing to wash out garments at night. It made up for another British institution which I did not appreciate—the toast rack. I have always wished to butter my toast when hot.

Eleanor made the most of the shops. In a wool store on George Street, a lady chose her words carefully, using a syllable between words, where a Canadian might use "Uh" she used, "Eh". Again, I wished for a tape recorder.

Outside a jeweller's next door, a man stopped us in the street and consulted us about a job offer he had had from a long-established Canadian Jeweller. We were able to steer him away from a deal that would have involved very poor pay.

We took in a musical recital in St. Giles Cathedral, by the castle. That was a church that, historically, had belonged to four different denominations. What impressed us that night was the timing—evidently common in Britain—of concerts. This one began at 6.30 pm. And I was amused by the stone statues. One commemorated the Duke of Montrose who died for Scottish freedom. But one on the other side was of the Duke of Argyle who made sure that the Duke of Montrose died for freedom!

Eleanor's mother and Danny, her grandson, were also overseas that summer. When we encountered them in Edinburgh, the idea was proposed that everyone get a change of company, with Eleanor going places with her mother, and Danny joining Morrey and me for a tour of the Highlands.

We had learned that Penny, of the Harbottle family, was to be the chief cook and bottle washer for a troop of players from the University of Edinburgh who were touring the Highlands with a farce. We three managed to catch up with them at Inverness. We took in the farce which was suitably entertaining and then met Penny at the side door of the theatre.

Inverness also has a golf course, and the boys managed a game, doing a good deal of damage to the turf while they were at it. In the morning, as we headed west, we couldn't miss the truck identified as The Loch Ness Investigation with telescopic equipment on the roof. Jokes about the Loch Ness monster, mixed with some remarks by credulous people, had recently occurred on the BBC.

Then we followed the Great Glen south-west and had lunch in Fort William. We came in sight of Ben Nevis which I did not attempt to climb, and passed through Glencoe, site of the historic massacre; and on south to Crianlarich, a highland centre where different railways used to stop at the top and at the bottom of the town. Here we managed to book a room for three at 4.00 in the afternoon. This left time to do some exploring, and we took a picnic supper and headed for Loch Voil.

I had known that Dad named his Fonthill residence after a favourite place in Scotland, but had neglected to get him to locate it for me before he died. In Edinburgh, I looked for it in vain in Tom Dale's *Guide book of Scotland*. But in Balquidder (Belcuiter, in Gaelic, Balwhidder, in my father's and his father's and his family's pronunciation) I found a tombstone of someone who was identified as a Ledcriech farmer. But no one there seemed to know what that meant. So we drove a mile up the lake and had our picnic.

Two weeks later, over dinner in London, Ian informed me (he has always been a great source of information) that Ledcriech was the farm house where the Ewing family, including my father and Aunt Daisy, his mother, went for holidays in the early years of the 20th century. And where was it? On Loch Voil, four miles from Balquidder! We had been three miles from it. A few years later, a realtor sent me colour prints of the property. It had become much grander than anything our ancestors would have been able to afford. There was even a gardener's residence!

From Crianlarich the next morning, we followed the west coast of Loch Lomond. There were occasional curves in the road that forced buses to make a three-point turn. After that, Danny stated and repeated a wish that he could acquire a tartan tie. Morrey belittled the idea. But we finally gave in and stopped. But none of the available ties suited Danny, and it was Morrey in the end, who bought one.

Then we were at Stirling Castle where there were huge banners saying, "Save the Argyles"[109]. The Labour Government had decided to save money by combining two companies of soldiers, but, evidently, it was at the expense of a great tradition.

As we approached Edinburgh, we needed a meal and, being a long way from a classy restaurant, we broke down and patronized a greasy spoon. The boys had fun mimicking what they imagined their grandmother Dillon would have said about such a place.

CHAPTER 51

# 1968 (2)

We drove south by the west side of England and Wales. We spent a night at a B & B in the Westmorland village of Shap. As we entered the driveway, an athletic-looking woman ran out to open the gate. She turned out to be our hostess, cook and waitress. When I asked her name, she replied in her local accent, "Miss-ees Jack-son."

The next morning we drove all the way to Chester. We walked on the city walls and had a musical treat at the cathedral. An organ recital was billed for that evening. But, as we planned to be deep into Wales by that time, we just visited the church. To our delight, the organist was rehearsing his program, which was almost as good as hearing the real thing. Melville Cook was to become very familiar to us in after years![110]

Ysbyty Ifan is a sheep village in Conwy County in the hills of Wales on the edge of the Snowdonia National Park. The name, we were told, means St. John Ambulance! We had booked accommodation with a Mrs. Hughes, and when we asked on the main street where she might be found, we were first directed to a Mrs. Hughes nearby. But when we mentioned a bed and breakfast, she said, "Oh you mean Mrs. Hughes, the minister." (Local parlance for "Minister's wife".)

Mrs. Hughes, the minister, lived at the top of the hill. She told us that she regularly had to polish a fantastic number of door-handles.

Betws-y-coed is a good town for shopping for things woollen, and we took advantage of it the next morning. We had plans to be elsewhere that night, but changed them in view of a poster announcing a concert to be given that evening in aid of the investiture of the Prince of Wales. So we booked a local B & B and headed north-west. Caernarvon Castle was a disappointment, especially as so many tourists had used corners of it as a physical convenience. It was also a bit disappointing that, due to repairs, the little train that normally carried people to the summit of Mt. Snowdon was going only halfway up, and therefore not worth using.

But the concert at Betws-y-coed was lots of fun. The performers were a choir from a nearby town who had never previously performed in the open, without the advantage of the echoes that walls and ceiling provide. They used an improvised platform in a field where ponies grazed. The opening chorus, the Welsh national anthem, brought the ponies galloping forward and whinnying as they came. But the MC encouraged the audience to sit saying, "The ponies haven't been everywhere!" The choir sang lustily. The grand finale was to have been *Hallelujah Chorus*. Then there was a quick consultation between the MC and the conductor and then the MC announced, "Before the *Hallelujah Chorus*, we have just enough time for *What a friend we have in Jesus*." That number went better. Then during the Handel, the accompanist, using an upright piano at the edge of the stage, got one beat behind on page one and stayed there!

The people of Britain were very helpful to us foreigners. Somewhere near Hereford, on a sunny day, I had stopped to consult a map. My window was open and a local resident asked, "Are you lost?" He supplied us with a lot of interesting information about the town we were in.

In the late afternoon, we saw over Hereford Cathedral. Again, the beauty of the building took on new lustre when evensong began.

Close to where the Wye River, a boundary between England and Wales, flows into the Severn, and then the Bristol Channel, sits the village of Chepstow. Here we had the bargain of the year. For one pound each, we not only got bed and breakfast but a dinner cooked especially for us! A feature of the establishment was a top-floor toilet with a tank at the ceiling. To flush it successfully, one needed a special knack.

By this time, I had acquired a fair amount of knowledge of

British roads. For instance, I found that, on a round-a-bout, it really mattered which exit one took if you didn't want to be moving at right angles from your intended direction. I also got to enjoy dual carriageways (what we, in North America would call four-lane highways).

The Williams had another delicious dinner awaiting us when we returned to Hayes, Middlesex after four weeks of driving.

CHAPTER 52

# 1968 (3)—Switzerland

In 1968, the Perréards were living in Versoix, 8 kms north of Geneva on the Lake of that name. Suzanne ran a primary school, while Victor served as assistant controller of the Geneva airport. Their house was roomy and easily absorbed three extra visitors. From that house, we were conscious of four kinds of transportation: steamers on the lake, buses and cars on the highway, frequent trains on Switzerland's electric railway system, and planes that were losing altitude as they approached the Geneva airport. Also from that house, you could see Mont Blanc when the clouds got out of the way, which didn't happen very often.

It was good to see Suzanne again and to get acquainted with Anne and Barbara who were ages 12 and 10. But the most memorable personality was Victor's. He was terribly proud of Switzerland and spoke all four official languages, as well as English. He was a warm, amusing, gregarious man with friends in most of its towns and villages.

During our stay in Switzerland, he organized a major trip to the Eastern part of the country. We rented a car and followed Victor as he led the way. Riding in our car with us was Suzie Krautschneider, who was spending the summer with the Perréards to improve her French and do some light housekeeping. In reality, a lot of what she heard and practised was English, though that probably did not come amiss. In advance of the trip, she had booked us into a chalet Bed and Breakfast on Mt. Pilatus, above Hergiswil, on Lake Lucerne. We reached the Krautschneider's home in Hergiswil after dark. Her father welcomed and fed us, but was a little aghast when he heard what Suzie had planned for us. Wanting to be sure we arrived safely, he drove ahead of us up the mountain so that we could follow his tail lights. Only in the morning did we understand his concern when we saw how steep the precipices were that we had skirted the night before.

At the chalet, we were introduced to straw-tick beds (very comfortable) and continental breakfasts. That morning, we had traded passengers in the vicinity of Lucerne. Morrey and I were driven by Victor through Hergiswil. It was raining heavily, but Victor pulled over anyway for a cordial visit with one of his many friends. And we got used to hearing his oft-repeated phrase, "I have a friend…" which preceded an interesting or amusing story or an introduction along the route. After a while, we only needed to hear, "I have a friend…" and we would smile and listen with great anticipation.

In Lucerne, we visited the Transport Museum. In the centre of a large room on a huge table was a model of the country, showing all the mountain ranges and all of the many railway branches, complete with tunnels. Model trains were constantly running, flashing tiny lights which claimed our attention.

As we rounded Lake Lucerne, we passed through Weggis, featured in the famous Swiss folk song, *From Lucern to Weggis Town* of which the chorus begins, "Holdiridia" which imitates yodelling.

*A Walking Song—Swiss Folk Song*

*From Lucerne to Weggis on,*
*Holdi-ri-di-a, hol-di-ri-a'*
*Care and labor now are gone,*
*Hol-di-ri-di-a, hol-di-a*

*Chorus:*
*Hol-di-ri-di-a, hol-di-ri-di-a, hol-di-ri-a,*
*Hol-di-ri-di-a, hol-di-ri-di-a, hol-di-a!*

*O'er the mountain trail we'll go*
*Hol-di-ri-di-a, hol-di-ri-a,*
*Lovely deep ravines below,*
*Hol-di-ri-di-a, hol-di-a.*

*Chorus:*
*Weggis leads to the highest hill,*
*Hol-di-ri-di-a, hol-di-ri-a,*
*Give a cheer, boys, with a will,*
*Hol-di-ri-di-a, hol-di-a.*
*(Chorus)*

From there we drove to Einsiedeln, a monastery town. The interior of the church is about as ornate as they get. Within that structure is a chapel. While we were there, a group of monks processed in and took their places in the chapel. There, they began singing in close harmony giving the whole place the same kind of atmosphere that I had experienced at Hereford Cathedral at evensong. At the end of town, we purchased a record featuring these singers. But I had been careless enough to leave it in the sun behind the back seat where it warped badly.

On our return, we paused at Interlaken where there was a magnificent view of the Jungfrau. It looked about one km away instead of the 30 it really was. When we returned to Geneva, I was able to read, in the papers, a story that must have been in progress as I watched the mountain. Four climbers had disregarded local advice and gone up during a storm, with disastrous results. Three men had lost their lives in a fall, while the one woman survivor had been found with frozen fingers and toes when a helicopter rescued her. Suzanne told us that would-be climbers often think they know better than the guides, with similar results, on Mont Blanc.

While we three did our travelling, Esther was a mother's helper in a very formal, upper-crust household. She may have improved her French, but otherwise the experience was not a happy one as they saw her as sort of a servant.

One day she was driving with Suzanne when the latter noticed a car with a Belgian licence. Immediately, she pulled over until the car in question had passed. In explanation, she said that, since there were no speed limits in that country, drivers tended not to observe the rules of the road in countries that had them.

Esther flew back to Britain with us and shared our last five days in and around London.

When I had first arrived in England in June, I had had to rely on taxi-drivers who knew English roads. After my 2300 miles on those roads, the situation was different. When we reached Heathrow from Switzerland, I sat in the front and told the driver exactly which turns to take as we returned to Hayes, Middlesex. The Williams were away at that time. But friends who were staying in their place still welcomed us back and cooked a scrumptious dinner for us.

*Hadrian IV,* which people told us we must not miss was sold out for the time we were there. But we did see *Canterbury Tales*. The earthiness of Chaucer's lines, the rough humour, and the bouncy tunes that the arranger had set made for great entertainment. That may have also been the day that we went up the Thames and took a boat down. These tourist craft, as it turned out, usually didn't guarantee their schedules. Traffic on the river and sculls practising for races held us up. So instead of floating all the way down to Westminster, we left the boat higher up and took the underground. Otherwise, we'd have missed much of the entertainment we had planned to take in.

During that week, we all had dinner again with Ian and Molly Richardson and their children, this time with Esther in tow. That was when I learned about the family connection with Ledcriech.

Sometimes during long flights I have felt claustrophobic. This time, as we returned to Canada, I sat for much of the flight in a seat at the front of a section with no seat in front of me, no doubt a rare privilege.

CHAPTER 53

# Commuting, 1964-1969

In 1964, since the family was still much involved in Burlington activities, I began commuting to my new job in Guelph. For four years, I used our Studebaker wagon which gave me 119,000 miles before I needed my second muffler, and for one year before we moved to Guelph, I used my red Volvo.

In this period, our cars were serviced by a Volvo dealership in Oakville, owned by a charming Hungarian-Canadian father and son who inspired confidence in both their sales—both cars had been purchased there—and in their mechanical work. My one complaint had to do with their courtesy cars which we were given to drive while our cars were being repaired. I tended to call them "discourtesy cars" since, in most cases, they were trade-ins that had not yet been checked over. One of them developed a flat tire and I found that the spare was also flat. Another one's motor purred beautifully once it was going but the starter wouldn't work, so that every time I stopped, I had to get to a phone and call the Motor League for a tow. And in another, I set off for Guelph in winter before discovering that the heater didn't work. You have to experience that to know what it's like. I'm sure, in these litigious times, they are more careful with the cars they lend to customers!

My favourite route to Guelph took me up the Appleby Line to #10 side road (now the Derry Road), west (to avoid Rattlesnake Point, the former shore of Lake Iroquois) to the Guelph Line, north past St. George's Anglican Church, Lever Brothers, the mushroom works, "Dad's" restaurant (now no longer in existence) and the hill that lay just before Campbellville and the mainline CPR. If I were headed for a school on the east side of Guelph, I would continue up the Guelph Line, past Ebenezer United Church, to #7 highway. For the other schools, I would use 401, a section that had then only recently been completed, and then follow Highway 6 to the city (now Brock Road).

But over the five years, I explored other routes. Sometimes I used #6 down to #5. Often I preferred the Centre Road which paralleled #6 to the east and led me into Waterdown. I became quite familiar with the Guelph Line below #10 side road. This involved a long curve at Lowville and hills that were part of Mt. Nemo. The journey usually took about 50 minutes each way. Since the sun was always behind me, visibility was usually good. But, when it wasn't, I was held up more often by fog than by snow. Black ice could be tricky, though, since it was invisible to the driver. Once as I was passing through Eden Mills, I started descending the hill at what I thought to be a slow speed. But I found that breaking started a skid and I had to rely on gearing down. Another time, I was approaching Guelph on #6. A trailer transport coming the other way caught up to a slow-moving small car, and, as the driver braked, his trailer jack-knifed across my lane. I managed to avoid being hit by him but I was thankful not to have left Burlington seconds earlier that morning!

Occasionally, I would head home down Victoria Road. At that time, it was not paved south of the Arkell Road, and, on one afternoon, it was snow-covered. I was peacefully coasting at 30 mph and, just as peacefully, slid into the ditch, and had to phone for a tow.

In June, 1964, Joe Gruzleski, the secretary and at that time the only office employee of the Guelph Separate School Board, took me on a quick tour of the seven schools that were then operating in the system. Strictly there were eight, but St. Agnes and St. Stanislaus, on the hill, were complimentary, with St. Agnes teaching the primary grades and St. Stans the juniors. Three more schools were added while I was on staff. The principals, in 1964, consisted of two lay women, one man newly appointed, and five nuns. When I retired, in 1982, there were two women (both lay) and eight men in those positions.

In July 1964, I drove to Guelph for a Board meeting, since I would need a lot of text-books for September. The Board saw my point at once and ordered what I prescribed. One member of that board seemed to be taking advantage of the Board meeting to catch up on sleep. But Father Mattice, pastor of St. Joseph's Church, turned out to be one of my strongest supporters in that meeting and for my whole time in Guelph.

I had imagined that, coming into a Catholic system, I would need to get clearance for any sacred music I would use. I soon found out that I could use anything I could put across. The years 1962-5 were the years of the 21st Vatican Council or Vatican Two. As a result, 1964-65 was the year in which Catholic Churches began celebrating mass in English. They didn't have any repertoire of English hymns and for a while I was busy teaching dozens of tunes from the protestant tradition. Indeed, the first English language missal (the Catholic book which included prayers, hymns and responses) featured the Lutheran hymn, *A Mighty Fortress Is Our God*,[111] inside its front cover.

That year, a few of us went to St. Michael's College in Toronto to learn a new English mass written by Father Stephen Sommerville. The next month I tried to teach it to a teachers' workshop. In the end, however, what really sold was a set of folk-type hymns that were typically accompanied by guitars. It took a while for the clergy to accept this fare. It started in St. Joseph's parish, always the first to try new ideas. At one point, I overheard a student exclaim, "There's been a break-through in Holy Rosary!" I had little part in this development. I remained busy teaching traditional folk songs in the classroom.

In Canada's centennial[112] year (1967), someone suggested that we should organize a massed choir. Thus began my series of spring concerts that stopped only when I retired. To start with, these involved only Guelph Schools. Later, with the setting up of the county board, they added four, and then five, rural schools. Until the last two years, we used St. Joseph's Church for the concerts. For a few years, that meant lining the children up in front of the altar. When the altar was moved to the middle of the sanctuary, the choir was moved back to where the altar had been. This had the disadvantage of cutting off visibility for the section of the audience behind the new altar. But it had the advantage of improving the sound which could resonate with the wooden panels behind.

As the outlying schools adjusted to functioning under the larger board, which began operating in 1969, some interesting situations developed. The local board that had run the four-room Sacred Heart School in Kenilworth finished their last year with a surplus of $6000. The inspector, who became assistant superintendent of the new board, urged the principal, Sister St. John, to spend this money, since any that was left on December 31st of that year would simply disappear into the general pot. But the sister, having, all her life, made two pennies do the work of four, couldn't imagine that kind of expenditure. She bought a record player for $175 and thought she was being extravagant! I would at least have hit her up for a new piano. But my jurisdiction didn't begin till after the New Year when the money was no longer available.

CHAPTER 54

# Outers Camp in NW Ontario

In 1966, I took Morrey and his Norquay cousins to the Quetico Outers Camp near Atikokan[113] in Northwestern Ontario. A teacher at the Atikokan High School had founded a wilderness camp[114] for the students. At various parts of the year, students would go into the bush and learn to survive should they ever be stranded there. They used snow-shoes in winter, canoes in summer. Part of the exercise involved having each individual staying by themselves for between 36 and 48 hours.

On returning to town, the campers would be debriefed about their experience—promptly before they got together and develop a stereotyped answer. Then they would be interviewed again two weeks later. The teacher told me that, typically, at the first interview the campers would complain of the hardships they had endured. But, at the second interview, they talked only of the glory of having survived the ordeal.

The camp this teacher organized for younger children took place at a resort on Eva Lake, about 16 miles east of Atikokan by highway #11. Eva Lake had the advantage that most of the lake, being uninhabited, was considered drinkable.

Morrey and the three Norquay children whom I drove to Eva Lake in the Norquay's Studebaker were at an interesting stage. Over the two previous years, Morrey and Sara, who were born in the same month, had developed a warm friendship. But, by that year, with the emotions of puberty kicking in at 13, that friendship cooled and there were verbal fights in the car. However, for many of the 50-odd hours of the journey there and back, I was driving four sleeping beauties—four, including Robbie, aged 11 and Naomi, 8.

Our first night on the way west was spent at Muldrew Lake. At that time, most of what we now call the Southwood Road was in gravel and I had to take the road's endless curves very slowly to forestall threatened car-sickness. That night, we were guests, at a cottage a little west of Sudbury, of Norquay relatives. The third night, we rented a cabin at Schreiber. On the highway north of Lake Superior, trucks often slowed one's progress. But we experienced some gorgeous vistas. By supper time the next night, we pulled into Eva Lake.

At the centre, we were made comfortable. One of the staff remarked, "We believe in two things: eating well and sleeping soundly." That was born out by the quality of the meals and of the mattresses. While the kids had their two-week course, I was given free lodging in return for minor jobs. Every night, we endured the sequence of deer flies while the sun was still high, black flies at dusk and mosquitoes when it got dark. That was in the camp. In the deep bush, I'm sure the bugs were much worse.

Each half day, the children were taught a different skill. These included tent-pitching, building lean-to shelters from brush, identifying edible plants in the forest, and using a compass to keep a constant direction when you have to go round a high hill. And I remember the director stating that healthy human beings can keep walking almost indefinitely. My one criticism was that the kids didn't get frequent practice in each skill. "How many of them would they remember a few weeks later?" I wondered.

But one compulsory activity they would never forget. Before the time was over, every camper was taken to a different point or spot where they would be entirely alone for over a day. They were given an orange, some fishing tackle and some means of cutting wood. Morrey's response was interesting. He reported that he had been so tired from the camp's activities that, after making a half-hearted—and unsuccessful—attempt to build a lean-to shelter, he lay down and slept the whole time! Fortunately, the weather was warm.

For the return trip, the Studebaker station-wagon was very full when all five of us people had packed in our dunnage.

Accordingly, we were very thankful for sunshine when, on the way to Port Arthur, we had to stop to change a tire. To get at the spare, we had to put several of our bags at the side of the road. I forget where we slept in Port Arthur (now Thunder Bay). I also recall that Jim Norquay had pre-booked some of our accommodation, though whether we always arrived on time to take advantage of it, I can't remember. Our next night saw us at Wawa, and I think we must have gone again to Muldrew, for it was a mid-afternoon when Jim welcomed us back in Toronto. I remember his typically warm welcome and his tone of voice as he used the one word, "Well!"

In October, 2005, the CBC featured a documentary on the immediate future of Atikokan. A major activity of the town is still the departure of a large number of young people in canoes. This has been the case since the Outers program of Atikokan High School was launched in the 1960's.

## CHAPTER 55

# Muldrew Lake, 1942-1997

At the time of World War II, at the cottage, our main building consisted of the original construction of 1929, with the long porch added. In addition, Mother had had a Mr. Russell do some internal alterations, removing a partition that divided the front room from a small bedroom, and closing off the porch door to the kitchen. The other building was the sleeping cabin which, as I have said before, had been built on a flimsy tent floor. The cottage porch still had only screens over the windows and no glass; when a storm arose, there were shutters on the inside that had to be closed, shutting out most of the light.

Enter Eleanor Ewing. I am very sure that the various improvements which have taken place over the subsequent years would never have been as interesting or innovative without her ideas and initiative.

In the 50's, while the children were little, we had August Shultz from Gravenhurst, uncle of Arthur[115], put windows in that porch. August was a trained carpenter unlike John McPhee, the farmer who had built the cottage and the cabin. August reported that no two of the joists between which he put the windows were parallel! The windows allowed a wonderful view of the westernmost area of the lake and the often-changing western sky. Many of our storms have come sweeping across the lake from that direction. In fact, soon after the windows had been installed, a thunder storm occurred, and the children were delighted to be able to look into the teeth of it without getting wet. It was great to see the gray waves with whitecaps and the beating rain on the windows.

Two of the narrow windows which had belonged to the original cottage led only to the porch. Plywood was nailed on the porch side, and shelves built on the other side where we

*Old cottage*

kept tumblers and other narrow objects. The windows closed over these objects.

On the other side of the kitchen, two similar narrow windows were at one point replaced with four large windows which swung upward for air. They had been the cast-off windows of a lady with a business on the Burlington Lakeshore. She charged us just $12.00 for the four!

At 75 South Drive in St. Catharines, my parents had had an interior French door which they didn't want to use. It became the north-west entrance to the cottage kitchen, replacing the fifth narrow window and giving us access to the outdoors and much needed light on that side.

Up until 1960, our cottage had to do double-duty as a boat-house in the winter. At first, our skiff rested on its side between front porch and kitchen and when we added the canoe, it lay on its side on top of the skiff. When the western porch came into being, the craft lived there in winter from 1933 to 1960, inclusive.

In 1961, August Schultz put up a boat-house so that we could have a separate building in which to store our craft over

*Boathouse*

the winter. In the summer, it would be used for extra living quarters. Indeed, for two-and-a-half summers after it was built, my parents lived there. This allowed them some privacy and they were able to be quite independent as they had a wood stove, a small Coleman gas stove and shelves and a table as well as their beds. In the afternoons, the children loved to go down and play cards or scrabble with them. A storage cupboard was built on the SE wall with access from the outside. Our neighbour, Alice Garrard, thought this cupboard was an unfair limitation of Mother and Dad's quarters!

I remember 1961 because, while doing the boathouse, Arthur Schultz also built our second out-house, and, while I dug the hole, I had a transistor radio on a nearby rock, bringing in CBC coverage of the founding convention of the NDP! I recall George Grube[116] opening *Mike Number Five* and Dorothy Steeves, one of the early legislators in BC, reminding the delegates of the battles of the CCF. George Grube, a professor at the University of Toronto, brought his family to Muldrew more than once in the 30's and 40's.

In the early 50's, Eleanor's Dad got a new out-board motor to use in Algonquin Park, and, since his old 3½ horsepower motor was still behaving, he gave it to us on the understanding that we would get a boat to take it. So we purchased a red fibreglass boat from Eaton's and were somewhat mobile from then on.

Of course, a used motor needs service, and we were lucky to have an excellent service man on the lake. Tom Belcher was a retired naval engineer who had a cottage on a high rock above the landing. He was quite a character. He used to refer to future events by saying, "By that time, I'll be underneath the daisies!" He had taken over a boat made by a Mr. Small which he called the "Queen Mary". It had an inboard motor and was probably the quietest powerboat ever seen on the lake. "Bring it in and let me have a look at it," was usually Tom's response when I mentioned any malfunction in our motor. He usually put it right, though after a few years, he told us that our motor was "reaching the point of no return".

Lil Belcher, about my age, who had married Al Rochon, was for many years the person from whom we rented our boat slips; and, in spite of her handicap—for one arm she had only a stub to which a hook had been attached—she ran the very important water taxi. In the early years, when we first arrived on the lake and when we finally left for the season, we used the community boat. But, from the 60's until our road was completed in 1994, we used Lil's boat taxi to leave. In the fall, the main problem was to fix the time when we'd be ready to abandon the camp and get into the boat. There were always last-minute chores that weren't anticipated but which would keep us from being ready to go. Lil was always patient and with obvious expertise, would hold her boat away from the shore until we were ready to go. This was no mean feat as we had usually pulled our dock up on shore.

In 1989, the Rochon cottage burned to the ground. Following this, cottagers got together a rather generous fund which facilitated the building of a new cottage. When the money was delivered to her, Lil was overwhelmed. She had had no idea that she had that kind of support on the lake.

Al, who did many jobs for cottagers, died in 1992 after a series of strokes. Lil continued to operate her taxi until the building of Fish Hook Lane and other private roads had rendered many cottagers independent of her services. She was very unhappy about this, and I wished that she could have kept a more active part of the Muldrew economy during the final six years before her death in 2000.

Our first telephone was located in the boat-house, the connecting wires coming in from the lake just behind it. Since the boathouse was not the main building, we were often not down there and so for the first few seasons, we kept having to check

*The Studio, West side*

for messages. Jane White remarked that it sometimes took less time to come over in her boat than to phone us and wait for us to phone back!

The studio went up in 1978. Many years earlier, when playing treasure-hunt with Eleanor, John Dale (about age 8, I believe) had confided in her, "When I grow up, I want to build a house on that point." That point was the second ridge southwest of the cottage. In 1978, John, then a 4th year student of architecture at U of T, designed the studio as the subject of his fifth year thesis project. In cooperation with Don Scott, a fellow student who had earlier apprenticed with a carpenter, it was built that summer. In this they were assisted by John's younger brother, Tom, and our niece, Naomi Norquay, who at that time was keeping company with John. I did all their cooking and was able to watch it go up, board by board.

When asked early in June if they thought they could have the building ready for an official opening on Civic Holiday week-end, they promised faithfully to be ready. They started off well enough. But, as the deadline got nearer, they had to set themselves daily goals and told me that they wouldn't eat dinner each night till that day's goal was reached. The second last night, the goal was completion of the stairs, and I not only had to light a Coleman gas lantern—this was before the advent of Hydro for us—but I had to hold their dinner until midnight.

The largest windows in the building had had a former life as storm windows in both John and Don's parents' winter households. That last evening before the official opening, the floors were treated, in a schedule of four-hour intervals, with urethane and varathane, and none of this could be started till a troublesome window was fitted and the resultant shavings swept up. So, that night, the whole crew set alarm clocks and got the job done just on time.

The studio was built two stories high, with a sleeping loft at one end accessible by a staircase with two 90 degree turns. When the construction was celebrated, before a number of other cottagers and families of the builders, the loft was used as a rather high stage. Naomi wrote a hit song and performed it with guitar. The chorus went like this:

> "It ain't no fun when I hammer my thumb
> And I nail my foot to the floor,
> When this job's done, I'm just a-gonna bum
> I'll never hang another damn door, Oh no,
> I'll never hang another damn door!"

For some little time, the Bill Dales had acquired the reputation of turning up late for meals to which they were invited. On that Saturday, parents of the builders were invited for a special commemorative lunch. With the influence of the Scotts, everyone came right on time.

From that day on, all guests of our camp have been asked to sign the guest book—a flat board, kept in the studio. At one point, a few years later, the first board got filled and a second one started.

Because our buildings tend to run parallel with the ridges of rock on which they stand, the four directions in the other buildings point toward the corners. But the studio was situated differently. As you stand in front of the largest windows, you look due north or due west.

For 20 years, Eleanor and I slept in the studio loft. There were real advantages for us to be able to retire early while younger folk wanted to stay up and socialize without disturbing us. Of course, this meant we had to have flashlights that worked, especially on dark nights in August. Sometimes, too, nature seemed closer in the studio. For years, I kept a badminton racket handy in case of bats. But I was only ever able to catch two: one that lighted on the back of my dresser, and another, when Sara Norquay found it on a window screen and managed to close the window over it, making it easy for me to remove the sleeping beast the next morning.

Then there were the mornings, two or three times, when we were wakened at 6:00 am by the rat-tat-tat of a woodpecker on the edge of the roof. And there was the evening that Eleanor had gone to bed early with her window open. I had to bring her a message, but couldn't make her hear because of a loud loon call in the adjacent bay!

Up until the 1980's, the Ewings were exhibit A on the lake for primitive cottage living. Then gradually we made improvements. First we got our second propane fridge and with it a gas range. Then a neighbour got electricity and gave us their string of gas lights. And one Christmas, Esther gave the men of the family a strange-looking present. It turned out to be an army surplus stretcher—two poles made of solid oak with canvas sheeting between. What was it for? Carrying 100-pound cylinders of propane gas from boat to cottage. It was very helpful in saving the backs of everyone who had to haul these unwieldy loads. The following June, Bruce and I carried the first of two such loads, and Bruce exclaimed, "That's July done!" A few years later, hydro became part of our lives—brought in from the lake at our second bay on the western side. From that point, it was a matter of adding appliances. In the studio, the coal-oil reflector lamps by which we had read at night were replaced by electric lamps also fixed to the wall above our heads. But we still kept the old lamps in case of electrical outages.

Until 1994, the routine for arriving at and departing from the lake was consistent. We drove to the landing, unloaded the car and loaded the boat at our rented slip, parked the car up the hill, and drove the boat to the cottage. As we never had a covered boat, weather was often a factor. Many days, we would arrive with our groceries from town only to have to wait until a storm had passed before it was safe to traverse the lake. But the building of Fish Hook Lane changed all that. Among other things, we have a different usage of our boats, since we don't need them to arrive or depart.

The creation of Fish Hook Lane was a story of great persistence in the face of major problems. If our neighbour, Ken Anderson, had not spent countless hours over two years, we would not have been able to build it. Several land owners had to be persuaded to let us route the road over their land; at least one held out for over a year. Then surveys had to be completed by the town, after titles had been searched. And a route over very rough terrain had to be found to service all the cottagers who had decided to participate. In the end, over 20 of us each paid $10,000 for our share of the construction which was done in an expert fashion by Don Robinson. And then we each got him to create our parking lots.

Three quarters of the 2-kilometer road is relatively straight. The last part, where it curves way around was the inspiration for the name of the road. Frankly, I had been cool to the idea of a road because of my concern about the number of pines that would have to be felled. However, I have found since the construction, that many beautiful trees are now visible that I was totally unaware of before the road went through. The road also made it possible for neighbours to go for daily walks. There are even some who jog every day.

CHAPTER 56

# Cars We Have Owned

My father sold his only car when I was 10 (a 1924 Chevrolet Sedan). So the issue of my getting a license to drive didn't arise when I reached the magic age. In the mid 1930's my cousin, Andrew Rutherford, and I were both working for Uncle Don one summer in Brechin. Andrew had a license and did some driving as part of his work, and sometimes I went along. Two or three times, he let me take the wheel—quite illegally, of course—but I got a bit of useful experience in that way on country roads. Andrew later recalled:

"…Being brought up on a farm had this one advantage and one of my memories was of trying to teach Don how to drive a car. It happened at Brechin where I was delivering groceries for Uncle Don, and Donald came to visit for a few days. Don came along with me one day and I was so happy to have the company. Then I thought how much easier delivering would be if I didn't have to drive. I convinced Don that driving was easy and got him behind the wheel and he was doing OK when a gate got in the way. Don hit the gas pedal instead of the brake and down went the gate. It was at Mara Beach. It was a good thing that the gate post was rotten as the only damage to the car was one broken head lamp. I had to take the blame as uncle Don knew that Donald couldn't drive a car.

It was a surprise to me when, some years later, he was driving to school, in a Volkswagen I think it was, and I never heard of him having any accidents."

I was not behind a wheel again until close to my 42nd birthday, when Eleanor and I took driving lessons. Eleanor passed her test on the first try, while I was given a couple of demerits—for street parking and in turning left at lights—and had to retake the test, passing the second time.

Our first car was a DKW (Die Kleine Wunderwagon—the little wonder wagon!). It ran on two cycles and three cylinders, and was known for its low gas mileage. Ours was a station wagon and we got a lot of use out of the rear storage area. In the long run, we had to judge our car to have been a lemon, since so many things had gone wrong during its life. We got it new at a dealer on East Plains Road in Burlington, but got most of our servicing at a dealership in Oakville.

One Sunday in December, after we'd had the DKW for about five weeks, I took my parents for a drive, promising Eleanor that we'd be back by dark. We headed out Cedar Springs Road and, as the sun dipped, pulled into a side road to turn round. But, as I tried to put the gear-shift—a lever at the wheel—into reverse, the lever came loose in my hand. When I knocked on a farmer's door to phone for help, I was told of a garage to the north, down the hill on the Cedar Springs Road. A man from that garage arrived with a handful of screws. A screw that should have joined two bars under the hood had come off and was somewhere back in the snow. But the DKW had screws with German threads and the one this man put in only just got me down to his garage. He then found something that fitted better. But, of course, the place where we had got the car wasn't open on Sundays. When I got there on Monday afternoon, I was told that this would not likely ever happen again. I wondered, "What kind of checking had the car received before being sold that this would happen at all?"

Another evening when the DKW had been guilty of one of its failings, we happened to be in Oakville and dropped into our dealership and asked if the problem was necessarily typical of the make. Our mechanic, in his soft, reassuring tone of voice, assured us that it was not, and proceeded to make a simple adjustment. He had won our confidence and was our service agent for this and the next two cars.

Before we had had the DKW for a year, we drove it to Oshawa for a dinner in honour of A. E. O'Neil. That was the occasion at which I was present in three capacities—as a former student, as the son of a former teacher and as the husband of another teacher. It was also the occasion when Dad told of Mr. Comrie, a very stern janitor, who found Dad and several other new teachers in one of their rooms after school one day. This was in the fall of 1926, the year Mr. O'Neil took over after a period of indifferent discipline. Mr. Comrie, having taken the measure of Mr. O'Neil's leadership, told them, "You fellows have got to make good or get out."

The night of Mr. O'Neil's dinner was one of equinoxial rains. Our windshield wipers had failed soon after we had left Oshawa and I had to stop repeatedly to wipe the windshield by hand.

Generally, the DKW was difficult: With just three cylinders, we were very conscious of the loss of power if one cylinder cut out, especially if we were climbing a long hill!

The DKW was pressed into service at Muldrew at an early stage. It appeared that a natural gas fridge that had been converted to propane was available. But we took some time to think over the decision of whether to upgrade to this convenience. We went off to the lake where our refrigeration was still the old cold hole in the ground with a wooden cover. That week we stored a ham there that we planned to share with guests on the Sunday. Alas, we had a storm with heavy rains and the water filled up the hole ruining the ham. The next morning, Eleanor took off in the DKW wagon to get the gas fridge.

For a few years, my Uncle Don (Haig) owned a motel and gas station on #11 highway opposite Orillia. One day we set off from the lake to visit him. En route, I noticed liquid drops on the windshield, although there was not a cloud in the sky. At that time, there was a very obliging garage owner on the side of #11 just south of Washago. He soon discovered that my upper radiator hose had worn out. One of the features that made DKW's unique was that its upper radiator hose was conical in shape unlike the ubiquitous North American cars in which radiator hoses were typically cylindrical. The man phoned garages in Orillia and Barrie, even the DKW place in Barrie, but failed to locate the right hose. Eventually, he was able to contact the importer in Toronto. He was first told that the soonest he would receive the part was the next day. But he explained that the Ewing family would be stranded if they were not served that day and the importer reluctantly agreed to put the part on the next bus. We were picked up for the day by Uncle Don's assistant. But I often wondered how we might have fared if this had happened half way across Northern Ontario.

We followed the example of the Norquays in the make of cars we bought. Their DKW had not been a lemon and served them well in Alberta. But the importer of parts from Germany took advantage of the scarcity of competition to fleece the many dealers across Ontario, and, one by one, they abandoned the make. The Norquays' next choice was a Studebaker, then being made in Oakville. Eleanor's mother also drove a Studebaker Lark which had served her very well. I got to drive the Norquay vehicle when I took Morrey and the three Norquay kids to an Outers Camp in Northwestern Ontario. Perhaps it was that experience that led us to get our Studebaker wagon. I used it for four of the five years in which I commuted to Guelph. The many miles of highway driving may have been the reason my first muffler lasted me for 125,000 miles!

I got both the Studebaker (in 1964) and my first Volvo, four years later, at Meray Motors. I had been told that the way to buy a car was to offer $200 less than the asking price. That approach worked with Mr. Meray, Sr. "Can we make a deal, Meester Ewing?" He didn't lower the price but threw in some extras that I wanted. But four years later, when I offered less than the fixed price for my first Volvo, his son, Andy Meray was a tougher negotiator and insisted on the full price. One of Andy's Hungarian-English expressions was, "I think so it is."

The Volvo Company used to boast that their cars lasted an average of 13 years on Swedish roads. Three of our four Volvos exceeded that. It was true, also of all four, that the motor outlasted the body. The body of my last one, bought in 1984, had better attention than any of the others, but, when I sold it 21 years later, it still had a well-functioning motor.

The red Volvo saw me through the last of my five years of commuting, and then served as I began driving to Fergus, Elora, Arthur, Kenilworth and Mount Forest. It also served to take me to a number of out-of-town NDP gatherings, including the Sudbury Convention in 1974 where I drove with a full load of passengers. It also took me to a Provincial Council meeting in the United Auto Workers Hall south of London. At that meeting, the provincial president, Pat Chefurka of London, introduced Jane Bigelow, Eleanor's first cousin, then mayor of London, with great pride. And her tone of voice matched her words.

And the red Volvo allowed me to circulate the NDP Newsletter. This was edited, and then typed on a stencil and run off on the mimeographing machine at the Steelworkers' office. The Steelworkers, although affiliated with the party, did little to help our election campaigns. But they were willing to make their office facilities available on an on-going basis. Our newsletter was published monthly—mimeographed—and was distributed for more than ten years.

During that period, we took the newsletter to hundreds of people—members—and many others, who had indicated support at election time, for instance, by taking signs. The city was divided into many districts, and a deliverer recruited for each district. The bundles were put together, and, on a Saturday, I would set off to deliver the bundles, putting some 30 kilometers on the car. Usually, about half the deliverers would be home, and often they would want to talk. After all, we got together seldom enough.

This wasn't a very efficient way of getting the letters out. The deliverers could be very human. Those left in doors often disappeared before they were read. But it kept a number of people involved between elections, and this hasn't happened since the letters are printed and mailed.

Since 1967 until I stopped driving, Eleanor and I have had two cars. While I was commuting to Guelph, Eleanor had the opportunity of leading the music in the public schools of Milton. This lasted only for the two years it took the Burlington Board of Education to realize that Milton was receiving what no other part of the jurisdiction could be granted, and to bring the service to an end. But, to get there, Eleanor needed a car, and she acquired a Cortina, a British-made Ford.

Those two years were a very special example of the light that Eleanor revealed to a community. The stories I heard from her and others told of some wonderful work and of a high degree of appreciation from staff.

When we moved to Guelph, Eleanor got her Volvo, a full navy blue sedan. She used it to get to her new job which was to lead the music education in the public schools of Elora, Arthur and Kenilworth. One of the teachers in the Arthur school offered Eleanor a bed in her home, in case she was ever stranded in the village by weather. In January, 1971, she had occasion one day to take advantage of that offer. A severe snowstorm began at the beginning of the school day.

In that same snowstorm, the Separate School superintendent and his assistant both arrived early to visit St. John School, in Arthur. Their business finished, they started south, but experienced a white-out on the highway and were lucky enough to be rescued by a truck-driver and returned to the village where they spent the next night in the Convent.

The school bus drivers, when they had arrived at the schools in the morning, declared that if they didn't immediately take the students home again, they might not be able to do so. The public school principals phoned the Board office in Guelph for permission to send the children back. But the officer who might have given permission was not in his office, and by the time he had returned, it was too late to send the buses back!

The villagers rose to the occasion nobly. They opened their homes to all the children. It seemed that, the larger the family, the more kids they took in to bed down on the living room floors, probably because they were used to having crowds of kids around.

Farther south, the ploughs made roadside walls that made it dangerous to turn out from side-roads since you couldn't see left or right on the highways. At one point, highway 6 was closed north of Guelph, and a wall of snow appeared where traffic had to stop. It made me think of Shakespeare's *Julius Caesar*, "A lioness hath whelped in the streets!"[117] A story circulated in Guelph that some people had begun digging out a Volkswagen only to discover that another vehicle was buried underneath!

In the summer of 1973, Eleanor and I used the blue Volvo to make our first tour of the Maritimes. We descended the St. Lawrence, spending a night at St. Jean Port Joli, passed through Edmonston and saw upper New Brunswick by descending the valley of the St. John River. After a night in Fredericton, we crossed to PEI. I recall being tremendously impressed with the CNR ferry across Northumberland Strait. It loaded simultaneously on two levels and thus made excellent time.

We had booked accommodation in advance, using a travel guide. In some cases, we had to re-book because we made unexpectedly good time. We arrived at the outskirts of Charlottetown and drew up in front of a house where we had booked our first night. Eleanor was not impressed with the outside appearance of the house and declared, "I'm not staying here." "Well," I said, "You'd better go in and tell them." But when she had met the people and had seen the inside of the house, she changed her mind completely. Indeed, we stayed there three nights while we explored the island.

Our host, Mr. Macleod, was an inspector of seed potatoes, and told us many stories about PEI. According to him, the PEI MacLeods (spelled m-a-c) were Protestant, and the McLeods were Catholic—the reverse of the situation in Ontario. Sometime in the 19th century, the Catholics of one electoral district had ambushed the Protestants on their way to a polling station, causing deaths and injuries. As a result, Catholics had since been forbidden to represent that district in the Legislature—talk about the sins of the fathers!

We took in an excellent show, *Anne of Green Gables*, at the Centennial Hall in Charlottetown. At Amherst, NS, near the NB border, we visited Pat and Len West of Burlington. Len's American firm had appointed him manager of a new plant which had been built to take advantage of a Government grant made to stimulate the Maritime economy. After a very short time, the company abandoned the plant! From Amherst, we re-crossed the border to hear a chamber concert on the campus of Mount Alison University in Sackville.

A few weeks earlier, Eleanor had listened to a CBC interview with the mayor of Amherst. He had been asked about people's difficulty in remembering to spell the name with an "h". He remarked that most people wanted to get the "h" out of Amherst!

We next headed for Cape Breton, staying two nights at Normandy Lodge in the Margaree Valley. We had decided that, on the day between, we would visit the Louisberg Museum if it rained, or follow the Cabot Trail if it were sunny. Sunny it was. I was at the wheel, and Eleanor began to get squeamish about the twists and turns and hills of the road. However, we kept going until it was shorter to go on than to return, and we managed the whole Trail. I remember picking up a Newfoundland radio station from the tip of Cape Breton, and descending hills on the West side.

The next day it did rain, all day. We drove all the way to Digby, thinking that there were really long distances in these provinces that had looked so tiny on the map of North America. I also came to realize how much of Maritime land is still in forest. We lunched in Truro and chose just the right restaurant and time to see a famous phenomenon. The tidal bore is caused by the Bay of Fundy's very high tides. At a certain time, the surface of the river has two simultaneous levels and the bore is the dividing line between the levels which is constantly moving up river. We were shown to our table just as the bore went past.

That night we took a motel and got up in time to be on the dock of the Digby-St. John ferry by 4:00 am. While we waited in line, we tried the car radio and found at least 40 stations which came in clearly but had nothing we wanted to hear. In Western New Brunswick, we visited relatives of Lloyd Yeomans, then proceeded through New England, spent a night beside Lake Champlain, crossed back to Canada at Cornwall, and thence home.

The blue Volvo served as the vehicle on which Morrey learned to drive, and in which he got his first license. Eleanor used it to begin her music teaching in upper Wellington County. We finally sold it in a very informal manner. I met the purchaser down-town, where he gave me ten $100 bills!

My red Volvo did me for 13 years. For my next car, I bought a used Volvo—the only time I have bought a used car. I had used it as a courtesy car and liked the way it handled. But I bought it without realizing that the oil tank had a leak. Nevertheless, I used it in my visit to Timmins in 1983 (see chapter 72).

In October, 1984, with Aunt Mary's help, I bought my brown Volvo, which lasted me the 21 ½ years in which I kept driving. Lawrence Motors advertised some of the previous year's cars. When I phoned them, they had two left. When I got to the dealership, they only had one. I had always driven with stick shift. This car had an automatic transmission which meant that, for a time, Eleanor was happy to drive it.

One of our first trips in this car took us to a dinner at York University where Eleanor's sister, Marg, was being honoured. On our way back, another vehicle drove across my path so that I couldn't avoid hitting it. The insurance covered $4200 in body repair. The motor was not damaged.

The following summer, I drove to an NDP convention in Ottawa, where Eleanor joined me for a foray into Quebec as far as Quebec City.

Over time, this car "got to know me". My biggest help was,

of course, Hamilton's Corner Garage. People spoke disapprovingly of their untidy yard, where every trade-in was kept and used for parts that were used to save customers money in repairs. However, I found that I could always trust them in their assessment of my car's condition and in their service in putting things right. If I needed a new headlight, new wiper blades or the repair of a tire, they would drop everything and serve me promptly. I came to see the brothers Hamilton—Bill (body and sales) and Jim (service) as friends.

I was once rear-ended, and had difficulty with the other party's insurance company which wanted to write off my car as irreparable. On Morrey's advice, I threatened to appeal to the Ontario Insurance Tribunal and won. I believe the company felt that settling with me would cost them less.

Another time, I needed a Drive Clean certificate, required at that time by the provincial government. This program was aimed at ensuring that automobiles met certain minimum emission standards. For older cars however, there was a provision in the regulations that if the car failed after a certain amount of work done on it, the car would be given a provisional pass, which meant that you could continue to drive it but you couldn't sell it to someone else. My car failed. Hamilton's did some work on the motor but it failed again. On the fifth try, it passed, but by then they had almost given me a new motor. They predicted that my gas mileage would improve. That summer it certainly did—by 50%!

Bought in 1987, Eleanor's Toyota has lasted over 20 years. Every now and then it needs body work, but we gladly pay the cost as it's cheaper than a new car. Meanwhile, I stopped driving in June, 2006. I carry senior's tickets for the Guelph bus service, costing $13.50 for ten). And I have an account with Canadian Cab for taxis when it's inconvenient for Eleanor to take me places.

CHAPTER 57

# Supervising Music in the Separate Schools

In 1964, I was ready for a new job, and applied, among other places, to the Separate School boards in Oshawa and Guelph. The first was interested in me because they "preferred a qualified non-Catholic to an unqualified Catholic", but offered an inadequate salary. But, when I quoted them (as "another board") in speaking to the Guelph board, they responded that that was also their position. A contract was then signed.

In July, I attended a meeting of the board, held then in St. Agnes School beside the Church of Our Lady, to request a set of texts and was given exactly what I wanted. Subsequently, Joe Grusleski, the secretary, gave me a tour of the seven schools the system had at that time in Guelph. For five years, I commuted to these schools from Spruce Street in Burlington. It took me around 50 minutes. The sun was always behind me, and I was held up more often by fog than by snow.

I soon got straight about a few stories that I had heard at the expense of Catholic schools. For instance, it was said that pupils spent so much time praying that regular subjects got short-changed. The first class I entered, a grade 5, began the day with 45-seconds on their knees, and then quickly resumed their seats ready for their teacher's first instructions.

All teachers and principals soon got to know that I wasn't a Catholic. But I was never conscious of pressure to change my beliefs. On the other hand, I found plenty of evidence that I was regarded as belonging to the Separate School community. I once met the Bishop of Hamilton diocese who was delighted to hear that I was a United Church elder. On another occasion, I attended a concelebration of mass in the Church of

Our Lady when, during the passing of the peace, all the teachers around me shook my hand with great warmth.

This job gave me scope to apply my love of organization. I divided the year into eight phases and prepared a mimeographed course for the year in each grade. In each phase, I gave the teachers a choice of songs. In September I would get teacher lists for each school from the board office. Then I would phone each principal to learn which half days in each week I should avoid using for visits to his/her school. I would then make myself a two-week timetable for visiting every class, allowing for a visit every two weeks or every four, depending on the amount of help each teacher might need. Next, I would tour the schools to meet each teacher and give her/him a copy of the course. This would use the first week.

I had also to be sure that every teacher had the equipment needed. That included the appropriate text-books and a pitch-pipe. Getting them all to use a pitch-pipe was a challenge with some teachers who preferred to guess at the pitch. Other equipment took longer to acquire. Eventually, I got an autoharp for every school floor. I was constantly tuning them. I also worked simple chording into my courses so that small children could use this means of adding another dimension to songs their classes sang.

The Orff instruments gave the songs another dimension. Designed for children by the 20th century German music educator, Carl Orff, the xylophones, glockenspiels and metalophones can be played with arm movement which is more easily mastered than the finger movement needed for piano and violin. To store and move these and other smaller percussion instruments, I copied a design from Scarborough and had one cart used on each floor.

Then there were the cassette tapes. For creating the master tapes, I had a monthly session with Esther. There were plenty of good recording voices among the teachers, but Esther outdid them all in her ability to read music. My secretary sometimes was exasperated by having to make copies of my master tapes, using somewhat primitive equipment. But during each phase, I would distribute copies for the teachers, and collect a set of old ones. Some music supervisors would develop permanent "libraries" of tapes in each school. But I found the tapes were more likely to be used if they were available for a limited time.

One year, Esther performed at assemblies in some of the public and separate schools in Guelph. In the latter case, teachers and pupils were able to meet the "voice in the tape." But music in the public schools was then a very hit-and-miss affair, and Esther found our children much more responsive to what she had to present. The regular classroom practice made all the difference.

I never worked myself out of a job. I believe that my visits provided routine and encouragement for the teachers who had a million other things on which to focus. But, in the 18 years of my sojourn in the separate schools, the great majority of the teachers in my jurisdiction did outstanding work in the classroom. Many of them grew in their ability to get results. And while my efforts might sometimes have been dispensed with, the consistent work of the teachers was what counted in the children's development.

This was illustrated one year when a grade 4 class had the misfortune to lose three successive teachers during the year. In the process, little music was taught. The next fall in grade 5, it took a lot of effort to get the children caught up and accustomed to regular practice.

In June of each year, as the school momentum was at a low ebb, the temptation was strong to stop teaching music early. I used a plan that did something to counter that. At the end of May, I would ask the teachers to review the songs they had taught since the beginning of September and select the four they thought the children could do best. I went round asking to hear the four they had chosen. Although some of the results were not as good as I would have hoped, I never said so. I just picked the two best and asked them to sing their choices for a closing assembly which I somehow scheduled for each school before the year's end. I really believe that both teachers and children were glad they could end the year that way.

Perhaps the most flattering remark I ever heard from these schools came from a Kindergarten. Unlike other non-Catholic teachers, Mrs. Maisie Russell was allowed to teach religion to her class. One day she told them: "You know we can't know everything. But there is one who does and who is that?" A child put up her hand and asked—"Mr. Ewing?"

Many times, we demonstrated the superiority of the old-style classrooms with cloak rooms. When we came to performing an echo song that began, "Down in the well," the grade two children couldn't wait for the chance to take their turn doing the echoes from the cloak room. The acoustics were just right.

One summer, one of our teachers, Dorothy Beitz, toured Egypt and came home loaded with Egyptian artifacts. When I went to see her before school began, she exclaimed, "Welcome to Egypt!" One of her treasures was some special dress material, which she had sewn up in Guelph to fit her. One Saturday, she took the bus to attend a teachers' seminar in Toronto. On her return, it had been raining when she got off the bus at Norfolk and Macdonnell. She didn't see a car coming and it hit her. She was rushed to hospital, where she was told that her dress would have to be cut from her back. But this was the special Egyptian dress, and no way would she have it cut. I never heard the rest of that story!

CHAPTER 58

# The Separate School Concerts

We managed to have Christmas assemblies in almost every school. I used to encourage the teachers to start preparing early in November. That didn't preclude teaching other material in that month. Since the excitement of performing can drive the words and notes out of students' heads, I knew that elementary school children needed to be very familiar with songs that they would perform for others.

The literature of Christmas music is especially rich, and there were songs of quality in our books for every stage in the children's development. Enough of these are appealing that they will stay with the children most of their lives. In my opinion, that is not true with *All I want for Christmas is my two front teeth!* Each year one teacher came up with a version of *The Little Drummer Boy* (not in our books), and I would make the most of the rhythmic elements involved. But it was not my favourite music.

At the concerts, we used to alternate the performances of individual classes with leading the audience in singing well-known carols. I believed in making *Silent Night* move fast enough that the children could feel the 6/8 rhythm. And of course, we always had fun with *The Twelve Days of Christmas*.

Whenever possible, the teachers conducted their classes, and when needed, I accompanied them on the piano. Also, when possible, I accompanied them without looking at a book. Having worked with the material used, I usually did some basic chording. Of course it was better still if a child could provide the support with an autoharp, or with Orff instruments in which case the piano was not needed at all.

In the fifteen years in which I had spring concerts with massed choirs, I gradually fine-tuned my planning. Usually, about 300 of the grades 5 and 6 in my jurisdiction volunteered to belong to the choir before the March break. At first, this involved the seven schools in Guelph, a number that gradually grew to eleven as more schools were opened. Later, children from four, and then five, county schools were bused in. The concert was held about the first of June, for thirteen years in St. Joseph's church, and, for the last two, in the Church of Our Lady[119].

The program, which lasted just over an hour, followed a fairly consistent pattern. It would start with a group of 3 or 4 songs for the whole choir, usually a group that was sacred in emphasis. One song would be in unison with piano accompaniment. One would be in three parts unaccompanied. One would be a canon or round, again unaccompanied, and one would be accompanied by a battery of autoharps, preferably with one player from each school or the accompaniment would involve tuned Orff instruments[120].

To add to the program, the choir was divided between the schools on the east side of Guelph and the schools on the west side. Each would learn and perform a set of songs with the same variety as characterised the opening group. Through the month of May, these choirs would rehearse separately both their own songs and the ones they would do together. When the county schools joined in, they had to be rehearsed entirely in their own buildings until the dress rehearsal.

One song was always reserved for all the boys in the choir. They were always outnumbered by the girls. But forty or fifty of them gave a good account of themselves.

Then we always did a song involving the audience. The words were on the program. After the choir had sung a verse or two, the audience were asked to join in on their verse, then stand and sing it by themselves—accompanied, of course, on the piano. Then it would be the turn of the children to applaud their parents. One number was attempted on the xylophones, glockenspiels and metalophones that were regularly used in the schools.

The program would end with a rousing unison song, often by Rogers and Hammerstein. Once it was, *You'll never walk alone;* another year, *June is bustin' out all over,* another year, *Oklahoma.*

Preparing for the concert meant almost as much planning as organizing the program. I first persuaded one of the more musical members of the staff of each participating school to teach the notes of the songs involving the pupils of that school. Then Esther made me tapes of all the material to be used, and I would deliver the relevant tapes to these teachers. With part-songs, each school group would learn one part. From the March break until the end of April, I would spend half an hour every two weeks with each of these groups. Sometimes I would need to eat lunch in the car as I drove from school to school for this purpose.

In May, the East side choirs would practise together each week at 4:00 o'clock in St. John School, while the west side choirs would gather in St. Joseph.

Then came the dress rehearsal, held on the day before the concert. I enlisted one principal each year as choir marshal. In order to get those singing each part close together, I had to give the principal a very complicated plan. That would send some people up the wall. But I don't remember one principal who didn't rise to the occasion. The singers spent almost as much time practising coming up from the parish hall in the right order as they did in putting the songs together. As well, this had all to be accomplished in one morning and we had to hope that the boys and girls still had the energy for school classes in the afternoon.

Reserving the church for this rehearsal was never guaranteed. I was always told that if the church were needed for a funeral, that would have priority. Was it just my luck that that never happened? Or did the priests just want us not to take this availability for granted? When we were rehearsing, the Blessed Sacrament, a vessel that lay in a recess high in the church wall, would be removed, making the church what one priest termed, "just a hall."

Publicity was done mainly by the choir members themselves. They would be reminded in lots of time to get their parents and other family members to keep the concert night open. Then, at a late rehearsal, I would call for volunteers in each school to go round inviting all the teachers. The students would fall over themselves to be selected for this purpose.

And would the children like the songs I put before them? I remember one boy who dropped out after one practice, declaring, "I don't like the songs." But usually the girls and boys liked them well enough after they got to know them. After all, "pop" songs are ones that are heard many times a day. These children had to know the songs "backwards and forwards and upside down" before the concert.

One year, for a variety of reasons, the music was not going well in a grade 6 class. At one point, I referred to two of the songs some of them had learned for the previous year's spring concert, and watched their faces change from boredom to enthusiasm. They had made those songs their own, and, no matter what happened later in their lives, they would never entirely forget them.

In September, new teachers would appear and have to be introduced to what we would try to do in music. When I asked one of them whether she liked music, she replied, "I remember being in your choir."

CHAPTER 59

# Our Homes in Guelph

In all four properties we have occupied since coming to Guelph in 1969, Eleanor has used her considerable talents in effecting major renovations. In 44 Dean Avenue, the attic was made habitable while we were there. With the other three places, we undertook bridge financing so that most of the work could be done before we moved in. So impressive was Eleanor's work in each case that a realtor friend told one prospective buyer that "every room is an adventure", and later on offered Eleanor a job advising others in how to renovate the houses they bought. Eleanor appreciated the offer but didn't follow up on it.

In 1969, real estate was sluggish in Burlington, and it took the whole summer to complete the transactions. We bought the Dean Avenue house from an agricultural economist who was moving to the agricultural farm in Ottawa. 44 Dean Avenue was not far from number 17 where Professor Dan Jones had lived, having built the first cottage on the south arm of Muldrew Lake. Our nearest neighbour performed the traditional courtesy of calling in soon after we had arrived. This man was a Mennonite who had recently retired after a long tenure as head of the poultry department of the Agricultural College. One of the decorations in our front hall was a chanticleer, a large model of a rooster that Eleanor had acquired at a northern antique store. The following day, the man's wife remarked that she had chided her husband about having nothing in their hall to show for his career!

At first, we occupied the first two floors of the house. There was a stairway to the attic that had a floor, but nothing else. When Eleanor was through, the floor had been carpeted, there was a bathroom on one side, with book shelves on its outside walls; the front and back windows were properly framed; there was a crawl space around the perimeter and the walls and ceiling had been plastered. When this work was done, because the interior had followed so closely the exterior contours of the roof and sloping eaves, I was able to count about 100 different angles and surfaces of the plaster. This became our master suite.

When we lived at 44 Dean Avenue, squirrels were something of a problem. After the attic renovations, Eleanor and I slept up there. On all sides of us, there was a crawl space which the little animals had managed to enter. We invested in a "have-a-heart trap", which we baited and placed in the crawl space. One night at 2.30 am, I was wakened by the sound of a squirrel struggling in the trap. I got up and carried the trap to the back stoop, whence I took the beast in the car the next day to a spot which I hoped would be sufficiently remote that it wouldn't return. Was that the time I let one go by the Speed River, saw it jump over the bank, and concluded that, if it had the ingenuity to get into my crawl space, it would likely survive in the river? Another time I even encountered some baby squirrels on our front porch and had one crawl up my sleeve for shelter!

In 1971, Aunt Muriel moved east from British Columbia and accompanied Mother and Aunt Mary to Florida. In their absence and with their permission, I used Mother's power of attorney to sell her house in St. Catharines and buy one a short block from 44 Dean Avenue where the three sisters lived for two years. In 1973, Mother was too ill to accompany her sisters to Florida, and stayed with us. By then, she had lost her memory and knew little of what was taking place. One day, she tumbled down the front stairs but was not hurt since she had been well padded with her dressing-gown, and had fallen in a state of complete relaxation. In late February, she died.

A year later, Dr. Flora Little retired and decided that 264 Woolwich Street constituted more house than she and her daughter, Jean, needed. We managed to buy this house by selling both 44 Dean and the house Mother had had. I managed to set up the mortgage so that it would be entirely paid up eight years later when I would be retiring at the age of 65.

We made three major changes to 264. The Littles had subdivided some rooms with partitions to allow them to practise medicine at the front of the house. They had put a partition in the 27 foot living room to give their nurse a separate room and had put a partition in the dining room to create a waiting room and an examining room. We removed both partitions restoring the living room and dining room to their former gracious size and we took down a partition from the main hall.

Upstairs, we changed a sleeping area into an apartment for my two aunts. In a room that had been mainly used for storage (a "glory-hole" as Eleanor's mother would have called it) we had a heavy cupboard and a shower removed, to make a kitchen and breakfast nook. One of the bedrooms became my aunts' living-room. The generous hall-way became the dining-room when company came. Aunt Muriel died of cancer a few months after moving in. But Aunt Mary was to note that the 12 years she had lived there constituted the longest period in her long life that she lived in one place.

At the back of the ground floor, kitchen cupboards were added, and a two-piece bathroom was enlarged with a bath-tub added. The bath-tub sat in its wrappings in the kitchen for at least two weeks after we moved in. Up a back stairs from the kitchen were two extra bedrooms and a bathroom, an area that saw good use during those 12 years, both for guests and for roomers.

As we began life at 264 Woolwich, Eleanor's mother, Madeleine, had been spending her last years in her Mississauga house. She was still driving, and sometimes she drove to Guelph. On one of those occasions, I was expecting her at a certain time and became concerned when she hadn't arrived an hour after that time. When coming up the Hurontario Highway, she had been following an open truck laden with objects that were not tied down. A mattress fell off and, before she could stop she had driven over it, and it became wedged under her car. She managed to drive into a service station. But the manager refused to extract the thing because it didn't belong to her! Only when a police car pulled in did she get authorization to have this done.

After the sale of the Dillon house, Madeleine spent some time with us. As she needed help in getting around while waiting for access to a nursing home, we employed and housed a Mennonite girl of 20 for three months. Florence Martin was ideal in the role. Mother had entered a difficult stage, and Florence seemed to know just how to handle her on each occasion. Florence undertook a couple of projects with her which included quilting as well as reading aloud to her. These activities brought them great enjoyment.

In that period, we registered with the University of Guelph department of Off-campus Housing and they sent us a wide variety of visitors. Their length of stay varied from the two days in which an English professor from the University of Western Ontario gave guest lectures, to Beta O'Hara. Beta came from Kenya on a CIDA grant. She had never previously been out of Kenya, had never seen snow and had to be helped to find winter clothes. She came to us for a weekend while someone else cleared out a room. But we got to keep her for 14 months! She was great company. As a special project, she made a quilt, finishing it before she left.

Andre was in his early 20's, hailed from Poland, and stayed for several months. His English was a bit inadequate. When I asked him what his special interest was, he replied, "The pregnancies of peegs." We took him to Muldrew where he did his best to be helpful. Once when I began sawing a log, he appeared at my elbow and said, "I cut". Another time, when I had managed to lock myself out of the boat-house and needed to get over the partition from the boat-house cupboard by climbing a ladder, he again appeared and said, "I go."

Most of our tenants confined themselves to the room they were using, the bathroom, and the kitchen (where we often fed them). But one gentleman had other ideas. He claimed to represent the oldest Christian Church in the world. The Church of South India was reputed to have been founded by the apostle Thomas a few years after Jesus' death. But this strange character was quite capable of turning up in the room where you were dressing if he suddenly needed something.

We had a graduate student from northern Greece whom we didn't much like. When comparing Canadian customs with those with which she was familiar, she would not say, "In Greece we did so-and-so…" but "In Europe…." A student from the Collingwood area stayed for a year. She had a head-on collision one day in winter as she was setting out to drive home and encountered a white-out. I don't think she was badly hurt. A couple from India stayed a few days. They had lived for 17 years in Yorkshire. The wife was a good pianist and once sat down at my piano and played the Chopin *Fantasie-Impromptu*. A very black man who was a professor of veterinary science visited the Guelph department for a few days. When speaking to us, he used impeccable English. But, while he was here, his son was killed while riding a motor-cycle at his home in Jamaica. During the resulting long-distance calls, the professor used a Jamaican dialect that was almost impossible for us to understand.

In 1977, after the separatist government was elected in Quebec, Norman McLeod, the new public librarian, stayed with us while he found housing for his Montreal family. That same summer, Morrey ended three years in British Columbia on a motor trip with two Ottawa friends that took him first to the Yukon, then back east. He had told us he would be arriving on a Sunday at about 2.30. We assumed he meant pm. But at 2.30 am he and his friends crept into the house and headed for the beds at the back of the house upstairs. Norman McLeod sat up in bed and used the typical librarian's greeting, "May I help you?"

There was a garden at 264 which included some raspberry canes. There was a cherry tree where we had an annual race to get them picked before the birds had them stripped. And tiger lilies lined the driveway, making it hard to avoid stepping on them when getting out of one of the cars. If I forgot my key, I had a way of getting onto the house. A ladder from the garage got me onto the roof of the back porch. From there, I stepped onto the roof of my bedroom, which led to the outside door of Aunt Mary's bathroom which was usually unlocked.

For a time, we had a problem with pigeons which would roost immediately above the front door, necessitating daily cleaning of the steps. After some very uncharitable thoughts (inspired by *Poisoning the Pigeons in the Park* by Tom Lehrer[121] which would, no doubt, have been unappreciated by the local Humane Society), we got someone to put metal screening around the spots where they would otherwise roost. I never asked Dr. Little how she had dealt with the problem!

While we lived at 264, I had a number of group meetings. Some groups were Presbytery committees; others were NDP executives. At one of the latter, Bob Rae, then provincial leader but not yet premier, presented me with a life membership in the NDP.

While we were boarding university visitors, Aunt Mary had many guests of her own. She managed to be aware of any relatives, however distant, who were registered at the university. She would invite them for meals, and glad of a home away from home, they would usually accept.

After 12 years at 264, we were glad to move to a smaller house, where we could accommodate Aunt Mary, but not university guests, and that would cost us less in taxes and heating. 133 Glasgow Street North was also made of stone, had an extensive side lawn and a double garage. The garage needed new doors and we immediately ordered ones that were electrically controlled. But it was a full year before we were able to make room in them for the cars!

The move was only about one kilometer. Yet several of our new neighbours went out of the way to welcome us to our new street. And we had our new status nailed down by being invited to a community meeting where we would protest to the city the action of a landlord in subdividing a house into a rabbit-warren of apartments.

This move was our first in which we paid less for the new house than we received for the old. The difference paid for the renovations we had done before moving, besides adding to our investments. When viewing the Glasgow house, we found some of the rooms depressingly dark. Lighter curtains and paint worked wonders.

The design of the house suited Aunt Mary well. As she was then glad to take her meals with us in the kitchen or dining-room, we saw her more often than we had previously. But we still had her help in the kitchen when she assumed responsibility for washing the pots and pans.

On the left, as you entered, you encountered our main living-room which even had enough length for Eleanor's parents' 27-foot Persian rug. It also housed the piano which was used on more than one occasion for family recitals. It was even the scene of an *a cappella* recital for a paying audience by "Artisan", a Yorkshire trio we had first heard at the Lunenburg, NS, Folk Harbour Festival. I can still picture daughter-in-law Sharon almost dancing as she held Annie during one of the more rhythmic songs.

The basement had been partially finished by the creation of a recreation room at the foot of the stairs. It was there that I put my desk which had been my father's over 30 years before that. This was also where Esther introduced me to my first computer. Unfortunately, the room was subject to periodic flooding, a condition that was only solved when our favourite carpenter finally arrived at the solution of building a new floor, 4 inches above the old one. The room was also the scene of Presbytery committee meetings, before and during my term as chair.

The trees on the property produced more leaves in the fall than I had ever seen anywhere else. We had three large trees on our property alone and our neighbours had their own trees. Once a year, the city collected, with giant vacuum cleaners, any leaves that had been raked beyond the curb. Of course, we would sometimes get the leaves past the curb, only to have the wind blow them back before the city trucks arrived. It didn't help, either, that some of the trees didn't shed till after the collection. And then there was the rain that turned the leaves into a pile of muck.

One year, children of friends saw a huge pile of leaves on my side lawn and asked if they could play in them. I agreed, provided they had all those leaves outside the curb by a certain Sunday night. They promised and proceeded to bring a large canvass sheet to build a "house". But, on the Sunday in question, it was raining hard, and it was the father of the children who came and helped them comply with my condition.

Another event resulted from the age of one of our trees. One Saturday, which Eleanor and I spent in Toronto, the sun was shining and there was hardly any wind. But a huge branch collapsed across the road, and Aunt Mary told us that city trucks took three hours to clear the street so that traffic could move. Fortunately, the tree in question sat on city property and the city paid for the clean-up.

*133 Glasgow Avenue*

One other difficulty I encountered made us glad to make our next move. There was a single driveway that divided in two in front of the garage. I got to put my Volvo on the left side. But often in winter, as I was backing out, I would skid off the drive into a snow bank, which meant a lot of shoveling and sometimes delay until I was towed out.

The 1997 move involved the most amazing real estate transaction I have ever known. Through Agnes Gelb who had already moved into the Village on the Green, we heard that No. 103 was for sale, although it had not yet been listed. Brad Douglas showed us the unit one morning; we made an immediate offer and had a deal by that night. Then, the next morning, before we could list 133 Glasgow, Brad brought round a young couple who were looking for that kind of property. Again, they offered and we had a deal by night.

The "deals" were in late February and possession was not till April 8th. That gave us time to be thorough when considering what to keep and what to dispose of. For instance, while I still had, and valued, Dad's set of the Scott Waverley novels, I decided that, since I had not looked at them in the previous ten years, I probably wouldn't in the next ten, and so they went to the English Department at Trent University in return for a tax receipt. Facilitating this arrangement was Len Conolly who had been a close neighbour while he was at the University of Guelph, but had moved to be President of Trent in Peterborough.

In this move, we ran away from some problems—expensive repairs to the chimney, a lot of outdoor work. We also lost some advantages—I had always enjoyed hanging my washing on the back line to give it a fresher smell. We have not been able to do this on Water Street. And we had loved our next-door neighbours—David Howlett of the Anglican Church in Rockwood, Lucy Reid, the university chaplain, and their delightful children. More than once, one of them knocked gently to ask permission to recover a ball that had strayed to our property.

Another advantage of the Woolwich Street and Glasgow Street houses was the fact that we were within walking distance of the downtown area. That meant I could walk to Chalmers Church, the Credit Union, housed for many years in the Cooperators' building, various shops, and, before my retirement in 1982, my office in the Separate School building. The latter applied only when I didn't need to depart for a school for which I needed my car. The walk from Water Street was possible when I could spare the 35 minutes required. In practice, I have rarely done it. We are actually closer to Harcourt Church where I go monthly for meetings of the Guelph and Area Cluster.

The very extensive renovations which Eleanor planned for the Water Street house involved walls and floors, adding a shower and toilet to the laundry room, moving the door to the garage from there to the far wall of the family room, and removing a row of bricks from under the hearth to allow our favourite rug to fit the living-room. Our Cambridge contractor, who was working to a time limit set by our plans to move in on a Saturday, was exemplary. The actual work was finished by the Thursday night. Then one lady was assigned to spend the Friday cleaning the place from top to bottom. The condominium couldn't have been more ready for our move.

This move reduced our total floor space from 2300 square feet to 1700. We didn't manage to calculate accurately enough what that meant in terms of the furniture we could keep. At least two large chests of drawers were carried to the top floor and taken down again. A cabinet with a glass front in which I had kept my music proved to be too tall to clear the low ceiling of the family room and was sent to Morrey's house. However, the final organization has made us enjoy the locale immensely.

Eleanor and I disagreed over the location of the piano. In the Glasgow house, the piano's position in the living-room facilitated many events that were built around it. On the other hand, it has been just as well that Eleanor won this argument. In the family room, I can practise to my heart's content, while Eleanor can sleep on the third floor without being disturbed.

The vista from our windows on the north-west side is very special. Between us and the Speed River we look on bush; colourful wild-flowers in the spring, and the river in winter. In the morning of a sunny day, the line of sunshine is determined by our roofs. There is an infinite variety in the moods we experience in that direction.

## CHAPTER 60

# A Tale of Two Churches

When we reached Burlington in 1955, the minister was announcing his departure for a Florida church within the year. Keith McMillan arrived and continued at Trinity or Wellington Square until 1968. I don't remember his sermons, although some members accused him of shouting. He and Mary were kind friends, and we agreed on most issues. After they had left, I was able to say at a session meeting that it would be a long time before any other minister knew this congregation as well as Dr. McMillan.

From 1968, Keith preached for a time in Streetsville United Church. He later did pulpit supply for another minister who was on maternity leave. That situation was fairly uncommon then.

While we worshipped at Trinity, there were two Sunday services. At 9.30 the assistant minister, Jeff Preston, was in the pulpit and Eleanor's Junior Choir was in the choir loft. Keith and Gordon Douglas' Senior Choir led the better-attended service at 11.00. Sunday school was held during one of these services. Keith used to talk of parents who were still in their pajamas when delivering their kids. In Wellington Square, the two choirs occupied the transepts.

Leslie Cust, sometimes called, "Patchcord Pete", was our expert sound manager. The bag of tricks he put together at one end of St. Paul's Hall in Wellington Square was impressive. He must have wept, some years after we left, when vandals took a crowbar to his equipment.

Les was somewhat unorthodox in his views. One Sunday night, when we had a wide-ranging discussion of denominations, Les ventured to suggest that the Unitarians were to be admired, only to be shot down by our deaconess who insisted that the Unitarians didn't believe that Jesus Christ was the Son of God. I often wished that I had challenged her to explain!

Another time, during nominations to the Music Committee, Les nominated Sheila Richards to represent Junior Choir parents. The way things had worked, several members of the Senior Choir had been on that committee, but the Junior Choirs were not represented in any way. This time he was shot down by Murray Fisher on the grounds that the constitution didn't provide for such an inclusion.

Murray Fisher, although rather set in his ways, was a tower of strength in the congregation. I forget which positions he held besides clerk of session. Once, the guests of one of Morrey's birthday parties were shown over the Fisher Hatchery. I recall Murray showing us the grinder where the chicks' beaks were blunted. He explained that the chicks were like cannibals. The hatchery would be a bloody mess if this procedure were not followed. Eleanor remembers that after the visit, the children at Morrey's party refused to eat the egg salad sandwiches that had been prepared for them. Eleanor and Fran Tovee quickly slapped together peanut butter and honey sandwiches instead!

The Fisher farm, on the edge of town, had great potential because of urban expansion. Many builders were reputed to be trying to buy it. Once at a bridge party, Murray's sister, Edith, was asked about the rumours. "They say your farm is priced at $1 million, Edith. Is this true or not?" After she had demurred for a while, one of the ladies persisted, "Come on Edith, is it true?" All she would say was, "Well, you know what they say!"

During the 60's, the senior choir raised the funds for the installation of stained glass windows across the South wall of Wellington Square Church sanctuary. The artist, Yvonne Williams[122], was an old friend of Eleanor's and a superb creator. The windows were a *Te Deum*, illustrated by many regional activities. The nine panels were magnificent on a sunny day, although only the ministers and the choir got to see them without turning round. But they created a display with wonderful ribbons of coloured light.

For a number of years, Yvonne lived alone with her mother. She would write and sign Christmas cards for them both. One year, she found time only to sign her own name. An old friend of her mother's who happened to live in France, made the wrong conclusion. She wrote, "I regret that your mother is no longer with you." When she saw the letter, Mrs. Williams insisted that Yvonne correct the misunderstanding. "What if she got to heaven and found I wasn't there?"

In Guelph, we shopped around for over a year, while my aunts and my mother immediately joined Harcourt Church which was by far the nearest United Church to where they were living. One day in January, Eleanor said, "Let's join Chalmers. Anna Pond is the organist." We did so, only to find at the end of January that Anna Pond was resigning. She said that she couldn't get over her let-down when, after a big effort at Christmas, members in the choir stopped coming in the new year.

The Music Committee which had the job of replacing Anna was chaired by a professor named Ib Nonneke. (A nephew of his was the NDP leader in Alberta.). I recall that Ib tangled with Taylor Evans in at least one Session meeting, but that he stood his ground. The young person appointed, Mark McDowell, had impeccable musical qualifications and was very exacting in his insistence that choir members watch him. One of the strong tenors asked him whether he was to watch him or watch the music. Following Mark's response, he walked out. Mark stayed only for one year, and I heard later that he was directing the music at Bloor Street United in Toronto. When I next ran into him, he had given up music for flying!

For five years, the music was run by a partnership. Young people of 25 years of age or less were offered free singing lessons with Arlene Barnum, provided they would join the church choir and attend regularly. Eleanor directed the choir. Together with a handful of older singers, this gave the church a choir of about 28. In this period, Eleanor was able to use some of her favourite repertory, and work on choral quality she had not been able to experience for a long time. Different organists occupied the console during her tenure including one with an eccentric habit of slowing way down at the end of each hymn verse.

Once a youth service was scheduled and the full choir took part with an anthem that contained lots of syncopation. At the next session meeting, someone objected that a youth choir hadn't been used. He hadn't noticed that at least three-quarters of the choir were young people.

Two pieces Eleanor used included the a capella *Hallelujah* by Randall Thompson and Keith Bissell's setting of the poem, *When the Song of the Angels is Stilled*. Our rendition had to be some of the best that Chalmers people had ever heard.

During those years, Eleanor and others organized a series of Sunday afternoon concerts called *The Merry Organ* named for the phrase from the chorus of the carol, *The Holly and the Ivy*[123], each annual series of five concerts sold for a low price (ranging from $5 to $7).

> *The holly and the ivy when they are both full grown*
> *Of all the trees that are in the wood,*
> *the holly bears the crown*
> *The rising of the sun and the running of the deer*
> *The playing of the merry organ, sweet singing in the choir.*

Tickets could be purchased only for the series. Even if a subscriber could only attend one or two of the five, they got a bargain. Each year, over 400 tickets were sold (I lost track of the phone calls Eleanor made for that purpose!). Thus the performers could enjoy both the superior acoustics of the Chalmers sanctuary, and a good house. The performers were always of a high caliber. Once, the *London Sinfonetta* was featured. They finished with the Mendelssohn *Italian Symphony*. The eight members of the woodwind section, whose score calls for virtuoso playing in the finale, sat on the pulpit platform. Esther took part on three occasions, once paired with Eleanor

James, once with Glyn Evans, once with Katya Pine.

At different times, people from different United Churches met in Chalmers to sing hymns. In the early 70's, we had Stanley Osbourne introducing us to the *Red Hymn Book*[124]. He was on the joint Anglican-United Church committee that produced the book. Since it was published during discussions around possible union between us and the Anglicans, the book was intended for use in both communions and, in general, was so used. I recall Don Barnum asking why the Amens of the *Hymnary* had been dropped. I don't remember the answer!

Another night, several choirs joined forces in a hymn sing with the altos and tenors singing from the respective galleries. Different choir leaders took turns in directing the combined choirs. Eleanor got to direct Keith Bissell's setting of *Christ Whose Glory Fills the Skies.* Calling for a crescendo on the notes used for "glory" she inspired a thrilling rendition.

Before that series began, the organ received a major overhaul. As someone appropriately remarked, "Our Casavant organ[125] has been kept together with binder twine for many years." The price of this work was in the neighbourhood of $35,000. Taylor Evans' part in raising it was positive. He addressed members of the official board, "We can't expect our members to be generous if we don't show the example." The goal of raising the fund in two years was oversubscribed!

Was Taylor's participation a good thing? On the one hand, he could be counted on to support cultural endeavours. (His wife, Isabel, sang in the choir for many years.) On the other hand, it showed the domineering position that Taylor occupied in the congregation. He sometimes gave people a tongue lashing, and many members got the habit of doing what he wanted lest they be on the receiving end of it.

Another incident showed how bad this situation could get. At a certain service in July, it was announced that the Music Committee was ready to propose the appointment of a new organist. Our assistant minister was new and called the Official Board to meet after the service. After considerable discussion, Taylor pointed out that, since the Music Committee was a committee of Session, not of the Official Board, this meeting could not ratify the appointment. It mattered not that about three quarters of those present were elders. But it did matter to many of those present that their lunch was being delayed. After a lot of talk, Taylor moved ratification, subject to agreement of the Session. The Official Board then adjourned and the Session was called, and, while the appointment was then ratified, Taylor opposed it because there had been insufficient notice of the Session meeting!

Around 1980, I led a group discussion one night in the course of which I asked everyone present to say what they thought Chalmers was doing best. When it was Taylor's turn, he talked only of what Chalmers had done in the past.

Doug Sloan was minister of Chalmers from 1968, a little before our time, until his retirement in 1989. A Welshman named Jones stayed for only a year, but we thought he brought some interesting perspectives. A Welshman of a different sort, Rupert Evans, tended to preach at length, but he made the time worthwhile. He left us to become New Church Development Officer of Waterloo Presbytery, in which position he created Westminster United in Waterloo and Southwood in Guelph almost singlehandedly.

Some years, Chalmers members have been invited to attend what was sometimes called a retreat. One year in the early 80's when we met in Arkell United Church, Doug Sloan asked us to take a look at a book by Lyle E. Schaller, *The Passive Church*[126]. In one chapter, Schaller asks church members to do an exercise to determine the extent to which we were a passive church. We had to rate ourselves, in a scale of 1 to 10 in about 53 aspects. One point involved the question of whether there was one layman who dominated our affairs. On total score, where the totally passive church got a score of 160, we gave ourselves 119 which was pretty high.

More than once in the early years that we belonged to Chalmers, I was tempted to transfer either to Dublin or to

Harcourt because I was attracted to some specific preaching or music. I always changed my mind when I considered the Chalmers people I would be letting down. And I now realize that, if I had yielded to that temptation, I'd never have experienced Diane Clark. Perhaps this was an example of the old saying, "Farther fields are greener."

One development in Chalmers involved Rupert while I was chair of worship. It was our job to plan the celebration of the church anniversary held around the beginning of November. Rupert suggested that we honour those who had belonged to Chalmers for at least 50 years. This sounded like a good idea until we tried to make a list of those to be honoured. The church records didn't go back that far, and we had to depend on the memory of two older women whose information didn't always agree. However, we proceeded with the plan, and it seemed to be appreciated. Afterward, one gentleman remarked, "This was very nice but I didn't really qualify." And a woman remarked, "You missed my brother!"

In the 70's, the Sloans purchased the church manse on Glasgow Street from the church. This created what became known as the manse fund. Afterwards, the church's annual budget was often balanced by dipping into that fund. As often, Taylor Evans did his best to make us feel a little guilty for doing that because the fund wouldn't last forever!

CHAPTER 61

# Other Friends

Eleanor's out-going nature is well-known and she has had a wonderful gift for making interesting and creative friends. But, among these friends, there has always been one or two that at any one time was extra special, friends with whom she had much in common, friends with whom she had been especially comfortable, whom she would see almost daily and with whom she would spend a lot of time.

Of course, this process didn't begin with our marriage. Eleanor's first teaching job had taken her in 1942 to Ingersoll High School. The public librarian in Ingersoll at the time was Betty Crawford[127], whose interests lay not only in literature but at least to the same extent in the arts. As a water-colour artist, she has long been admired in our family, several of her works being displayed on the walls of our successive homes. One of the delights of her visit was that she always came with her sketch pad and water colours and even, on one occasion after a visit to Muldrew Lake, sent her thank you note on the back of a water colour sketch of our bonfire. Betty was one of our close friends, right up until her death in the spring of 2003.

When we established our first married home in Regina, Norah McCullough[128] came into our lives. On meeting Eleanor, Norah mentioned that she had known Dorothy VanLuven, an Oshawa teacher who had taught me Latin and Art, and had been a colleague of Eleanor's on the Oshawa Collegiate staff between 1945 and 1947. As the secretary of the Saskatchewan Arts Board from about 1946, Norah was part of the Adult Education structure and was almost always present at frequent gatherings at the home of David Smith, the Adult Education Director. As part of that group, she was one of the witnesses to my carrying my wife over the threshold in January, 1948. But Norah soon became a frequent visitor to our apartment.

I remember that she applied her creative talents when drying the dishes, she chose wonderful ways to put our dishes away. In her work, Norah traveled the province to promote the arts. That year, Eleanor became the editor of the Arts Board Newsletter.

While we were in Ottawa, Eleanor, as I had mentioned before, was reunited with Suzanne Butler. Suzanne visited us at both Muldrew and Goderich before she made the trip to Geneva where she met her husband, Victor Perreard, and became a permanent resident of Switzerland. Since then, Suzanne and her family have been wonderful hosts whenever any of our family visits Europe.

Two years is not a long time in which to develop lasting friendships. But from 1953 to 1955 we happened to live in the north end of Goderich, and a lady who lived across North Street from us, named Mary Howell, was a frequent visitor.

In Burlington, one of Eleanor's favourite friends was Mary McMillan, our minister's wife. Through her, we came to know her family, Bruce, Donny and Margy, the members of Trinity Church, and then Wellington Square, the largest congregation to which we ever belonged. Mary was ever aware of the duties and privileges of her position as the minister's wife.

Another very important Burlington friend was Fran Tovee, with whom I had been a neighbor when we were babies. As a member of Port Nelson United Church and the community it served, Fran kept us in touch with the doings and thinkings of that part of town. Her husband, Harold, worked for Westinghouse in Hamilton. He was a great devotee of model trains and had quite an extensive set-up in his basement. Through him, Morrey developed a lasting interest in this activity which he has passed on to his son, Alexander. In 1961, Harold died in hospital where he had been sent when he didn't seem to be recovering from flu. After his death, cancer cells were found in his stomach. A couple of years later, his son Bobby needed hospitalization but resisted because he said, "That's where people die." I remember that there were always dogs in the Tovee household.

The longest friendship of this sort has been with Agnes Gelb and it is still in full swing. Its beginnings were interesting. In 1971, Eleanor and Agnes met as parents of cast members in Benjamin Britton's opera, *Noah's Flood*. Esther played one of Noah's daughters-in-law and Agnes' son Martin, was one of the animals in the ark. That work brought many people together from many different spheres of Guelph life. And one of the most satisfying has been our connection with Agnes.

These two have faithfully worked together in furthering many causes. And when Agnes completed her Masters Degree, Eleanor hosted a party in her honour. Together they have explored back roads, craft shops, and antique stores ranging from Ontario to Vermont to England.

With the way I have tended to concentrate on my activities, a less resourceful wife might have had reason to find time hanging heavy on her hands. But Eleanor has always had great friends with whom time was well spent and great projects to complete together.

*Agnes Gelb with Eleanor*

# Part 3—

# Retirement

CHAPTER 62

# Presbytery

As long as we lived in Burlington, there was no question of my involvement in Presbytery. Halton Presbytery met during the day, and Wellington Square Church was always represented by retirees. However, I do remember that Wellington Square contributed an annual $10,000 to the Halton Presbytery Extension Fund for New Church Development. Since my involvement during the 80's and 90's, I have seen very concrete results of that fund. During our first 13 years in Guelph, Waterloo Presbytery was similarly unavailable to me, and, as such, I didn't think about it very much.

When I was finally elected a representative from Chalmers Church in 1984, I noticed several things. First, the different churches that hosted my first five meetings all used different hymn books. The former Evangelical United Brethren Churches, of which several are located in our area, came into union in 1968 with the provision that they could keep their own hymn books. Some other churches had never ordered the Red books and still used the old Hymnaries. And one church in our presbytery even had an old American book which they preferred.

Secondly, the regular worship period, which was scheduled for 11:45 am, was not attended by everyone. The court divided into committees which met during the morning, and, if a committee felt their time allotment was insufficient, they simply cut worship.

Thirdly, the committees reported during the afternoon, and the attendance started to dwindle from noon on. Members often found that they had better things to do than listen to boring verbal reports that didn't directly affect them. As a result, the last committee to report sometimes found that their audience was extremely slim.

On one occasion that year, a report caused a stir. A diaconal minister had asked permission to perform sacraments, and Reverend Ray McCaul, chair of pastoral relations, announced that the committee for which he was reporting had refused. The ruling was challenged and overturned.

In Presbytery, I first joined the Christian Development (CD) Committee. In the winter of 1985-86, a group of us began to plan reforms in the way Presbytery functioned. By May, the committee had endorsed our proposals, and in June, at a meeting in Belwood Church, we took them to the full court. One was to establish an (agenda) committee, to plan the timing and content of each meeting and to lay out the main features of future meetings. Another was a requirement that all motions, except those affecting procedure, be presented visually, either by mimeographing, or through an overhead projector. When a motion was simply read, there was often misunderstanding, and time was lost through irrelevant discussion.

At the presbytery meeting, we had a problem. The CD committee was to be the last to report. How could we persuade members to stay till that time? Elizabeth Eberhart-Moffat devised a name tag, shaped like a light-bulb, with the caption, "I'm staying for the CD Report." This device worked and the motions were passed.

One development that made the changes easier was the fact that Reverend Bob Hyde, minister of Barrie Hill and Speedside, became chair of Presbytery in that month. Not only did he support the changes, but helped us to put them into effect. In September, when Elizabeth, Reverend Sam Wigston and I were meeting to plan something else, we needed to consult Bob about something and he thereupon appointed us to constitute the new (Agenda) committee, along with the chair-elect of Presbytery. The arrangement for this involvement of the chair-elect worked well, since becoming involved in the working of the court gave her/him some intimate knowledge of the organization he/she was to chair.

A later change was the adoption of the docket system. Inspired by the example of a Presbyterian presbytery in California, this system distinguished between the Consent Docket (those unlikely to produce disagreement) from the Decision Docket (those requiring debate). When the Consent Docket, which included minutes and necessary formalities, was presented, any member might request that an item be removed to the Decision Docket where it could be discussed. The rest of this docket was then passed with a single motion, and time was saved. In practice, the Pastoral Relations Committee has made the most use of the Consent Docket, listing all the proposed changes in the pastoral charges.

Finally, presbytery meetings were moved to the evening. The local church provided supper at 5:15 and the meeting began with singing an hour later. We have tried to make table groups a functional part of the meeting. To that end, caterers have been asked to leave a few tables near the door unset, to accommodate those who couldn't be present for the meal. But that request has rarely got through.

CHAPTER 63

# Conferences

All members of our presbytery are automatically delegates to Hamilton Conference which meets annually in late May or early June, in a different location each year. Since Esther was born on May 27th, and Eleanor on the 31st, I have sometimes had to juggle dates carefully in order to work in birthday celebrations and meetings of Conference.

In 1984, we met at Brock University in St. Catharines. The president, Reverend Beverley Johnston of Port Nelson Church, had engaged a lady from his congregation to perform a special function. Mrs. Buchanan had studied the history of the churches in what is now Niagara Presbytery and at frequent intervals she appeared on a side balcony and read a vignette from that history. Thus proceedings were never dull. Our theme speaker was Reverend Bob Smith, whom we successfully endorsed for moderator.

Sexuality was already very much on people's minds, since our conference had asked General Council for advice about a lesbian who was asking to be admitted to the order of ministry. When a motion was passed, Irene Evans Parker, Conference secretary, would use her strong microphone voice to make it clear just what we had and hadn't done. I took an active part in debates. Afterwards I was congratulated for being so active at my first conference meeting. I didn't tell them that I had got my training in the NDP!

In 1985, the delegates, who usually numbered around 500, gathered in the University of Waterloo. Conference always finishes with a New Ministries service where people are ordained, commissioned or received from another denomination. For communion by intinction, people were asked to line up to receive the elements from one of these people. In this case, one of the ordinands had bused in a large number of friends, all of whom lined up to receive communion from him. As a result, the whole operation took about 45 minutes longer than had been planned. In subsequent conference meetings, planners preferred to avoid communion altogether!

In 1986 my offer to lead the music at Conference was accepted. Unfortunately, conditions were against me. The president for that year, Mary Ann Connell, had arranged for us to meet in the arena of her home town of Palmerston. The piano, an ancient upright, was quite inadequate for leading singing in such a barn of a place. The acoustics of the place left a lot to be desired. Finally, music time on the agenda occurred only at the beginning of half days, when delegates were slow to come in out of the beaming sun. The result was less than satisfactory.

But I have other memories of that meeting. A new song, celebrating the United Church Women, was introduced, *Called to Become*. The author of the words was Anne Squire. The song was set to Robert Fleming's[130] tune *Concord* which later appeared in *Voices United* with the words, *Let There Be Light*. They are quoted here with her permission.

> *Called to become—*
> *Called to become God's daughters ('family' in mixed groups)*
> *Called by the words of scripture*
> *Called to respond in faith.*
> *Called to become—*
> *Called to be free in Jesus,*
> *Called to be free to serve him,*
> *Called to respond in love.*
> *Called to become—*
> *Called to become God's people,*
> *Called to a life of service,*
> *Called to a ministry.*
> *Answer the call—*
> *Answer the call to service,*
> *Answer the call to freedom,*
> *Answer the call to love.*

The meals were served, in rotation, by women from a number of nearby small-town churches, with all the virtues of rural cooking. And a by-product for me of the occasion was a workshop I was able to attend, in advance of Conference, in Bloor Street United Church in Toronto. It was led by the Argentinean musician, Pablo Sosa, who also has two wonderful tunes in *Voices United*.

In the years in which General Council meets, commissioners are elected at the conferences. It was then the rule that those who had been previously elected by the presbyteries—a fixed number of lay and clergy—were automatically included in conference's allotment. But the others were always elected at conference to make up the total of 38. In 1986, I was elected by acclamation in Presbytery. The next three times, I was defeated in Presbytery, but elected at Conference.

In June of '86, those of us who were going to General Council from Waterloo Presbytery circulated a letter to the congregations asking whether they had any messages that we should take with us. There were four responses, all on the subject of Inclusive Language, the hot topic of the day. In three cases, a church board had passed a motion condemning it. The fourth was a letter from Reverend John McTavish, then of Calvary Memorial United in Kitchener, explaining the two sides of the issue and pleading for tolerance from the supporters of each. John and I don't always agree theologically but I have admired him since that time.

In 1996, Reverend Diane Clark was received into the United Church from the Presbyterians, having completed all the requirements for that step. That year, we were meeting in Port Dover on Lake Erie. No one has been more loyal to everything the United Church stands for than Diane at Chalmers in Guelph.

CHAPTER 64

# The Big Issue of Ordination of Gays and Lesbians

In 1988, the United Church had to wrestle with an issue that had the potential to be one of the most divisive in its history. I refer to the issue of the ordination of gays. Views within the church represented a broad range of beliefs. On one extreme, there were those who believed gays should even be denied membership. At the other end of the spectrum were those who were practising a gay lifestyle and believed that they should be denied none of the privileges of the church.

This issue has long been confused by many conflicting views, much of it based on ignorance and a deeply embedded tradition. Both extremes tend to have a deep mistrust of the other. While one extreme raises accusations of chauvinist intolerance, the other extreme has raised accusations of dreadful sinning.

In 1988, the National Church asked congregations to wrestle with the implications of this issue and sent a statement out for members to debate. That spring Chalmers' members took their turn.

As Chalmers members filed into their meeting, one of the woman members remarked, "This statement goes against everything we've been taught." It occurred to me later that I should have responded, "Our teachers gave us the best that they knew. But when they were teaching us, they didn't know the truth about sexual orientation, that it is not a matter of choice but a "prenatal and irreversible preference".[131]

One story I have heard follows a pattern that apparently has occurred many times. A girl grew up in the United Church in a small Ontario town. As she became old enough, she taught Sunday School and got involved in other church activities. She was generally admired in the congregation. When she finished high school, she took a job in the city. But at Christmas she came home. While there, she went with her parents to a church meeting at which the homosexual issue came up. When she entered the room, there were smiles all round. She listened as one member after another spoke violently against homosexuals. Then she rose to say that they were talking about her, because she was a lesbian. The subject was quickly dropped because, when they found that this young person, whom they admired, was gay, it made them reconsider their views.

Those who insist that homosexuality is a sin often argue using biblical references. In fact, only six of the 66 books in the Bible mention the subject. As Reverend Ken Gallinger has commented, biblical writers were much more interested in economics than sex. There is no mention of the subject in the Gospels or the Book of Acts, places where most Christians seek guidance.

It pays to look closely at the story of Sodom and Gomorrah in the book of Genesis. In trying to prevent what he feels is the larger sin of men raping his male guests, Lot first offers these men a chance to rape his daughters. (Of course, women were seen as expendable in those days.) But the men in this story were not condemned because they were homosexuals, but because they wanted to rape his guests. There's plenty of mention in the Old Testament of heterosexual rape (rape of a woman by a man). Of course, any kind of rape is a sin.

Leviticus generally is full of admonitions and rules that do not make a lot of sense in today's world. For example, Leviticus calls homosexual intercourse an abomination and in another part of Leviticus, declares that if anyone is found to be wearing a garment composed of the product of both plants and animals, as in cotton and wool, he is to be stoned to death!

In the New Testament, Saint Paul mentions the practice in three of his letters. One biblical scholar points out that Paul was not aware that his readers might include homosexuals. He was telling heterosexual people not to get involved in homosexual practice, and that has to be considered good advice.

Nowhere in Scripture are homosexuals condemned as such. But one fact I consider relevant. Jesus was constantly befriending people whom society had considered impure or sinful. Publicans and sinners, he said, were as much the children of God as anyone else. In our society, people favouring the fundamentalist approach to the Bible often denigrate gays and lesbians in the same way. Would Jesus have refused them his love?

At General Council, all commissioners are traditionally assigned to one or more sessional committees to consider the issues before the Council in smaller more intimate forums before being considered by the full body. The sessions are divided by subject area. In these sessions, consideration is given to the petitions and resolutions that have been sent to General Council in order to make recommendations to the plenary session. In 1988, the sessional committee that was to handle this issue was carefully chosen to represent every conceivable viewpoint. In view of the magnitude of their task, they were asked to arrive in Victoria, the scene of Council, a full two days before everyone else. They not only came early, but they met far into the night.

That committee made an early decision that they would make no recommendation to the plenary session that was not the result of consensus in the committee—a tall order considering the variety of opinions and the passion with which they were held. The committee prayed together, sang together, read scripture together and was silent together. They spent countless hours reading the hundreds of petitions that had come in and classifying them by content. They set aside a statement that had been circulated in the spring and declared it not to be the policy of the church. Finally, someone asked what existing policies of the church might be relevant to the issue. They found two. One said that any person could be or become a member of the United Church of Canada if they promised to obey Jesus. According to the other, any member was entitled to be considered for ordination. The committee then recommended reaffirmation of these policies. In the plenary session, the recommendation was then subjected to endless debate. One night a motion to adjourn at 11.30 pm was defeated! But after a few minor amendments which had to do with wording rather than substance, the new statement was passed by about a two-thirds majority.

One reaction to the committee's presentation that probably turned things around in the general session was that of former moderator, Reverend Clarke McDonald. Clarke had been negative in his attitude four years earlier. But on hearing the committee's presentation, he felt the committee had sounded the right note.

But of course, just because something passes at General Council doesn't mean that there is an automatic acceptance across the congregations. In fact, there were pockets of great bitterness across the church. One minister phoned his organist to give him the hymns for the following Sunday, only to be told that the organist in question was resigning over the issue. Another commissioner announced that, even though she thought the final motion was right, she was voting against it for fear of repercussions back home.

Many in the media just didn't understand what we had done. The Guelph Mercury stated that Council had changed the church constitution, something Council didn't have the power to do. That paper also published a picture of Trinity United in Guelph with a zigzag line down the middle—a too-graphic depiction of a supposed split in the entire membership of the United Church. Emmy Beauchamp, then a long-time active lay-person in Trinity lost no time in getting in a spicy letter-to-the-editor about the reflection on the integrity of this particular congregation.

The fact that General Council had not really changed its policy, but had re-affirmed the old was lost, not only on the media, but on a lot of members as well[132]. This simply showed a great lack of understanding of the church's structure. General Council had, in effect, indicated confidence that the lower courts (presbyteries) could handle the situation. People seemed unable to realize that ability to be considered for ministry merely meant starting a long discernment process, at any stage of which candidates could be stopped from going further.

Curiously, about a year after the 1988 Council, few people seemed to want to talk about the issue. My guess is that some realized that their claims were not valid, but wanted to save face. But probably most were simply tired of an issue that seemed to divide people so bitterly.

Two organizations have kept the issue alive. The "Community of Concern" refuses to recognize sexual orientation and lists many types of damage that they say that gays do to the church. They have been guilty of stirring hatred among church groups. "Affirm" (the name has changed from time to time) seeks to support gays and lesbians in their efforts to work in the church in a meaningful way.

One of the fears that anti-gay spokespersons expressed many times was that a floodgate would be opened allowing many gays to occupy our pulpits. It is known that a considerable number of gays have been ordained while remaining in the closet. But, over the several years since 1988, as far as I know, only three newly ordained or commissioned ministers have been openly gay.

CHAPTER 65

# Chair of Presbytery (1)

After being involved in several reforms in the way Waterloo Presbytery functioned, I got the idea that I would like to try chairing it. Soon I heard that Barbara Bitzer of Kitchener had been nominated, and I had to bide my time since I admired the way she did things. Indeed, I admired the way she chaired Presbytery. Two other considerations affected my actions. Barbara was followed by members from Cambridge and the rural North-West. It was time for a Guelphite. In addition, it was a long time since an election for chairperson had occurred. Usually, the nominating committee found someone willing to do it and that person was elected by acclamation. This time the nominating committee found one person, while some of my friends supported me. One of these, Bill Elliott of Chalmers and treasurer of presbytery for ten years, used to say that my reports from presbytery meetings to Chalmers were exemplary.

I found, however, that campaign methods that were commonly used in the NDP were not acceptable among people I knew in the church. It was not okay to campaign for yourself. However, at the meeting in Dublin Church that April (1991), Elizabeth Moffat distributed her own flyer in my support. Later, she confessed that she had forgotten to include my last name! But it did the trick. I defeated another layman of the same age (I was 74!), though by what margin I was never to know.

That same evening, Nancy Argenta and her mother paid us a visit—at 133 Glasgow North, two minutes' walk away. Somehow, I managed to take in both events.

The chair-elect took office in April, and became chair 14 months later. According to our reforms, he or she chaired the Program Committee, thus getting the feel of the court for a year before taking over. In June of 1992, I felt ready to begin when I was sworn in at the beginning of my first meeting as Chair.

That meeting happened in the gym of First United Church, Waterloo. The agenda—timed as was usual in this court—was long—so long that I had omitted to give time to a request by Reverend Derek Parry, of Lincoln Avenue Church in Cambridge, to deal with a complaint. At about 10.00 pm, as I was about to give the benediction, Tom Watson moved that Derek's complaint be given 10 minutes. He presented it; Keith Tudor, chair of the relevant committee, responded and Derek's motion was soundly defeated.

Of course, I felt really badly for this mistake in my first meeting. In the dreams I sometimes have, I see myself handling things expertly. In one of these dreams, I asked, during consideration of the agenda for an amendment to that agenda, adding the requested item, with the suggestion that the mover stipulate the timing of the insertion. Ah, if only!

At this meeting I tried successfully a method that I strongly believe in. When Presbytery changed from meeting in the daytime to using an evening starting with supper, we chose Monday as the day in the week with the least conflicts with congregational activities. What had not been taken into account was that, for most ministers, Monday was their day off. So on this occasion—a Monday—we were voting on whether to switch to Tuesdays in the fall. I asked the table groups to discuss the matter for five minutes, with everyone at each table being given the chance to give an opinion, and one representative to record the number of votes each way and report. The verdict was positive by a large majority. But everyone had had his/her say, rather than the meeting being swayed by the opinions of those who felt able to address the whole meeting. This use of table groups is commonly used in Hamilton Conference and in General Conference. I have tried in vain to persuade those planning NDP conventions to use the method.

A further source of tension occurred at this meeting. The

Presbytery's Extension Council works to make it possible for new congregations to be created with the necessary acquisition of land and construction of new buildings. This happens where new population development has occurred, but the Extension Council tended to be independent of the Presbytery in its decisions, digging in its heels at times.

In this instance, a recently established Church had built too small and was now hugely overcrowded—so much so that one Sunday school class had to meet in the minister's office! But the congregation's plan, promoted by a rather uncompromising layman, was seen by many to be much too expensive. The motion called for approval of a Presbytery loan. The protagonists were both on their feet at once and I had to adjudicate.

On another point I was less successful. One of the reforms we had passed was that all motions except procedural motions must be visibly in front of the members, either duplicated, or shown on an overhead projector. It has not been an easy rule to make stick. At this instance, I let the New Church Development Committee present four motions orally. What I should have done was to offer the Committee chairman acetate and tell him that we would deal with other business while he wrote out his motions. This time, the discussion was less focused than it should have been. As people were leaving, someone called my experience my "baptism of fire."

# CHAPTER 66

# Chair of Presbytery (2)

One of the jobs of the Chair of Presbytery is to arrange and conduct covenanting services for new ministers. These need to happen as soon as possible after the people have begun their work. The chief hold-up in arranging these events is that they can't be held until a warrant or official approval arrives from the Conference office. Then a date must be found to suit both the congregation or pastoral charge and the members of Presbytery. Then a speaker needs to be lined up. When I was chair, the minister concerned usually invited someone who knew them from past association. That is the procedure now. But, for a while, it was mandatory that the speaker be a member of our Presbytery.

Around the time I was chair, a new form of covenanting service had been developed. I preferred the old form because there was a definite point at which the minister was received.

The participation of as many members of the congregation as possible is important because symbolic gifts are presented and they need to represent the congregation's genuine acceptance of the new covenant. And members of Presbytery (the presiding court) need to be there because the court is part of the covenant.

One of these services at Trinity in Elmira was set by the congregation for what turned out to be a foggy night in the first week of December. The only member of Presbytery present, who did not belong to Trinity Church, apart from me, was Reverend Fred Hagle who was the speaker. The assistant minister being covenanted was Kate Young, now at Windermere in Toronto.

Most covenanting services are held on Sunday afternoons or evenings. Occasionally, they are held during the regular Sunday morning service. There are two drawbacks here: most other ministers can't be there, and the offering, which should go to the work of Presbytery, is difficult to split with that of the congregation.

My first covenanting service was for the three-point charge of Ebenezer. There was an informal atmosphere. Normally, the Secretary of Presbytery is supposed to bring the new minister forward, but this year, the Secretary couldn't get up because of recent surgery. I was able to suggest that Reverend Doyle Prier could get to the front on his own. Symbolic gifts were dutifully made for Eden Mills and Arkell as well as Ebenezer.

I inherited a stole which the wife of Reverend Norm Watson, a former chair had sewn. At first I didn't wear it, being insufficiently aware of its importance. But Paul Bitzer, Barbara's husband, who is also an active NDP member, took me aside and persuaded me that, if Barbara, another layperson, had worn it, I should too.

A by-product of the fact that almost all churches worship on Sunday morning is that I couldn't be faithful to our own minister and get out into the presbytery to hear others. But, as the chair of Presbytery, I felt it was important to visit other churches. Once a month, I paid a visit to one or other of them, mostly specializing in churches that had had some difficulties which had come to Presbytery's attention. I forget the order, but these included one where factions had been continuing to war since the retirement of their authoritarian minister. The then senior minister had me assist in the laying on of hands which constituted the official appointment of their youth leader. This youth leader surprised and pleased many of us by his success in carving his own niche at this church and avoiding entanglements with the various factions.

Then there was a church where the leaders were so eager to get rid of their minister that they deliberately neglected badly needed repairs to the manse. They also kept referring to presbytery decisions about their church as dictatorial. I was not surprised to hear that the next minister they chose was a woman who commuted from Dundas and who wouldn't need to use the manse.

One minister had served at a church for seven years before developing a terminal disease. In February of my year as chair, a service of appreciation was held which he conducted! I attended that service and afterwards commended the congregation for the heartiness of their hymn-singing. Six weeks later, I noted the same quality of the hymn singing at his funeral service, when I read scripture. It was one of the psalms and I chose to read it dramatically.

A tricky situation arose in another church in the presbytery. The timing was wrong for re-appointing the minister after his ordination. A vote had to be taken after the morning service, which I conducted as the independent representative of presbytery. The music leader whom I had known and admired in Presbytery, told me the positive vote left her greatly relieved.

The chair of Presbytery also served as a member of the Program Committee which was chaired by the chair-elect, Katharine Edmonstone. The energy with which she operated from the tiny Presbytery office on Franklin Street in Cambridge gave me lots of confidence about my wisdom in nominating her for the job.

People sometimes sympathized with me because, as chair, I had to deal with so many problems. What I found was that I could so enjoy the positive way the committees sought to solve these problems that it more than made up for the unpleasantness of the problems themselves. The problems included a diaconal minister who had a relationship with a member of her congregation who not only broke with her, but sued her former partner. A Presbytery committee brought healing to the minister, though she had, of course, to leave her job as the relationship with the congregation had been too impaired for her to continue to be effective in this charge. Love was applied to a situation that began with guilt.

CHAPTER 67

# General Council (1)

The national governing body of the United Church of Canada, called General Council, consists of about 390 commissioners elected by the conferences. This council meets every two years. The Conferences are allotted commissioner positions according to their memberships. In most cases, Presbyteries within each Conference each elect a certain number, while the rest are elected at the Conference annual meeting. There is always a 50/50 split between lay and clergy.

During my involvement, the business of General Council was handled through about 16 sessional committees, each of which was assigned a particular subject area to study and review ahead of the plenary sessions. These committees considered petitions that had come from the lower courts, and resolutions from other organizations of the Church, and made recommendations to the whole Council. All commissioners were assigned to particular sessional committees, and each committee had representatives from each conference. Many cross-country friendships resulted from this association.

In 1986, I chaired the committee on Communications and my very able secretary, far more knowledgeable than I, was Ralph Milton of Wood Lake Book Publishers in the Okanagan. At our first meeting, remembering how hard it was to remember names, I tried a new departure. When a name was announced, I had everyone repeat it. (On a later occasion, when we had a visit from Gordon Nodwell, retiring chair of the Observer Board, Ralph mimicked my practice by having everyone repeat his name in the manner of a group of children, "Good morning, Mr. Nodwell," we all chorused to lots of chuckles and grins.)

The table groups to which we were assigned for the plenary sessions were also representative of every conference, of both clergy and lay people, and of both genders. I have often wished that NDP Conventions were organized so that people were mixed up in this way. It helps you to understand points of view that are different from your own.

The 1986 Council was held at Laurentian University in Sudbury and we were accommodated in the residences. On the first evening, we assembled for worship in a hill-side stadium overlooking Ramsay Lake. We were warned to dress warmly, but I forgot, and, during the proceedings, I began to shiver violently. Someone behind me saw my predicament and loaned me a windbreaker.

During the service, a representative of each of the 12 conferences brought forward a stone characteristic of their area, while the scripture reading spoke of the Twelve Tribes of Israel. In 1988, we created the All-Native Circle Conference, and from then on, the number 12 no longer applied. But, at this service in Sudbury, out-going moderator Reverend Bob Smith, began his sermon by telling the story of the Bishop who, at the beginning of a service, commented, "There's something wrong with this microphone" to which the Anglican congregation answered automatically, "And also with you!"

At that 1986 Council, the ground for the new All Native Circle Conference was laid by the Apology. Bob read a carefully worded statement, making clear what it was about. The early Christian missionaries had preached European culture along with the Gospel, and had regarded native traditions as intrinsically evil. In apologizing, we undertook to respect native culture. That is too brief a summary of what was meant and the vote on the statement was less than unanimous. But most found the accompanying ceremony deeply moving. One evening, we all paraded to where the natives had their camp fire, humming *Amazing Grace* as we went. The proceedings lasted long into the night.

The General Council workbook is a heavy, voluminous tome. I tried to devise a scheme for carrying about only the pages we would need for the agenda of the day. But I failed to take everything into account, and ended up lugging the whole thing in the bag that United Church Women in Sudbury had made for us.

In the midst of the 9-day Council, we had an afternoon free, and I set off to walk round Ramsay Lake. It proved to be impossible, for the road I followed ended in private property. Two dogs, one large and one small, undertook to see me off the premises and followed me all the way back to the residence where I had to speak firmly to prevent them from coming in.

Education for the ministry of the laity was an idea that was initiated enthusiastically at this Council meeting. From here on, theological knowledge would not be confined to the clergy. At the Conference level, I became involved by chairing a conference committee called "Learning on the Way". Congregations were each to put an amount into a common fund which would be used to permit lay people to take courses. I even got to give the main address on the subject at a service in Palmerston United Church. (I got paid $100 for my pains, and then lost that much on my way home in a fine for being late in renewing my car license!) "Learning on the Way" was finally eased out of existence for lack of funds but not before many individual laypeople became deeply involved in the study of our faith.

The election of the moderator was, of course, a major event. The different ballots were run off one morning, and while we waited for the counting of votes, the Sessional Committee on the Manual reported. The least interesting report was thus scheduled when no one would want to be absent. I ended up getting all the pages of my copy of the report in the right order. But I knew nothing of the changes we had made!

Three of the candidates for moderator were women. One man, Clifford Elliott, who was making his second try, had my vote. But he was again defeated. Ann Squire of Ottawa became our first lay woman to be elected moderator.

Previous Councils had made the installation of the moderator a very solemn occasion. This time a jazz band was used and it was great fun. A very rhythmic *Hallelujah* was introduced and became the theme song that was repeated throughout the evening.

Besides electing a woman as moderator, this Council moved significantly in the direction of inclusive language, a move that triggered some violent reaction across the country. For instance, a Vancouver newspaper ran a headline, "King of Kings Becomes Queen of Queens!"

But we practised what we preached. In the opening worship, the 6-verse hymn, *Unto the Hills* was used. In the version we were given, in verses 1, 3, and 5, God was referred to as "She" and "Her". In verses 2, 4 and 6, we used "He", "His" and "Him". It was hard at the time to contemplate the best way to solve the problem of the lack in English of 3rd person pronouns that are gender-neutral. Of course in subsequent years, some very fine poets have addressed themselves to the task of upgrading the language to reflect not only inclusivity but also our modern culture and this has made more graceful amendments available to us.

The process whereby the Manual has been changed at Council has appeared to me to be altogether too cumbersome to be democratic. There was altogether too much detail for the commissioners to make judgements. In effect, therefore, we trusted the sessional committee to do the job. At the 1990 council, I got a motion passed which recognized that fact at the beginning and saved us the time that might have been spent approving much detail we had not seriously thought through. Some people found that helpful. But I don't flatter myself into thinking that the change was permanent.

CHAPTER 68

# General Council (2)

At the General Council meeting in 1988, Eleanor accompanied me to the University of Victoria, where we were comfortably accommodated in a residence room, with meals served in a dining room that, on a clear day, overlooked Mount Baker. We flew west two days early with the intention of seeing something of Vancouver Island, and especially its west coast. On the Monday morning, as we set off in a rented car, the rain began. Before we reached Parksville, the rain was coming down heavily and the clouds were low. We realized that we would see nothing, whether mountains or sea, and we returned to Victoria, and contented ourselves with visiting the shops, where I acquired one of my all-time favourite sweaters.

Eleanor took in many of the Council events, including the installation of the moderator. (Much later, remembering the effectiveness of Bruce McLeod's keynote address to Council, she invited him to address our local celebration in Guelph of the 75th anniversary of the founding of the United Church. The effectiveness of his speech on that occasion significantly contributed to its success.)

The first event, on the Wednesday morning, saw 300 of us lining the football field at 6.00 am to watch and take part in a long native ceremony. For these people, time has a different meaning from our conception, and most of us had to leave before the proceedings were finished if only to get breakfast before the general session began at 9.00. But, before we left, we had all been issued a pinch of tobacco, and we all lined up and took turns shaking hands with several elders and reverently dropping our tobacco into a small fire. It felt like communion.

Almost the first order of business at the general session was the dedication ceremony creating the 13th conference called the All-Native Circle Conference. The natives involved arrived, with a slow, regular drum beat,—about 45 minutes late (by OUR clocks!). This conference is the only one not defined by geographical boundaries. It doesn't involve the Maritimes or British Columbia where natives are not as involved with the United Church. The four presbyteries, however, ARE distinguished by geography. "Great Lakes Waterways" comprises Montreal and Southern Ontario. "Keewatin" is NW Ontario and Manitoba. "Plains" is all of Saskatchewan, and "All Tribes" is all of Alberta. The conference has a "Speaker" in contrast to the other conferences who have "Secretaries".

The 1988 Council was memorable in two significant ways. Many remember it as the time when the All-Native Circle Conference was created. Others remember it as the occasion where we settled the sexuality issue.

The contest for moderator was colourful. The conservative viewpoint was represented by a Mr. Clarke of London. He was eliminated on the third ballot leaving what Eleanor called, "The Poet, Walter Farquharson" and the "Storyteller, Sang Chul Lee", a Korean United Church minister who ultimately was elected. In her final address as moderator, Anne Squire said, "I thought I knew this church" and proceeded to talk of the outlandish behaviour of those who get emotional about an issue and take it out on the person at the top. She stressed that "We have ordained homosexuals for years and now we have to decide whether to do it consciously." When Lee was called to the stage following his election, he was asked how felt. He said, "I'm scared." Said Anne, "You should be!" and brought down the house.

Afterwards during a chat, Don Gillies reminded Lee that he would now be addressed as "Right Reverend". Lee replied that he hoped that no one would call him "Wrong Reverend!"

For some years, Sang Chul Lee had ministered the Korean Congregation that used Bloor Street United Church in Toronto. He had been born on the Siberian side of the Korean border. His first contact with the Christian church had happened when he joined a group of ten boys who had walked out of their school in protest against their treatment and had been accepted by a Methodist school. His first inspiration came through his exposure to the writings of Toyohiko Kagawa, the Japanese leader who ministered to the poor in a Tokyo slums. During the Korean War, he was permanently separated from his family who remained in the north while he went to South Korea. He was introduced to prayer in a church where everyone prayed aloud at the same time. He emigrated to Canada with his wife and three daughters. When their daughters married boys of other races, they had to remind him that he had preached that people of all races were all children of God.

Before the election when he was asked about the sexuality issue, he said he had always assumed that it was "white man's problem" until one day when a woman in his Korean congregation had phoned him in great distress. Her husband of 17 years and father of three teenage boys had suddenly told her that he had to leave their marriage since he was gay.

Normally, Council has to deal with about fifty to eighty petitions from the Presbyteries and Conferences. In 1988, in response to a paper that had been circulated on the impact of sexuality on ministry, there were over 900. I have already written about the process of the sessional committee on the ordination of gay and lesbian candidates. I know that I was on a different committee but the seriousness of the sexuality committee has overshadowed that experience in my memory.

It is the practice of General Council to invite theological reflectors from outside our communion. One of those in 1988 was Jordan Pearson, a distinguished retired rabbi from Toronto. He spoke several times and brought a welcome perspective to all that was going on.

Before Council finished I had decided whom I wanted to support for a future moderator. Marion Best chaired the famous sessional committee whose decision to recommend reaffirmation of the two principles the church had had since its inception led to our main decision. Others had the same idea I had. But Marion thought it wise to wait six years before letting her name go forward. She was elected by a large majority in Fergus in 1994.

CHAPTER 69

# General Council (3)

In 1990, on the first morning of the Council meeting held at the University of Western Ontario, while the agenda was being considered, someone moved that speeches from the floor be limited to 90 seconds and this was carried. My first reaction was to wonder how a person's point of view could be adequately expressed in that much time. As the rule was put into practice, however, I was convinced. A large electric monitor was placed at the edge of the stage. As a person began to speak, the second count started at 90 and worked down—89—88—87, etc. If the speaker got to 25 and still had another point to make, he/she made it immediately in order to get it said. At 03, Sang Chul Lee, the moderator, said, oh so politely, "Thank you" and the speaker sat down, having made her/his point without wasting time on irrelevancies.

I must admit that the rule is harder to manage without this expensive monitor. But I found that, with the rule itself, commissioners showed a degree of discipline that doesn't characterize most church meetings.

In 1988, the statement that was made on the sexuality question in Victoria was re-examined by a committee chaired by Don Linkletter. In the course of deliberations, Don stressed the difference between hearing people's submissions and agreeing with them. The committee recommended complete endorsement of the earlier statement and this passed much more easily than it had in Victoria.

And then there was the Community of Concern. In the cultural field, COC is understood to refer to the Canadian Opera Company. In left-wing political circles, it means Council of Canadians. But, in the United Church, since the autumn of 1988, it has indicated our conservative wing. They are not only anti-gay; they're fundamentalist, and, as we found out in

London, very intolerant of those who don't accept their ideas. During Council, they holed up in Huron College and issued daily newsletters for general distribution. These were so full of innuendos, extreme points of view and violent attacks on leading figures in the church who were present at Council that one of their more moderate members arose during one morning session and distanced himself from what that day's newsletter had said. It was a revelation to some commissioners to find such behaviour present in our church.

The following winter, I attended a COC meeting in Waterloo, just to be informed of what they were saying. They had brought in two former politicians who proceeded to attack the United Church on so many points that one wondered why they wanted to remain in it. Did they want to destroy it, or did they want to take it over and run it their way?

One evening at the London General Council, an address was given to a large audience by Archbishop Desmond Tutu, one of the great men of our time. Words of his that stayed in my memory included, "If someone says that he doesn't believe in God, that's alright. God believes in him."

The children in Council, which that year included Timothy Moffat of Saint Luke's in Cambridge, one day took over morning worship. I forget the details, but a mature theme was very effectively presented. One evening, the United Church Youth of Oxford Presbytery presented an operetta, built around creation and what mankind is doing to it. It included some very catchy songs like one that used the words, "good, good, good" from Genesis and drove home the points made. The Children in Council had an important part. The then minister of Chalmers in Kintore, a man who had had difficulty in deciding whether to make a career of music or of theology, used his talents both to compose and rehearse.

In the vote for moderator, the runner-up from 1988, Walter Farquharson from a rural charge in Saskatchewan, a poet with many hymns in use across the church, was elected. Another candidate was Jim Sinclair of North Bay, now General Secretary of the church. When Walter's election was announced, it was immediately proposed that one of his hymns be sung. We chose one that was to be found in the green *Songs for a Gospel People*, a book that had been published by Wood Lake Books in the 80's as a supplement to the *Red Hymn Book*. Many of the same hymns were later included in the more complete *Voices United*. Walter was the speaker at his own installation.

One Sunday in the subsequent year, Walter addressed a large congregation in Wellington Square Church in Burlington. He was not one of those for whom a rural Saskatchewan charge was a stepping-stone to a city church. He spent his entire career in the Salcoats area where he began. On this occasion, he told a story that occurred in a senior's home in that area. A young fundamentalist minister was conducting worship. At one point, he repeated the term, "Miserable sinners" over and over. Finally, one of the women brought her cane sharply to the floor and said, "Young man, shut up!" This was Walter's mother.

One day in London we were treated to a dramatized version of the *Apocrypha* story of *Daniel and Suzanna*, acted out by Joan Wyatt and Cliff Elliott. The story as presented continued past the scriptural tale to include Suzanna's forgiveness of the scoundrels that had tried to rape her.

The adult choir that took part in much of our worship at Council was put together by Alex Clark, my predecessor in the schools of Goderich 37 years earlier, and Eleanor's predecessor as organist of North Street Church, who had become organist of Metropolitan in London. At one of our worship periods, a large linen screen had been stretched within a frame across the stage. In front of it, on a wide table, ashes were strewn. We all paraded across the stage, putting a smudge of ashes on the screen, symbolizing our confession of sin. While we did that, the choir sang repeatedly one of the Taize hymns. I believe it was the one now included as 466 in *Voices United*. It was very moving.

My residence at this meeting of Council was Rosemary Bartlett's house in Southern London. When driving there, I usually found my way without difficulty. At another time, I got thoroughly lost by assuming that parallel streets got you to the same destination. One night I learned the hard way that no on-the-street parking is allowed anywhere in London. When I phoned the authority, I was told that I should have found that out by reading the signs as I entered the city. As I had entered it from the North, rather than via #401, I had not been aware even where the city boundaries occurred.

It was at that Council that Elizabeth Moffat reported as outgoing chair of the Board of the *Observer*. When people expressed dissatisfaction about national policy, especially on the sexuality question, the *Observer* bore much of that criticism. People refused to take it. There were even some congregations that refused to have the magazine delivered within their bounds, though there were usually individual members who subscribed directly. Intolerance of others' views has seemed, in recent times, to be more prevalent in our church than in the population at large. On the other hand, there have always been people who have made our church great. Other denominations, notably the Lutherans, have thanked us for tackling the sexuality issue first.

CHAPTER 70

# General Council (4)

On our way to Fredericton in 1992, the news was circulated that a man whose name escapes me had just died of an accident. He had been a tremendously effective stewardship officer who had divided his time between Waterloo Presbytery and one of the London Presbyteries. He had fallen down his cellar stairs and hit his head on the cellar floor.

Council met this time at the University of New Brunswick, on a hill overlooking a wide stretch of the St. John River. Two or three times a day, we walked—or were driven—up that hill from the university residence where we were quartered.

One of the 'gofers' who waited on our table and a few others nearby, was a gracious black man who had come all the way from Bermuda to volunteer. The Bermuda Methodists had at one time joined to become a Presbytery of the Atlantic Conference of the United Church. They have tended to be conservative—like the African branch of the Anglican Church.

The theme of this Council came from a Psalm, *"There is a river whose streams make glad"*[133], etc. All worship periods related to it. On the final day, someone asked about what to do with the accumulated paper. A response: "There is a river!"

A major question this Council was to answer concerned our view of scripture and its place in the life of the church. I participated in the sessional committee that considered this. Our chair was Marion Pardy, a minister from Gower Street United in St. Johns, Nfld and, eight years later, Moderator of the United Church. When the discussion of scripture came to the floor of the whole council, I got a chance to contribute my thoughts in saying, "We don't worship the Bible. We use it to worship God."

At this Council, the United Church of Canada inaugurated

a covenant partnership with the EKV, the Evangelical Church of the Union in Germany. The EKV has existed mainly in what used to be called East Germany, where they lived under persecution by the Communist regime. A group of ministers from that church graciously assured us that any of our members would be welcome when visiting Germany. Through Reverend Carl Sievert of Kitchener, Chalmers has since established contact with a small EKV congregation near Berlin. Linda Paul, whose mother was German, has been our point of contact.

Reverend Rod Sykes was, at that time, a minister at Trinity, Kitchener. He had been at Wilmot, in Fredericton, and was warmly welcomed back. Council had the moderator's installation there. Since the man being installed was Stan McKay, the first native to hold that post, native customs were, of course, worked into the ceremony. Rod told me that, being originally from 'Upper Canada', he was never chosen in the Maritimes to go to General Council. He now serves a church in Calgary.

Coverage of Council affairs was done nightly by *The Spirit Connection*, and, if we remained in the hall after the evening session, we were able to monitor it on a large screen in the main hall. Back in the 80's, when United Church Television was first mooted, I was from Missouri about it because of the cost. The Anglicans were, too, and have never taken part. It was at the 1988 Council that, in the Communications sessional committee, I was convinced of its viability by a man who later became general communications secretary. It was launched as *The Spirit Connection* in the fall of 1990 (or 1991?) on the Vision Network with Mardi Tindall and Bruce McLeod as hosts. It has continued successfully over the years since then.

The Vision Network is unique among broadcasters in that it provides an outlet for a wide variety of religious organizations on the understanding that none of them will attack any others. As far as I know, this rule has never been broken.

From Fredericton, I flew in a small plane to Halifax. It was a long time since I had been aware of propellers, rather than jet planes. I got into Halifax airport before I was expected. While

Morrey and the five-year-old Alexander eagerly watched for me in the lines of those arriving, I was able to greet them from behind!

At the beginning of the Fredericton Council, representatives of the conferences brought bottles of water from large rivers of their areas and dumped the water into a common pot. At the end of the Council, they were given their bottles back with the mixed water inside.

Two years later, in Fergus, Ontario, the opening ceremony saw conference representatives bringing something distinctive. Commissioners from each conference identified themselves, and after each group had done its thing, everyone sang the chorus of the hymn that begins, *"Come in, come in and sit down, for you are a part of the family."* When the thirteenth group had been welcomed, moderator Stan McKay commented, with great effect, "What a family"!

I was not a commissioner this time. But, living close, I volunteered in the office and got to sit in on the major events in the main hall. The host presbytery, Waterloo, had invited its congregations to contribute squares to a presbytery quilt, and the result, having been sewn together, was presented to General Council. This was formally received during the proceedings. The quilt was hung in different churches of the Presbytery afterward.

This was the Council meeting at which Marion Best felt that the time had come to allow her name to go forward, and she was decisively elected as our third woman moderator. Our first woman moderator, Lois Wilson, spoke at her installation.

This was also the Council that determined that Council meetings would henceforth be held at three-year intervals, where they had been two. To ensure equal representation from all parts of the church, the church has always paid the full expenses of those taking part, and this has used valuable M & S money. To make that money go farther, meetings have been spaced farther apart.

Deliberations this time were carried on to a much greater

extent at table groups. Someone remarked that it didn't make for good television. But it made sure that voices were heard, not only of those who felt able to use the microphones, but everyone with anything to say. The native custom of the talking stick was used, whereby only the person in the group who was holding the stick was allowed to speak. But all had a turn holding it.

The concluding worship ended with the African hymn, *"We are Marching"*.[134] People moved around the room as they sang. As everyone went home immediately afterwards, the fact that the hymn was endlessly repeated was a sign of the extent of the enthusiasm of everyone concerned.

Local arrangements are always an essential factor at meetings of General Council. When the locale was in our bailiwick, we got a chance to experience the process. Before the locale is chosen, usually before the previous meeting, it is thoroughly investigated for the adequacy of the facilities, as well as the possibilities for billeting. Since Fergus is not a university town, residences could not be used, and billeting became that much more important. Indeed, the use of Fergus hung in the balance for a while because people took their time in offering their homes.

Our local arrangements were headed up by Katharine Edmonstone, my successor as chair of Presbytery, and later to be chosen president of Hamilton Conference. She was at that time minister of the tiny Conestoga Church which later closed. At Council, she wore a gay straw hat. Without knowing her, one might have thought she was looking after a strawberry festival. But by then, her thorough preparations were well in place and she could afford to relax.

CHAPTER 71

# Prayer Cycle

Back in 1992, when my chairmanship of Waterloo Presbytery enabled me to belong also to the Executive of Hamilton Conference, the president referred casually to the prayer cycle. I wondered what it was, but had no idea that I would later get deeply involved with it.

For many years, the Conference has issued an annual list, naming a different congregation or pastoral charge to be prayed for on each Sunday in the year. It also gives the Presbytery in which the church is located and the church phone number. Since this conference extends from Fort Erie in Niagara Presbytery to Tobermory in Bruce, there are now 238 such charges.

The secretary of Chalmers Church had for some time been identifying the relevant church in our Sunday bulletins. Some time in 1999-2000, it was suggested that the exercise would be more meaningful if we knew more about the charge concerned than just its name. That's when I began the job of phoning the charge about three weeks before the listing to get acquainted with a minister or secretary who could tell me about the charge. Then I wrote a paragraph and E-mailed it to Chalmers Church. More recently, thirteen other ministers have asked me to include them in my E-mail.

Things I immediately ask about are the church's origin—how long ago it began, which denomination was involved and interesting points in that history. The majority were organized by circuit-rider Methodists, a few as early as 1790, including Appleby United, near where we lived in Burlington, where an interesting legend persists. Such churches were of course honoured when Egerton Ryerson paid them a visit. But, owing to the lack of modern means of communication, they never knew when he would be coming. He just turned up on his horse. When he appeared at Appleby church, then located on what later became the Queen Elizabeth highway, a lady would blow her conch shell and the farmers would come running.

Some churches had Presbyterian origins, like First Church, St Catharines, which was organized by the Buffalo Presbyterian Presbytery! Many others began as Evangelical United Brethren. That denomination affiliated formally with the United Church in 1968. But, in some areas, the influence began much earlier. Of course, a number of United Churches have been organized more recently to establish a United Church presence in newly built up areas. Here a large percentage of members are people with no church experience who want to get to know their neighbours better.

The older churches tend to have pipe organs; some of the smaller ones have reed organs where the air is produced by pedalling. Around 1900 in Edinburgh my father as a boy had the job of physically pumping air into the church organ during a service. I can imagine that that practice was once common in Ontario. By 1950, electronic organs were bought for many new churches. At that time, they could not compare in quality with pipe organs. Some have been greatly improved since, though I will never admit that they can match the tone of the better pipe organs.

In these days of declining attendance, it is good to hear that some churches are experiencing actual growth. In some cases, suburban churches are the beneficiaries of movement outward of members from the cities. The new members are not farmers, but commuters and retirees. In a few other cases, charismatic leaders are drawing people from the community. It is not my role to enquire about the theology that is being stressed, though this undoubtedly has an influence on attendance. In particular, I would like to know more about the message that is being received by those who come to 'alternative' or 'contemporary' services. In one pastoral charge, the fundamentalist outlook was too obvious to be ignored. The first time I contacted them, the minister obtained my E-mail address and told me pointedly what he thought I should know. No phone interview for him!

Three patterns of outreach are common. Many rural churches support Food Grains, an organization with a good reputation for keeping overhead costs down as they help feed Third World people. Often, the local church or some of its members, donate land where the grain is grown. All United Churches within a radius of 15-20 kms of Hamilton support Wesley Urban Ministries. Part of that consists in giving leadership, every so many weeks, in worship at the WUM centre. Finally, more churches are supporting Beads of Hope which helps to fight Aids in Africa. I notice that most congregations which help in these ways also give generously to M & S.

Every now and again, I encounter enthusiasm. A young lady who ministers to a small town church in Bruce Presbytery likes her job and wouldn't trade it for any other. In other churches, music is taken seriously and involves several choirs. The music director is referred to as 'terrific'. And, after getting cold statistics from the secretary of a Hamilton church, I spoke with a former minister who told me how much the members of that church enjoyed working together.

Some contacts involve personal interest. I had occasion to call Cooksville United, where Eleanor grew up and where we were married. First Church, St. Catharines, was where Mother and Dad went during Dad's last 11 years. Christ Church, Mississauga, was organized from two smaller churches by the father of a prominent member of Chalmers. Congregations in Waterloo Presbytery often have ministers or members whom I have come to know from Presbytery associations and who are valuable sources of information.

The ease with which I make contact with a church varies considerably. Sometimes a secretary will refer me to a congregational web site where I find far more material than I can ever use. Sometimes I encounter a minister whom I have met, who knows me from letters in The Observer, or who is flattered that someone outside his church will show this much interest in what they are doing. Sometimes a problem is identified which indicates something particular they would like prayed about.

Sometimes it is hard to get an answer to a call to a small rural church. It helps if the outgoing message gives the private phone number of a minister. Often it doesn't, and it may take a week to make contact. But only once in four years have I failed completely to do so.

And are my paragraphs read? I had confirmation that they were a few years ago when I reported a story on Port Rowan United near Lake Erie. A long-serving, much-revered minister passed away during the 1890's, and was buried on the church property. Ten years later, the church property was sold and another acquired down the road. But the remains of their favourite minister couldn't be left behind. So they disinterred his remains and re-buried them on the new property! Brian Clark, our minister's husband, couldn't restrain his laughter.

A few ministers have referred to this work as "a ministry'. I doubt that I should dignify it with that title. But I have certainly found out what the Prayer Cycle is.

CHAPTER 72

# "Pack-Ratting"

In the NDP, maintaining membership levels has always been a problem because of the time involved in each riding. During the 70's and 80's, a system was developed which produced large numbers of new members in certain ridings. A few dedicated people were recruited at the provincial level to do the work, a few days at a time, for little more than basic expenses. Ridings qualified that were able to produce large lists of contacts, and undertook to provide billets and facilities (including phones) for the pack-rats. After retiring in 1982, I served in seven different areas. In three of these, I belonged to a team. In the others, I was on my own.

In the team efforts, someone was in charge, making sure that sound procedure was followed, and making the decision to end the exercise when results were starting to diminish. A frequent captain was Marion Simpson of Hamilton, whose husband was a professor at McMaster University.

Always the first hours were spent on the phone, approaching the contacts we were given and making appointments to visit those willing to consider membership. Contact lists varied in quality. Sometimes one would phone for more than an hour before making one appointment. Sometimes that much effort produced all that one could handle in a day. Times of the appointments were necessarily flexible—arrivals estimated, for instance, between 7.00 and 7.30 p.m.—since time required to get from one address to another in unfamiliar territory could only be guessed. But, if the person visited had another appointment to keep, children to put to bed, etc., this was carefully noted on the appointment card.

About two-thirds of the appointments produced memberships. Some people merely wanted to inquire more closely about party policy. Some turned out not to be the joining kind. Others were lonely and welcomed any visitor. They would listen to your spiel before revealing that they had no spare money. However, while memberships had minimum rates, especially for those fully employed, the member was always asked to decide on his/her rate of contribution.

I spent a week in Timmins. This riding had a proud record of membership. I recall a Provincial Council meeting, many years earlier, at which a large group of delegates from that riding paraded across the stage, their positions earned by the signing of more than 1100 members that year.

In Timmins, I visited a home where the parents were trying to concentrate on my message in spite of interruptions from a couple of undisciplined kids. The mother shouted: "Watch TV!" I refrained from interfering. I also attended a Sunday service where the preacher had been a long-serving MPP of our party.

On returning south, I chose to use highway 118 to Sudbury, instead of 11 from North Bay. After affecting the rather rough crossing of the main line CPR, the motor of my green Volvo died. Unlike southern Ontario, the northern area doesn't have farms where one can phone for help. But a kind motorist took me to the next service station at Cartier, Ontario where a Volvo mechanic from Sudbury happened along and helped me arrange a tow to the Volvo garage in Sudbury. I rode the tow to Sudbury where I got a bus to Toronto. Some of my NDP colleagues were staying in Timmins for another week and I managed to get two of them who were driving together to head for Sudbury at the end of their week where one would pick up my car. Meanwhile, I slept at the home of Esther and Bruce who happened to be attending a special event at Wellington Square Church in Burlington the next morning—as was Eleanor. Luck was with me.

Elliot Lake was a hastily established town which was built in the 1950's to accommodate employees of Dennison Mines. The houses were often described by their occupants as 'poorly built' with many flaws. The streets were also poorly planned, with many corners that were made dangerous by abrupt turns and steep hills. Crutches and casts with some new members told the story.

The streets were named arbitrarily at one time. Several had the names of trees. Another area featured the world's larger cities—"Paris Avenue, Tokyo Boulevard", etc. Still another area had the names of past Prime Ministers—three Liberal, three Conservative. Nevertheless, these houses were also the result of flimsy construction. Two short streets, holding former trailers, were named "Cul-de-sac one" and "Cul-de-sac two". I was informed that this type of home was cheap to buy, but difficult to sell for what they had cost.

One of my appointments took me north of the town to a trailer camp. En route, a cliff was clearly visible from the road. On it in large white letters was the sign, "Vote Hall CCF". Since the NDP replaced the CCF in 1961, the election referred to must have been in the mid-fifties.

From Elliot Lake, I drove to part of Algoma to work for two days in the neighbouring communities of Blind River and Iron Bridge. I was able to operate from the home, in Iron Bridge, of a retired officer who had once been in charge of fire-fighting for all of Northern Ontario. He not only let me phone for appointments from his home on the first day, but he rode with me on the second day while I made my calls. Since he knew the people concerned, this enabled me to do a reasonably successful job.

One thing held me up, however. Before I could start on my rounds, an 18-year-old boy, who was chronically epileptic, had a seizure as he was walking on a road with swampy ponds on each side, walked into the water and was drowned. Since many of the local people were inter-related, the lad had some of my contacts as relatives who naturally didn't feel like talking politics.

One thing I encountered sounded familiar. In Guelph, we were represented at Queen's Park for 30 years by Harry Worton whose support was mostly personal. In Algoma, the NDP member for many years, Bud Wildman enjoyed the same, uncritical support. One of his constituents told me he didn't care what Bud's party was; he was a "good man".

I got up early on the third day and drove to South Baymouth on Manitoulin Island, on time to catch the Chi-Cheemaun. Unfortunately, I had difficulty staying awake on the long drive from Tobermory to Guelph. More than once, I had to let in the rain to prevent drowsiness. Alas, while much of Bruce Peninsula is reputed to be beautiful, the route of highway 6 is extremely monotonous.

Of Chatham-Kent, I remember little except that some of our best contacts were in Wallaceburg, and that I managed to work in a meal at Anna Dorland's, Rae being away at the time. It is as well that I saw her then, for I never saw her again before she died in 2002.

Hamilton East was interesting. I was billeted with a retired high school teacher who had a house to himself in Hamilton West. Since his retirement, he had given up driving, putting his money into taxis. His place was conveniently situated for work in Hamilton East, because of the system of traffic lights on the one-way arteries of King and Main. Set your speed at just over the speed limit and you can do about 25 blocks without stopping.

I remember telling the Hamilton East riding president that "I have been going among the poor". But I recall a visit with an Italian-Canadian who had found the funds to create a marble hearth. At the end of 1979, minority Prime Minister Joe Clark had produced a budget that neither the Liberals nor the NDP could support. As NDP finance critic, Bob Rae moved the vote of confidence that brought the Government down and precipitated a February election. This citizen was unaware of Bob's involvement in that move. Said he, Bob Rae (by then provincial leader) is all right. But Broadbent should have let Clark show what he could do. I got his membership. Was I wrong in not correcting his misunderstanding?

I worked in Toronto Rosedale for only two days, this time

doing renewals. One was a daughter of Christina McCaul Newman who wrote "Grits", an analysis of the party which has ruled Canada for more years than any other. Another was a Mr. McLeod, whom Morrey had had as a professor at U of T. Morrey has a hilarious story of this man's constant habit of feeling his pockets for his tobacco accessories while he lectured.

Finally, I worked on my own in Simcoe East, having volunteered to work there from the cottage one summer. In 1975, a teacher had come within 1500 votes of winning that seat for the NDP. I did my phoning from his home in Marchmount, but during his absence. I probably put more kilometers on my car in this area than in any other. But I met with many interesting people.

Eleanor was once given for Christmas a book called The Back Roads of Ontario. Immediately, she found that a majority of these roads were familiar. Few of my roads were the same as hers. Still and all, "I've been around."

CHAPTER 73

# The Bob Rae Government

In 1990, the NDP won 74 of the 130 seats in the Ontario Legislature. No one was more surprised than leader, Bob Rae. When Liberal Premier Peterson called the election, the NDP was in 3rd place in the opinion polls. After his huge win in 1987, Peterson obviously misjudged the popular mood. But, with the unpopular Brian Mulroney in power in Ottawa, people weren't having Harris at that stage. Bob Rae's campaign was effective, but not more so than in two previous election contests. This time, it worked.

The party was not ready for power. For one thing, many nominations had been made merely with the aim to have the party's colours flown in each riding, rather than searching for cabinet material. When Bob chose 27 people as ministers in October of that year, a few, of course, were outstanding. One thinks first of women—Evelyn Gigantes, Marion Boyd, Frances Lankin, Ruth Grier. Among the men there were Floyd Laughren, who was finance minister throughout the regime, David Cooke, Bud Wildman and Brian Charlton. Then there were some who learned the hard way and developed into quite capable ministers. But, inevitably, Bob had to try a few whose abilities were unknown and had eventually to be replaced.

For another thing, the members were unprepared for the possibility that some of the party's promises could not be realized in a first term, or could be done only in part. At the convention that was held just two months after the Government took office, one member complained bitterly about action that had not yet been taken about her favourite issue. A resolution was passed condemning the Government for failing to reduce university fees. At the same time, it became more difficult to maintain membership levels that had been achieved before the 1990 election.

Thirdly, no one had expected the financial restraints under which the Government had to operate. The deficit inherited from the Liberals was larger than had been expected. The arrival of the worst recession since the Great Depression of the 30's cut seriously into Government revenues. Finally, the Mulroney Government in Ottawa chose that year to cut transfer payments to Ontario by over $4 billion. At this point, Bob Rae took a stance for which I believe we should all be grateful. Any other government would have passed those cuts on to the municipalities, school boards, hospitals, universities and other institutions that depend on the province for their very existence. Bob refused to do that. At the same time, taking a leaf from the Saskatchewan CCF Government of the 40's and 50's, Bob and his colleagues went to great lengths to avoid seriously increasing the provincial debt. Taxes were raised somewhat, though not for the lower brackets. And cabinet members were told each year that they would have to operate with less money than the year before. This was managed. This became the first government in Ontario history to finance administration in any one year with fewer dollars than the year before.

This government made two decisions that resulted from the financial situation, for both of which they were widely criticized, and both of which undoubtedly contributed to the party's crushing defeat in 1995.

The first was the decision not to proceed with public auto insurance. This had been a central plank in the NDP's platform, and action on it would probably have been as popular as it had been in the west, if only because most voters would have benefitted. But Floyd Laughren explained that it would have meant borrowing $1.5 billion just to set up the plan, even though that would have been recouped over time. Also, since private insurance is more labour-intensive than government insurance, unemployment would have increased. It was already at an unacceptable level. Beyond that, a rumour has never been confirmed or denied that one of the American insurance companies involved threatened to sue for a huge amount under NAFTA if the government plan went ahead.

The other decision has been known famously as the Social Contract. The government decided that $2 billion had to be found from cuts to the civil service, to be realized either by lay-offs or by a temporary wage reduction of 5%. Since the Government was opposed to increasing unemployment, they legislated the cuts, and then negotiated the terms under which the cuts were to happen. This legislation, I believe, was a major mistake, because it involved breaking union contracts that were in force at the time. As it turned out, union members reacted angrily. Julie Davis, secretary-treasurer of the OFL, felt it necessary to resign as NDP President, and the issue undoubtedly contributed to the party's loss of seats in the 1993 federal election.

I believe that the Government, instead of legislating the cuts, should have informed the locals that lay-offs were a possibility which could be prevented in each local by reduced incomes, but that, since contracts cannot be altered except by mutual consent, they awaited their pleasure. Unions could not then have complained because they had agreed to the changes. As it has turned out, the Social Contract has been sited ever since as an excuse to withhold support. They, of course, ignore Bill 40 which had outlawed the use of scabs during strikes and had made it easier for new unions to get organized and achieve a first contract. Bill 40 was condemned by the Ontario Manufacturers Association. Around this time, I canvassed a lady who said she was a life-long Conservative. She told me, "Bob Rae has ruined Ontario." I asked her how he had managed that. "By making the unions too strong," she replied. This viewpoint was, of course, reflected in the initial actions of the Harris Government in 1995. They repealed not only Bill 40, but every other piece of labour legislation then in existence.

The Bob Rae Government took action on a number of issues, action which no other party would ever have taken. Besides Bill 40, they saved several northern industries from closure by persuading management and unions to downsize.

This included Algoma Steel in Sault Ste. Marie, a firm which is still considered viable in its present scale of operation. They introduced Pay Equity, involving 420,000 women. They enacted Employment Equity, giving women an equal chance at employment, but without setting quotas. They expanded Child Care. They helped car industries bring new contracts to Ontario. They organized and funded an Ontario Parents' Council. They built tens of thousands of units of affordable housing, some of it in Guelph. They passed Rent Controls with teeth. They established a computer health network to prevent the use of drugs harmful to individuals. They ended waiting lists for bone marrow transplants and for cardiac care. For the environment, they rewarded reduced waste, increased the penalties for harmful emissions into our lakes, and gave a tax credit for initiatives in Research and Development. They legislated permission for midwives to practice in hospitals.

One of their major initiatives was called *Jobs Ontario*. Employers and community organizations willing to expand or build were promised capital assistance if they would undertake to employ an agreed number of welfare recipients whom the Government would have trained for the purpose. This proved to be a useful program for Guelph's artistic community.

Through the 80's, Guelph's arts community set out to get a civic centre—ultimately called the River Run Centre. The original budget called for the city to pay $4 million, the private sector $4 million and the two senior governments $2 million each. Faced with great financial difficulties, the provincial government was reluctant to pay their $2 million. Indeed, for a time, all communications to the Ministry of Culture were ignored. In June of 1992, I attended the federal NDP Convention in Halifax, and after Bob Rae had spoken, I managed to ask him to open communications over the Guelph Centre. Two weeks later, several of us joined the Mayor of Guelph in interviewing Rosario Marchese, then Minister of Culture. Whether it helped or not, I got to speak at that interview. Eventually, the $2 million was approved, though this may not have had anything to do with this interview. But someone realized that it qualified under the *Jobs Ontario* program and so we got our funding.

In 1995, the NDP were badly beaten. On the ballots, of course, they were defeated by Liberals and Conservatives, for these people had considered the election of 1990 a disaster which must never be repeated. But they would not have had it so easy had it not been for the many people on the left who somehow thought that Bob Rae had betrayed their cause. They were vocal throughout the regime, and they didn't stop when the '95 election was looming. They gave the Government no credit for the good things they did. Thomas Wolkom, a left-wing commentator of the Star, similarly, gave them no credit. People like Maude Barlow, Linda McQuaig, and Naomi Klein, writing and speaking along the same lines as the NDP, refused to get involved with the party. But party members like Buzz Hargrove talked openly of Bob having "torn up the party platform".

I believe that our ministers were unskilled in handling the media. But the CBC, which I use constantly, frequently gave more credence to the critics than to the government, and, just as often, failed to seek comments from the government in response to the criticism. When the legislation on mid-wives was passed, we got a story on people who were adversely affected, although there was no attempt to explain the purpose of the legislation. And when Bill 40 was passed, the CBC quoted as news an opinion of the Ontario Manufacturers Association to the effect that the Bill would result in half a million lay-offs.

But I have one final observation. I had supposed that any votes our MPP Derek Fletcher would get in '95 would be party votes. But I found that he had developed a personal following. When canvassing with him, I found that he had become quite skilled at helping individuals from a government point of view. The provincial average for the NDP in that election was 21%. Derek got 26%, the highest vote we had ever got in this riding except in 1990.

CHAPTER 74

# Cabinet Ministers

One hot night in July, 1930, as I was about to go to sleep at Kenmore, Uncle Don and Aunt Muriel's farm near Cobourg, Mother brought me the bad news that the Conservatives under R. B. Bennett had won the federal election. I recall three of the ministers Bennett appointed.

Mr. Rhodes was minister of finance. One day he was approached by Ted Garland, one of the "Ginger Group" of MP's who had been elected in the 20's by the United Farmers of Alberta, who had joined the CCF in 1933 but was defeated by the Social Credit landslide in 1935. Ted asked him a question on finance. He replied, "You come along and talk to my deputy: I don't know anything about finance." H.H. Stevens brought out a report on *Price Spreads and Mass Buying*, and made comments that brought Bennett's censure. He eventually resigned and formed his own political party. The Secretary of State was a right-winger named Cahan. Someone quipped that "Bennett may be able to can Stevens, but Cahan can't".

At one point, Mackenzie King had a minister of Finance from Saskatchewan named Dunning, leading to the expression, "the Dunning budget". In the 30's, Mr. Dunning moved to provincial politics and contested a by-election. The CCF was then on the rise in the province and won the by-election. Another seat was opened for him and the CCF beat him again!

After 1940, King's successive finance ministers were Walter Harris, who in 1940 defeated Agnes MacPhail in Grey North, and J.L. Ilsley. In 1935, he made Jimmy Gardiner Minister of Agriculture. Jimmy had been Premier of Saskatchewan. In 1945, the CCF came close to defeating him in Melville with Louise Lucas, a very highly respected woman, as the candidate. Traditionally, the second-in-command of the federal government was a cabinet minister from Quebec. For a long time, that person represented the riding of Quebec East. It had been Laurier's seat and, in the 30's and early 40's, the Quebec lieutenant was Ernest Lapointe who served as Minister of Justice. From 1945, Louie St. Laurent held that seat and that position and served as Foreign Secretary. Other Liberal ministers were Chubby Power, of Quebec, who tended to be progressive, and Eugene Whelan from Windsor whose brother in Regina served in Tommy Douglas's CCF Cabinet. When running for leader, Eugene once made a speech that could have been made by a member of the NDP. When St. Laurent became Prime Minister in 1948, Lester Pearson was brought in to be Foreign minister, won a by-election in Algoma, and, after St. Laurent's resignation in 1957, went on to beat Paul Martin, Sr. for the leadership. Jack Pickersgill began his career as a trusted member of Mackenzie King's office. In 1953, St. Laurent made him a cabinet minister and then he won a seat in Newfoundland serving thereafter as that province's representative in the cabinet. Diefenbaker enjoyed making a pun on his name: "Who picked Pickersgill?"

In 1934, Mitchell Hepburn swept to power with the Liberals in Ontario. Two of his ministers were more progressive than the others. They were Arthur Robuck, Attorney-General, who represented the old Bracondale riding in central Toronto and David Croll, Minister of Social Services, from Windsor. In 1937, the newly organized Auto Workers Union at General Motors in Oshawa struck. At issue was the right of Canadian workers to decide who was to represent them in collective bargaining. The fact that the international union, UAW, had organized the union was used by Premier Hepburn and others to declare that "foreign agitators" should be kept out of Canada. These two ministers sided with the union and were promptly fired by the premier. Both were later appointed to the Canadian Senate.

In 1941, Oshawa's Gordon Conant, Attorney General, became premier after alcoholism forced Hepburn to retire. Conant didn't stand for re-election in a leadership convention. That convention gave a big majority to Harry Nixon of Brant. Nixon had been elected in 1934 as leader of the Progressive Party, but had been included in Hepburn's cabinet from the start. (This is reminiscent of Mackenzie King's action in 1921, in resolving minority government by including members of the 65 Progressives from Western Canada in his cabinet) But Nixon's tenure as premier was short-lived. In the election of 1943, the Liberals were relegated to third place. In the 70's, Harry's son, Bob, served for two elections as Liberal leader.

When The CCF under Tommy Douglas swept into power in Saskatchewan in 1944, he appointed the two members elected in Regina to cabinet. One was a man named Williams who became Minister of Labour. Williams brought in Ken Brydon from East Toronto as Deputy, who drafted labour legislation that was hailed as exemplary by progressives throughout North America. The other was Clarence Fines, a former public school principal, who became provincial treasurer. He inherited a province that was almost bankrupt and gradually made it fiscally strong. A banker was to ask federal leader M.J. Coldwell "where that man got his training in finance". In the 50's, when ministers wanted to spend government money, Fines would ask them if they wanted to be beholden to the banks, because their cause was not served if the public debt became unmanageable. Bob Rae, when premier, was to quote him on that.

Douglas' first minister of agriculture was George Williams who had led the party through the 30's. His highways minister, who developed a public bus line between Regina and Saskatoon, was Jack Douglas of Biggar. His attorney-general for many years was Corman of Moose Jaw. He had a weekly radio broadcast, on one of which he told his constituents that, as he entered cabinet meetings, colleagues would exclaim, "Here comes Moose Jaw"! In 1935, Social Credit swept Alberta, both provincially and in the federal sector, winning 15 out of 17 seats in Alberta and two seats in Western Saskatchewan. Corman was one of those two Saskatchewan MP's. Fortunately, he "saw the light" before Douglas came to power!

The Education minister, Woodrow Lloyd, began as one of the weaker ministers but grew in the job. In 1961, when Tommy became federal leader, Lloyd succeeded him as leader. In 1948, when the CCF was narrowly re-elected, two ministers lost their seats: Oakland Valeau of Social services in Melfort, and Joe Phelps in Salcoats, an outspoken radical.

During the First World War, Britain's Prime Minister Lloyd George was succeeded by Herbert Asquith, the last Liberal PM in the country's history. A minister in his government was Russell Rea, whose son, Walter, married my Aunt Mima. About 20 years later, when I was having lunch with J. Campbell-McInnes while preparing for a Hart House Songster, my host drew my attention to a framed certificate which indicated that he had been knighted by the King of Italy. "Does that make you feel different?" he asked. In response, I told of our connection with Russell Rea. "You don't know what you're saying", he exclaimed. "Russell Rea gave me my first addition." This would have been the beginning of his singing career in England.

In 1929, Ramsay MacDonald's second minority Labour Government was elected. In 1931, he formed an all-party coalition to deal with problems of the Depression. At the time, Walter Rea was a Liberal MP and was appointed Comptroller of the King's Household, which meant walking backwards in his formal uniform before the King at state occasions. This ended a year later when the Government abandoned Britain's traditional free trade policy which led to the withdrawal of the Liberals from the Coalition. Soon afterward, MacDonald resigned and was succeeded by Stanley Baldwin of the Conservatives though both MacDonald and his son, Malcolm, remained in the cabinet. But in the next election, Labour supporters showed their resentment for their leader's "betrayal" in forming the 1931 coalition by defeating both. In that same election, Walter Rea lost his seat to a Labour candidate, and was subsequently created a baron.

In 1941, when Winston Churchill became Britain's wartime Prime Minister, he formed an all-party coalition. Labour ministers in that government, notably Clement Atlee, Herbert Morrison (formerly chair of the London County Council, a much more important post than "Lord Mayor"), and Ernest Bevin, all got valuable experience before Labour took over government four years later. Bevin, Minister of Labour in the coalition, began by asking how many Britons were classified as unemployable. He was told 300,000. His department went to work, retraining and matching people to jobs till they got the number whittled down to 10,000, with the rest helping to relieve the great shortage of war workers. That record has never been duplicated in peace time!

After Atlee became PM in 1945, Bevin became foreign secretary. Was Morrison Chancellor of the Exchequer or House Leader? Two other important ministers at the time were Aneurin ("Nye") Bevan, from Wales, who, after Labour's defeat, led a major revolt in the party; and Jenny Lee ("We wept for joy when the mines were nationalized").

The victory of the Ontario NDP in the election of 1990 was not expected, in or outside the party. Candidates were nominated on the basis of having a standard bearer in every riding, not whether the nominee was of cabinet material. As a result, Bob Rae had to "scrape the bottom of the barrel" to complete his cabinet. A few were obvious choices. Marion Boyd, who had defeated Premier Peterson in London, went to Education; Ruth Grier from Etobicoke took the Environment, Evelyn Gigantes from Ottawa went to Health; Frances Lankin of Toronto's east end had Social Services, and among the men, an old labour warrior, Bob Mackenzie of Hamilton headed Labour; Floyd Laughren of Sudbury took on Finance; Bud Wildman from Algoma had Natural Resources; Dave Cooke from Windsor had Housing, Howard Hampton from Fort Frances became Attorney-General and Richard Allen of Hamilton had Colleges and Universities. Others had to be tried out. Some had to be replaced. Others, like Marilyn Churley, were subsequently appointed and did well.

As individuals, most of these people did a very conscientious job. Because many labour unions turned against the party over the Social Contract, because big business was angry that the NDP were ever elected at all, and because this government failed to follow through on measures like Auto Insurance that might have made it popular, few of them received the credit they deserved.

CHAPTER 75

# The USA and Me

World War II was a watershed in that the United States replaced Britain as the biggest foreign influence on Canadian life. Even the word, foreign, took on a new meaning. Before that, the organization of international unions was denounced as the work of "foreign agitators". Since WWII, people tend not to speak of Americans as foreign, regarding them as belonging to the same society as our own.

As I was growing up, I was aware of several good things that were American. First there was music. Listening to the Sunday afternoon broadcasts of the New York Philharmonic, which were carried on CFRB, was such a necessity for me that I quit Sunday School to listen; and my mother once told me that I had my priorities wrong because I wouldn't go for a walk with a friend at Philharmonic time. Through those concerts, I got to know many great soloists and many great conductors like Bruno Walter, John Barbirolli and Arturo Toscanini. After the latter "retired", he formed a new Orchestra for NBC. Interestingly, after he retired from NBC, the members of the NBC Symphony insisted on continuing for a season without a conductor.

Leopold Stokowski of the Philadelphia Orchestra was another of my heroes. One summer, he brought the orchestra to the U of T arena. Always in the habit of beginning on time, he raised his arms the instant he reached the podium. Expecting the national anthem, the audience rose. But he was several bars into Brahms' *First Symphony* before they found their seats.

Then there was Walter Damrosch. Born in Breslau, Germany, he was a long-time conductor of the New York Symphony, a rival of the Philharmonic. My experience of him came through the Music Appreciation Hour which NBC aired on

Friday mornings for those schools that would use them. My school was never one of these, so I would be glad any Friday morning I had a cold that was bad enough to justify my staying home from school and listening to Damrosch.

Mid-week, the Orchestra of the Curtis Institute of Music in Philadelphia broadcast for 30 minutes. On one such day, the music was Mozart's *G minor Symphony* and it was the fourth time I had heard the work. That evening I got to go on one of Miss Emsley's concert trips to Massey Hall where we heard Paderewski. The concert included some great melodies. But what ran madly through my head on the way home was the *G minor Symphony!*

Also, at a young age, I became aware of American preaching. In the 30's, what we heard consisted mainly of the sermons on NBC radio by Dr. Harry Emerson Fosdick, minister of the Riverside Interdenominational Church in New York. Only recently have I become aware that Dr. Fosdick had organized that church, following the destruction by fire of a large Presbyterian edifice, that the sanctuary resembles that of a cathedral, and that the church, having today 2200 members, is that rare combination of adequate funding and service to the social minorities of the city.

One sermon that I can never forget was about believing in the veracity of our finest hours. For illustration, Dr. Fosdick recalled a time when, as a little boy, he was misbehaving badly. His father put up with so much of it, then he would say, "Where's Harry? I haven't seen him all day." He meant, of course, that the real Harry was polite, considerate and everything one would expect a child to be.

Dr. Fosdick was also a pacifist. He once said, "There are worse things than war—and war produces all of them." Fosdick's broadcasts, *National Vespers*, were heard not only on radio from coast to coast, but by short wave around the world. From one of the BCFS Camps during World War II, I wrote him, telling him, among other things, of the decision I had to make whether to turn him on from 4.30 to 5.00, or to hear the last half hour of the Philharmonic. "In the end," I said, "You won out." I became one of his many fans who actually got a reply, in which he spoke of his "unwitting influence" on me over that period.

Dr. Fosdick had a summer substitute—I recall the name, "Coffin" as one. But there was no radio at the cottage at that time. Anyway, we looked forward to hearing Fosdick again in the fall. We also read a number of his books. Three of them were called *The Meaning of Faith, The Meaning of Prayer* and *The Meaning of Service*. They were edited in the form of daily devotions, with weekly summing up. Dad read some of them aloud to the family.

In 1939, when I went to Chautauqua, NY to study piano, I heard other American preachers who were featured on Sundays in the amphitheatre.

I was also aware of American religious leaders who visited Canada. I believe Stanley Jones was one of these. Jones had views that were arresting in his day. But I found his books rather arbitrary. He would talk about a certain kind of spiritual value and he would write, "There are three," meaning that he could think of three.

At another time, Mother reported an incident that took place in New York. A world-famous Christian leader, Dr. T. Wellington Koo, was addressing a service club dinner. A member of the club was detailed to greet their guest and to make him at home, but was not told anything about him. At the table, the member saw that his guest was Chinese and behaved according to habit. As the first course arrived, he asked him "Likee soupee?" At the second, "Likee fishee?" Dr. Koo said little, but was finally called on speak. The address was, of course, given in eloquent English. When Dr. Koo returned to his seat, he asked his neighbour, "Likee speechee?"

In recent times, I have been greatly influenced by American leaders of Christian thought. The one, who stands out above the others, is Dr. John Shelby Spong, former bishop of New Jersey. He says that his family originated in the fen country of eastern England where the ground was spongy—hence his name, 'Spong'. Other leaders, notably Marcus Borg, belong to the Jesus Seminar, which is representative of most of the Theological schools of North America.

In 1933, Franklin Delano Roosevelt began 12 years as president. Canadian politics of the time had nothing to equal the New Deal. It involved a number of programs that served to make the Great Depression more bearable for average people. The Tennessee Valley Power Authority has been rightly called socialism applied to a limited area. And it really worked.

A loyal Republican millionaire was my great Uncle John McLeod, who had a lumbering business in Buffalo. He would come visiting his brother in Highland Home in his Cadillac car. One trip occurred during the 1936 presidential election. His prediction was that Governor Landen would "just make it" for the Republicans. But Roosevelt got a huge majority. Symbolically, the Democratic donkey leaned away back in laughter in the presence of the very worried Republican elephant.

Eleanor Roosevelt, who survived her husband for many years, had a successful speaking career in her own right, appearing at a meeting in Regina while we lived there.

Of course, jazz got its start among what was then called the Negro population in the Deep South. As I was growing up, preference for jazz or classical music was highly polarized. You took sides. Mother once ventured to express her love of the great classics in the presence of her hair-dresser, only to be told, in an acid tone of voice, "Tastes differ." In 1944, when Joe Grant was expected to join the staff of the Lemon Creek High School, students asked me, "Is he classical or popular?" For Japanese-Canadian teens, embracing the latest songs from the Hit Parade was considered an essential element of being Canadian which was of great importance since they had, been undergoing great hardship, ostensibly because they were Japanese.

Soon after we were married, Eleanor and I read aloud a book of American history which gave us an appreciation of the better aspects of American life.

Some years since that, I tuned in by radio to a Democratic national Convention. The votes for the presidential nomination were being recorded, state by state. As the spokesperson for each of the fifty states stood up to announce the breakdown of votes among their delegation, he/she gave a slogan that marked off that state as being different and special. It almost made me want to do the grand tour and see for myself!

Against this background, it was all the more devastating to hear of the witch-hunt carried out under the leadership of Senator Joseph McCarthy during the 1950's. Many admirable American citizens were subject to character assassination, being accused of Communist sympathies. Many others who might have spoken out were intimidated into silence. Ironically, in 1946, when McCarthy was first elected as a senator from Wisconsin, defeating Lafayette of the Progressive party, Communists in Milwaukee urged labour voters to support McCarthy!

Canadians played a part in destroying McCarthy's influence when CBC broadcast a play satirizing the whole process. A lot of Americans tuned in.

Of course, the term "witch-hunt" originated during the late 17th century in Salem, Massachusetts where women were treated with unbelievable cruelty.

Racism has long been deeply ingrained in American practice. In the South, it is rare for a white murderer of a black person to be convicted. But a black person who was suspected of killing a white person was almost always executed. Illegal acts of persecution are committed under the disguises of the Ku Klux Klan. This is worst in the South. But it occurs in almost all parts of the USA. People of Hispanic origin are also subject to discrimination.

It has therefore been a great source of joy to hear of the Civil Rights Movement and of the leadership of people like Martin Luther King. This has brought out the best in thousands of Americans who now found a vehicle to express their innate sense of justice. Whenever the American Government does something I abhor, I know that thousands of Americans feel as I do. When Ronald Reagan poured money into financing the Contras in Nicaragua, American visitors sided with the Sandinistas. When Lyndon Johnson pursued the War in Vietnam, many young people of military age fled to Canada. And throughout the incumbency of George W. Bush, the peace movement has developed many thousands of demonstrators.

For some years, I have subscribed to a magazine that is produced in Philadelphia and has given strong leadership in radical Christianity. *The Other Side* was started in the 70's by a group of people who called themselves fundamentalists but who wanted to carry their beliefs to their logical conclusions. This has led them to marketing products of Third World farmers, to defending the darker races against their persecutors, to opposing sexual prejudice, to portraying the essential humanity of people behind bars, to opposing war, to promoting new ideas.

Always the worst feature of American life, and of life in Canada and in the rest of the world, is the presence of the great corporations. Called "robber barons" in the late 19th century, the corporations have always opposed legislation that involved spending money on the quality of life. The exception, of course, happens when that spending helps the corporations do their work as in maintaining roads, or in controlling crime. The more enlightened corporations also recognize that, in the long run, they also benefit from healthy and well-educated people.

What I find most obnoxious about the corporations of the world, the majority of which have their head offices in the USA, is their sheer power—often more than that of governments. By financing political parties that can be counted on to protect their interests, by flattening small businesses that get in their way, by using the IMF and the World Bank to prevent debtor nations from taking measures to protect their people, and, now, by putting into place trade deals that penalize democratic governments for spending money on programs that could be seen as unfair competition to corporations, they manage an enormous influence in today's world. And that influence, in most cases, has an unfair and grossly negative impact on every day people's lives.

Of course, a lot of good people work for corporations, and a lot of good work is done through corporate organization. But, because the profit motive dominates this activity, any enterprise that seeks to improve the quality of life but does not promise a profit, is shoved aside. Accordingly, the USA has a huge underbelly of poor people, of people who can't afford medical service, whose children go to school hungry and have to try to learn in crumbling buildings, have to use homes with no running water or sewage disposal, if indeed, they have homes at all, who can't afford to be involved with the arts or who belong to arts organizations that are folding for lack of funds. The USA has the highest per capita prison population of all the countries in the Western World, and, of that population, the percentage of blacks who have been incarcerated is out of all proportion to the number of black people in the country.

I believe that what has been called 9/11 was an act, not of war, but of crime. Immediately, it should have been dealt with by an international police force. If no such body existed with sufficient authority, it should have been created by an international conference of all countries who would give it that authority. Those arrested for complicity (the on-the-spot perpetrators had, of course, committed suicide) should have been tried in an international court, where American citizens would take their lumps along with anyone else. President Bush has made it clear that his government won't agree to that.

To make the world—or even the USA—safe from repetition of an event like 9/11, there is no substitute for establishing good relations with all nations of the world. Those who planned this event did so in the context of a build-up of anti-Americanism that would guarantee broad support for it. Injustice and poverty have always bred crime. Making the world safe will take time. I don't expect to see it completed in my day but for authorities to go around arresting people just because their skin is dark or because they are of the Muslim faith, can only be self-defeating.

Given this atmosphere in our neighbour to the south, I am convinced that any activity that builds the quality of life can only make it easier for the powers of evil ultimately to be defeated. We must build faith in the value of the good things we do. And how much are we Canadians doing to help Americans see us as leaders, as examples, of the right kind?

I forget the movie, but I recall the scene. There was a campfire in the Deep South. A lot of black children sat around it as Uncle Remus regaled them with his yarns. At one point, one of the children exclaimed in a loud voice, "O Uncle Remus, you tell the best stories in the whoooooooooole—United States of Georgia!"

CHAPTER 76

# The UK and Me

When I was at Oshawa Collegiate (OCVI), our history teacher, Norman McLeod, spent a year in Glasgow in exchange for a Mr. Robb. I believe it was the latter who repeated a common saying that there are only two kinds of people, those who are Scotch and those who are sorry they're not. The English, Irish and Welch at least tolerate the saying since all are from the British Isles. But today, when the British are a minority in most of Canada, even that saying seems inappropriate.

We "Anglo-Saxons" still find it hard to adjust to the different cultures which colour our society. To some of us, it may seem outrageous that Christmas Carols can no longer be taught in public schools where Muslim, Jew and atheist families form part of the community; that the Lord's Prayer is regarded as a vehicle of Christian dominance. In time, it is to be hoped that movements involved in inter-faith dialogue will lead to mutual valuing of each other's cultures.

I grew up amid talk that Britain was the context of the best things in the world. The empire, more recently dubbed the "British Commonwealth of Nations", had the reputation of great benevolence in Britain's treatment of the other members. Undoubtedly, there were cases that justified that reputation. On the other hand, the main purpose of the empire was trade, which, until the Second World War, benefitted the "Mother Country." Two novels illustrated for me the darker side of British rule. One showed the attitude of the British to the "natives" of India—the "lesser breeds within the law". Until Britain elected the Labour Government of 1945-51, self-rule for India was considered unthinkable. The other told of the opium wars in China. In this, the British were no better than the French or the Spanish.

Perhaps it is a recommendation that they have been able to laugh at themselves. I haven't heard this kind of joke for a long time:

Two Englishmen, two Scots and two Irishmen were left on separate south-sea islands and re-visited a year later. The Scots had founded a bank. The Irish had fought and killed each other. But the English had not spoken because they had not been introduced! Or -

A Welshman prays on his knees and on his neighbours; the Scot keeps the Sabbath and anything else he can get his hands on; the Englishman is sure he is a self-made man, and is ever ready to thank his Maker!

A Highland chief was visiting an English nobleman on the latter's estate. The nobleman showed his guest his heraldry and his weapons collection. "My family," he boasted proudly, "has had the right to bear arms, for two hundred years!" "Hoot, man," replied the chief, "My family has had the right to bare legs for a thoosand years!"

It's a long time since I first heard those sayings. Obviously they pre-date inclusive language.

During World War II, CCF leaders looked for inspiration to the British Labour party. Around the beginning of the 20th century, that party was founded by Keir Hardy, of Glasgow, and others. After the First World War, Labour replaced the Liberals as one of the two strongest parties. In the 20's, Labour, under Ramsay MacDonald, twice formed a minority government. During the second war, Labour joined the coalition Government of Winston Churchill and several leaders got valuable experience. One of these, Herbert Morrison, had been Chairman of the London County Council, the largest municipality in the country. In May, 1945, when the general election was held, the ballots were not counted until after the international conference at Potsdam. When the ballots were counted in July, Labour had 48% of the vote to the Conservatives' 39%. Under the first-past-the-post system, this was enough to give Labour a very large majority. Under Clement

Attlee, this government carried out a large part of their program. The railways and the coal mines were nationalized, the National Health Service was established, covering even visitors to Britain on the ground that healthy visitors helped the permanent population stay healthy.

Whenever a left-wing government takes power arm-chair socialists are sure to find fault. They did this to the Attlee Government. And I recall being greatly cheered at a CCF meeting in Regina at the time when Mrs. Telford stood up after a trip to Britain and declared, "The Labour Government is doing a magnificent job."

Magnificent or not, that Government was reduced to minority status in 1950. Labour had come down from 48% to 46-1/2% while the Tories had 44-1/2 %. In the run-off election of 1951, Labour got 49% to the Tories' 48. But, since Labour vote majorities were larger, the Tories got a 20-seat majority. What had happened was that the Liberal party had effectively been jettisoned. If ever our voting system, largely inherited from Britain, needed changing, that was the proof of it!

For the next 25 years, it was always fun to tune to British elections, especially as the difference in time zones allowed us to follow their returns as they were announced. Of course, these tended to be slower than ours because their counting is done, not in the polls but at the riding headquarters. Furthermore, they don't issue returns till the final result is determined for the riding. This is possible because they have few ridings with great physical size. It also makes it possible to have immediate recounts where votes are close, whereas we sometimes have to wait for final riding results for two weeks or more, and long after the media has lost interest. In 1963, Labour leader Harold Wilson was able to assert at 1.00 pm on the day after the election that he had won power, although Labour had won only a 4-seat majority in a house with over 600 members.

I'm afraid that my interest in British elections has greatly waned since Tony Blair became Prime Minister.

Once, in the NDP, British Labour was mentioned as the wrong example. Michael Lewis, who gave our party important organizational advice, was stressing the importance of getting out the vote on Election Day. At the previous British election—was it 1968?—Labour had lost to the Tories by taking Election Day for granted. Michael blamed a "Lousy E-day organization."

Of course, British literature was an important part of my early education and consciousness. Performances and readings of the Shakespeare plays was a sine qua non. A different play was an assigned part of every high school curriculum. We had a lot of fun casting the parts of *The Merchant of Venice* in Harrison Murphy's fourth form class. In university, E. J. Pratt highlighted the symbolism of Prospero's line in *The Tempest*: "I'll drown my books."

Mother read some of the great novels aloud to me. Dickens' *David Copperfield* and *Nicholas Nickleby* portrayed the seamier side of 19th century life with which his finer characters had to contend. J. M. Barrie's *The Little Minister* and *A Window in Thrums* made us acquainted with the Charms of the Lowland Scotch, while R. L. Stevenson's *Kidnapped* and Scott's *Rob Roy* were of the finest adventures in that land. Dad used to advise readers to keep reading the first 30 pages of a Scott novel. That part tended to be dry. But by page 31 the reader would be hooked.

And then there were the poets. "Burns Night" in January is still a great institution in Canada. And they tell of the English poet, Alfred Noyes, "You can feel Burns, but you have to hear Noyes"!

And there have been leaders in other fields. In the 30's, I recall a re-broadcast of a talk given on the BBC by Sir Oliver Lodge. He was a strong believer in extra-sensory perception, and he told a story that took place in Glasgow. A business man had an office in an old warehouse belonging to a business that had been started by his father, then dead for many years. One day as he sat in his office, he heard his father calling him, whereupon he rose to greet his father. At that moment a rotted beam gave way and fell across his desk. He would certainly have died had he remained seated.

Four religious denominations had their origins in Britain. We don't remember Henry VIII as a nice man. But his quarrel with the Pope that led to the establishment of the Church of England probably made it easier for his countrymen to avoid being drawn, over the years, into many papal machinations on the continent. The C. of E. developed beautiful forms of service. But their adherents have tended to be very conservative. The part played by the Family Compact in the early history of Upper Canada is one that most of us prefer to forget.

John Knox did his preaching in the 16th century. When Bloody Mary came to the English throne, he fled to the Continent where he wrote a lot of letters. He gave it as his opinion that what was the matter with Queen Mary was that she was a woman, an opinion that didn't ingratiate him with the following Queen Elizabeth! A bit of dialogue in Barrie's *Little Minister* tells of a prevailing attitude at one stage of the Presbyterians. The comment had to do with "the paraphrases", the metrical treatment of the Psalms. *The Psalms of David* (as read, of course, from a prose Bible,) "rise straight to Heaven, but the paraphrases stick in the ceiling of the Kirk"!

By the time Presbyterianism was exported to Canada, there were four Presbyterian sects, all of which found their way to this country and which had to be united in the 1980's. In Guelph, Knox and Chalmers, though located on the same block, belonged to different sects when each was founded.

In the 17th century, John Wesley began life as an Anglican and was a priest when he started preaching in the open air, declaring that "the world is my parish." He was soon denied access to most Anglican buildings. Undoubtedly, his followers achieved a level of commitment that was not characteristic of most Anglicans. In 19th century Upper Canada, the Anglicans didn't build new sanctuaries until they could afford stone structures, while the Methodists were content with the cheaper frame buildings, of which they built many more. Their circuit riders carried their message out with great energy and the Methodists soon outnumbered the Anglicans many times. A majority of our United Churches had their start in this way.

The 17th century also saw the founding of the Society of Friends, called pejoratively at the time, 'Quakers'. They are known for their skilful use of silence in worship and for their pacifist stand. Many have been left wingers politically. But some American Quakers, notably the Penns of Pennsylvania, have been very successful in business. *The New Commonwealth*, the first organ of the Ontario CCF, had a columnist who called himself "The Quaker preacher", though he was anything but dogmatic in his views. The British Columbia village of Argenta was formed as a deliberate Quaker village. Our friends, the Herbisons, went there from the United Church in 1962 and have been a tower of strength to the community.

I've also been aware of inspired peace leaders from Britain. A group of us in Regina once brought Muriel Lester to speak at Metropolitan Church. The minister was no pacifist but found common ground with her as she had been a member of the London (England) County Council. A story she told had nothing to do with peace. Commenting on chair people who had introduced her, she mentioned one speaker who said that the audience needed to take his introduction with a dose of salts!

The panoramic stories of Edward Rutherfurd give one a great view of British history as it applied to certain areas. The cities of Salisbury and London and the New Forest are each represented over 1000 years. Different ages are represented by mini stories that have plots of their own. Different families play roles that are similar in different episodes, though they are always affected by changes that have taken place. Most characters are fictitious, though famous people appear as part of the circumstances of the time. Two facts that surface have to do with the period when Jews were not allowed to live in Britain, and the high percentage of English people who are descended from the Huguenots, who fled from the intolerance of Catholic France. In the 17th century, most people drank tea which had been smuggled into the country.

Some of the best detective fiction depicts the geography, history and local customs of Britain with remarkable faithfulness. One thinks of Sherlock Holmes, Peter Wimsy and Hercule Poirot in times past. More recently, Ann Perry has given us a vivid picture of Victorian Britain with its sharp class distinctions, and Elizabeth George depicts racial tension on the east coast, although she now spends most of her time in California. Indeed, so many stories are set in that interesting country that, to get one's entertainment from fiction is to become pretty familiar with the British countryside and its people.

And what would our culture have been without the Gilbert & Sullivan operettas? These ten or so creations have become a separate genre—so much so that when Thomas Crawford tried introducing something called *San Toy* to the Victoria College Music club repertory as a change from the Gilbert and Sullivan shows, people thought the club must be about to fold. Norrie Frye called it "laundry Chinese." The one Gilbert and Sullivan I produced was *Trial by Jury* which we did at Regina Central Collegiate.

## CHAPTER 77

# Recent Use of the Piano

During my teaching years, I kept playing at music I liked or found to sight-read. But, except in the summer, I didn't find time for disciplined practice. When I retired, I wondered whether I could find a teacher who would relate to my situation. While I thought about it, I decided to try staging a recital on my own. In the spring of 1984, I did a full program in Chalmers Church and invited an audience from far and wide. I remember that Frances McLeod appeared. Not everyone was pleased. For instance, Eleanor cringed with every wrong note.

I forget why I was not always able to practise at 264 Woolwich Street and used instead Agnes' house on King Street when she was not there. The program: Bach's *Prelude* and *Fugue in E+* from Volume 2 of the WTC; the Beethoven *Moonlight Sonata*; Schubert's *Impromptu in E flat*, Schumann's *Arabesque in C*, Brahms' *Intermezzo in A Major*, Palmgren's *Valse Mignonne*, Jean Coulthard's *Quiet Song*, and Derek Healey's *Carousel*. I worked hard at this event. My lack of focused practising over the years did show. For example, in retrospect, I think I grossly underestimated the time that needed to elapse between first managing to play a piece from memory and finally feeling comfortable with that memory. One relies too much on motor memory which can be unreliable. Succeeding years have, I hope, taught me to do that right.

But, after this event was over, Aunt Mary folded me into the warmest hug I'd ever received. She almost ran into my arms. It was the effort that impressed her rather than the fine points of the result.

After that, I studied with Sister Emma in her studio in the Loretto Convent. She had accompanied my massed choirs, and I soon related to what she had to give me. It was she who introduced me to the Pro Musica group. I was the first man to join this collection of amateurs whose musicianship and technique varied from one to another, but who all needed an audience which would be the focus of their efforts. The original group included teachers and rank amateurs. Our format has changed little since that day. We meet in each others' homes on the second Tuesday morning of each month, not including July, August, or September. Everyone plays or sings for not more than ten minutes, no one criticizes, and (hopefully) no one apologizes for not doing better. But the days we meet tend to serve as objectives as we practise. And we usually enjoy each other's contributions.

Sometimes, members call me the star of the group—my technique is better and I practise regularly the year round. So why do I belong? Partly because I so enjoy the fellowship, partly because I like accompanying my partners, but also because of the unreliability of my physical nature, which means that I can never be sure that I'll not stumble. This can only remind people of my fallibility, something the Pro Musica people can be counted on to overlook.

From time to time, people in Pro Musica have left town while others, including men, have been introduced to the group. Before performing, each of us talks about the music and its composer. Mary Mitchell, a retired language teacher from high school, tells us things we tend to remember. She is terribly humble about her piano technique, although she has a wonderful sense of phrase.

In 1988, Sister Emma was forced to reduce her commitments, and recommended me to Valerie Candelaria with whom I have happily studied ever since. I have always set the agenda for every lesson. I try to have the notes learned before I take something to her for interpretation. I also make sure I take the same music to her at least a second time. There are so many points

*Don with piano teacher, Valerie Candelaria*

that can't be worked into one lesson.

To expand my repertory, for a few years, I made annual visits to the Canadian Music Centre on St. Joseph Street in Toronto. This is a marvellous library. Hundreds of works by Canadian composers are arranged alphabetically under categories, such as piano music. I would browse through this section and pick out about 20 pieces that looked interesting and possible to play. At the front desk, I borrowed the pieces for up to two months by merely giving my address. At home, I would narrow the stuff down to around four. I could then purchase a copy in the usual way from a music store, if it had been published. If it had not, then the Music Centre would duplicate the music and bind it between hard covers at cost.

I also have studied some of the great classics that I had long wanted to learn. But I have always given the greatest amount of time to reviving music I began long ago. Each time I brought back a work, I have managed a section or an aspect that I never quite managed before. Some of these works have had what I call a third or fourth incarnation.

Valerie and others have remarked that I am playing better in recent years than I did when I was first retired. I like to think that is true. What is certainly true is that, in my multi-faceted life, nothing is more satisfying than the process by which daily practising allows me to experience what I imagine the composers wanted to say.

In all this I have a confession. I never do what has been called technique. When I was growing up, practising scales, octaves, chords and arpeggios was considered essential. Indeed, at one stage—I believe I was coming up to the Intermediate exam—Miss Emsley decreed that I should spend at least one third of my practice time on technique. Of course, as one practises certain passages of a Beethoven Sonata, for instance, incidental examples of technique creep in. But I've been managing what I do without the formal technique. Should I apologize? At least my teacher has not complained!

Some of this satisfaction has originated from the accompanying that I do. This has led to my having a bigger part in the Pro Musica programs than my own solos would allow. There have been singers, a violinist, and players on flute and clarinet. And, at the cottage, I seem to have acquired a cello partner. To some extent, this activity helps me to make up for the school work I no longer do.

*Pro Musica Group*

Now and again, Valerie Nichol, my church choir leader, and the other Valerie in my life, lets me play a solo before or during a service. It's what I'm about.

In October, 2004, I did one of the half-hour recitals of the Chalmers series. Because I had been mistakenly scheduled for the spring series when I would not have had sufficient time to prepare, I worked on the fall presentation from the previous July, and, but for Barrie Cabena's work, I put in the program only numbers I had been at for years. Four people accepted my invitation to hear me, and their remarks were flattering, to say the least. Barrie liked my interpretation of his "Five-and-a-half Winter Potatoes" and remarked how I had made the piano sing. Murdo and Elizabeth McKinnon were delighted. And Allison McNeil gave me huge hug and was still raving when I encountered her a week later. This time I did not stumble during the memorized work. It would be nice to think that I had finally arrived at my full potential. But will I ever know?

CHAPTER 78

# Pianos I have Known

As a youngster I recall practising on a Gerard Heintzman upright which had relatively loose action, compared with Miss Emsley's grand on which I had my lessons. Sometimes Mother would announce after supper that she would do the dishes if I kept playing. That was likely only one way in which she motivated my practicing. Once when I was preparing for a piano exam, Dad came to me with pencil and paper, confessing that he had not kept track of my work, and asking me to put him in the picture as to what my pieces were.

Every couple of months, Miss Emsley would have her pupils come to the house to play for each other. Sometimes the first player would stumble. Then a number of others would follow her example. It was as if it were contagious!

She also organized trips to Toronto to hear world-famous pianists. Thus in 1931 we heard—and watched Paderewski—in Toronto's Massey Hall. Five years later, we experienced Arthur Schnabel in the Eaton Auditorium. Both times, the piano used was a Steinway grand. So I assumed that Steinways were always instruments of quality, until 1939 when I went to Chautauqua to study piano. For practice, I was assigned an instrument in Piano Village, where each of 20 huts had an upright Steinway piano, many of them very inferior.

Once, in Oshawa, I attended a public recital at Simcoe St. Church. Before it began, someone asked me to raise the top of the grand piano. Miss Emsley was present and watched me try. Next morning at a lesson, she started by showing me how—and how not—to raise the top of a grand piano. She had almost had a heart attack watching me in the church, afraid that I would let the thing slip from my hand and crack the sounding board.

Once, as a boy, I was given a lesson in manners where other people's pianos were concerned. Our family visited the Millers who had long-standing connections with the Haigs and who lived on a farm north of Bowmanville. I was asked to play on their piano which turned out to be badly out of tune. I mentioned the fact, and was scolded when we got home for being rude.

In chapter 10 I mentioned trying to practise on a common room piano in Gate House. Thereafter alternative arrangements were made through my teacher whereby I practised at the home of the Conservatory janitor, behind the main building. The janitor had a strong accent. One day as I arrived, he remarked, "Och—still r-r-rainin"!

In the second year of our Honours Music course, we had a section on the Physics of sound, and, one afternoon, our professor arranged for us to see over the Heintzman piano factory in West Toronto. We were told there was not a single nail in the pianos they made. They used glue that was stronger than the wood it joined. And what was the glue made from? Tapioca! One of my favourite desserts at home had been tapioca pudding.

In 1937, while I was studying with G. D. Atkinson, he told me of a lady with a Gerard Heintzman piano to sell. I spoke with Mother and Dad about getting it to the cottage. In the end, we paid $30 for the piano, $40 to have it repaired, and $50 for storage and delivery to Thirlestane. The movers, Tippett-Richardson, told us, at first, that their trucks couldn't negotiate the gravel roads that we used at the time to get to the lake. But, after twice failing to appear according to schedule, their driver did, indeed, deliver the piano to our landing. I had been out meeting family and was told by Ken McPhee that my piano was on the dock. It wasn't as heavy as he had imagined. "Oh, it won't blow away or anything, but it's not bad." Ken took the piano up the lake in an in-board motor-boat that he had made. He got it into the boat himself, and, while Bill Stevens and I helped him get it up the rock and into the cottage, he lifted one end himself. "Let me get under that," he said.

A few years later, during a university term, I was invited to have tea with some ladies who were entertaining Aunt Mary. In the course of the conversation, I related the troubles I had experienced with Tippett-Richardson in getting my piano to the cottage. The next day, Aunt Mary told me that, after I had left, the ladies had a good laugh. One of them was married to the original Mr. Tippett!

In those days, noisy motor-boats were uncommon, and people would often drift by in canoes in the calm of the evening. If I missed playing the piano on any one night, I would hear about it the next day from my neighbours!

This piano had very tight pins, and while four years would sometimes elapse between tunings, it would hold its tune well enough that other instruments could still be used with it. Our first tuner was a Mr. Freeman who, at the time, was serving the Muskoka area, but had lived in Cooksville where he had tuned the piano on which Eleanor had practiced. To arrange his visit, we corresponded and he agreed to come for $4.00. But he totally disregarded my stipulation that he should tell me when he was coming so that I could meet him by boat. One day we went up the lake on a picnic and returned to find my music moved and a bill on the piano. He had "hitch-hiked" across the lake and back!

After World War II, when my efforts to reach Mr. Freeman were unsuccessful, I heard of a Mr. Thackeray who also lived in Cooksville but would come to Orillia when enough business had been lined up for him. I arranged for him to come to the lake one afternoon. That day, my parents were arriving with relatives and I took both skiff and canoe to the landing. On reaching the dock, I met Mrs. Unwin who told me there was a man up the hill who was looking for me. "I think he's a piano tuner," she said. I went up and met the man who had brought his wife. When helping them into the boat, I ventured to introduce them to the family. "Mr. Thackeray," I said. "Freeman's the name," he countered! Mr. Thackeray had taken ill while Freeman was responding to a letter I had sent him. I later received a postcard from Mr. Freeman telling me he was coming on the previous Friday!

We proceeded to the cottage where Mr. Freeman tuned while Mother got dinner. Then we all sat round the table. Freeman, by this time, was organist at Huntsville United Church. He had just married one of the sopranos and was on his honeymoon! But Eleanor recognized him and asked if he had tuned pianos in Cooksville. "Yes," he said, "and there was a lawyer." He remembered tuning Eleanor's parents' piano and being totally charmed by Eleanor's Grandmother Yeates whose age he always tried to guess and which she would never tell. Of course, her Grandmother Yeates' hair remained black, regardless of her age, until the day she died so it was difficult to guess. And she was a wonderfully charming lady who was always very attractive to the gentlemen. Mr. Freeman tried even at this late juncture to find out her age. But Eleanor stayed loyal to her grandmother's intentions and wouldn't even give him hints.

At Regina Central Collegiate, I inherited a number of initiatives which my second predecessor, R.J. Staples, had made. One was the acquisition of a transposing piano. A brass plate below the keyboard indicated middle C and four keys to the right or left. A lever under the keyboard would move the entire 88 ivories to left or right. To allow for this movement, the ledge at each end was hollow. The middle peddle acted as a clutch to release the lever.

The advantage of the instrument was that the player could change the key of a song to suit the voices concerned without having to transpose. It was played by a lady who had been hired to accompany classroom singing of semi-popular songs. I also used it on occasion for concert performances by special groups. On one such occasion, the accompanist forgot to adjust the setting between songs with the result that a boys' number was effectively killed.

At our Regina apartment, we were able to store someone's

piano for use. That meant having it in the kitchen where Eleanor would stand her cook-books on it! Of course, the piano had to go back when we moved to Ottawa.

In Ottawa, we acquired a grand piano from Aura Bender, a piano teacher who had been given a new grand and wanted her old one to go to someone who would appreciate it. When we observed that we were unable to pay her, she said something about paying her later, but nothing definite was arranged. In July, 1951, we rented our house while we would be at the cottage, and departed in that direction. But soon after we got to the cottage we received a message from our tenant: "Your piano has arrived."!

This rather ancient Heintzman had 19th century legs, but a good tone. It was well used at our Christmas carol parties. In Goderich, Eleanor used it for teaching. In the Carolyn Street house in Burlington, it had to go in the dining-room. In 1969, when we left for Guelph, we sold the Heintzman to a Hamilton man who had to have windows removed in his house for the piano to be hoisted to a second-floor room.

We bought our Yamaha grand piano for $1,900, reduced from $2,000 because it had been twice rented out for concert performances. Today, it would have cost many times that figure. In Guelph, it has graced three different living rooms and a ground-floor family room. At 264 Woolwich and at 133 Glasgow, I would sometimes use it to entertain a family gathering. The Pro Musica Group has used it in all three locations and of course, it was used for rehearsals, either for my solo performances or for voices and instruments that I accompanied.

In 1955, soon after I took over the music of three public schools in Burlington, the secretary of the School Board took me to a home to inspect a piano they were considering for a kindergarten. It turned out to have a crack in the sounding board. When I pointed this out, the secretary replied that it was only for a kindergarten!

In Guelph, whenever the Separate School Board needed to build a new school or add to an older one, I would hit them up for a new Yamaha. At that time it was possible to buy an apartment-sized upright piano with castors that allowed even a child to move the instrument for about $815. This price lasted a few years but one year the price rose to $1,000, the next year to $1,500 and the next to $2,200 after which I had to conclude that we could no longer afford the product. But those pianos were well used. They were certainly better than the pianos of some parish halls where the upright would often be badly abused. Indeed, I once had to accompany the classes of Holy Rosary School at their Christmas concert on a piano on which a third of the hammers were broken!

At the spring concerts that I put on for 15 years, I always made sure that we had the use of a good piano. Not all the music involved the piano, but when it did, its function was essential.

CHAPTER 79

# Music That Has Touched Me

At the Oshawa Collegiate & Vocational Institute, where I spent five High School years, there was little music. Leonard Richer maintained an orchestra that played catchy tunes. Indeed I believe they were expected to play that fare. Once, during an assembly, Mr. O'Neill, the principal, asked the orchestra that was waiting to play in front of the stage—to play 'something lively'. But classroom music was to be a thing of the future. However, Violet B. Smith, head of the French Department, would use class time to encourage music in the community. And Laura Jones, the German teacher, once got my hopes up—unjustifiably—that the school would one day let students hear (at 11.00 am on Fridays) the NBC Music Appreciation Hour of Walter Damrosch. I heard that program at home when I was too sick to go to school. Mr. Richer once quoted Shakespeare in saying that Mr. O'Neill "had no music in his soul".

There were, of course, special musical events. Harrison Murphy, an English teacher, once thrilled an assembly by playing Grieg's *March of the Dwarfs* on the upright piano.

Miss Emsley, my piano teacher from the fall of 1926 to the spring of 1936, sent me, during my first year at university to HER teacher, G. D. Atkinson. Mr. Atkinson once described the relationship between his family and the Emsleys as one of love. "If Phillip (his son) had been older, we know what would have happened." Phillip acted as choir marshal at Sherbourne Church although he was rather an immature person whom the members indulged for the sake of his Dad.

G.D. spent a day a week teaching at the Ontario Ladies' College in Whitby. One year, his pupils did exchange visits with Miss Emsley's in Oshawa. When we visited the Ladies' College, I recall G.D.'s comments on my playing, "You need to get your nose out of your playing." Taking him somewhat literally, I said something about the distance of my face from the keyboard. "No, I mean mentally." For a year in Toronto, he had a chance to develop his idea. I studied with him, practised in the janitor's residence behind the old Conservatory at College and University, attended the student recitals he had at his home, and sang in his choir at Sherbourne United. At one of these recitals, I played Palmgren's *Valse Mignonne* and was congratulated by another student who exclaimed, "O that's how it goes!" At Sherbourne, I sang beside Harvey Doney, a strong baritone soloist whose wife was Jean, one of Mother's many first cousins. At Whitby that Christmas, Harvey came in singing *The Boar's Head Carol* with everything he had.

In the summer of 1936, before I started university, I was hired as a counsellor at the YMCA Camp Pine Crest, near Torrance. I wasn't taken on for my musical abilities, but I became the accompanist of two fellows who played the violin rather well. It was with Dave Emeny (the object of a lot of puns!) and the native Arthur Moses that I first got to play the slow movement of Bach's *Concerto in D minor* for two violins. And we must have played some of the old violin warhorses, because one night we were taken to a strawberry celebration at someone's cottage on Lake Muskoka. I remember splashing confidently in the dark in big waves in a luxury motor launch on our way to the event.

After my first, unsuccessful year at U of T, I gave up piano study to concentrate on university studies. However, I began participation in an activity that I never regretted undertaking. The Songsters that happened in the Hart House music room on alternate Sunday evenings were more special than just any song-fest. As leader, J. Campbell-McInnes gave us the benefit of long experience in the folk song field. As one of two pianists, I thought my first effort was pretty bad, but was told I had done well. I kept at it for four years and considered it an excellent course in learning to be an effective accompanist.

I forget who suggested that I apply to study with Austin

Conradi at Chautauqua, NY in the summer of 1939. I do remember that G.D. Atkinson advised me to use the Bach *Prelude and Fugue in C minor* from the first book to prepare for my audition, rather than something more advanced. I took his advice, but not Mr. Conradi's as to the Beethoven *Sonata* I would study with him. While studying the *Appassionata*, I learned from him the importance of subordinating some notes to others in my phrasing.

There was little music to be had during my year in the BC Forest Service. One day I had an altercation with the lad who was doing some of our cooking with regard to whether the available radio was to bring in some symphonic music that was available, something I was hungry for. On week-ends, I sometimes visited the Herbison family in Vancouver. One Sunday afternoon, Agnes took me to a Stanley Park band-shell concert of the Vancouver Symphony.

In my second and third years in Lemon Creek, Joe Grant's little radio brought in a lot of good music—frequently but not reliably. It was then that I became aware of the Sunday evening half hour concerts of a chamber orchestra in Winnipeg that were carried on the CBC's Western network. The theme music was the music by Fauré called *Après un Reve* which I didn't find out till many years later was originally written as a song.

From 1946, my school work always involved music. The only music outside the schools that I recall in Sault Ste. Marie was that I often played the piano in the Church of All Nations. Once I accompanied the choir in the hymn, *Jerusalem*.

In Regina, I belonged to the 80-voice Regina Male Voice Choir under our friend, Lionel Allen. The accompanist was the young organist of the Catholic Church on the west side of town. (Sometimes I wondered how he managed some of the seemingly difficult accompaniments, till he revealed to me some of the short cuts he took.) When the choir was performing, there were always a few members whose gestures while singing were worth the price of admission to watch. Lionel was a great believer in competitive festivals, and one year he entered the Male Voice Choir in the Winnipeg Festival. All winter, the choir kept raising funds to go. One night we were told that, with the money raised at that time, we were assured of getting only as far as Indian Head! The choir got to Winnipeg, though without me, as I had to teach at that time. But they were opposed by a hand-picked choir that rehearsed for only three weeks and beat our people by one mark. The loss did little for the Regina Choir's morale.

Once on holiday in Toronto, I took in a brilliant recital by a young pianist named George Haddad. Later in Regina, I heard that he had done the Grieg *Concerto* with the Regina Symphony. But our friend, Hilda Allen, reported that he had played a single line instead of a line of thirds called for in the score. With Hilda, that was an unforgivable sin.

But I have fewer memories of concerts in Regina than in Ottawa. I have mentioned the visit of the Royal Ballet doing *Swan Lake*. We once took in a recital by Kathleen Ferrier whose records we cherished and whose early death from cancer we bemoaned. We would often go to the home of Fritz and Aura Bender where he and his string quartet would "try to play" some of the classical masterpieces. Allister Crandall was conductor of the Ottawa Choral Society whose *Messiah* we took in. (I remember fondly his interpretation of the final page of the Amen chorus). Lastly, I recall hearing a performance of *The St. Matthew's Passion* by a choir of 30 or so, sung from a choir loft high in a wall of St. Andrews Presbyterian Church, the church where MacKenzie King had worshipped. After the very large Toronto Conservatory Choir, we found the intimacy of the performance refreshing. This applied especially to the chorus, *Lord, is it I?*

In the 1950's, the Toronto Symphony invited, as guest conductor, Sir Thomas Beecham, of British fame. Still a dynamic conductor at an advanced age, he referred at the end of the concert to Sir Ernest MacMillan's impending retirement. He said that, while one should assume that all North American symphony orchestras were well trained, "it is not true. I have conducted them." He then went on to praise Sir Ernest's work with the TSO, saying how he had "knocked them into shape", or, to put it more kindly, "licked them into shape." (I was reminded that Norrie Frye had once informed us that, in Elizabethan times and before, people had actually believed that bear cubs were born spherical, and that the mother then had to lick them into the shape of bears!)

Our time in Goderich was very much filled with music—with my work in the public and high schools, with participation in the Huron County Festival (I once figured that I was involved with a quarter of the four hundred odd events of that festival!), and with Eleanor's work at North Street United Church in Goderich. I remember there was a male quartet a group of high school boys had formed at the suggestion of my predecessor, Alex Clark. I never felt I had much influence over them because they had once performed on the Wingham TV station and felt they had arrived. But they were pretty good. One evening at North Street, the guest preacher was the minister of Yorkminster Park Baptist church in Toronto. The quartet sang *Lonesome Valley* and he was impressed. "I like those boys," he said. Once in the Festival when a Goderich choir and two out-of-town choirs had sung the same number, I was invited, after the adjudication, to conduct the three choirs together. We did a concert of the public school and invited Dr. G. Roy Fenwick to come. Dr. Fenwick (Esther called him "Dr. Friendly" after listening to his CBC music broadcasts) used his position as Provincial Supervisor of Music to put Ontario school music on the map. More than once, I was employed as a result of a reference from Dr. Fenwick. In his brief remarks at the concert, he claimed, "I really shouldn't be here, because I am a very busy man. But I wanted to stop in on my way from Pembroke to Ottawa!"

In Burlington, I dimly recall being asked by a group in Aldershot to play the piano part of a Schumann quintet. I found it technically difficult, though I greatly enjoyed getting to know the material. I don't believe the group had any intention of performing the work. But I did attend at least three rehearsals. I've completely forgotten who my colleagues were or whether they thought my contribution was valuable. If I were doing it again, I think I would insist on having my score available for individual practice well in advance. THAT would have been a rare opportunity in those days.

In the 1960s, Seiji Ozawa became the conductor of the Toronto Symphony at a relatively young age. One night we drove to a concert in Massey Hall to hear, among other music, the *C Major Cello Concerto* of Haydn with Piatagorski as the soloist. The work has since been performed often. But, at the time I believe it had been a late discovery. The Hall had been set up with special runways on which men in rubber-soled shoes ran about with TV cameras, for the orchestra was making a tape for a CBC telecast. We got to hear the Haydn twice since there was a minor flaw in the first take and the artists needed to improve it. Of course, we made a point of taking in the telecast when it was broadcast.

I remember a story about Ozawa that Esther told me. He and his wife lived in a house in Rosedale that had belonged either to Sir Ernest MacMillan or to Leo Smith. One morning, he came out at the same time as a lady who lived nearby. Her car wouldn't start and Ozawa offered to help. He soon had his head under her hood, and at one point the lady said she hadn't learned his name. "Ozawa", he said. "Oh, are you the son of the maestro?" "I AM the maestro," he replied.

He had this boyish look for many years. Once on TV he was leading the orchestra in *Beethoven's Ninth Symphony*. During the scherzo, the rhythm of the first theme is very steady. I remember Ozawa conducting with his head.

I first became aware of Elmer Iseler while taking a summer course in Jarvis Collegiate in the early 50's. He brought a high school choir from, I think, Earl Haig Collegiate where he was having a lot of success in selling contrapuntal music. Soon afterward, he organized a chamber choir called The Festival Singers, named, I believe, because of its initial connection with the Stratford Festival. The group was widely appreciated, partly because of rather frequent appearances on the CBC. At some point, Iseler gave up his teaching job to give full time to this choir and the much larger Mendelssohn Choir.

There is no question that Iseler had supreme musicianship and made a great contribution to choral music in Canada over a long period of time. One night, we went to Roy Thompson Hall for a performance of Bach's *B minor mass* by the Elmer Iseler Singers with chamber orchestra. Iseler conducted entirely from memory and it was a stellar performance. On the other hand, his human relations left a lot to be desired. The Board of the Festival Singers, a professional group which he had founded, once refused to renew his contract. The group tried rather ineffectually to carry on with another conductor for a year, but then folded because Iseler had the connections to get the performances and the contracts with orchestras, concert organizers and the broadcasters. Iseler then formed the Elmer Iseler Singers which lasted till his death. I was told that he ruled the group with an iron hand. It was his position that, if any member tried to find out what another was paid or if any member told anyone what they were being paid, he/she would be fired.

During the 80's, immediately after the opening of the Centre-in-the- Square, we subscribed for one season to the concerts of the KW Symphony under Raffi Armenian. The first concert consisted of the Beethoven *9th Symphony*. At the beginning, a presentation was made by an executive, whose words were clearly audible though there was no microphone in sight. During that season, Midori played the *Brahms violin concerto*, Janet Auger played a rather dull double bass concerto, and Anton Kuerti did the *2nd Brahms concerto*. A drummer began Ravel's *Bolero* using only a dime for the opening rhythm. Another time, Raffi featured the *Prelude to the First Act of Wagner's Lohengrin*. I hadn't heard it for many years and had forgotten what a wonderful shape it had, highlighted at one point by a clash of cymbals. One night, Aunt Mary used

Eleanor's ticket, and we greatly appreciated the fact that we could be home by 10.30.

One Sunday afternoon, we went to the Centre-in-the-Square Art Gallery for a concert of The Canadian Chamber Ensemble, which consists of the first desk players of the Symphony. The program was Bach's *The Art of Fugue*. Raffi was entertaining in his initial comments. He said, "This is basically vocal music; it's religious in tone and it was never meant to be performed—but by that I don't mean that you should all go home!" This is the work, of course, that was never finished and stops in mid-phrase. On this occasion, James Mason, first oboist, and Jan Overduin, at the positif organ, finished off with a lovely chorale. A few days later, I was able to tape this performance from the CBC.

For three seasons, we subscribed to concerts of Tafelmusik, held in Trinity-St. Paul United Church on Bloor Street in Toronto, a building that had been specially renovated to improve acoustics for these concerts. For instrumental works, Jeanne Lamon led with her violin while Ivars Taurins played viola. For choral works, Taurins is the conductor of the Tafelmusik Chamber Choir.

With only 19 regular players, they became familiar as individuals. Harpsichords are commonly drowned out, but Charlotte Neddiger once played a harpsichord concerto with orchestra playing so lightly that we could appreciate the soloist's brilliance. Similarly, one night two recorder players were accompanied in such a way that we could enjoy their light tones throughout. And I always thought that Christine Mahler was a wonderful name for the first cellist. On occasion, this choir and orchestra would perform a major choral work. We went to Yorkminster Park Baptist Church for *The St. Matthew's Passion*. Musically, the performance was splendid. Had it been performed in English, I would also have found it to have been great as a religious experience.

When Guelph's River Run Centre had been completed, and the KW Symphony began performing regularly there, we subscribed, glad not to have to go out of town for such concerts. This is an orchestra that plays well for any conductor, and there have been some outstanding guest-conductors. I soon began an argument with the orchestra's management because more substantial works were programmed for Kitchener than for Guelph. Initially, I was told that music that was brass-heavy couldn't be performed in our hall. But, now that we have an acoustic shell, the argument is given that, because some Guelph subscribers take in concerts in both places, the music has to be different! Nevertheless, the first concert of this season had the same program in both locations.

One summer, the Canadian Youth Orchestra, under Mario Bernardi, played at River Run. *Brahms' Second Symphony* allowed these youngsters to display their amazing talents. One young lady played French horn and would have graced any orchestra one could name.

A few years ago, the KW Symphony featured an English lady cellist in the *Elgar Concerto*, a performance that stood out among any I have heard. Jim Allen and I have enjoyed the slow movement in an arrangement for clarinet, a fact that made the professional performance more special still. I wish I could remember the soloist's name.

The Guelph Spring Festival began the year before we moved to Guelph. When driving around Guelph between schools in that first year, I became aware that Benjamin Britten's *The Prodigal Son* was being done. The third of his religious operas, *Noye's Flood*, which was presented in the Church of Our Lady in 1971, was of special interest to us as Esther played the part of one of Noah's daughters-in-law. She was easily the most expressive singer in the cast (spoken like a biased parent!). Eleanor brought a school class from Elora to one of the performances. Afterwards, Alan Monck, who played Noah, spoke with the class. One of his questions was what they liked best about the opera. Several blurted out, "The church!" They had never been in such an edifice.

One year, the Montreal Symphony Orchestra under Charles

Dutoit performed in the large university gym. There were many criticisms of the locale. Among other things, it was noisy, and the air was stuffy. However, the music got through to me. If this was the only way this orchestra could be brought to Guelph, I felt it was justified. The concert began with Beethoven's *Egmont overture*.

Another year, a group of musicians in War Memorial Hall gave the premiere performance of Oscar Morawitz's *Harp Concerto*. In those days, one could speak to performers after the concert. I asked this composer when the second performance would be. "Oh aren't you nice," he replied. In fact, it was repeated in Winnipeg six months later. So often a premiere is also the final performance.

One of my idle dreams would involve persuading the Musicians Union to do something they would never do. When a premiere was scheduled, so goes my dream, the performers would make a tape of the work a week ahead. Then a local radio station would play the tape every morning at breakfast time. The audience, then, would hear the premiere as something that was really familiar and would give the work a really mature judgment. It would thus have a much better chance of being programmed again. My dream!

Then there was the Bach Aria Group which gave their audience a rich treat. But one duet always stands out. Lois Marshall, her body moving freely to the music, and Maureen Forrester, standing very still, finished the evening with *Wir Eilen Mit Schwachen* by Bach. A few days later, the CBC broadcast the same program from Toronto. Not wanting to stay up till it was finished, I set the tape recorder going and went to bed. But I was in doubt about whether my tape was long enough. I found out the next day how lucky I was. The tape ran out one second after the last note was recorded!

I have many more memories of the Guelph Spring Festival. Eleanor would have many more, serving, as she has, for years on the Board. Suffice it to say that, for over 30 years, it has been a great source of enrichment.

# CHAPTER 80

# The Glasgow Orpheus Choir

Soon after we were married, we began collecting phonograph records. The records of the day were very breakable. Jim Norquay told us at the time, that someone had said, "Before I was born, my mother sat on a gramophone record and smashed it all to pieces. But it didn't affect me, didn't affect me, didn't…!"

We made a point of using thorn needles, instead of the more popular steel products, so as to slow the wear in the grooves. The records played at 78 revolutions per minute and came in 10-inch discs that played for about 3 minutes on each side or 12-inch ones that played for 4 to 5 minutes.

One of our favourites was the Glasgow Orpheus Choir, conducted by Sir Hugh Roberton. The Oxford Companion to Music speaks condescendingly of this choir as an exception to the generally poor state of music across Scotland at the time. In our opinion, they demonstrated a very special musicianship indeed. I later heard that most of the choir members could not read music, which made their performance all the more amazing. Most of their numbers were sung a capella with perfect tuning and diction.

*By Cool Siloam's Shady Rill*, set to the tune *Belmont*, was sung very slowly, letting the harmony have its full effect. Alternate verses used a "faux bourdon" with the melody in the tenor. After the last verse was done, they hummed the music for another verse—as if they wanted this music to go on forever. Similar treatment was given to *The Lord's My Shepherd* (sung to the tune, *Crimond*), and to some of the more reflective folk-songs. The slow tempos displayed superb phrasing and breath control.

Several wonderful Scottish folk-songs were included: *Ellen Vanin, I Live Not Where I Love, Bonnie Dundee, The Herdmaid-*

en's Song, *The Presbyterian Cat*, *Dear Isle of Mull*, *O Can Ye Sew Cushions?*, *Sea Sorrow* (a Highland song that begins like *Rock of Ages!*), *The Iona Boat Song* and *Smoor the Fire*, speaking of the custom of banking an open-air fire at night, carried out as a religious ritual.

The piano was used only when the instrumental part was an essential part of the work. This was true of Bach's *Jesu Joy*, of Handel's *Haste Thee, Nymph*, and of Elgar's *White Waves on the Water*. The latter was done by the women alone. The men sang *The Old Woman* alone, singing of the beauty of her face.

The other parts of the British Isles were represented by the Irish *Londonderry Air*, the Welsh *All Through the Night*, and the English *Turtle Dove* all rendered with the same love given the Scottish ones.

Two compositions by Hugh Roberton, heard here, had a wide circulation. *All in the April Evening* had a pastoral scene reminding the writer of the Crucifixion. *Go, Lovely Rose* was a setting in eight parts of a poem by Edmund Waller. I later used this successfully with a teen-aged group in Goderich in the Huron County Music Festival in 1955.

Finally, three numbers featured the rhythms of dance. They all conveyed a desire in the listener to move. Who could remain in his/her seat through *Stumpie will be married in the morning* or *The Dashing White Sergeant*?

We kept these records in a large brown album with an imitation alligator pattern. At one stage, when I was disposing of these very heavy records, I copied them onto a reel-to-reel tape. Later, I copied all 29 songs onto a cassette tape. The sound, of course, is not stereo. But the contagious enthusiasm of the singers, the clear diction, and the fact that each rendering has the freshness of a new day—all are still fully evident.

CHAPTER 81

# Bach's B Minor Mass

The almost flawless performance on the afternoon of March 20, 2005, in St. George's Church in Guelph, by the Elora Festival Singers and Orchestra under Noel Edison has triggered a host of memories. In the mid 1930s, during one of the Easter holidays in which I visited Tom Dale in Toronto, he took me to a performance in Massey Hall of this work, probably Bach's greatest, by the Mendelssohn Choir, then conducted by Harry Fricker[135]. (At the time, Dr. Fricker was organist at Metropolitan Church. And, for one year, he conducted a special choir in Oshawa to which my father was able to belong.) While at my first introduction to the Mass, I was much less able to judge the level of performance, it was still quite a marvelous performance. On our way out of the Hall, Tom quipped, "I couldn't have done better myself!" A music critic observed that an organization that could manage a major work like this shouldn't waste their time on lesser works—like the *Messiah!*

A few weeks earlier, Leonard Richer, Music supervisor of Music for the Oshawa Public Schools, and a member of the Mendelssohn Choir, came to my father for help with the Latin. It was some years later that I realized that ecclesiastical Latin used in oratorios and other sacred works, was pronounced quite differently from the Caesarian Latin that was used by Virgil and other authors, pronunciation that was taught in the classroom. But perhaps Mr. Richer was interested mainly in the meaning.

Over the years, I know that I have more than once listened to the *B Minor Mass* on CBC Radio. But it wasn't until the early 60's that I got a chance to take part in it. I forget the name of the other bass that used to drive me from Burlington to rehearsals of the Hamilton Bach-Elgar Choir. But, at the time, John Sidgwick drove each week from Toronto to direct us. I got to know the *English Horn obbligato* for the bass solo, "Quonium tu solus sanctus", particularly well since John would play the last bit frequently to prepare us for the spirited and rather demanding chorus, "Cum sancto spiritu" that followed immediately. And the penciled reminder, "Memorize," is still in my copy where the bass section had to sing a rather tricky 12 bars alone. John didn't want us to stumble in public and spent a lot of time drilling the passage.

But I still remember more vividly the night John was sick and his place was taken by Elmer Iseler. Iseler was then still a high school teacher and had not yet become famous for his work with the Festival Singers or with the Mendelssohn Choir. On this occasion, he rehearsed the Sanctus, and he made two points that stuck with me. (1) On long, sustained notes, he wanted us to consider the end as we began and to think about how we were going to get there, letting our tone grow or diminish. (2) For the music of Bach and other baroque material, we were to use a 'white tone' or one without vibrato.

In the 80's, Eleanor and I got to experience Elmer Iseler again much later in his career. It was a performance of the *B minor mass* by the Elmer Iseler Singers in Roy Thomson Hall. What sticks in my memory is the fact that Elmer conducted the work entirely from memory. With a work of that complexity, that is no mean feat. I found that out one time when I got to conduct a chorus from *Messiah* in Chalmers Church. With a fugue—and the *B minor mass* is full of them,—you must know the order in which the sections enter every time they enter, plus the passages when the main theme is not in progress.

In 1983, we were in Geneva and the Perreards had got tickets for us of a concert whose content they had forgotten, but turned out to be the *B minor mass*, sung, of course, in that universal language, Latin. What was especially noticeable was the great coordination between singers and orchestra. So often with North American performances, since musicians union members have to be paid for rehearsal time, there is only one joint rehearsal. We heard that in Geneva there had been two. (I also remember the elaborate fire regulations for the hall which was made mainly of wood!)

But I have to say that, in Noel Edison's performance the voice-instrument coordination was especially well done. Also well staged was the movement of the choir. During solos and duets, they were seated in the choir stalls of the church. But they were always back in formation and ready to start when each chorus was about to begin. One was frequently reminded that the Elora Festival Singers constitute the core of the more famous Mendelssohn Choir of Toronto which Noel Edison also conducts.

The mass is, of course, based on one of the ancient creeds, documents which I refuse to repeat when called for in church. These creeds concentrate on telling the history of how Jesus came into the world and the details of his death, hardly mentioning his ministry. However, in the context of the Latin words and Bach's music, I can find my own meaning. I can imagine that Bach, a Lutheran, was able to give the words meaning of his own. Whatever his inspiration, he managed to use the well-known words on which to hang his greatest music.

CHAPTER 82

# Musical Activities since Retirement

For me, school music has always been based on the conviction that the great majority of children are capable of appreciation and participation where fine music is concerned. In Sault Ste. Marie, I remember the words of my boss, David Warner-Smith: "When entering a school class in a competitive festival, teachers should never 'pick out the roses' ", that is, the star singers in the class. The entire class, including the out-of-tunes, should be included. They'll all benefit.

Of course, it greatly helps if children are taught to sing in tune when they are very young. But applying the principle to people in general, I have often taken part in music leadership outside the school system when average people were involved. With some school musicians, that has meant becoming organist and choir master of a church. Indeed, my mother hoped that the organ lessons I had from Gordon Douglas in the early 60's would lead to that for me. As it turned out, those organ lessons ended when Dad died and I never got back to it. But I found other opportunities.

At Muldrew Lake after the war, I found that there were many children about, that I didn't know. So I organized a small junior choir which occasionally sang at the Sunday services where they sat on the rise of ground below the highest cliff. I regularly picked up some of the children in our red boat which was propelled by the 3 ½ hp motor given to us by Eleanor's Dad. It always got us there, though sometimes a little late. I believe the junior choir lasted about three years. In the long run, it proved too difficult to work around various families' holidays. However, the occasional member of that group still remembers belonging.

In Ottawa, I played for Ted Nicholson's after-dinner sing-songs. In Goderich and in Guelph, I took part in the respective church choirs, and was sometimes asked at rehearsals to take the male section to another room to rehearse while the ladies specialized in music that involved them alone.

In the early 60's, Eleanor's youth choir at Trinity Church, Burlington were asked to do a recording of folk songs from Trinidad and Brazil to enhance mission studies of those countries in the church across Canada. I did the arrangements of several of those songs for SAB. They seemed to work well for the purposes we had in mind. On the recording, the songs were done in their complete form and then with the parts sung separately to make it easy for amateur groups to learn.

I don't remember when Chalmers Church began having annual men's services in February. But for several years, I had the privilege of directing a male choir for the occasion. Always, men would turn out who were totally unable to sing in tune, as well as some who thought they couldn't sing at all but who managed not too badly when combined with men who sang well. A few strong singers always encouraged the others. I tried to combine one or two new songs with old familiars. But I always made demands in terms of interpretation. I probably had ideas that were too ambitious for the amount of practice time that was available. We had to work after church on a few Sundays in the New Year. Sometimes the annual meeting or another event prevented. And when the men had to be rounded up, Jack Kirkham was a great help. One year, Nick Kaethler was our guest soloist, composing endless verses with biblical reference while the men did the *Amen* chorus.

Then, one year, I made a major mistake. It turned out at the final practice that one of the Trinidad folk songs I had been teaching them was not yet familiar enough to use. I should have left it out. But I went ahead and, of course, the number broke down and the men were embarrassed.

The following year, without a word of explanation, I was told that the Men's club had decided that Joe Carere would in future lead the men's choir. Whether the previous year's embarrassment, reluctance for demands to be made of these men's singing, or a desire by men's service organizer to use his son-in-law led to my summary dismissal, I will never know. Of course, it was not a paid job, and one can't complain. But later, when thanking people on his departure from the congregation, Don Martin expressed thanks that I thought he could sing!

Several years ago, I ventured to have a bit of a hymn-sing before the service, with a view to making some hymns more familiar. It didn't seem to be as widely appreciated by those present as we might have hoped.

In 2003, Eileen Burnes, balancing the double duty of taking minutes and leading the hymns, asked me to take her place at the piano. For that year, I had great enjoyment, not only playing for the hymns, but conducting an informal time for ten minutes before the meetings in which I sometimes ventured to treat the assembled members as a choir, inviting them to harmonize a hymn, or to vary the dynamics at other times, using an easy round. Indeed, the resulting sound was sometimes compared with a choir.

However, by the summer of 2004, a new secretary had taken over, with the added position of chair of agenda, and I was told that my services would not be needed. Someone had remarked that my sessions resembled a music lesson! Again, my job was not paid, and I imagine that, now that she is retired as secretary, Irene is glad again to be the pianist. But I didn't enjoy the politics involved. I really think that, if the majority of Presbytery had not enjoyed my efforts, they'd not have responded so wonderfully.

Another experience has been sheer joy. Once in November, 2004, and once in January, the organist of Chalmers, Jane Davidson, has asked me to take her place in conducting the Thursday choir practice and leading the music for the following service. Both times it has gone well, and both times, choir members have thanked me warmly.

CHAPTER 83

# Overseas, 1983

I have not shown as much interest in travelling as Eleanor. It's not that I don't enjoy the activity once I get away. It's rather that I feel more tied to the routine of life at home. In my activities of church, NDP, piano, concert-going, writing, and family, I find it more satisfying to keep building each week on what was achieved the week or month before. In July and August, when many of my routine activities are in abeyance, I expect to spend a lot of time at the cottage. But that, in a way, is a routine of a different kind which I am loath to miss. So in the last 36 years, while I have crossed the Atlantic four times, Eleanor has gone many more—visiting with Suzanne Perreard, touring with Agnes Gelb, or doing things with Esther on one of her many trips. As for flying, I shall probably do it again. But it won't bother me if I don't.

Our host in 1983 was my wonderful cousin, Ian Richardson. He and his boys were living at the time with a family of wonderful friends in South London. Ian had a story that I've re-told many times since.

The Pope visited President Reagan and commented on the three phones he had on his desk. The president explained that one let him communicate quickly with the Pentagon, the second with the Kremlin, and the white one with God. So the Pope asked to use the white one, Reagan agreed and the Pope asked and was told that the call would cost him $50. "Fine," said the Pope and paid up. A few weeks later, the Pope was visiting President Ben Gurion of Israel. Again there were three phones, one to his chief of staff, one to the President of Egypt and one to God. Again the Pope asked to speak to God and then asked the price. "Fifty cents," said the president. "Why is it so reasonable?" asked the Pope. "Well, you see, it's a local call."

Eleanor and I visited the Aldeburgh Festival on the coast of the North Sea, and getting there involved four kinds of train. First, we took the commuters' train, where every station saw people getting out of their compartments and slamming the doors noisily. Then we used the Underground to get from one London railway station to another, and there was great squealing of wheels as the ancient train rounded curves. Then we boarded an interurban train that was both comfortable and fast, though I seem to remember that we rode in a more luxurious coach than we were supposed to. Finally, we changed to what, in Canada, we would have dubbed a 'puddle-jumper'. We paid the conductor in cash and he made our change from a huge facility at his belt.

We were taken to our B&B in a very rattley Volvo taxi. We took in two concerts, one involving Peter Peers whose records we had played for years. Murray Perahia was to have played, but was ill.

The outstanding feature of this visit to England involved going, in Ian's car, to Ludlow near the Welsh border This town has a castle ruin, as you would expect, at the edge of a cliff, which would, of course, have helped with defence in medieval times. The Anglican Church was named after St. Lawrence, who was known as the 'Laughing Martyr'. According to a display in the parish hall, Lawrence was burned at the stake, and, as the stake revolved, he was heard to ask, "Aren't you going to finish me off?!"

A short distance north of the town stood an ancient church in which an enclosed room had been built near the front of the church for the convenience of the local lord, to enable him to sleep through the sermons!

Ian had rented a cottage for 3 or 4 days. One wall of the structure was the actual cliff below

*Ludlow Castle, Shropshire*

Ludlow Castle! At the front door, you entered a tiny living-room. To your right was the kitchen which had a cliff wall. Next to the wall, stairs led to the 2nd floor which consisted of a good-sized bathroom and a master bedroom. The stairs to the two tiny bedrooms on the third floor were very steep, and one needed to trust one's weight to a heavy rope instead of a railing, to make the climb.

With this cottage as our base, we explored the area. For some distance, we followed Offa's Dyke Path, an embankment that had been built in the ninth century by a local English king to keep out the 'wild Welshmen'. Some of it had been destroyed. But it is in evidence along at least three-quarters of the Welsh border. One day as we were hiking along it, we met a group of Londoners one of whom quoted, "Hail to thee blithe spirit." I was proud to be able to reply, "Bird thou never wert!"[136]

Another time, we were exploring country roads, many of which lay beside high hedges. Running ahead of us was a sheep with her lamb. Unable to find any break in the hedges, the animals held us up for what seemed like a mile before they sighted a driveway and dashed across in front of us to make that exit.

1983 was an election year when the Labour Party hit rock bottom. The Social Democrats were enjoying a good deal of popularity. But I recall that Ian was proposing to do 'strategic voting'—going Labour to try to get rid of Mrs. Thatcher, rather than supporting the SD's which had an excellent platform. If it were today, how would I have voted there?

I sometimes get claustrophobic on a plane. If the atmosphere has become too warm, or I have eaten a meal but the trays have not yet been removed, or I have a middle seat and there is no way I can get out, I sometimes get a bit desperate. But, on our flight home that year, I was lucky. Two aisles converged in the front part of the plane, and, at that convergence, I was allowed to occupy the single seat from which I could stretch my limbs at will.

CHAPTER 84

# Trinidad and Tobago, 1989

Noor Hassanali came of an East-Indian, Muslim family in Trinidad, but attended Naparima Presbyterian College where he acquired a respect for the Christian gospel that stayed with him all his life. During World War II, he came to Canada instead of England to study law, and, through a mutual friend, came to know Eleanor's family, where he made his home away from home. On graduating, Noor returned to Trinidad to begin a law practice. He married Zalay, and when he visited Canada a few years later, he brought his family. Our children were part of the circle where Zalay taught some of her country's charming folk-songs. *There's a Brown Girl in the Ring* was one that has stood out as a family favourite over the years and latterly even found its way into my curriculum for kindergartens.

These friends came twice to Muldrew Lake. Once we took Noor to our open-air service where Reverend Lavell Smith was preaching. He was utterly charmed, as he was another time in Toronto when Eleanor took him to one of Sir Ernest MacMillan's performances of *The Messiah*. Another year, the Hassanali family rode to Muldrew in my Volvo, and, as we encountered the many hills of the Airport road, we would all guess the distance to the next hill on the horizon, and improve our skill as we went along.

Back home, Noor rose in his profession, and when he retired, he had become his country's chief justice. Shortly thereafter, there was a change of government and the

*Hassanali Family, Noor Hassanali, seated in center*

new Prime Minister, having been a fellow-student of Noor's, invited him to succeed a British appointee as the country's president. It was in February, 1989, during the first of Noor's two five-year terms that we accepted an invitation to be guests of the President.

The plane that took us to Trinidad carried a lot of natives of the island who were returning for *Carnival*. An engaged couple were on board, and everyone present was invited to the wedding. When the plane touched down, the passengers cheered loudly.

Zalay met us at the airport in one of the President's cars, and Noor met us on the front steps of the President's residence, a sort of palace amid large grounds. Our bedroom had 12-foot ceilings, and the huge ballroom had a ceiling 25 feet high. Such was the climate and the absence of insects that one side of the building was entirely open. That night, we were given dinner in a small dining room where we were served after the President. They explained that this happened as they were still training the servants in protocol. One of three flavours of the ice cream dessert was mango.

In our two-week stay, we never left the grounds except in an official car. The fleet of cars that Noor inherited were in bad repair, and Noor instead got several new, low-priced cars and disposed of the old ones. When we went driving with Noor or even with Zalay, we were escorted by a police motor-cycle, often driven by an attractive black woman with a white helmet. She would go ahead and ensure that we didn't have to stop at traffic lights. Our driver would slow almost to a stop to avoid—we were never sure whether it was speed bumps or pot-holes! Cars drive on the left side of Trinidad roads, undoubtedly a throw-back to British rule. However, I doubt if that accounts for the terminology whereby our 'minibuses' are referred to as 'maxi-taxis'.

On the President's table, we could always find the local publications of the Presbyterians, the Anglicans and the Catholics. In this way, one could access dogma which the same denominations would often refrain from mentioning in Canada. For instance, the column in the RC paper in which a priest answered questions stated that Jesus could not sin. You can imagine how I wished I could have taken him on!

Eleanor adjusted to the local diet better than I. For instance, she developed a great fondness for a type of small banana that we were offered. I'm not sure what it can have been that I ate, but I missed a trip to the east coast one day because I was indisposed. At one of the performances of *Carnival*, the president's party retired at intermission to a dining room where a full dinner was served at around midnight. I restricted myself to a glass of water.

We were taken to most of the *Carnival* events. The spectacle was indeed impressive. For instance, contestants made costumes so elaborate that they had to be wheeled onto the stage. The difficulty for me was that the *Carnival* planners had been bitten by the bug that said that loud was beautiful. We were constantly regaled with a tremendous wall of sound. I tried putting plugs in my ears, but they wouldn't stay in. So my memory of that aspect of *Carnival* was decidedly unpleasant. However, it was indeed pleasant to be introduced to members of the cabinet—all black, of course.

The population of Trinidad and Tobago consisted at that time of almost equal numbers of East Indians and people of African descent (about 43% each) with whites and Asians making up the rest. The second group was not called "Blacks" as in the USA, because, as Zalay put it, "We're black, too." Instead, the older term, "Negroes", was used. The main political parties corresponded roughly to the racial groups, with the East Indians and Negroes alternating in power fairly often.

Noor's son, Khalid, held an important position with a Trinidadian oil company. One day, we were taken to visit his cottage on the south coast. We were shown the new mosque he was financing in his town of San Fernando. Also included in that trip was a visit to a great pitch lake in SW Trinidad. The product was exported world-wide, but was something of a problem for local residents who were finding that vehicles that are parked for any length of time would sink into it and have to be pulled out. Khalid's family visited the President's house in Port-of-Spain more than once while we were there. Adam, then six, was a lot of fun.

Official visitors were received in the ballroom. Port-of-Spain and St. Catharines, Ontario had a twinning arrangement. Accordingly, we encountered St. Catharines visitors while we were there.

One day, we were taken to the Caromi Swamp, a wild area south of Port-of-Spain, where we were taken by boat to watch the departure, from a great tree, of a large flock of scarlet ibis. The timing was vital, as this would happen every day at about the same time. Before leaving for Trinidad, I was advised to take a sun hat for a country that is just 10 degrees north of the equator. So I invested in a Tilley hat. But our day in the swamp was the only time I needed it. The rest of the time I was under shelter and in range of beautiful breezes from the sea.

Another phenomenon, that we observed, fascinated me. Cows and white ibises typically would maintain a partnership. The cow, trudging through tall grasses would stir up insects which the ibis could then eat. For its part, the ibis keeps the cow's hide clear of harmful insects. I was told that, while each creature would go its own way at night, in the morning, the same cow would rejoin the same ibis!

Tobago has long been an integral part of the country, and therefore part of the President's jurisdiction. We flew over to this island with Noor one day and slept in a bed the Queen of England was said to have occupied. One morning, I joined Zalay in the warm waters of the gulf. Using a snorkel, I observed the amazing variety of colours that distinguish the small fish. Of course, only someone who had never swum in salt water before would be surprised at the presence of the showers you use to get the salt off your body after swimming.

That afternoon, Noor had business. So he sent us with some of the servants in a van to the far end of the island. That road was full of hills and sharp turns. We were glad the head cook of the President's house was a skilled driver. Someone mentioned hearing a hymn on the radio that he liked. It turned out to be *Blessed Assurance* which we had learned long before. Together, we recalled how it went and ended up singing it in time to the twists and turns in the road. At the small beach at the end of the island, our driver told us stories about events that had taken place there during World War II.

The same car that took us to the airport was to pick up the next Canadian visitors to the Hassanalis. After Zalay had introduced us, she had another duty to perform. The people then took occasion to ask us about protocol in the President's house. By that time, we had almost forgotten there was such a thing!

CHAPTER 85

# Norway, 1990

The Norwegian Coastal Steamers serve the inhabitants of a very long coast-line by carrying people and goods on a regular basis. But a major part of each ship is reserved for tourist passengers. We were two of those passengers in September, 1990. Each evening, a different ship leaves Bergen on the 11-day cruise that passes in and out of fjords, between islands, and across the occasional bit of open sea, till it reaches Kirkenes, on the Arctic Ocean near the Russian border. The timing is arranged so that towns that are passed in the night going north are seen in daytime on the way back.

Our boat, the Vesteralen, was, in 1990, the newest and largest of the fleet. It was very comfortable, although, on two occasions, we encountered huge waves, causing Eleanor to lose—or avoid eating—her dinner. On speaking to the captain the next morning about the 'storm' we had had, I was told, "That was no storm. It was just the open sea!"

Friends had told us of breath-taking beauty of the train-ride from Oslo to Bergen. But our affable travel agent insisted that we would not be guaranteed connections on the train. So we flew to Bergen. We had expected a four hour wait between planes in Heathrow. But there was a bad hold-up at Pearson. We were given first class service in compensation. But, at Heathrow, we had to be rushed in a bus from one terminus to another to catch the flight north to Bergen. We liked the Bergen airport which we reached about 11.00 am. But our baggage had not changed planes in England, and it was finally delivered to our hotel at 11:15 pm.

Our agent had insisted on booking us into Bergen a full day before we boarded the ship. If the plane was delayed, he reasoned, we couldn't get on another ship. But the day we were there, Grieg Hall where the Bergen Symphony performs was not open. So we walked, and went up the side of a mountain by monorail. We could have enjoyed living in Bergen.

On the ship, we were paired with an English couple at all of our meals. They had retired to the Cotswolds after the husband had had a distinguished career in the civil service. Illustrating one of our topics of conversation, when we got home, they sent us a book about various privies in Britain! Surely we didn't bring that up at table!

Our guide for the journey came on the public address system two or three times a day. He spoke first in Norwegian, then in German—there were a number of German passengers—and, by the time he got to English, we were giving him full attention. He would tell us when we would be docking at the various ports and—most important—when we would have to be back to be sure we weren't left behind.

One of the German passengers was a civil servant who hailed from Bonn and turned out to have a son at the University of Guelph. The Berlin Wall had recently come down, and, as a civil servant, he hoped that Bonn would not soon lose its status as temporary capital of Germany. Of course it did shortly thereafter.

There were special on-shore excursions which we could make at extra cost. We took some, skipped others. On our way back, we docked at Tromso at midnight and were bused to the Northern Lights Museum. There we were ushered into a hall where a film was shown on the dome, with reclining seats for comfort while looking up. I recall that, even in the months when the sun never rose, people skied and played hockey by the light of the stars reflected in the snow. Their eyes got accustomed to the dim light. There had been a superstition that, if children were out when the Northern Lights appeared, they would be scooped up and away if they waved at them. We saw three children waving their handkerchiefs and their mother bundling them inside. Then, at the very end of the film, we saw a solitary child waving her handkerchief at the Lights.

On the way north, when we stopped at Tromso in the daytime, we saw over the *Cathedral of the North* which had a very steep roof and a wonderful set of windows. We also learned that the University of Tromso had been established the same year as the University of Guelph.

Another of the 35 ports we visited was Molde, which I understand means "roses". Before the last war, everyone in the town grew roses, and as steamers were entering the fjord, the passengers would pick up a strong aroma from these plants. During the war, the Nazis destroyed the town including the roses. After the war, the town was re-built and the people determined to re-establish the roses. A German horticulturist was engaged to find a species that would do well in that climate. The roses were planted, and they bloomed beautifully. However, this kind had no aroma.

A feature of the return journey was the Troll Fjord. A little bay between high cliffs, but with colourful plants growing out of the crevices, was evidently once the scene of people's terror. After five or six ship's lengths, we arrived at a kind of watery cul-de-sac. The ship stopped and began to turn around so slowly that at first I didn't notice the movement. Then it looked as if the prow would scrape on the rocks. But we were, of course, in expert hands, and I'm sure the visit had taken exactly the time that had been planned. I particularly delighted in the Troll Fjord. It probably brought us closer to nature and its beauties than any other part of our trip. What in bygone ages was seen as a place of evil became for us a delight.

Of course, this far-northern country is made habitable by the Gulf Stream. I have more recently heard reports that the Gulf Stream is weakening. It is not likely that I will witness this in my lifetime. But, if it happens, all of northern Europe would have major climate change.

Half of our journey lay north of the Arctic Circle, and the crews would always make a big thing of it. We crossed it early in the morning, and the passengers were invited to compete in naming the hour, minute, and second that it was crossed. That evening the result was announced at a dining-room gathering, and we were each initiated (with cold water down our necks) and certified as visitors to the new area.

1990, of course, was the year that Bob Rae brought the NDP to power in Ontario. We used the advanced poll, because Election Day found us well up the coast of Norway. Needless to say, news services in that part of the world didn't mention events in Canada let alone what was happening in one of the provinces. So at 9.00 pm on the day after the election I phoned Morrey at his office in Toronto (it was 3.00 pm there), and he gave me the run-down. He began by listing some of the ridings the NDP did not win—Kenora, Port Arthur, and Cornwall—before telling me that we had taken 74 of the 130 seats. The call cost me $44.00 for eleven minutes. It was well worth it. The joke was made for some time afterwards that, if the NDP wanted to win an election, I should be sent on a trip to Europe!

CHAPTER 86

# Scotland, 1997

Morrey had talked for several years about his wish to visit Scotland with his father. We finally agreed on a time and reservations were made. Since Ian Richardson was to join us and give us the benefit of his knowledge of the country, he offered to have us go in his car, to save expense. But Morrey had already rented a car, and we stuck to that plan. While preparing for the trip through a land where rain is a big part of the climate, I couldn't help thinking of the Robert Louis Stevenson poem about rain: "And the rain it raineth every day". In anticipation, I got the best raincoat I have ever had, and shoes that would keep out the wet. It rained for only five minutes while we were in Scotland, but the equipment has been useful ever since.

Morrey and I were to meet at Pearson Airport, in time to get on a 9:15 plane for Glasgow, on a Friday night in July, 1997. But Morrey had come from Halifax that morning and was rather devastated to find that his largest suitcase had not arrived on the Toronto carousel, and that, moreover, it still hadn't come on later flights that day. So we boarded our plane without the baggage Morrey needed most. Morrey shared his problem with the staff of the Air Canada plane and was advised to contact the Air Canada supervisor at the Glasgow airport. He did so, and was assured that the problem would be solved. We left the agent Robin Richardson's phone number in Edinburgh since we would be spending the week-end there. There were numerous phone calls made until, on the Monday morning, Morrey was finally notified that his suitcase had reached Glasgow. He drove back and picked up the article, taking it triumphantly into Robin's house, with the remark, "Now I can sleep in pyjamas!"

I have always been interested in people's accents—not in

any scientific way, but in ways I can enjoy hearing them. I was once on a canoe trip with a German, and I was soon exclaiming, "My weurd". In a store in Burlington, one of the cashiers had an English accent I loved to hear. Since a cashier doesn't really have to say much, I would always try to think of ways of engaging her in conversation. On a phone-in radio show, I found that a cooking specialist had a particular way of talking that I liked, even as I ignored the content of her advice. In 1968, when our family toured Britain, I regretted, not that I didn't have a camera, but that I hadn't brought an unobtrusive tape machine for collecting accents. In Glasgow in 1997, there was a counter with a large 'B&B' sign over it. As we needed accommodation for Pitlochry the following Monday night, we asked the young lady to book for us. Business was brisk and she had to talk to four different parties, which meant a lot of talk. I could have listened to her all day.

It was farther from Glasgow to Edinburgh than I had remembered. As I sat with Robin's road instructions and Morrey drove, there seemed to be a lot of roads. But the house and grounds that Robin and Sandra owned were well worth the trip. Robin told me that there is a cultural division between North and South Edinburgh. He grew up in the North, Sandra in the south; and he only persuaded her to live in the North by finding a home this attractive. The house has several rooms, all on one floor, and the grounds are attractive, including a lily pond. I can never quite get used to the lack of screens on doors and windows in Britain. On Sunday, dinner was served outside, and no one worried about insects.

One of the guests at that dinner was Helen Richardson, Robin's mother, who lived in Harbottle. (She was affectionately referred to as Helen Harbottle to distinguish her from Helen Reid, Robin's aunt.) Robin's mother had come up to Edin-

*Ian Richardson*

burgh by train. I applied the word, jolly, to her manner. She must have been wonderful to live with. Ian, my first cousin, had also come by train and thus connected with our trip. Ian, Junior, and his brother Andrew—both sons of Robin from his first marriage—were there. At that time, we didn't find as much in common with these lads, partly because they hadn't realized that the occasion was a party. Of course, Penny was there. I had previously met her in 1968 at the stage door of an Inverness theatre, where she was 'chief cook and bottle-washer' for a troop of actors from the University of Edinburgh.

It was the next morning that Morrey had to return to Glasgow for his baggage. As Sandra was then working in Glasgow, he gave her a ride. Her parting shot was her expression of pleasure that in Morrey she had found a new friend.

On the Monday morning, we set off across the Forth Bridge and soon stopped at Dunfermline (where "the king sate, drinking his red, red wine"), and from there I phoned Eleanor. One of our stops showed us the pass of Killicrankie where Rob Roy is alleged to have jumped the river in one of his bold escapes. The resort had three stages of development—by horse-drawn vehicles along the road at the bottom of the valley, by railway halfway up the hill, and by the highway at the top. Charts and pictures make all this plain in the building that now welcomes tourists.

From there, our route, designated by Ian, took us past Queens View over the Loch Tummel and Loch Rannoch. ("Sure by Tummel and Loch Rannoch and Loch Aber I will go"—I have never located Loch Aber![137]). Another stop was Fortingal, an ancient stone church where, according to local legend, Pontius Pilate had once visited!

The local yew trees are supposed to be thousands of years old. A story my father once told me concerns a wealthy Scottish laird who travelled to tropical lands and picked up two samples of yew trees and returned to instruct his gardener to plant them in the hope that they might survive in the rugged Scottish climate. A year later, the gardener reported that the yew trees were dying. "Throw them on the scrap heap," he was instructed. But two years after that, the laird was inspecting his lands and discovered two little yew trees that had taken root and were thriving!

We spent a night in a hotel in Crianlarich where Morrey, Dannie Dillon and I had slept in 1968. He and Sharon had slept in this hotel in a previous year after booking elsewhere. They had gone to this hotel to eat although they had been told on the phone that they had no room vacancies. But, on appearing in person, they had been told that, after all, they did have a room.

Despite the modern roads, one is keenly aware of the majesty of the Grampian Mountains as one passes through them. We were heading for the Isle of Skye, and while we lunched in Ft. William, we didn't waste a lot of time there.

Two impressions stand out regarding our movement through the Highlands. One was Morrey's skill as a driver. I'd known, of course, that he was a good driver. But, as he guided us along twisty, one-lane roads, always driving on the left, of course, encountering small widenings of the road marked, 'passing places' at intervals of half a kilometre or so, and even managing, within those restrictions, occasionally, to overtake and pass slower vehicles, I had to express admiration in a new way. Once we encountered a small herd of highland cattle, standing right across the road. As we passed between the animals at a slow speed, I could have grabbed a horn through the window of the car, a temptation, however, that I had little difficulty in resisting!

The other impression concerned the other vehicles on the road. Like our rental car, they were almost all of recent vintage. Indeed, the only cars I saw that were more than about four years old were some that were heading down Edinburgh streets toward an antique show. Jim Sylph told me afterwards that British law kept older vehicles off the road. I gather that my car, by then 13 years old in Canada, would not have been allowed in Britain.

In Skye, we rented the same accommodation—in Broadford—two nights in a row, while we explored the island. We first drove to the Town of Portree where Morrey carried out his mother's instructions to buy me a woollen sweater. I asked for blue and I am wearing the thing as I write, although I have already had to add leather elbows.

We then proceeded up the West shore, around the north end, and down the East side. Before we got to the north end, Ian was briefly confused, thinking we had already headed down the East side. However, he was quickly put right. What he afterward confessed, and which was simply not true, was that he had misdirected us.

Near the north-east corner of the island, we detoured up a valley between mountains and parked where we could see a mountain with a U-shaped top called Quiraing which means 'wind'. On that day, the place was living up to its name as a huge gale was coming in from the Minch. We learned that hikers commonly climbed to the bottom of the U, then went round the mountain to the point of departure. Morrey walked to the top of the U and back, having to successively climb and descend in order to get there. It was apparently not dangerous. But Ian and I were glad to see him re-appear.

Farther down the east side we saw a famous rock figure that stood clear of a mountain slope. It is known as The Old Man of Storr. It was shaped like a man but about three times as large.

*Highland cow*

The next day, we encircled the Cuillins. I couldn't help singing, "O the far Cuillins are putting love on me."[138] We admired them from different directions but were never able to view a peak. They all wore little clouds at the top which looked likely to be a permanent feature even in good weather. On the seaward side, the islands of Eig and Rum were clearly visible. Also on that side, we experienced the only five-minute shower of our trip. One minute, the shower was over the sea. The next it was on us.

From Skye, we visited Loch Morar. Morrey had invested in a phone card, but found that it didn't work on all Scottish phones. The one on Loch Morar didn't. From there we crossed the bridge to the Isle of Mull and drove south to our B&B at Craignure. Our hosts had lived all their lives on Mull and knew its history well. Their back-yard ended at a high rock cliff which displayed a fascinating variety of wild plants. The next morning, I committed a faux pas by announcing that Morrey and I would "do" Mull that day. Our hosts were horrified at the implication that it was possible to see the island in only one day!

From Craignure, Ian took the ferry to Oban and the train to Edinburgh as he had other obligations. Morrey and I made a reservation for the same ferry for that night, and set off to encircle Mull. The main shore of Tobermory is picturesque with a church spire in the middle which turns out currently to indicate a craft store. As we drove counter-clockwise around the island, Ben More always loomed up in the middle. Everywhere, there were sheep near the road. Even though occasional fences appeared with gates on the road through which the creatures couldn't wander, I marvelled that the owners were able to keep track of their flocks.

Fionnphort, at the SW corner of Mull, had the ferry to Iona. From there, the island of Staffa with Fingal's Cave was clearly visible. Another time we'd go there. As it was, our timing in catching the Craignure ferry was much too tight. I visited the famous Iona church with its

*Tobermory, Isle of Muir*

display of unique materials. But I'd love to have actually dialogued with some of the people of Iona.

After a night in Oban, we drove east, past the Wallace monument, to Minathort, where we took Penny's advice to get some pottery for Eleanor; thence south to Edinburgh and Penny's party. One of the young men present defended the British custom of driving on the left. It originated, in the days of horses with right-handed horsemen using their right hands to fight on-coming antagonists (I think I have that right). But he went on to accuse Napoleon of getting people on the continent to drive on the 'wrong' side!

At our hotel near Glasgow where we spent our last night in Scotland, the girl at the desk had another lovely accent. However, I heard her utter only one sentence before we had to leave!

As we flew over Greenland, a remarkably clear view of the coast of that great island was visible, including the location of some fjords. Tiny white dots on the water may have been icebergs. I made good use of my disposable camera.

Some time later, Morrey left me for the plane washroom and seemed to take a long time to return. He finally appeared and relayed an invitation to the pilots' cabin. Flying over Labrador and Quebec was the more boring part of the flight, and the Air Canada pilots were glad of some conversation. They even let us stay while they made their landing at Pearson Airport. I was truly impressed when they lined up the centre bar of the windshield with the centre line on the runway. Since 9/11, alas, conversations with air pilots while in the air are no longer possible.

I recall one of the phone calls Morrey made to his family from Scotland. Plainly, he never takes them for granted! And love is never forgotten.

CHAPTER 87

# British Columbia, 1999

I had toyed for some time with the idea of visiting the Kootenays, since at least four sets of friends were living within driving distance of each other. Esther became interested, and managed to clear a week in June of 1999 for this purpose. We made reservations on Air Canada, with change at Calgary to a smaller line that would take us to Castlegar, and Esther used Jim's frequent flyer status to get us seats in business class When we picked up our rented car in Castlegar, Esther announced that the family had decreed that she would do all the driving. A few years earlier, I might have objected. At the time, however, I was aware of Esther's driving skills and was quite prepared to be chauffeured. And in fact, it saved us a lot of money to have only one registered driver.

Bob Forshaw had been a professor of hog production at the Ontario College of Agriculture. He was an Anglican and a long-time member of the NDP, though he is conservative about some issues. On retiring, he returned to his native Grand Forks, BC. He had long been in the habit of phoning me frequently to get up to date on what was happening in the Ontario party.

We flew out on a Monday. On the previous Friday morning, I received one of those phone calls, though I was busy and couldn't talk long. But half an hour later, his sister called to say that Bob had just fallen on the cement floor of his front porch and broken a hip bone. He has a large body and the fracture didn't surprise me. But the call, made while they awaited the arrival of the ambulance, was to insist that we should still stay at his house when we arrived. When we reached Castlegar, we were met by a niece of Bob's (a nurse) who repeated the invitation and told us that Bob was in the hospital at Trail. At the hospital, we could see Bob for only 20 minutes, but he suggested that we contact his sister, Betty Tolarico, in Grand Forks. We arranged to go and see her the next morning. We spent that night in Rossland at a Swiss-style B&B, where up-to-date maps and pictures of Switzerland covered the restaurant walls, and we arrived in Grand Forks the next day.

Betty Tolarico turned out to be a very interesting person. After a good visit, she showed us Bob's house in the next block and gave us a key, so that we could sleep there on the Tuesday night. Both houses are located on a hill that overlooks the town to the north and west. Betty had to leave for an appointment, and, at about 11:00 am, we picked up some lunch makings and headed across into Washington State. We passed forest that had been burned over not long before and, since the elevation was high, we encountered snow in June. Later we came within sight of a widening of the Columbia River that is called Franklin D. Roosevelt Lake and the famous Coulee Dam; then followed that river north to re-enter Canada and return to Grand Forks. At around 4 pm, we took another suggestion of Bob's and connected with the Funk family, NDP members and friends of Bob's, who gave us a tour of the town.

On the Wednesday morning, we had time to stop for photos of some of the gorgeous scenery. As we headed up the Slocan Valley, we stopped at Lemon Creek, which I hadn't visited since I had left it in June, 1946. Of course, the tar-paper shacks of the Wartime Relocation Centre were long gone. But there was a tourist lodge which we visited and where I shared my story with the middle-aged proprietors who were much interested. They showed me a cement icon from the garden of Reverend Tak Komiyama who had been our minister in Lemon Creek. Knowing that they had lived on Dogwood Street, I was able to determine just where the settlement had been all those years ago. Lemon Creek—the creek, that is—as it turned out, was in spate and Esther was able to get some good shots of it.

Slocan City had developed considerably in the 53 years. I don't believe there was a bridge over the Slocan River in my day. Now there are two, both of which we used. The beauty of

Slocan Lake throughout its length was as evident as it had ever been. The highway, however, was much wider, straighter and safer than I remembered it. We reached our accommodation in New Denver in the late afternoon, and immediately related in a big way to the lady who ran it. We managed to phone Stan Rowe that evening, and later met him and his partner in one of New Denver's streets.

Throughout this trip, I couldn't help noticing how quickly my friends all became Esther's friends. Stan was one. In the 40's when he had taught high school in New Denver, we knew him as John. But, in one of the offices he had worked in during his career as a federal civil servant, there were several people named John, and he began using his middle name. His marriage broke up at the time of his retirement, and he moved back to New Denver. His partner, Katherine Chumiak, was a charming lady whose brother was an NDP member of the Manitoba Legislature and has since become Minister of Health. On Thursday we had lunch in their little house, and Esther sketched the lupines in their front garden. Since the house had only four rooms, Stan had built a one-room place at the bottom of the garden where he kept his computer and other office equipment. At night, Katherine took us on a hike along the shore of the lake, which gave us a slightly different mountain vista from the one we had at first taken in.

On Friday morning, Stan showed us over the Nissei Memorial Centre, a museum commemorating the experience of the Japanese-Canadian war-time evacuation. Among the pictures on display, Esther was able to find me in a shot of the Lemon Creek School—and knew for sure that my story was true!

*Top: Overlooking Slocan Lake, 1944*
*Bottom: Stan Rowe*

The next day, we drove to the house in the woods where Miranda Hughes and her family lived. Many years earlier, Daphne Hughes had founded and directed the Suzuki String School of Guelph. Where many Suzuki schools had developed string players who played accurately but with little expression, Daphne's products tended to be really musical. These included the four Hughes children, all of whom became sufficiently proficient to manage concertos. Miranda, the oldest, was probably the best. But at university, she switched to medicine, became a doctor and married one. Wherever they lived, she was able to play in the local symphony. In New Denver, her husband works full time as a doctor, Miranda does medical work two afternoons a week to keep her hand in, but teaches several violin pupils, and leads a community orchestra (Stan plays clarinet in it), and a string quartet. She is also bringing up three children and teaching them at home! We had hardly got in the door when her five-year-old daughter got out her tiny violin and played her entire repertory of four pieces for our benefit! Miranda's parents, who had moved to New Denver for retirement, were in England when we were there so we were unable to see them.

On the Friday afternoon, we headed out highway 17A toward Kaslo. On the way, we visited Sandon, and what we found didn't jibe with what I remembered from the 40's. Stan told me that a huge flood and subsequent looting had changed things. But I think that the actual place we visited in 1999 was a piece away from what I saw in the 40's. Shortly before reaching Kaslo, we sighted a bear cub at the side of the road.

Kaslo, on Kootenay Lake, was where a Mr. Green had lived. His son, Howard, was a long-time MP for Vancouver South, and had served in John Diefenbaker's cabinet. He was one of a number of politicians who had clamoured for the so-called return of all Japanese-Canadians to Japan after the War. When the Government quartered over 1000 Japanese-Canadians near Kaslo, the family resented it. However, Mr. Green needed frequent medical attention and one week-end, the white doctor was out of town, so that Mr. Green had to summon Dr. Shimo-Takahara. Reportedly, he liked Shimo so well that he wouldn't have the other doctor back and his long-standing prejudice came to an end.

From Kaslo, we drove around the north end of Kootenay Lake to Argenta. This village, consciously created by the Quakers some decades back, bore little resemblance to New Denver. There are no streets. People's residences are nearly all hidden by trees. We first encountered the community hall and post office. The next lane on the left belonged to the Herbisons.

I had got to know Agnes and Hugh Herbison at Victoria College, Agnes graduating in Sociology, Hugh becoming a United Church minister. We were all pacifists and ardent members of the CCF. After their marriage, Hugh was called to Vanderhoof, BC. As a pacifist during the War, Hugh was not accepted by his parishioners; he tried other occupations but finally settled into high school teaching. At one point, he headed a government commission on the Doukhobors, though I don't recall that his constructive suggestions were seriously considered by the Social Credit Government. The couple had five children, all of whom excelled in Music. Nancy, the youngest, has become world-famous as a soprano, singing under the name of Nancy Argenta, since there was already a soprano named Nancy Herbison. At the time of our visit, Wendy was teaching violin in Nelson. For many years, Agnes taught piano and directed the music of Nelson United Church, commuting from Argenta where they had lived since 1962.

Our sleeping arrangements for the Friday and Saturday night in Argenta were with an interesting family, who were local members of the same Quaker community as the Herbisons.

Our visit with Agnes was as fruitful as ever, and, again, Esther related to her strongly from the first moment. Agnes had both a grand and an upright piano.

*Agnes & Hugh Herbison*

At one point, she got out a book of *Schumann lieder*, and, for the first time in many years, Esther sang songs she had learned in the 70's. It brought tears to my eyes, for she seemed to have forgotten nothing. I had deliberately refrained from criticizing her neglect of this activity in recent years because she had been engaged in so many other things she was good at. But I had forgotten just how much joy her singing had once brought us. Agnes commented to Esther that in giving up performing she had deprived the world of a great treat.

Wendy put in an appearance while we were there. In recent years, she had not only organized a district string ensemble of high quality, but managed to stage a local performance of *The Magic Flute* with her brother David as Tamino.

On Sunday morning, we were guests at the regular Quaker meeting. For half an hour, they sang hymns with Agnes at the piano. Then followed an hour of mainly silence although it was understood that individuals could share inspiration as they felt moved to do so. After the hour, there were community announcements with discussion of the same. A small youth group was proud of their activities.

For our last night, we switched our accommodation from Nelson to Castlegar to be near the sight of our departure. I understand that air pilots didn't enjoy landing or taking off at Castlegar because of the nearness of surrounding hills and the frequency of high winds in the area. I don't know whether the nervousness was shared by frequent passengers.

I've not mentioned the mountain peaks we sighted, especially at New Denver and at Argenta. The Herbisons made a pun on the name of the one they saw from their house. Peaks are things to which I can't be indifferent. I'm sometimes disappointed because local inhabitants can't name them.

This trip with Esther was a lovely experience, as I was able to share much of my life with her. She was, and is, a very special travelling companion.

CHAPTER 88

# The Danube-Main Rivers, 2001

Shortly after what is now referred to as "9/11", someone asked me whether I felt less safe about flying than I had before this event. I answered, "About 3% less." Evidently, the others who had booked onto the same river trip as we had must have felt the same. For when the travel agent assured us that we would be leaving on—was it September 16th, almost all of the passengers appeared at Pearson Airport on schedule. One of the fellow travelers whom we met at this rendezvous was Emerson Lavender for whom Eleanor used to supply-teach at Nelson High School in Burlington when he was principal.

I found the night flight to Frankfurt didn't allow for the kind of sleep that was satisfying in the following day. After experiencing Frankfurt's enormous airport, we were bused across a wide section of tarmac to where our Lufthansa plane was ready to take us the short distance to Budapest. From there, we were bused to the river where our boat awaited us. I declined to join the bus that had been laid on to give the passengers some experience of the city. Instead, I lay down for a couple of hours, and then went for an extensive walk.

Our river boat had the strange name, Calypso, and nobody knew how it had got the name. The river boats were very long and low for passing under bridges. One could walk the upper deck, but we were warned to duck for the bridges. While we were tied up in Budapest, a Swiss boat tied up beside us. We could see through from our dining-room to theirs; the waiters wore the same uniforms in both. And their passengers used our hallway to get ashore and back.

In our first night, after dark, we were taken up river to see the lights at some of Budapest's key buildings.

The program for our cruise up the Danube and Main Rivers included a number of free side-trips where we were guided by people who had mastered English as a second language. Their English was excellent, though, occasionally, they would use a phrase that was not quite idiomatic. For instance, one of them went from the word "restoration" to "restorate" instead of "restore". I fear that, in their place, I would have uttered many more boo-boos than they.

The first side-trip was the one in Budapest which Eleanor took and I missed. She was greatly impressed with a horse show. The second one I took, while Eleanor felt the need to rest at that time. The young lady who guided us through Bratislava, the capital of Slovakia, had a wonderful voice for the purpose. Between lectures, I remarked that she would want always to avoid laryngitis. I had to explain the term. Later, as she was bidding us good-bye, she asked me, "What was that disease you mentioned?"

When describing tapestries, she used the term, amour, where we would say cupid. She also told us a story to illustrate how frequently national boundaries changed in Europe. "I was born in Hungary, went to school in Austria and I am now subject to the Government of Slovakia. Yet I have always lived in Bratislava!"

The trip took us through more than 60 locks. Some were much deeper than others. The ones with the greatest distance from high to low occurred on the canal that linked the two rivers. The shores of the canal were also designed to allow easy pedestrian movement. Several times we were cordially waved at from the shore.

In the lower river, in Hungary and Slovakia, the freight boats we met tended to be old and rusty, while the ones that appeared in Austria and Germany looked much newer. That was just one sign we encountered of varying economies.

The largest city on our route was, of course, Vienna. One morning we had a short visit to the shops of a main street. Al-

*Main River, interesting shoreline*

most everything for sale had some relation to Mozart, which amused me in view of the terrible struggle Mozart had to survive on a tiny income. While we were there, the bells of St. Thomas Cathedral sounded the hour—a very deep boom!

Great concerts are, of course, available in that city—if you plan to take them in. The one that was laid on for us happened in an attractive baroque hall. But the musicians had obviously played the same program for tourists many times before and were thoroughly bored—and sounded it!

At Passau, our first German city, we were introduced to the largest pipe organ in the world, but were there at the wrong time to hear it. At Bamburg, we were told that the local symphony orchestra was the best in Germany, though, of course, we never heard it!

At Nuremberg, we were driven past the buildings where the famous trials were held, and past the huge stadium where Hitler used to harangue the crowds. We were also told at the time that Nuremberg was now a stronghold of the leftist Social Democrats.

Toward the end of the trip, the side trips became more frequent. The boat would proceed while some of these trips were happening; then the bus would overtake the boat. Since river boats have a shallow draught, they are able to pull into the side of the canal, where there was no dock, using a long gangplank to allow the passengers to board.

We went down the Main River (pronounced 'mine') which empties into the Rhine a few kms below Frankfurt where we left it. The river boats regularly move up the Rhine to Switzerland and down it to Amsterdam. On the last day of our tour, we skipped two side trips, finding the life and verdure of the river more enjoyable than more cities.

The journey was a good introduction to the sites and life of Central Europe. We reached Frankfurt early in the morning. A major convention was going to take place, requiring the use of our boat that evening as hotel space. We were hustled out early to allow staff to prepare for the guests.

CHAPTER 89

# New York City, 2003

Before February, 2003, I had visited New York only once. In the 70's, Laura Margaret McLeod had been our hostess. As she inhabits small quarters, it has been her policy to let guests make their own sleeping arrangements while she looks after their entertainment. On that occasion, she took us to a performance of *Carmen* in a hall that had no centre aisle, but plenty of leg room between the rows. Then we went to a concert of the New York Philharmonic at Avery Fisher Hall in which a new work was included that had been developed from *Alice in Wonderland*. At Carnegie Hall, we heard the Boston Symphony under Seiji Ozawa, formerly of Toronto. To top it off, we were treated to dinner by Laura's friend Michael Borrello, a liberal Catholic who thought it wonderful that I, a Protestant, could be employed by a Catholic school board, as I was at that time.

In 2003, I became more aware of the geography of Manhattan Island. Maps and guides had previously been supplied by Esther and Jim, so that features like La Guardia Airport and 38th Street became easier to find.

After we had arrived at Pearson airport, it turned out that I had forgotten my passport. A Canadian official warned me that the Americans might not let me through. But I guess I was just lucky in the American lady who put me through She merely asked me where I had been born.

New York taxis are an institution in themselves. Registered with a municipal authority, they are all yellow and are a favourite means of transportation by many New Yorkers who, like Esther and Jim, prefer not to try to negotiate traffic and park expensively in this crowded metropolis.

Esther's and Jim's apartment is on the 53rd floor of a very high building. It is very pleasantly laid out, although it is rather a long haul from kitchen to dining area. From their dining table, you look out on the East River with its traffic of tugs and other small craft. On the near side of the river is the United Nations Building, which 'scrapes the sky' below the level of the apartment. Across the river is Long Island.

Our Valentine's Day visit to New York began on a Friday. A visitor to the apartment was Jessica Heald, who had been married in the previous June, but did not take her husband's Italian name. She was full of good spirits, and was optimistic about the company she and John were forming to market their skills. Since then they have moved to Toronto.

On the Saturday, a major protest rally was being held in New York to coincide with others across the world who wanted to head off the War on Iraq. The protesters failed to get the mayor's permission to march down the streets and had to assemble only in one place. Obviously, the authorities had little faith that orders would be obeyed. A load of sand was dumped across the main entrance to the United Nations building, effectively preventing traffic from approaching the building. A coast guard boat anchored opposite. And when Esther and I took a cab late Saturday morning, we passed one street corner where 30 police had been assembled. Later, four cruisers dashed by, sounding horns that were meant to scare.

On the Saturday morning, Esther and I went to Carnegie Hall where an orchestra was holding a dress rehearsal before an audience who had been issued passes. The orchestra, called Orpheus, operates without a conductor and has their members take turns in occupying key positions like concert master or first desk cellist. During rehearsal of each work, a member goes to the back of the hall and reports to his/her colleagues on what he heard. That morning, some very interesting new music was being played with terrific results. Especially featured was a clarinet concerto by Aaron Copland. On returning to Canada, I ordered a CD by Orpheus, but was disappointed to find only hackneyed numbers on it.

From Carnegie Hall, we went to the Riverside Church,

which had been Dr. Fosdick's preaching place. A conference of choral leaders was taking place, and we just missed a concert by an outstanding choir. It was happening in the enormous sanctuary which resembled that of a cathedral. Free brochures about the history and life of the church were very revealing.

Eleanor and Jim had gone in a different direction, and we had vaguely hoped to meet for lunch. We were surprised, therefore, to notice them in the cab behind us as we were planning a lunch stop. I had left one of my good leather gloves in a cab, so purchased a new pair along with shirts.

That afternoon Kate Brennan called. I had got to know her at Esther's Harmonic Convergence event at Muldrew a couple of years earlier. This had been a gathering of members of an e-mail network of people world-wide, which supported the philosophy of Matthew Fox. Kate was also a strong believer in peace and the importance of pacifist activities.

That evening it snowed. The ground had been dry. But now traffic was stalled by great drifts. The whole Atlantic seaboard was affected. In Canada, we take this sort of thing in our stride. In New York, it was rare enough to be devastating, partly because there is no place to put the snow!

Still, Esther, Jim and I got to church. They had been attending Christ Church (United Methodist). The shape of the front was different. When not singing, the choir was seated behind a permanent screen with the people at each end just visible. Of course, they came out to perform.

That evening, Cousin Laura came to dinner and we caught up on McLeod news. The youngest of four daughters of my great Uncle Jim, she had graduated from The University of Toronto—she had more than once been my date—but had spent the rest of her life in New York as a chartered accountant. In her time, she had run the finances of the Metropolitan Museum of Fine Art. Officially, she retired years ago. But she keeps taking on more jobs. Perhaps she is happier that way.

Our departure from New York was delayed from Monday to Wednesday because of the snow.

CHAPTER 90

# Britain, 2005

My first cousin, Ian Richardson of London, England, has been suffering some memory loss in recent years, and, having always had a tendency to self-deprecation, had not been enjoying life as he had before. Jim Sylph thought that I could do him good by a visit. So, one April, I teamed up with Esther on a trip that she managed to combine with service to clients in London.

Before flying, we spent a night in a hotel in Malton that has the same name as the very different one we used on Cromwell Road in West London. The latter was a rabbit warren, having been constructed from a group of former residences. Our room keys were little cards. With me, sometimes the card would work, sometimes not, and the card had to be used to get us through hall doors on the way. More than once I did get lost and had to be rescued by one of the staff.

However, once reached, the room was comfortable. One morning, Esther had to serve a client and left me on my own. Momentarily, I thought of using my Underground pass to visit some of London's sights. But the moment passed and, three hours later, Esther found me fast asleep!

I was intrigued by the way those passes worked. At a post that formed the gate to the trains beneath, you enter the pass into a slot, then, three quarters of a second later, and you retrieve it on the other side of the post! But, of course, once having done that, you can ride forever!

In our nine days in the UK, we arranged with Verena to visit Ian but of course we didn't want to tire him out. So we went there on a Friday afternoon for tea which turned out to be a full course dinner. And we went there for real tea the following Tuesday afternoon and visited also with Colin who came in from work on his bike. We had a jolly visit both times and

I could only hope that my visit fulfilled its purpose, where Ian was concerned.

On the Friday, Esther and I had to get to Ian's house on Woodwarde Road independently. For me, that involved changing from the subway to a train at London Bridge station, an enormous building with endless passage-ways. In the end, the train had been cancelled, and I used a cab all the rest of the way. Esther now has a great deal more experience of London than I, which is just as well. When we first crossed a busy street, she made sure that I realized that fast traffic from the left would come by just as I was about to step out!

One night we had dinner with both Colin and another cousin, Donald Reid. In 1936, my parents attended the wedding of Helen (Ian's sister) and another Donald Reid. This Donald came from that family and is a charming fellow. Now I have adjoining e-mail addresses with that name, the other being the husband of a first cousin on Mother's side!

On the week-end we flew to Edinburgh where we were guests of Penny, who showed us some of "Auld Reekie" in the gentle rain. In the apartment, we tasted her very special soup. She also hosted a Sunday afternoon gathering at which we met Andrew's Chanda whom he had recently married, his mother Patty and her interesting partner, Richard Robertson.

Moving between London's Paddington station and Heathrow, we sampled a marvelous modern train. It ran the whole distance in 15 minutes so smoothly that we had to look out the window to realize that we were moving. And, to cap it off, we were able to check our baggage from Paddington to Edinburgh, and this in reverse. Alas, that service has been withdrawn since the more recent London bombings.

I believe our journey home went smoothly or at least uneventfully. But I then resolved that I had just had my last trip across. The joys of arrival are no longer worth the effort of getting there. At the same time, I am deeply aware of the degree to which flying has made crossing easier, compared with the previous adventures involved in crossing the Atlantic by ship.

# Part 4—
# A Few Considerations

CHAPTER 91

# The New Cottage

What we called the old cottage had been built in two stages by John McPhee in 1929 and 1933. It had, of course, been built for Dad, Mother, Alec and me. (Funny to realize that, then, Eleanor didn't even exist for me and hadn't heard of our lake. Stranger still that Esther and Morrey and their descendants hadn't even been conceived. How much joy lay ahead!)

At any rate, as a family, we decided that we should either renovate the old cottage or build a new one and when we contemplated the fact that adding on to the old cottage would simply create a bigger playground for the mice, we decided in favour of a new building.

At the end of the summer of 1997, the piano was taken out the front door after a 60-year stay. That fall, the place came down—quite unwillingly, as it turned out. We had always thought of it being a frail building because when you lit a

*Moving the piano out of the old cottage after 60 years*

light inside at night, the mosquitoes would come in through the cracks and when you lay in bed in the dark, you could hear the mice scuffling around in the cupboards. With that vision of frailty, we had thought that when three walls had been removed, the fourth would collapse easily. But it took six men with chain saws to drag it down! It was as if its function in resisting countless storms was not suddenly going to be abandoned!

Morrey sat down with us and helped us figure out how we could pay for the new structure. He also played an important part by engaging Andy Mathers, a retired architect, who managed to do the job to our satisfaction without even seeing the site until after the building was up.

As we were conferring with Andy over various projected plans, he used the term, "phantom corridors" to indicate the routes people would be likely to use within the building to get from A to B. It was an important consideration, and, for the most part, I believe his predictions were right.

Morrey had to get the Gravenhurst Town Council to pass a severance to allow us to build higher than the by-laws would normally allow. He drove up especially for the occasion. We also took advantage of our having had a cottage on the given site, because the new rules required building a minimum of fifty feet from the water. As it is, we have a magnificent view of the lake from two directions.

This was the year I had an operation for an aneurism late in June, and showed a rapid recovery by appearing at Thirlestane by the end of July. That summer, Esther and Jim camped in the boat house while Esther, week-end after week-end, advised the builder, Bob Smallfield, about details. The fridge and microwave were being stored in the sleeping cabin and were thus available for use. The electric stove was there too but the wiring in the cabin was not appropriate to plug in the stove. Cooking was done on a two-burner propane stove as well as an electric kettle, both set on the boat-house steps. Of course, a real dinner happened at least once a week in Rosemary's cottage.

In fact, Esther says that for much of that summer, Rosemary hosted her for dinner and Esther often took food over to contribute. And some of her most fun dinners were the 'camping out' that they did on the boathouse steps. This was only one of many ways in which Rosemary helped with the project.

In my previous experience, when a new building was erected on the lake, the exteriors had to be painted—or at least stained—before the snow arrived. In this case, every board was painted on the ground before it was put in place. To achieve this, Esther hired the Houlihan and Brown teenagers who were old enough to paint but not old enough to have summer jobs. And I'm told that the scene resembled that one in Mark Twain's Tom Sawyer when kids were vying for the privilege of painting the fence.

For many years, the Ewings enjoyed the reputation on the lake of being the #1 example of primitive living. Then, in the 80's, we began 'disgracing' ourselves. For a couple of years, Bruce's father's "luxury launch" a 35 hp boat, formerly stored on Rideau Lake, was tied up at our dock. I forget which year our dependence on propane gas was brought to an end by our being linked with hydro, brought to us by water from the Garrards through our second bay. Then came the phone which was brought from under the lake to the boat-house. But indoor plumbing had to wait for the new cottage. The new cottage floor was built higher than the old one, to allow for a hot-water heater underneath. The ground-floor bathroom was available in the first year, plus a

*Top: new cottage, Bottom: Pro Musica visiting the new cottage*

shower, Jim's special gift, for the upstairs bathroom which was completed the following year.

Indoor plumbing, of course, meant establishing a septic tank near the parking-lot. Grass that we had not seen there began to grow and so did wild-flowers which were encouraged. The bulldozers had brought up some large boulders which have made handsome boundaries, on the cottage side of the parking lot.

The kitchen cupboards, more convenient by far than any we had previously enjoyed, were built by a Gravenhurst specialist. After the job, he remarked that, while he had been accustomed to finding that builders usually made their framework with inaccuracies amounting sometimes to ⅜th of an inch, with Bob's work, he found all measurements to be exactly right only needing to use one little shim.

On Labour Day week-end, the architect present for the first time, the cottage was officially opened with Morrey as the proud MC. On Thanksgiving week-end, we used it for the first time. Rosemary Bartlett and Suzanne Perreard joined us, and we enjoyed a full turkey dinner with all the trimmings. With electric blankets on all the beds and brand new flannelette sheets, as well as fires in the new wood stove, everyone was very snug.

## CHAPTER 92

# Animals and God's Other Creatures

Except for six months in Lemon Creek, I have never had a pet. Because of Morrey's allergies, there was never a pet in our family home, except for an abortive attempt on his part to raise guppies. But my encounters with what are sometimes referred to as 'dumb animals' have usually been happy.

The collie dog that lived at Kenmore, my Uncle and Aunt's farm was called Jack. He and I got along well. But, when Alec appeared on the scene, Jack was jealous of the baby, who was the centre of attention, and bit him twice. When he sold the farm, Uncle Don arranged to take Jack to Uncle Jim McLeod's farm at Highland home, about ten miles away. I was a passenger in the Ford when he drove him to his new home. But the dog was allowed his freedom while my uncles visited. When we got back to Kenmore, Jack was there ahead of us!

During my school days in Oshawa, I went on numerous country walks, and, as often as not, a farm dog would attach itself to me. And I would have to tell the animal very firmly that it could not come into our house.

At Muldrew Lake, I have tended to favour those creatures that don't come into the cottage. Whether that is why I am not a fisherman, one can only guess. As a teenager, I twice pulled in a 4-pound bass, once off Dales' Island, once off our point. But that was the sum total of my efforts in that field. However, I have always treated mice as an enemy, whether adults or babies. But, while a squirrel did get into the old cottage a few years ago, I have usually liked having squirrels and chipmunks around. Not so raccoons. For a time, people made pets of baby raccoons, then released them into the woods as they grew up.

Of course, they had not been taught to survive on their own and had to invade cottages as their only source of food. When one tore a hole is our screen-door and demolished a basket of peaches, and then had the temerity to return mid-morning, I grabbed a broom handle and ended its life. Some people thought me heartless. But I have failed to repent. I have not dealt with skunks or porcupines in this way. But, of course, I did everything else to discourage their presence.

In the 30's, Dad and I hiked several times from Green Point to what is now called Pidgeon Bay, following two ridges of rock. Once, on our return we encountered at close range, two baby eagles. We were delighted, although the eagles plainly were not!

In 1928, Margaret Dale and I found a frog at the back bay of the island that measured fully a foot from head to tail. I used to love the evening symphonies the bull-frogs made with their "r-r-rump". We have always loved the whip-poor-wills who have, alas, not now been heard for many years. But the loons have been a different story. I don't always hear their four different calls. But they do sound. I have often heard a mournful cry turn suddenly into a laugh when a period of wet weather ends and a fresh west wind begins. And I have often admired the vigour of a loon's wings as it flies purposefully from one area to another.

In 1945, in Lemon Creek, Helen Hurd's and Gertrude Hamilton's cat had a litter and Joe Grant and I got one of the kittens. Its favourite resting-place was in my bed by my feet; its favourite activity was crawling up my pant-legs. At first we fed it from a saucer at one end of the kitchen. Then one day we changed the location to the other end of the bed-room. But, before he would touch his milk in the new location, he insisted on visiting the old location to be sure no food was there before returning to the new place. We put him out at night and welcomed him back in the morning. But one morning he wasn't there and we later found his body with the marks of dog's teeth in his fur.

I was only once bitten by a dog. During election canvassing, I noticed a police dog in the window. The dog got to the front door before his master, and when the door was opened, the dog lunged at my belt before the man could control it. Luckily, I was wearing a jacket of tough material and was not hurt. At another time, a resident marvelled at how I had got past a dog that was tethered on the front lawn. But, I wish I had a dollar for every house where the owner had to spend over a minute overpowering the noisy brute before I could say a word.

In Chapter 21, I told of Uncle Don's clever dog. One day in the back yard, I denied this animal some food because he had just been sick. My uncle had to educate me, one who had never had a dog of my own. He said, "Perhaps you don't know, Donald. A dog can be sick and go on eating without doing itself any harm."

CHAPTER 93

# Eleanor & Our Many Moves

One often hears about the hardship that arises when someone's employment necessitates a move to a new community, and usually that person's spouse is reported to find the uprooting quite devastating. They find their old patterns of life hard to duplicate, and it sometimes takes them a long time before their new life is enjoyed. In some cases, the situation has even led to divorce. Eleanor has been quite different.

Since 1948, when Eleanor and I were married, she followed me through four different moves. In each case, she entered energetically into the new situation, quickly made strong friendships, and undertook projects, and sometimes jobs, that made good use of her talents and enriched the community into which we had moved.

When we arrived at our Quebec Street apartment in Regina, a group of friends were there to see me carry Eleanor over the threshold. It helped that, in the four months that I had lived in Regina, I had made contact with the adult education group who tended to gather at the home of the director, David Smith. At our wedding in Cooksville, Dorothy Van Luven, with whom both Dad and Eleanor had taught in Oshawa, observed, "Don knows Norah McCullough." Eleanor hadn't heard of her then. But Norah was part of the group at our door, and she quickly became the friend we saw every two or three days at each other's homes. (I remember how Norah showed great originality when putting away the dishes she had helped us wash!)

Very early in our stay, our landlord started turning down the thermostat during the day. Eleanor soon took a part-time job in the correspondence branch of the Department of Education. She said it was to keep warm during the day. But I'm sure that she also felt that she needed to keep active. The office where she worked was run in a very dictatorial manner, employees being treated like children. But she stuck it out for a few months.

At one point, Eleanor accepted an invitation to lead a choral group in the University Women's Club. A member of that group was wife to the "tin soldier" who ran the correspondence branch—and altogether made up for him, I was given to understand.

Eleanor's main project in Regina was to assist Norah at the Arts Board. Through this activity, she got to see something of Saskatchewan. Mostly, she edited the Arts Board newsletter, and one issue—on orange-coloured stiff paper—was a selection of Christmas carols from many lands.

We also got to know the Howards. He was a retired lawyer who gratuitously advised us, in our difficulties with landlord Vasilash, that we were entitled to quiet possession. Mrs. Howard took a keen interest in the arts.

One day, Eleanor exclaimed, "Look who's coming next month!" and she mentioned an international celebrity. "To Regina?" I asked. "No, to Toronto!" Had she treated Regina as just an extension of Ontario?

However, Eleanor did feel closer to home when we moved to Ottawa in 1950. During our year on Bay Street, Bill Dale moved to the National Gallery. He stayed with us while finding lodgings. He came often with his viola for the "Chamber Music Society of Lower Bay Street" and finally produced his friend, Jane Laidlaw. Gordon Jocelyn was teaching at Fisher Park High School and dropped in often till he was able to bring Joy and the children to Ottawa.

We also made the acquaintance of the Milners who had the apartment below ours and with whom we did reciprocal baby-sitting. When the Royal Ballet brought Swan Lake to a large down-town movie-house, the Trembles (ticket agents) refused mail orders and opened the box-office only on one Tuesday morning. Eleanor organized several of our friends to take turns in the line-up from 7:00 am.

Eleanor had two successive music jobs in Ottawa. She became an accompanist for children's choirs when John Sutherland was music director for the Public School Board. She was also, of course, an ATCM, and only stopped playing due to arthritic fingers a few years later. One year she directed the Junior Choir of Glebe Collegiate, housed in the far end of the High School of Commerce building. At the local competitive festival, the choir won first place due to her interpretation of *Cherry Ripe*.

And, of course, it was in Ottawa that Suzanne Butler came into our lives. She was working on her first novel which was subsequently published as *My Pride, My Folly*. On several occasions, Eleanor sat down with her when the wording of some passage was being finalized. I recall one session:

> *Eleanor: This would sound better.*
> *Suzanne: But that isn't what I mean!*

While in Goderich, Eleanor found satisfaction in dropping in to school choir rehearsals of mine and offering suggestions. Since I was involved with many kinds of preparation for the annual Huron County Music Festival, this gave her a lot of scope. In the spring of 1955, I was involved with about 100 of the 400-odd entries. There were several different massed choirs from the different grade levels. There were double trios, duets and solos from each of under 8-year-olds, under 11-year-olds, under 14-year-olds.

Goderich had an amateur men's chorus called the Harbouraires. In Cyril Hampshire's adjudication of this group in 1954, he said, "What basses!" Afterwards, Eleanor told him, "You can't have them!" The best of these basses were also in the North Street Choir.

The move to Burlington was more long-lasting. A few months after our arrival, Trinity Church needed a new leader for the Junior Choir. I received a phone call from a man named Sam Ferguson whom I already knew. He offered me the church job, but I put Eleanor on the phone. It turned out that the Junior Choir comprised a rather unmanageable crew of over 60 kids. One of Eleanor's earliest decisions was to split the choir into a Training Choir of grades 2 and 3 and a Junior Choir of Grades 4 to 6. At that stage, Trinity had two Sunday services; the children's choirs were in the loft at 9:30 and the Adult Choir at 11:00. I recall the Training choir singing a tune to *Jesus Bids Us Shine* that was much more colourful than the one that was better known. The Junior Choir had lots of wonderful anthems, like the Alta Lind Cook setting of *Gentle Mary Laid Her Child*, with a descant by Harvey Perin; but also lively folk songs like the Uist folk song. Both were used in Christmas and spring concerts.

One of these concerts raised money which was used to create a singing scholarship. Later, the Women's Association added to the fund, so that more than one singer could benefit. Once the singer was launched, parents would pick up the cost from the second year on. In the second year, Esther won one of the two places. George Veary, of the Anglican cathedral in Hamilton, who made the decisions, insisted that Esther had to overcome the handicap of being the choir leader's daughter, but in spite of this, she was an obvious choice. The teacher of the female scholarship winners was Helen Simmie, and parents took turns driving the kids to Toronto once a week.

As the more reliable choir members grew older, Eleanor was able to organize a Youth Choir which sang in three parts. One year, as part of a national study program, Eleanor was asked to do a record of music from Trinidad and Brazil, which were being studied. I dug up and arranged folk songs from these countries, and the junior and youth choirs practised them for the recording sessions. Then Esther, Eleanor James and Don Story, all scholarship winners, recorded the individual parts so that amateur groups across Canada could learn to do the songs in parts. Eleanor's colourful introductions rounded out the project.

The biggest event of the Youth Choir was *Let There Be Joy*, a ten-minute work which Eleanor commissioned Keith Bissell to compose. The words came from a book of Prayers from the Gaelic, edited by Alexander Muir. The music was scored for SAB Choir, soprano and tenor soloists, flute and cello obligates, and accompaniments by organ alternating with Orff xylophones and glockenspiels. The performance was dedicated to the founders of Trinity Church and the attendant publicity had the effect of filling the church. Of course a lot of other music was used to fill the program and the more traditional stuff tended to be better appreciated than Bissell's modern harmonies. But, for those who took part, *Let There Be Joy* was loved. Esther, as soprano soloist, was troubled with threatened laryngitis, and Keith gave an alternative to the high note that formed the climax of the work. But, on the occasion, her voice soared and the note was beautiful.

Through the decade that Eleanor gave to this enterprise, Gordon Douglas was organist and sometimes gave good support. But he tended to play politics in a way that marred a lot of the experience. For instance, when an alto or a bass was doing well in the Youth Choir, Gordon would sometimes raid this group for his Senior Choir. He was a good organist, but an indifferent choir master.

## CHAPTER 94

# What If?

Have you ever wondered how history might have been affected if one event had turned out differently?

What if my brother, Alec, had not died of a streptococcus brain infection in 1934? We were told that a drug came onto the market the following year (was it penicillin, or sulpha?) that might have saved him. What if it had become available that much sooner?

Alec was judged to be a delicate child. So something else might have taken him away. But let's suppose that he became stronger in his teens and actually lived to 2004 and beyond. Would his interests have coincided with mine? Comparing us as children might give us clues. I was learning piano while he was learning violin, though on a group basis. I loved to have my back stroked; he couldn't stand it. One day he came home from school, devastated to find that our mother wasn't about. Today, we would be used to people's comings and goings. But, on this occasion, he fairly grabbed me and sobbed, "Do you know where mother is?"

Would Alec have caught our mother's interest in peace? Would he have embarrassed our Dad by refusing to attend a meeting of high school cadets? Would he have enlisted in World War II, perhaps been killed in action, perhaps survived with a permanent injury, or perhaps just with a different perspective on war from me?

What occupation or profession might Alec have taken up? Would he have been a success at it? A professional success? A financial success—or both? Would this work have taken him to the other end of the world, to many different places, or close to home? Might we have become partners in the same work? On the other hand, might we have perceived each other's work as mutually exclusive?

What sort of marriage might he have had? Might he have found a wife who shared his convictions right down the line, with the danger that their offspring might become intolerant of those who are different? Might she have shared so few of his beliefs that the marriage wouldn't last? Or would he have been lucky like me in finding a spouse whose basic values were the same, who sharply disagreed on many specific points, but who helped me build a relationship based on mutual respect?

What sort of first cousins might Esther and Morrey have had? Nieces and/or nephews? Wouldn't Aunt Mary have enjoyed them!? Alec would now be around 15 years retired. Would he have started his memoirs? Would he have been cleverer than I in figuring out mechanical things? Would his grandchildren have been teaching him to manage a computer? Would his dwelling depend as heavily on electrical supply as my house is?

Who would have been the main influences in Alec's life? Who would have influenced his political thinking as J. S. Woodsworth did mine? Who would have got him thinking about his faith as Jim Finlay did for me? Would some professor have given him guiding principles for his chosen field in addition to a whole raft of funny stories? Would there have been another Healey Willan? And would someone have spurred his creativity just by being the devil's advocate from time to time?

And how would Alec's presence have affected Muldrew Lake? He and I shared five summers there. But he died before getting involved in any of our canoe-trips. Would he have had my luck in interesting his descendants in the place? If so, would he have acquired alternative property on the lake? Or would the larger number of family users have affected the building of the new cottage? Perhaps even the timing of the new cottage?

And what if Bobby Kennedy had not been assassinated in 1972? Would he have defeated George McGovern for the Democratic nomination, and, with his personality, would he have defeated Nixon as President? Would the country have thus been spared Watergate, and some of Nixon's other acts of misrule? Would a longer tenure of Democratic government made it easier for someone like Reagan to get in four years sooner? What would Bobby Kennedy's legacy have been? Would it have been more beneficial for the common man in the USA than his brother's had been in 1960-63?

What if the American presidential election of 2000 had had a different result—it almost did? Here my speculation has a negative aspect since I don't recall Al Gore's attitude to things. Would he have given the corporations a massive tax-cut with consequent service-cuts bringing misery to many more Americans than before? Would he have opposed Kyoto and similar measures to save the environment? Would he have refused to cooperate with other nations in ridding the world of landmines? Would he have declined to participate in a world court where American citizens would be subject to judicial decisions on the same basis as people from the Third World? Would he have induced Congress to pay America's full dues to the UN, and recognized the UN as the supreme international body?

What would have happened on 9/11? Would American foreign policy have created the atmosphere in which terrorists would feel the time had come to strike? If so, would and could American authorities have deflected the second plane before it reached the tower? Would the President have invaded Afghanistan and/or Iraq? Would Tony Blair have done it alone? Would the movie, *The Passion of Christ*, have had the wide appeal it has had if wars had not occurred in so immediate a past?

Suppose Bob Rae had set up the Social Contract by negotiation, rather than by legislation? If any action had been taken which involved the consent of individual unions, would the 'Social Contract' have been a weapon that unionists and other idealists have used against the NDP ever since?

Suppose Bob Rae had proceeded to set up Government Auto insurance? Suppose rumoured lawsuits under NAFTA had been made by an American Insurance Company? Suppose, then, that Bob had been unwilling to back down and had called an election, would the voters have sustained him?

If Employment Equity had been introduced nearer the beginning then the end of Rae's mandate, might the idea have taken root and been harder for Harris to slash?

Suppose Peter Kormos had not been dropped from the NDP cabinet. Would the Government have been stronger or weaker?

Throughout the NDP mandate, there was a significant body of left-wing opinion which refused to support the government, and gleefully looked forward to our defeat—likely at that time by the provincial Liberals. Would they have come round if Bob had put his reputation on the line over insurance? Or does it matter what this group thought?

In 1974-75, Morrey was making plans for post-graduate work, after working for the BC Government for over three years. Following various applications, he was accepted by York University in England, before getting into Harvard. Suppose he had gone to York. Would his employment opportunities have been different when he finished? Would he have settled—and perhaps married—overseas? How would that have affected our trips to the Old Land? Might his influence within the family have been less? What would Esther be doing now if she could not have joined her brother in a business partnership in Toronto?

Suppose there had not been a convention in Halifax on a certain week-end in the fall of 1980, forcing him to find Sharon in her apartment? Suppose he had not even thought of getting in touch with that acquaintance in Ottawa who steered him to Sharon. The mind boggles!

Another question: People argue about what really happened during what we call the Resurrection of Jesus. But what if it had not taken place at all? To start with, the Disciples, all of whom had returned to their former occupations, would probably have stayed there. And would we, 2000 years later, have even heard of Jesus?

Would the Hebrew religion have spread in the way Christianity did? Would Emperor Constantine have taken it over for his military purposes as he did Christianity? In the absence of the Roman Catholic Church, what would the middle ages have been like? What would the architecture of the ages have looked like? Would those universities that were founded by churches ever have started? Would great music have been more sterile without the Christian religion for something to build around? Would the institution of marriage have flourished? Would the patriarchy that dominated biblical society and came to characterize the Catholic Church have been more or less a feature of our world? Would you or I have been conceived?

Or, failing the Resurrection, would God have found an alternative way of steering us toward the idea that love is what works in his world? The fact that the Resurrection did happen (and ultimately the only proof of it was the changed lives of the apostles) has always given encouragement to people who have taken a stand on something and apparently lost out completely. "Where, grave, is thy victory?" Indeed. And did Christ die to save us from our sins? Without the Resurrection, we'd never have known.

CHAPTER 95

# Second Thoughts— After the Event

Most people regret something in their past. My greatest regrets have to do with situations that I might have handled differently, if only I could have thought it out in advance. In other words, hindsight has been so much easier than foresight.

As a member of Carleton United Church in Toronto, I was not very active because my university studies took so much of my time. But I did manage to attend a meeting of the Music committee when something controversial was coming up. The Sunday broadcasts on CKCL had gone on for some years, and someone had noticed that a few of the older women in the choir who were seated near the microphone had squeaky voices, and it was suggested that the young man who had taken over leadership of the choir should move these ladies farther back. The committee took no action because, since the ladies in question held prominent positions in the congregation, referring to them as inferior singers might have serious repercussions all round. I left the meeting thinking the committee was shilly-shallying. More mature thought suggested the obvious solution. If the choir leader were to announce a general change in the choir seating-plan, no one should feel picked on. Besides, why assume the worst interpretation on the part of the ladies in question? They might be painfully aware of their shortcomings. But 'obvious solutions' don't jump into one's consciousness all at once.

A few decades later, Jack Kirkham was chairing a meeting of the Chalmers congregation. Taylor Evans sat near the front where he could have some control over the way things went. Jack made a ruling to which Taylor objected. But he didn't

445

move to overturn the ruling because he had no assurance that his motion would pass. I tangled with Taylor over this. But the perfect response didn't come to me till far into the night: "Mr. Evans can't have it both ways. Either he moves censure and takes a chance on what the meeting does with his motion, or he should graciously accept the ruling of the chair." And I might have added that, when he chose, few people in Chalmers knew better how to be gracious.

CHAPTER 96

# Money

In a life as long as mine, inflation has to loom large. Somewhere I still have a scribbler from the 1930's in which my mother noted every detailed expenditure. I remember 'butter, 20c.' At that, the price for a pound has increased only about 30 times since my childhood years. However, in December, 1926, when Dad bought his first house (near the northern boundary of Oshawa) and assumed his first mortgage, the price of a two-story brick house with three bedrooms and, of course, just one bathroom upstairs, the price was $3600. It would have cost about 100 times that today. In July, 1926, Dad bought the only car he ever owned, a 1924 four-door Chevrolet Sedan, for $600. It worked well except that the clutch kept losing teeth which had to be replaced for the car to move. In December, he decided that driving was not his 'thing', sold the car for $400 and bought the house. The car probably retailed new at about $900. Today the corresponding car, much improved, would likely cost $30,000 new. Finally, I remember that a letter would pass through the mails to anywhere in Canada for 3 cents, while an open postcard could be used locally for 2 cents. Comparatively, the 2006 cost of mailing a letter for 49 cents is probably a bargain.

My high school years all occurred during the Great Depression. Teachers' salaries in Oshawa were cut by one third. Yet my parents always seemed to manage financially. Mother used to tell me, "Your father always has money in the bank." When Alec died, the brain specialist in Toronto billed him for $500, explaining that he was cutting his regular fee of $1000 in half because the operation was not successful. How Dad found that kind of money in the 30's, I will never know.

From all this, I learned to make one penny do the work of two. Up until 1936 when I left for university, as a school student, I got my hair cut for 15 cents. When I went to Toronto, I asked older students to tell me of a good 25-cent barber, but was told I wouldn't find a barber within ten miles of Toronto that charged less than 40 cents! After one year in Burwash Hall, and two in an attic room on Bloor Street, I applied to get into the Campus Cooperative residence. When considering the question of whether I would be accepted, I told Mother that the coop was for poor students. "How poor do you have to be?" she asked.

My father-in-law used to say during the fifties, "Before the war, we lived on an inadequate income. Since the war, our income has been more than adequate." During and after the war (II, of course), he was employed in labour relations representing management. The contrast between his standard of living and mine in this period was hard to ignore. He spent a lot of money building a new house in the centre of the orchard. On the other hand, as a conscientious objector, I worked in the Forest Service on 50 cents a day plus my keep. As a teacher in the Japanese-Canadian camp, I was limited to $50. a month. When there was first talk of our marriage, I received a letter from Eleanor's Dad saying that he thought Eleanor would expect "a minimum of gracious living".

By this time, my parents had retired. Knowing they were less well-off than he, Dad Dillon was always generous, helping with things like transportation. Once, while driving me into the city, he referred to a trip across Ontario that my parents were planning, and told me to offer his services in driving them there. I said something about this being "hard to ask." "You didn't ask it, did you? Well shut up!" Then, in a gentler tone, he said that he never offered to do anything that didn't give him "a lot of pleasure".

Meanwhile, my parents were generous in their own way. When they had retired and were managing on a limited income, I was struggling to find my feet. From time to time, Dad would slip me a hundred or two, just because he had managed to finish a carefully planned month with that much left over.

With me, the addition was always gratefully received.

In 1951, we bought our first house—at 30 Pansy Avenue in Ottawa. Neither this purchase nor the subsequent one in Burlington in 1956 could have happened if Aunt Muriel, then living in BC, had not loaned us the down payment at 5% interest. Between March '56 and November '58, when we got our first car, we accepted a great many rides to the centre of Burlington from generous neighbours. Even after that, I would sometimes accept one of those rides, so Eleanor could use the DKW during the day.

It was some time after I was teaching in public schools before I was able to give Eleanor much of that "gracious living". But she never once complained. She would respond to the shortage by seeking—and finding—means of supplementing our income. Less than three months after I took her to Regina, she got employed by the correspondence branch of the Department of Education. Later she worked for the Arts Board. In Ottawa there were other projects, and, in Goderich, she was, for a year, Director of Music at North Street Church and she did piano teaching. For ten years in Burlington she worked very hard as leader of the junior and youth choirs of Trinity, then Wellington Square, churches. Before leaving Burlington, she taught music for two years in the public schools of Milton. After arriving in Guelph, she taught in several of the public schools of Wellington County. And, in five of the 70's years, she directed the choir of Chalmers church. These activities not only brought in much-needed income. They also allowed her to give her own kind of leadership and to be so much more than just a housewife.

When Esther and Morrey left home, we, of course, paid a substantial part of the cost of their university education. But, following that, they were both financially independent of us, and, after they got established, were earning more than I had ever earned as a salaried teacher.

Still, I was able, after our purchase of 264 Woolwich in 1974 and the building of the "Studio" at Muldrew in 1978, to pay off both mortgages before my retirement in 1982. In retirement, I have enjoyed one of the best teachers' pensions, besides the available government pensions. In addition, in 1982, I was able to buy an annuity with a bonus from unused sick-leave, and from that to make annual donations to about 25 of my favourite charities.

Eleanor and I have long had agreement on which kind of expense each would cover. In 1986, we sold our Woolwich Street house and bought a smaller one on Glasgow Avenue ending up with a bit left over. That helped us take a couple of trips to Norway in 1990 and on the Danube river in 2001.

Meanwhile we continue to live frugally supporting, as we can, our church and other charities as well as the NDP.

CHAPTER 97

# A Loner

Once, when Eleanor and I were getting acquainted, she characterized herself in words from Kipling's "Just-so Stories", as the "cat that walked by herself in the wild, wet woods." More typically, Eleanor has been an out-going gracious, person. For instance, on hearing someone making music, she would often ask, "Do you mind if I make a suggestion?" And as guests are arriving for a party, Eleanor has always managed to convey great pleasure that they have arrived. On looking back, I feel that I have been the lone operator far more often.

It was Dad who got me in the habit of taking long, country walks, "to get fresh air and exercise." But far more of my walks were taken alone. After school I would go up a branch railway line that seldom saw a train, sometimes trying my skill at balancing on a rail. On one such occasion in winter, I rubbed my ears vigorously when facing a bitter north wind, but forgot to rub them after I had turned around and was enjoying the relief of having the wind behind me. Of course, my ears froze and had doubled in size by the time I reached 602 N. Simcoe Street.

On Saturdays, there would be longer walks. Occasionally, my McLeod cousins would go along. This happened when we walked all the way to a lagoon several miles east of the Oshawa access to Lake Ontario—there and back! But I often did that sort of thing alone.

On the 10-minute walk to high school, I would put on my "ten-league boots" and pass everyone else on the street. Perhaps I sometimes walked with someone else, but I have no recollection of accompanying dialogue.

From the time we were married, I got the breakfast. Indeed, for a time, Eleanor didn't get up until I brought her coffee. Accordingly, I developed a system for doing it—and other meals too—with built-in variety. The system depended on twice-weekly shopping. Occasionally, Eleanor would do some imaginative shopping that resulted in a dinner party or other social occasion. Then it was back to my less interesting but reliable system.

I applied the same systematic organization to supervising music. I like to think that my system worked—for me. But it wasn't anything that someone else could usefully adopt. Before the end of my last year before retirement, I took my successor with me on my rounds for a week. He found that he couldn't stand "the pace," and in the fall, he set up a much more relaxed routine.

It was the same when I organized spring concerts for my grades 5 and 6 classes. My organization of rehearsals over two-and-a-half months was elaborate, and strictly something that only I could operate. Then I made a very complicated plan for the order in which the children were to stand, and one of my long-suffering principals had to put it into action. The plan always worked. But I'm sure the principal was glad when it was over.

When I ran an election canvass, I began by adopting a plan that I got from organizers like Michael Lewis. But the plan I used would be mine, and I would stick stubbornly to it till the election was over.

My activity with the Conference Prayer Cycle was entirely a personal development. It was started in response to a suggestion by a member of Chalmers Church that the prayers would be more meaningful if more were known about the churches being prayed for. But the means of obtaining that information, the questions I would ask, the way the story was told and the method of distribution of the material were all my own. Ann Fleming, formerly of the Conference office, has called this a special "ministry". But I suspect that it will die when I have to give it up.

It has been said that, if you want to develop workable new

ideas, don't use a committee. But, in most cases, good ideas that come from individuals are better developed by a committee. Since I have been such a loner, that has not always happened. And the systems that have worked for me will work for others only when they are liberally interpreted according to circumstances.

This has a big effect on my success or failure in asking others to carry out my wishes. In 1954, I prepared a group of high school students to take part in a provincial high school choir that was conducted in Toronto by Don Wright. Good Friday seemed like an excellent opportunity to rehearse the group, and I arranged for them all to come to our house at 9:00 in the morning. Somehow I had thought that they could simply rehearse throughout the day. But I found that by noon they were exhausted. In my plans I had imagined that finding the time was all that mattered. I just hadn't considered the kids' capacity. As it turned out, they achieved what I wanted in the shorter time. But I hadn't got inside their skins, as it were.

When selling NDP memberships, my success is often due to finding people who hadn't joined only because they had never been asked. I have been less successful in getting busy people to help me do the same job. It would be nice if we could find a way to share these tasks.

CHAPTER 98

# Books

My earliest memories feature being read to. I know my parents both did it, though, with Dad, I recall mainly books of devotion like Harry Emerson Fosdick's *The Meaning of Service*, *The Meaning of Faith*, etc. But somehow, Mother's readings have stayed with me.

I'm sure it started with the nursery rhymes. Once when I was little, there was an appeal for children's books to be donated to the poor. My parents gave me a choice of two books that I would part with. I chose my copy of the Arabian Nights, keeping something that wasn't nearly as dramatic.

Of course, I was started on such English classics as *Alice in Wonderland* and *Through the Looking Glass*; then the books of *Winnie the Pooh* and other creations by A. A. Milne. The Pooh characters so typified people we knew that we have kept referring to them long after those first readings. For instance, Tigger couldn't seem to find any food he liked, but finally tasted and liked Roo's medicine. Said Pooh, "So that's what Tiggers like." In his earliest years, my grandson, Alexander, would refuse all manner of foods, especially cereals. Then one day I was eating bran buds. He tried them and liked them. "So that's what Tiggers like," we said.

When I was quarantined for three weeks in my Oshawa bed—I think the complaint was whooping cough—my mother read me J. M. Barrie's *The Little Minister*. Each day I couldn't wait for the next chapter. I recall something of someone's description of the gypsy girl, "She was snod, but no unca snod. She was kippit up to the nines. She was gae orra put on." This is, of course, a Lowland dialect.

At one point, a conservative member of the little minister's church reacts to the introduction of paraphrases, the re-writing of the Psalms in metric form, so that they could be sung.

"The Psalms of David rise straight to Heaven," he said, "but the paraphrases stick in the ceiling o' the kirk!"

*David Copperfield* was my introduction to Dickens. Bob Nixon, a cousin, and a voracious reader, once asked me if I had got to the place where Steerforth was drowned. As I didn't yet know that Steerforth was to meet that untimely end, this rather spoiled that part of the story. But, since David Copperfield's first marriage was unsatisfactory, but his second one very happy, I could never forget the emphasis with which Mother read from the last page, "O Agnes, O my soul!"

Growing up, I read several historical novels by G.A. Henty. *Bonnie Prince Charlie, With Wolfe in Canada,* and *With Clive in India* were three of the titles. Then there were the *In Search of...* books by H.V. Morton. I think my favourite was *In Search of Scotland*. I remember the epitaphs, recalling the Jacobites: "Here lies James Stewart. He'll rise." Another one:

> *Here lies Peas*
> *Under the grass, and under the trees.*
> *Of course not his body,*
> *It's only the pod.*
> *He's burst his shell and gone to God.*

And I forget the name of the young Scot who published an encyclopedia at an early age. A family reaction was recorded in the book: "Your father always kenned ye were a fool. But noo the hale world'll ken!"

From France, of course, came Dumas' *The Count of Monte Cristo* and *Twenty Years After*. In the former, the hero escapes from the Chateau d'If, by communicating with another prisoner, and taking that prisoner's place when he died, so that when they threw what they thought was a dead body into the Mediterranean Sea, he survived by cutting off the weight that was supposed to sink him. Scenes like that were always more vividly portrayed in the book than in the film version.

From the USA came many books. In Mark Twain's *Tom Sawyer*, Tom and Becky being lost in one of the great caves of

Kentucky was again better in the book than in the film.

An American named Winston Churchill (no relation to the English leader) produced a number of novels that came my way. The titles all featured the letter C, for example, *Mr. Crew's Career*. A Canadian series appeared about Scottish settlers in Oro Township on the west side of Lake Simcoe. In one, *The Silver Maple*, there was a lot of Scottish dialect. 'Roarin' Sandy's Archie' was one of the characters. It also told of naughty stunts like that of the boys who would quietly sneak out of church as the minister was beginning the long prayer, race around the concession and be back before the prayer was finished. I've forgotten the author's name.

High School English, in the upper grades, was divided between authors (literature) and composition (grammar and writing). I was always better at composition. I once, in grade 10, got 100 in a grammar exam. I liked the systematic following of rules. My difficulty with authors was the fact that I was such a slow reader. The study of a novel would be over before I had finished reading it. The Shakespeare plays I found easier, especially when we acted out the parts. One year, we were studying *The Merchant of Venice*. I got to attend a professional performance in Toronto and in class the next day I was allowed to act the part of Shylock in a scene with Tubal. I overacted, of course, in imitation of what I had heard in Toronto. But I had to admit it was fun.

Another day, in a grade twelve class (we called it fourth form), we had a visit from the principal. We had been studying a long poem (Was it Browning's *My Last Duchess*?) and some students had been finding it heavy going. Mr. O'Neill urged us to "master the stuff". His interest in language appeared another morning at an assembly. A few days earlier, King George V had made the first of a series of Christmas broadcasts. Mr. O'Neill found that the text was a masterpiece and said so.

Then, of course, there was Robert Louis Stevenson. *Treasure Island* was first, followed a few years later by *Kidnapped* and its sequel; then by *The Master of Ballentree* and, among other south sea stories, *The Bottle Imp.* The latter is based on a notion that, while in one's possession, the object could be used for all sorts of magic purposes, but that, if you owned it when you died, you would go to Hell. There was also the difficult rule that it could only be sold for less than you paid for it. Of course, the price got down to a British farthing and the owner despaired of selling it. However, someone found a smaller currency and decided that, since he was going to Hell anyway, he might as well have some fun by buying the thing!

In Sunday School, we were given passages of Scripture to memorize. Someone once gave me a sumac bowl in return for committing *I Corinthians 13* to memory. And, every Sunday, we learned a *Golden Text*. Of course, those were the days when the *King James Bible* was the only translation used and, frequently the text was chosen for its literary value alone.

In school, we always had poems to learn by heart. There seemed to be a consensus among educators that certain poems, or the poems of certain authors, were superior to all others. Perhaps, it was just recognized that, to have verse available in later years simply enriches one's experience. Once, in Ottawa, when Bill Dale and I were constructing some shelves, I started on Tennyson, "How dull it is to pause, to make an end, as though to breathe were life." He responded with Shakespeare, "There is a divinity that shapes our ends, rough hew them how we will!" And why does this still come to mind, "Along the line of smoky hills, the crimson forest stands"?

Another branch of reading has involved detective fiction. I suppose it began with Conon Doyle's *Sherlock Holmes.* What was the attraction? Was it Holmes' cleverness in solving mysteries? Was it the way he proved conventional wisdom wrong? Was it the charming interplay between him and Watson? Was it the phrases of speech that no one else thought to use? Was it the depiction of earlier times in England? Who will ever know? But I relished the phrase, "Elementary, my dear Watson."

Then there were Dorothy Sayers' Peter Wimsey books. Bunter, from his different station in life as Peter's butler, is always an essential part of the detection. *Murder Must Advertise* which deals with the realm of commerce, mentioning "the tremendous commercial importance of the relatively poor", and *The Nine Taylors*, built around the tradition of change-ringing in Anglican Cathedrals, stand out. The developing relationship with Harriet, leading eventually to *Busman's Honeymoon*, made for interesting complications.

It seems that the best detective fiction has either been written by English or Scottish authors, or consists of stories that happen there. Why is that? Other countries have had just as clever criminals, just as clever detectives. Are the British more imaginative?

Agatha Christie created Hercule Poirot, the Belgian who made his name in England with his 'little gray cells', and Jane Marple, the unassuming villager, both of whom show up the slow-witted police by solving the mysteries in unconventional ways. I'm not sure that I ever really followed the detection, especially in the TV versions. What I enjoyed was the detective's air of superior intelligence, superior wisdom and quiet dominance. You just knew that this person had to win in the end.

I have enjoyed Ann Perry's picture of Victorian life when the class system was in full flower. Elizabeth George portrays, vividly, racial tensions in modern England. And Brother Cadfael is Ellis Peters' way of depicting mediaeval life along the Welsh border. In all of these, the background enhances the story.

In general, however, I most enjoy fiction when there is character development. For me, a happy ending is only satisfactory if the ending is the result of a development in at least one character, rather than outward circumstances. That is even true of Dick Francis' ingenious stories built around English racing.

Three novels with a different structure have recently (in 2006) been published. *Bel Canto* by Ann Patchett explores human relations in an artificial situation. A large gathering of notables from around the world, and speaking many different languages, attend a dinner held in "a South American country" at the mansion of the vice-president. The occasion is a birthday party for a Japanese business man and the gift, the contracting to perform of a world-famous soprano. After her performance, the whole party is taken hostage by three terrorist generals and a group of teen-aged gun-wielders who hold the guests hostage. While negotiations with the government proceed, four-and-a-half months go by and in that time marvelous personal relationships develop. For once, a happy ending is not needed to keep one reading.

One of a series of "who-done-its" by the Swedish author, Henning Mankell, features Linda, daughter of the detective, Kurt Wallander. Linda has graduated from Police College, but cannot don a police uniform for several weeks. Meanwhile, she manages to solve a major mystery, as if she were already in harness.

It is not often that a group of ne'er-do-wells who settle in a condemned house are portrayed as detectives. But Fred Vargas makes the story sound plausible. Vargas, an unassuming young Parisian lady (does "Fred" stand for "Frederica"?) has seen her works translated into many languages.

CHAPTER 99

# The Stratford Festival

Round about the year 2000, the Stratford Festival priced itself out of my market. Over the years, I had come to count on some of the best entertainment anywhere in that setting. But, when prices exceeded $90 a seat, I decided that I could more easily buy quality entertainment elsewhere.

We had moved to Goderich by the time the first Stratford season was under way in 1953. We didn't get to it that year. But we got well filled in by Gordon Jocelyn. Joy Jocelyn's father had been principal of the old Stratford Normal school (as we used to call teacher's colleges), and his house, located both near that institution and the site of the Festival, is still in family hands. Gordon was employed that season as a dresser to Sir Alec Guinness, and in the Martin house after the performances, he would regale friends with stories of life back stage.

In the first four seasons, the plays were presented in a big tent which proved to be less of a limitation than might have been expected. The superb acting that occurred under Tyrone Guthrie's direction, the stars like Alec Guinness, the innovation of the thrust stage and the costuming by Tanya Moiseiwitsch drew audiences from far and wide. The doubters, who had questioned the entire project from the time it was first proposed by Tom Patterson, were effectively answered in the first two seasons.

The tent did, of course, present problems. When it rained, for example, the resulting roar almost drowned out the actors. And rolling away the huge canvas at year's end required unbelievable energy. It was later noted that someone had insured the thing against theft!

The first play we saw in the tent was presented in the second season. I believe it was the ancient Greek play, *Oedipus Rex* by Sophocles. The acting was splendid. But here I have to confess a limitation. I don't fully enjoy a play that depicts the steady deterioration of a central character. This happens in *Oedipus*, which I saw again on the same stage many years later. Another was featured in the first season. With *Richard III* I was probably prejudiced by having first read *The Daughter of Time* by Josephine Tey in which Richard was exonerated, and ended being scandalized by his successor, Henry VII. My suspicion is that Richard's physical deformity led to widespread prejudice, which in turn resulted in a host of false yarns. It's argued that Shakespeare's play still made good theatre. Fine, but that doesn't work for me.

The other play in this category has to be *Macbeth*, though I suspect that the Scottish setting somehow mitigates the depressing feeling I get. Of course, it shouldn't. Scots have been among the most brutal in history. Just read Scott's *The Fair Maid of Perth*!

Over the years, I think I have most enjoyed the Shakespeare comedies. I remember a staging of *Twelfth Night* in which Malvolio reads the letter his enemies have written while sitting on a garden swing with his feet on the ground. At the words, "Go to, thou art made", he let the swing carry him across the stage. In the more recent performance, Viola, after wearing the male disguise of Cesario throughout the play, finally appears during the curtain calls, wearing a gorgeous white gown.

Organizational control of the Stratford Festival has had its ups and downs. One year, there was huge dissatisfaction with the Board's treatment of a director. Annual meetings, usually held in December, when the Festival Theatre was not otherwise in use, were sparsely attended, with an agenda just following predictable form. But this time, many members came from far and wide to try to turn things around. Morrey (in grade XII?) and I drove over from Guelph. There was a vigorous debate during which I discovered how easy the theatre acoustics made it to speak and after which I was thanked at the door for my remarks by actor Nicholas Pennel.

But the members were really not in control. The Board

had established so many proxies that they could easily defeat any motions made and prevent the election of any new board members. Nearly all the incumbents lived in Toronto.

For many years, I rarely took in a performance without encountering someone I knew—people in Burlington or Guelph that I hadn't seen for a long time, or other faces from the past. As we drove home after a play to Burlington, we often encountered night fog.

Once we were driven to a Stratford matinee by the Lapps. While Doug was director of Christian Education for Hamilton Conference, his children belonged to Eleanor's junior choir at Wellington Square. He used to exclaim about the wonderful songs she sent home through his children. Years later, when he ministered at Dominion Church in Ottawa, they treated us to a delicious dinner. On our way to Stratford, we had to stop to fix a flat tire just west of New Hamburg. An officer of the OPP stopped to see if Doug had everything he needed.

In more recent years, familiar faces have been less in evidence. Did this have anything to do with prices?

Over many of the years, the Stratford Festival has maintained a music program. Sometimes it has been a Gilbert & Sullivan presentation, complete with up-to-date political references. Once we took in a Sunday noon hour recital in the Stratford City Hall by Elly Ameling. She featured the Bach *Coffee Cantata*, in which she sang a strenuous objection to the banning of coffee in Germany in the 18th century. I recall dirty mugs ostentatiously placed all over the lady's apartment.

To avoid night driving, we have tended to prefer two o'clock matinees. At first we would use the lower parking-lot and eat our picnic on the island while watching the swans in the Avon River. More recently, we would arrive on time to park in the circle east of the Festival Theatre, picnicking at a park table.

The brass group that plays the fanfare to get people into their seats reportedly has a fresh set of notes written for each season. It is one of the many distinctive features of a great institution—one I have enjoyed patronizing for many years.

## CHAPTER 100

# The Roll-top Desk

Dad bought the roll-top desk while in Galt. The desk, made in Waterloo, is a most handsome piece of furniture. It comes in two sections. The lower part houses the drawers on each side of the person using the desk. Each side has three drawers 3 1/4 inches high by 12 1/4 wide and one at the bottom, 9 inches high. When the lower section is by itself, or if the roller is down, these drawers are locked. When the roller is up, its end presses against a spring at the back, releasing the wooden lock. Of course, this works only if the top is placed correctly above the bottom, something the movers had to do on each of the nine or so times the desk has been moved.

In Oshawa, of course, the desk sat in Dad's study. I was allowed to use the big drawer on the left. But I once allowed the drawer to become untidy with stuff sticking out. I was given so long to correct the fault or I would lose the drawer. I obliged very quickly!

One night, I heard Dad give a most unpleasant exclamation from the desk. He had been marking Latin examinations and when he came to my paper, he was hoping he could give me a high mark. Then he realized that I had completely missed a question worth 10 marks. Big disappointment!

The upper part of the desk has 12 pigeonholes and two small drawers. I know that Dad, with his orderly mind, kept the same purpose for each one over the years, and, in that I have been like him for every nook has its own, unchanging use, and everything is kept in its place.

I don't remember where the desk was in the house on the Niagara Street Highway, or in the house in Fonthill. But on South Drive, it sat against the wall in Dad's bedroom. When he died and Aunt Mary moved into the house, she slept in that bedroom and began to use the desk. When Mother and her sisters moved to Guelph, the desk entered the house on Caledonia. But, when Mother died and her sisters occupied the upstairs apartment in 264 Woolwich Street, the desk went to the sunroom that I made my study. Only after I had moved my things into the desk did I realize that Aunt Mary would have liked to have had it for longer. She mentioned it only once, but that was enough to give me a twinge of guilt.

On Glasgow Street, the desk occupied the recreation room in the basement. That made a problem when I repeatedly had water on the floor, before our carpenter built a new floor above the one that had been wet. It was also in that room that Esther introduced me to my first computer which had a table beside the desk.

In our condominium on Water Street, the desk stands against one wall in my third-floor study. On the other walls lie the computer and printer, my audiovisual machines, and Morrey's old photocopier in front of shelves, which contain books and my library of cassettes.

And what do I keep in the two big drawers? The left one has maps: an alphabetically arranged pile of city maps, maps of the provinces, and, at the bottom, a few National Geographic enlargements. The handiest of all are my local street map of Guelph, Cambridge and Kitchener-Waterloo, and my road map of Ontario. The right-hand drawer contains election results, provincial and federal, going back over many years, and all marked up with percentages of NDP votes. First things first!

CHAPTER 101

# Letters-to-the-Editor

I seem to have earned a reputation as a frequent contributor to these columns in various newspapers. Whether that means that I am verbose or just articulate, I have produced a considerable volume of stuff, less than half of which is, of course, ever printed. Newspapers with a wide circulation like the Star or the Globe and Mail accept, at most, three or four of my letters a year, while regional organs like The Guelph Mercury or the Kitchener-Waterloo Record print most of what I send them.

The computer has made the exercise a great deal easier. After I know what I have to say, typing it out, checking for errors, and sending it to the editorial offices will often occupy only about 20 minutes. If I decide that I want my message to go farther afield, I can send it to a number of papers across Canada in about a minute a paper, though whether any of them print it, I may never know.

Several factors affect the printability of a letter. One is brevity. Once, when support for Stockwell Day of the Reform Party was waning, Murdo MacKinnon had this letter in the Globe and Mail, "I was reminded of the old hymn[139], 'Day is dying in the west.' No comment."

Of course, the subject must be of current interest. Following the suspension by the Ontario NDP executive of CAW's Buzz Hargrove's party membership for publicly endorsing the Liberals, my letter explaining the need for the move got the most prominent place among letters in the Star.

Sometimes the identity of the writer is what counts. For instance, when an editorial has attacked the behaviour of a foreign government, a reply from the ambassador of that country will appear among the letters that paper will print. On the other hand, identity doesn't always have that kind of result.

465

In the 1940's, the St. Catharines Standard, a Conservative organ, ran an article greatly misrepresenting the work of the Saskatchewan CCF Government. Premier Douglas wrote a letter of correction which the paper refused to print.

What I find most frustrating is seeing an article which makes a statement which is patently false and on which I know the answer and being unable to get a reply printed. If other letters are printed which make my point, I tend to be satisfied. For instance, a recent column in the Globe and Mail accused the author of the Da Vinci Code of "marrying Jesus to a harlot." I wrote pointing out that nowhere does Scripture refer to Mary Magdalene in those terms. My letter didn't appear. But two others that did appear made the point. But, when the sexuality issue was at its hottest, a former United Church moderator had an article expressing several falsehoods. Neither I nor anyone else got an answer printed.

On two occasions, an editor wrote me refusing to print my letter because of the stand I took. In the late 1960's, talks were progressing towards a possible merger of the United Church of Canada with the Church of England in Canada. I objected to the draft of a Statement of Faith that was proposed to use, and said so in a letter to the United Church Observer. Al Forrest, the usually liberal editor of the Observer, thought it inappropriate for such a letter to appear while the fate of negotiations hung in the balance. If memory serves, Al later changed his mind.

On the other occasion, the editor made no such change. Reverend Kenneth Bagnell did extensive writing in both the Observer and the Globe and Mail. In 1972, the Ontario Provincial Council of the NDP met in Orillia to decide what to do about the Waffle which had been functioning as a party within a party. The motion, which passed by a large majority, called for dissolution of the Waffle as a part of the NDP. As was explained later by the president, no one was expelled from the party as a result; those few who left, did so on their own volition. But, in writing about the meeting, Bagnell stated that

Waffle members had been "expelled". As one who had been present at the meeting, I wrote to correct the statement. But the editor insisted that Bagnell had been right.

Many years ago, someone wrote an editorial in the Mercury commending my record of letters they had published over time. The only time they would refuse "partisan" letters was during elections. Evidently, they wanted to avoid accusations that the paper was biased. More recently, they have made a rule that no writer will have more than one letter printed in any given month.

Often I am phoned by someone in the office of a paper that is considering the printing of a letter. I am just asked whether I wrote the letter. Evidently, they have to guard against impersonation in this business. But it is pleasant to be able to speak to a real person.

I often wish that I could persuade more people with similar interests to mine to write public letters about them. They may not be widely read. But, if people are interested enough to tell me they see my letters, there must be some influence.

CHAPTER 102

# 2000—Celebrating 75 Years of the United Church

The United Church of Canada has served me well. It has allowed me to grow at my own speed. When, as a teenager, I didn't feel ready for membership because communion had not yet come to have meaning for me, I was able to wait until my university years when I found, in Toronto's Carlton United, a congregation that was truly a community of which I wanted to be part. When I could not conscientiously sanction World War II as most United Church members did, there was room for me and others where my stand was respected. It has provided pulpits for some of the finest preachers of the 20th century. And it has allowed doubters to grow into strong Christian leaders, able to understand the position of other doubters.

The United Church has taken unpopular positions on social issues, positions that have often enjoyed wider respect in later years. It opposed discrimination against our Japanese-Canadian minority when it was commonplace to blame them for the War in the Pacific. It gave strong support to social programs that were designed to help the poor, and strong support for nuclear disarmament. In 1988, it re-affirmed policies it had always had that allowed gays and lesbians to remain members after "coming out", and allowed any member to "be considered" for ordination. In all these actions, there were dissenters among the membership. Indeed, anti-gay prejudice has been used to justify expressions of hatred one would not expect to find in any church. But, through it all, our diversity has been respected.

In the year 2000, the church celebrated 75 years of operation. Nationally, this featured publication of *Fire and Grace*, a wide, hard-covered book in which a number of our best writers each told a different aspect of the church's life and history. In addition, Bishop Spong in the USA wrote of the warm welcome he had received in visits to Canada and of his admiration for our denomination; and a Lutheran minister thanked us for showing the way to others by the stands we had taken.

Locally, the celebration took many forms. But I doubt that it happened anywhere with more enthusiasm, or with more involvement of local church members, than it did in Guelph. Part of this was owing to the presence of the Guelph and Area Cluster where the idea was first brought forward, where the celebration committee was formed early and got to work without delay. But part of it was the imagination of the people on that committee which included my incomparable wife.

The committee began by booking the larger hall of the River Run Centre for a date in June, 2000 very close to the anniversary of the day in 1925 when our church was constituted in the Mutual Arena in Toronto. Not only were they smart enough to do that booking on time. But they were able in this way to secure facilities that must have been ten times better than the Mutual Arena had been.

They then booked former moderator Bruce McLeod as the preacher. There were objections from a few who were aware of what they considered "moral lapses" by Dr. McLeod in years past. But Eleanor—it was her idea—had heard Bruce speak at the installation of Sang Chul Lee as moderator in Victoria in 1988 and insisted that he would fit the occasion well. She was right. In his 15 minute sermon, he not only gave us a panoramic view of what our church had been, but made us enjoy it. He told of accompanying Bob McLure on a visit to the Near East, of suggesting to Bob that he save a strenuous walk by using a taxi and of hearing Bob's abrupt reply. "S'matter. You paralyzed?"!

The committee booked Barrie Cabena, then organist of Dublin Church, as conductor of a massed choir from our 12 pastoral charges and as composer of an anthem for the occasion. The cooperation of the different congregations in sending their best singers to take part in the 250-voice choir was tremendous, with the by-product of an increase in demand for tickets that finally filled that 800-seat hall. Barrie's composition inevitably contained some very modern harmonies. But, by the time we singers were able to manage the notes, we got to enjoy the music as much as the more traditional hymns that were also used.

The choir music was practised in many of the individual churches. Then we all gathered in Dublin Church for a massed rehearsal. I had witnessed similar occasions where confusion reigned. But our choir marshal, Beth McCracken, was organization itself. On arriving, each singer had to find his/her name on a seat. When she appeared, she gave us confidence, and Barrie was able to begin rehearsing within ten minutes of the scheduled time. There was similar organization at the final rehearsal at River Run. Said Barrie, "I have three messages for you. The first is to watch me. The second is to watch me. The third…"

The MC for the service was Andrea Buttars, John's second daughter and then youth director at Five Oaks. She trained a 12-year-old girl to read the scripture. Aware of the tendency of kids to read too fast, she had got this kid to read at a speed where every syllable was clear. Years before, Aunt Mary had found one Harcourt lady hard to take, since she was constantly pouring out her troubles to anyone who would listen, and Aunt Mary was good at listening. But the lady also told of a son and daughter-in-law who had travelled to Peru to adopt a baby. This "baby" was our reader in the River Run Centre. Aunt Mary would have loved it.

There was a junior choir, led by Margaret Hendriks. In previous years, when Marg was specializing in Orff music, she would disappoint some of us by doing public demonstrations for which the children were never properly prepared. However, her youth choirs at Harcourt church have been very well trained. On this occasion, the children did well. However, they were allowed a kind of fun that some observers thought inappropriate for a religious service. Only afterwards were we told that Andrea had made a deal with the kids. Children are not often asked to sit through a service as long as this one. But she got the cooperation of the junior choir by promising them this fun time. It worked.

Some church officials came from outside Guelph to take in this event. Eileen Burnes, then secretary of Waterloo Presbytery, was especially impressed. And well she might be for we had put on show samples of the best the United Church has to offer.

CHAPTER 103

# What Lies Ahead

I admit that this doesn't sound like a memoir. But I justify it because I am incorporating thoughts that date back for some years. First of all, I am claiming it as a privilege of age to concentrate on those activities that interest me. Keeping up with a modest program of solo piano practice, accompanying three or four players and singers, and attending a few outstanding concerts might be said to be enough to keep me out of mischief. But when you add researching and providing my own and six other congregations across Hamilton Conference basic information about a different congregation each week; leading the music for the monthly meetings of Waterloo Presbytery up until June, 2004; participating in the monthly meetings of Guelph and Area Cluster and Chalmers Church Council until that congregation folded as a separate entity, and the by-weekly rehearsals of Chalmers' Church choir, I might be forgiven for failing to notice the winners of the various athletic Cups. But when you add processing NDP memberships in Guelph-Wellington riding until February, 2005, attending the Saturday parts of quarterly meetings of the NDP Provincial Council, and sending letters-to-the-editor every week or so to one of a list of publications, you may understand why I rarely volunteer to belong to an ad hoc committee anywhere unless I get carried away and propose the thing myself. And I need only to add that I try to keep up with a host of wonderful friends and relatives, and that I take considerable pleasure in composing meals for Eleanor and me, to give you a little idea of 'What Lies Ahead'.

But, of course, there are limits to everything. Eventually, this life will be over and a new one will begin. At least, that is what I have long believed. Some writers, like Tom Harper, offer stories of Near-Death Experiences (NDEs) as proof of life after death. I don't need these proofs, though it's nice to have them fit the faith I already possess.

However, I have to express a couple of reservations about NDEs. When a person dies and revives a few minutes later with a story of what the other side was like, he/she probably has a subjective view of that experience. If she/he had died with a great feeling of depression or failure, then a new experience may easily be seen as positive. The same may happen if the experience is an example of the kind in which the person has always taken great pleasure.

But just how much does an NDE tell us? Assuming it is an accurate glimpse of the first few minutes of the next life, will that picture still remain ten years later? Will our concept of time apply to that life? And what does 'forever' mean in that context? What I have seen of basic changes in this life leads me to suspect that change will also feature in the next.

I've often heard people say of a recently deceased loved one, "He has joined his maker," or, "He's gone to live with God." I think I can understand this sentiment from the point of view of the African-American slaves. Since there was no great evidence of God in this life, it was good to believe he would be found in the next. But for us, can we not live with God here? And what would living with God be like in another life? Surely people don't mean that we would not have free will? If we didn't, it would not be the God I have come to know.

And what about being re-united with loved ones who have gone before? We don't know whether we will remember anything of this life or whether those 'loved ones' would be recognized. I don't relate to those cartoons that assume the conventional wisdom, even if I sometimes have to laugh.

I like to think of life after death as another stage in God's wonderful continuing creation. As the aspect of that creation that I most value has to do with the challenge to excel, I would expect to be confronted with challenges in the next life—after suitable preparation.

At my brother's funeral, our minister said, "Life is like a

tale that is told." All stories have an ending. I believe that new ones will always be ready to begin. In the meantime, I'll continue to enjoy the friends and relatives with whom I have been blessed.

# Part 5—
# FAMILY

CHAPTER 104

# Esther and Morrey Since 1970

Although it took Esther, like her father three decades earlier, some time to find her feet in university, she graduated with her Bachelor of Music in 1977.

While there, she was identified as a "singer" by Nicholas Goldschmidt and subsequently, in 1975, she accompanied the U of G Choir as soloist on a tour of England and its cathedrals. On that trip, she gave two recitals with trumpeter Len Hanna and organist Gerald Manning, and sang a piece that had been written for her by Keith Bissell.

During her university studies and for some years afterward, Esther was a soprano soloist with Melville Cook at Metropolitan Church. A highlight of those days included a CBC telecast of the Advent service from Metropolitan Church. The choir sang two *Magnificats*, one by Poulenc and one by Stanford. The latter featured a wonderful soprano solo which Esther sang with the choir.

In 1973 Esther married Bruce Mackay whom she had met at New College during her music studies. He had studied electrical engineering and, upon graduation, began his career at Ontario Hydro.

When introducing his wife to his family connection in and near Smith's Falls, Bruce told them she was a singer. At first, that made little impression. But, when Esther had done the solo on the CBC broadcast, which the CBC delayed for a week, Bruce was able to let his family know that they could see it on the following Sunday. On the morning in question, his grandmother tuned in to the program which not only featured the Metropolitan church choir but also the Toronto Dance Theatre. Bruce's grandmother turned it off because she was convinced that any service with dance in it must be Catholic and therefore the wrong program. By the time Bruce's dad understood what had happened and had driven over to find the program for her, Esther's solo was over. But the family was very impressed that she was on television.

It is an unwritten rule that people who marry into our family must relate positively to life at Thirlestane, our cottage on Muldrew Lake. In 1972, we had had glowing accounts of Bruce Mackay from Esther. But, that summer, he got to be subjected to the test. Having a summer job in Abitibi Canyon in Northern Ontario, he had to access the cottage by CNR on a train that was due at Gravenhurst at around 5.00 am.

Esther had obtained her driving license and told us she could meet Bruce without our help and accordingly set her alarm clock for 4:00 am. However, at 4:00 am a thunderstorm was beginning and I got to accompany her in boat and car. Of course, the train was late. But, when he had had some sleep, Bruce was truly appreciative of his fiancée's summer place.

As our son-in-law, Bruce soon became a strong member of the family. At the cottage, his practical advice was always appreciated, as was his physical help with the chores. During the 70's, we used propane gas to cook, refrigerate, and run some of the lights. At one point, we brought in the gas in 100-pound cylinders. At Christmas, Esther gave the men in her life a tall, slim gift which turned out to be an army stretcher which we used to carry these heavy cylinders from boat to cottage. The following June, Bruce and I performed the appropriate job. After the first trip, Bruce exclaimed, "Well, that's July."!

*Don, Esther, Eleanor, Breffney and Bruce at Memorial Pines*

Once, while opening the cottage at the beginning of the summer, Bruce and I found a mouse's nest in the coal oil stove and, carrying it outside, we dumped the contents of the nest on the ground. Suddenly the ground was crawling with babies. I began by stamping on them. But Bruce said he couldn't bring himself to do that. I was reminded of Robby Burns poem, *To a Mouse*. ("Wee, sleekit, cowrin, tim'rous beastie"!)

For his last two years of high school, Morrey enrolled in Guelph's Centennial Collegiate which had only 600 students at that time. In his last year, he successfully ran for Students' Council president. The principal was then George Hindley with whom I later did extensive committee work in Chalmers Church. During that year, Morrey and the Students' Council organized a careers day and astounded the staff when all of the guest speakers appeared on time!

At a University of Guelph social, about that time, I overheard Morrey tell someone that "my parents realize that I need to attend a university out of town". When he chose Trinity College at the University of Toronto, he was able to name several graduates whom he admired.

Upon graduating, Morrey was invited by John Brewin, a senior executive with the B. C. Attorney-General's Department, to be his assistant while he organized a law reform commission initiated by the Barrett government. That government was defeated in 1975. But Brewin was allowed to finish his work, and after the commission was established, Morrey helped operate it, supervising several field workers across the province.

In the summer of 1976, we visited him for two weeks. Morrey's apartment overlooked English Bay, where we witnessed sailors, ocean-going freighters, barges carrying saw-dust, small planes taking off for Victoria, and parachuters. Another apartment block was being erected that would have obscured this whole view in another year.

Morrey took us for a meal at the "Muck-a-Muck" basement restaurant which was unique. It was run by natives on a "Lip" grant. You made a reservation, and while you waited on the steps, a lady took your drink order. As you entered, you heard the waiters' feet crunch the gravel in the aisles. To seat your party, tables had to be cleared for each side to be raised on hinges to let you in. The menus specialized in the best BC native foods.

The following week, we spent two days in Victoria where we had tea with the Brewins—Gretchen, who was later to serve as Mayor of Victoria, followed by several terms in the B. C. Legislature and John who subsequently had a term as MP (NDP).

In 1977, Morrey left BC for Harvard University. But first he joined his Ottawa friends, the Shenstones, as they drove their van for a visit to the Yukon. At Harvard, he arranged to extend his stay from two years to three, to obtain two degrees: an MBA, and an MPP (not a Member of the Ontario Legislature, but a Master of Public Policy!) In 1980, we attended his Convocation, held in an out-door square, where we had to dump rain water from metal chairs before being seated. Also graduating was the daughter of former president John Kennedy. One graduating student gave a very eloquent oration in Latin.

In Toronto, Morrey was first employed by Canada Consulting. An early assignment was to act as a sort of "advance man" for a Parliamentary Committee, that was planning to travel across the country to meet with local businesses and governmental officials in major Canadian cities. In his own travel planning, Morrey was able to set up all of his meetings and most of his accommodation but could not find any room at an inn in Halifax. So he phoned Sheryl Kennedy (who later became a Deputy Governor of the Bank of Canada) who had lived and worked in Halifax, but was living in Ottawa. Did she know of anyone in Halifax who could help? She phoned an old friend, Sharon Barrett, who confessed that she had an extra bed in her apartment. Thus they met!"

The following June, Morrey attended a friend's wedding in California and on the way (!) he visited Sharon in Halifax, where they got engaged on the 29th. They were married on December 29th in Sharon's home-town of Sydney, and, a few years later, Alexander was born on November 29th.

At the wedding, the minister informed Morrey during the ceremony that "there is another man in Sharon's life" and took his time in identifying the man as Jesus! During the wedding, it snowed heavily, so that bride and groom had to spend their first night in the same building as the rest of us.

Nova Scotians have a great loyalty to the area in which they are raised, and with this marriage came an unwritten understanding that Morrey and Sharon would be spending a significant time each year in that province.

Accordingly, summer accommodation was rented each year, until 1993 when, rentals being unavailable in Mahone Bay, Morrey took advantage of a house for sale there. Now, each year, the family drives there late in June, returning Labour Day week-end. During that time, Morrey flies out and in on business. The family also flies there for Thanksgiving and Christmas.

After Harvard, Morrey settled in Toronto, working successively for three consulting firms. But after a few years, he and Esther formed a partnership called "The Change Alliance." This meant that, when an institution, company, or government department undertook major changes of structure, Esther or Morrey would help them realize the purpose with which the planning began. For several years, Esther had on her stationery "Improving people's capability." In this work, which takes them, separately or together, to many parts of the Western World, they have to sell their services. But there seems to be a good market for this kind of service. Morrey now uses the title, "Guided Futures."

*Morrey holding Alexander and Sharon holding Annie, c. 1992*

A few days after marrying Bruce, Esther began her Bachelor of Music program at the University of Toronto. During the next two summers, she worked as a teller in the TD Bank at the Fairview Mall. Next she got a job as a vocal itinerant, supporting teachers in the Scarborough Board of Education in developing their music teaching skills.

Esther worked to develop her singing career for about eight years. Then, in 1985, she decided that she should pursue other career choices. She rejoined the TD Bank for several unhappy months, and then moved to the Institute of Canadian Bankers where she worked part time promoting the banks' educational programs. After two years, she moved to working full time in the national office of BDO Ward Mallette, a chartered accountant firm. Following their merger with another firm in 1992, she managed professional development for the Institute of Chartered Accountants of Ontario. One Christmas, she organized a choir among the office workers. While there, she began her studies leading to a Master of Adult Education. In 1994, she left the Institute to join Morrey in the Change Alliance.

In 1989, Esther's marriage to Bruce had reached an end. But the way it was handled was exemplary. Two months after the separation, Bruce took me to lunch and showed me over the Hydro plant. He made sure that his parents didn't blame Esther for the separation, especially in the presence of Breffney and Caitlin. The following June, at her birthday party for Caitlin, Esther invited Mary, whom Bruce later married. And in succeeding years, as the girls went back and forth between households, their parents cooperated in every needful way. When illness prevented one from looking after one or both girls, the other would fill in. They went together to school parents' nights. And in 2005, when Breffney was married, both families gathered under one roof in fine good will.

In 1993, Jim Sylph came on the scene and in March, 1994, he and Esther married. Jim entered wholeheartedly into our life at the cottage. He has a tremendous personality. The expression of his political thinking began with the British Con-

*Jim Sylph*

servative party near Newcastle-Upon-Tyne, even successfully running for Town Council in Darlington. And although we have very different political views, I find it a great pleasure to find points of agreement with him. When the family gets together, he is the life of the party. And, on more than one occasion, he has served as a very effective master of ceremonies at family parties.

When we first knew him, Jim worked as the Director of Standards at the Canadian Association of Chartered Accountants. In those years, Esther, Jim and family lived on Fairlawn Avenue in North Toronto. I say "Jim and family" because he hit it off with the girls very early in the relationship.

Jim and Esther's wedding in 1994 was a joyous occasion. One of Esther's friends, Pat Lane, captured, in the toast to the bride, some of her finest qualities. The minister advised the couple to use humour in marriage. He mightn't have bothered if he had heard of the way they became officially engaged on a plane over the Atlantic. At the reception, it was announced that there was a competition—the winner would be the table who had done the best job of singing a song with the word "love" in it. The winning table would win a dinner at the location of their choice in Toronto. When the table with Muldrew Lake cottagers was informed that they had won, they were surprised to be given eight boxes of Kraft Dinner!

Esther's sale of the Lorindale house and Jim's sale of his Etobicoke apartment enabled them to buy the Fairlawn Avenue house. Joining Fairlawn Heights United Church proved a very satisfying move, especially since Eleanor Daly, one of Toronto's best musicians and composers, was—and is—the long-time organist. Esther, Morrey, Sharon and Annie have all sung in her choirs. In 2005, Esther gave a recital with Eleanor at the piano. The next year, Eleanor (Ewing) invited Annie to select a poem which she then commissioned Eleanor Daly to set to music for Annie's 16th birthday.

In 1998, Esther obtained a Masters of Education from OISE. Our dear Muldrew neighbour, Bill Alexander, was her thesis and academic advisor in this program.

In 1999, Jim was appointed technical director of the International Federation of Accountants (IFAC). Since the office is in New York, he and Esther were to move there. Jim moved there in 1999 while Esther stayed in Toronto to allow Caitlin to finish high school. Then, in 2001, when Caitlin went to study business at Wilfred Laurier University, Esther moved to New York to join Jim. This move to New York and Jim's new job meant quite a change in their daily lives. They sold their cars since it was too expensive to park a car in NYC. Since that time, they have used public transportation, and rented cars when they have come to Canada. Jim visits almost every corner of the world. This means that family get-togethers have to be planned far in advance, so that he can attend.

CHAPTER 105

# Aunt Mary

In the years 1971-92, in which she lived in Guelph, everyone called her Aunt Mary, although technically she had that relationship only with me and with cousins living elsewhere. But the word 'aunt' signified the role she played with a whole host of people who enjoyed her company. She was an attentive and sympathetic listener. People soon found that out, and beat a path to her door. The majority of these were members of her congregation, Harcourt United, and, through her, I came to know a lot of interesting people. These included successive interns who did the field work of their training for ministry at Harcourt United Church.

While in Guelph, Aunt Mary found out the names of Haig cousins who were studying at the University of Guelph and had them visit her, often for a meal. Sometimes when she became aware of boyfriends, they would be invited too. One of these boy friends got interested in Haig family trees, and traced mention in the Canada census of 1861 of my Great Grandfather's farm near Cobourg. He was fascinated to find that the children and the livestock were listed together!

Aunt Mary was often at Kenmore when I was little. Kenmore was the farm near Cobourg that was operated by my Uncle Don and Aunt Muriel until they found work they liked better. It was where we holidayed when living in Galt between 1921 and 1926. A favourite toy was 'the wheels', the chassis of an old baby carriage. Aunt Mary tells of a time when I was about two. I was climbing on the wheels, and, thinking this a dangerous pursuit for one so young, she warned me, "One

*Mary Haig, as a young lady*

of these times you'll fall." The next day, she arrived to find me climbing on the wheels again, but chanting, "One of dese times I fa', One of dese times I fa'!"

Aunt Mary had a wind-up gramophone on which I heard Scotch songs by Harry Lauder. But she took it with her in 1920 when she left for Formosa. That summer, Dad spent overseas, leaving in July, while Aunt Mary left in late August. I remember calculating that the two would need to say a big farewell before Dad left because he would miss her when he returned.

When I was little, someone told me a story which I associate with Aunt Mary although she failed to remember it in later years. It was about a little black boy called Pominandus who was slow-witted in funny ways. His mother sent him on successive errands and he applied her instructions about the last errand to the next. For instance, when he brought home a puppy, he should have pulled him home at the end of a leash. So the next time he dragged home a pound of butter at the end of a string. Each time he reached home, his mother exclaimed, "Po-min-andus, yo' ain't got the sense yo' was bo'n with." Of course, that story would now be seen as racist, in the sense that Little Black Sambo is seen as an example of how white people used to diminish blacks with this caricature. Does that mean that we have progressed in three-quarters of a century? About ten years ago, I caught myself using as a means of praise the expression, "It's darn white of you!" Reformed attitudes require reformed language as well.

I don't remember when Aunt Mary began to influence my thinking about religion. But it must have started before I was far into my teens, for it was then that she gave me my first New Testament in modern English by James Moffat. At that time the Bible as used in the church was almost always the King James Version, tremendously expressive, though somewhat dated in language. It had the advantage that, being universally used, more of it tended to be memorized. But, at that stage, I was more interested in meaning than in poetic values, and the Moffat version suited me well.

In our age, the missionary movement has often been criticized for the historic role it played. People have claimed that missionaries served to soften up the natives of foreign countries, thus facilitating imperial and commercial activities of their countrymen in those countries. They have also been accused of selling western cultural practices along with the religion they taught. In answer, Aunt Mary was always able to be specific, telling of the actual work in which she was involved, and of that of her colleagues. Then she would tell of the strong friendships with Japanese people that have lasted, years after they were formed in Japan.

Today, in the United Church, missionaries go only where they are invited by the local churches in the field. And 'mutuality in mission' means that Christian leaders from those countries also visit ours to bring us their special inspiration.

When Aunt Mary retired in 1958, she took an apartment in St. Catharines to be near my parents, and joined them in First United Church. When my father died, it was she who stressed the importance of my just being present in the South Drive house. Afterwards, she moved in with Mother. Suddenly, the dynamics of that home changed for Mother. Up to that point, she had been the nurse on whom Dad, with his headaches and other maladies, leaned. Now she was the older and frailer partner. The adjustment was difficult and, as her memory gradually deserted her, it led to many misunderstandings, in spite of her sister's loving care. Was her memory loss due to this situation, or would it have happened anyway? We'll never know.

Between 1920 and 1941, while I was growing up, my parents and I would see Aunt Mary when she was on furlough from the mission field. Travelling across the

*Mary Haig in Japan*

broad Pacific in an ocean liner, she always had a trunk. The upper part had a tray on which she would put Japanese gifts for various family members. She would teach me a few phrases from the Japanese language. I recall, "Tadaima" and "O ya-sumi nasai" but not their meanings.

Aunt Mary always seemed the strong person among us. On the farm, she would kill a rat if one was found among the grain. In Formosa, she was called on to kill a poisonous snake if one appeared and didn't hesitate to do so. In 1933, she appeared at Muldrew Lake having swum a mile on the Japanese Lake Nojiri. When Tom Dale and I organized an intergenerational expedition to Loon Lake, where we had previously built a raft, and where the picnic was to be on an island, it was Aunt Mary who suggested that those who could swim over should do so. Of course, she showed the example. She showed the example again in Newfoundland after an adventure in reaching a remote community. When she was asked to speak after a sleepless night, she didn't hesitate.

During my teens, I was always slow at my school work and sometimes my homework would not be finished when it was time for bed. On one such occasion, Aunt Mary advised me, "You get your rest."

During her missionary furloughs, Aunt Mary was often the preacher at country church services as she told of her work and that of colleagues in the mission field. Her voice rang out clearly, even in buildings with difficult acoustics. It was therefore a shock to realize in 1971 that an operation had damaged her vocal chords, reducing her voice to a loud whisper. That the operation occurred at all, we had to thank Dr. Flora Little, whom Aunt Mary had known in Formosa (Taiwan) in the early 20's and whose house on Woolwich Street we bought in 1974. Aunt Mary had decided to let matters (a sore neck) take their course. After all, she was already 79. But Flora told her, "Get on with it", with the result that we had her for another 20 years. She had had a tumour but the cancer never returned!

She had to use that loud whisper to full advantage one day when she was in Toronto. As she was going up in a department store escalator, she suddenly saw Morrey riding the down escalator. She apparently pushed her voice beyond the whisper, because she got his attention. Her voice did improve over the remaining years. But it never reached its previous volume.

In the late 40's, Aunt Muriel tried living with my parents. But it didn't work out and she soon moved to BC where she lived alone, some of the time on Pender Island in Georgia Strait, more latterly in the Burrard area of Vancouver. Through the 60's, Aunt Mary kept asking her to return to Ontario. In 1970, while Aunt Mary was visiting her, Aunt Muriel had her purse snatched, causing her to fall and break a hip. This time, after her recovery, she agreed to come east. But I became aware that I was not able to drive to St. Catharines as often as I should. So I got power of attorney for Mother, packed the three sisters off to Florida, and, in their absence, managed to sell her house in St. Catharines and buy one in Guelph, one block from ours on Dean Ave. While there, they began attending Harcourt church since it was within easy walking distance.

Mother died in 1973 and the next year, we sold the two houses on Dean Ave. and bought the Littles' large house on Woolwich Street. Major renovations enabled us to create a comfortable apartment on the second floor, and my two aunts occupied this until Aunt Muriel's death in 1985 left Aunt Mary alone.

We stayed 12 years in that house till in 1986 we moved to Glasgow Street for lower taxes and heating costs. Aunt Mary decided she had never in her life lived as long at one address as she had at 264 Woolwich Street.

Aunt Mary took a keen interest in music. It may have been Aunt Muriel who saw that her sisters didn't miss my massed choir concerts. At some of them they would encounter Father John Mattice of St. Joseph's Church. But at one, they didn't make it and Father Mattice asked me, "Where are the grandmas?"

After Aunt Muriel died, Aunt Mary maintained the interest. After retiring in 1982, I prepared and presented a full-fledged piano recital in Chalmers Church. There were many shortcomings in that playing, owing partly to the fact that I had not done disciplined practising for years, and to my delay in beginning to study with a teacher. But after the recital, Aunt Mary gave me the biggest hug I can remember. She fairly ran into my arms. What counted for her was the effort I had made, rather than the finished product.

Before my retirement, Aunt Mary and I played a lot of Mahjong, though she hadn't learned the game in the Orient. But after that event, we had a game around 4:00 pm. each day. And she would share with me any correspondence she had received from our many relatives as well as news from Harcourt Church. This way, I didn't neglect her, even though I tended to be busy. Aunt Mary would insist that I beat her most of the time in Mahjong. I refuted this by keeping track of the scores. Out of 100 games, one would win 51, the other 49. And the luck would alternate. For 10 days, she couldn't win; for the next 10 days, I couldn't.

Some of her friends would come over and make the game a threesome or a foursome. One of them loaned us a set from China that had no numbers or letters on the tiles. You had to learn the Chinese characters. I once tried playing with a table of translations at my side. It was remarkable how quickly one learned this when we had to. Before the 70's, Mahjong was not made in Canada and could only be purchased privately. Later, when western manufacturers got into the act, I didn't like their products. Instead of racks, the tiles were thick and were stood up on their edges, making it harder to conceal your hand. And the tiles were slippery

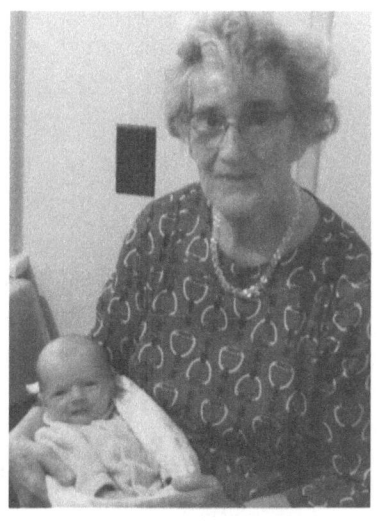

*Aunt Mary with Breffney Jane*

and wouldn't stack well. But then it's possible that the makers have already smoothed out these wrinkles since then.

Aunt Mary started taking her meals with us when we moved to 133 Glasgow Street, N. That house seemed to be made for her situation. As you entered the front hall, our large living-room loomed on the left. On the right was her small living-room which connected with her bathroom and her bedroom. Cousins who came to visit would sometimes take us aside and thank us for 'looking after' Aunt Mary. I would always answer that she looked after us. She regularly washed the pots and pans after dinner. She kept my mending and darning up-to-date. And she kept me in touch with many of the relatives. When she was about 95, she slipped on some ice outside our front door and broke her arm. The arm was soon tended to so that she didn't suffer much. But she didn't like depending on me to tie her shoe-laces. And she was no end frustrated because she couldn't get on with her knitting for a great grand nephew who was about to be born in Manitoba!

Aunt Mary remained canny about money. Once during her early 90's, Eleanor helped her shop for a new outfit. When they got home, Aunt Mary was somewhat aghast when she saw the price. Finally, so as not to seem ungrateful to Eleanor, she remarked that she would just have to live long enough to justify the purchase!

During the last year of her life when I was Chair of Waterloo Presbytery, I got to covenant with Harcourt Church and Reverend Jean Wright who had been called to the ministry there after filling in over the previous year. I was able, during that service, to share Aunt Mary's enthusiasm over the call. A search committee had been meeting for weeks but had concluded that they couldn't do better than to keep the person they had. Jean had qualified for the United Church ministry after serving with the Baptists. One day, Aunt Mary couldn't wait to tell me the news. "Do you know who has been called at Harcourt?"

Aunt Mary was as sharp as ever right up until the end of her life. A month before her body stopped functioning, she was in church. Five days before she died, a friend visited with her in her hospital ward, and together they went at a cross-word puzzle. When they had finished all but one word, the friend had to leave. But as she was passing through the door, Aunt Mary called her back. She had got the word!

Aunt Mary was valued at Harcourt up to the end of her life—and afterward. She was regularly picked up for church by the Whittakers, and this continued until less than a month before she died. On Friday mornings she was picked up for Bible study. On her last night, John Buttars and Jean Wright shared a vigil at the hospital. She left that church $6,000 which was used to buy copies of *Voices United,* the last United Church Hymn book, when it came out. She would have approved of that. Later a room was decorated in her honour at Five Oaks by the UCW at Harcourt.

CHAPTER 106

# Breffney Jane

We became grandparents at Thanksgiving, 1979. We were about to serve the big dinner at 264 Woolwich Street when Bruce phoned to give us the news. A few weeks later, I visited 30 Lorindale in Toronto, arriving in the early evening. As we sat in the kitchen, I asked where they'd put Breffney, and I was told to look down. There she was, sound asleep in a basket on the floor. I also recall that the diaper routine had improved considerably since her mother was an infant. At the same time, there was a baby seat in the family car, something we had never needed to consider since Morrey was already five when we acquired our first car.

Was Breffney one and a half or two and a half when her mother took her to tea at the Dicksons' log cabin on Muldrew Lake? Esther Dickson handed her a toy which she considered safe since no child could open it. Before she could turn around, Breffney had the thing open!

We played a game at a family Christmas party when she was little. We told her, "You call women, pretty, and men, handsome". At an unexpected moment, Breffney came out with, "Uncle Morrey's handsome," to which he quickly responded, "Right on!"

Breffney could play Mahjong from the age of three. One of the bamboo tiles has faded dye because Breffney, in a moment of inattentiveness on her parents' part, sucked on it.

Given names can be a problem for those who carry them. With some, like mine, the problem is that of distinguishing one from others of the same name who may be present. "Oh Don," doesn't always mean me. Others, like Breffney and Morrey, have to teach people both the

*Breffney with baby Caitlin*

spelling and the pronunciation. One day at Muldrew, when Breffney was three, I had an errand at the landing and took her along for the ride. While I did my business, I left her on the sand beach. When I returned, she was addressing some other children and saying, "No—BREFFNEY, not BREFF-A-NEE!" I have been given to understand, by the way, that Breffney is the name of a lake in Ireland.

Some things I can say about Breffney apply equally to her sister, Caitlin. Both experienced the life at the cottage from their earliest years, have responded with enthusiasm, and have come to take their full share of responsibility in making Thirlestane an attractive place. Both have consistently treated their grandparents with generous affection (I can recall them, as little ones, running into my arms on their arrival at the lake). Both have always treated 'Grandpa's porridge' as something that you eat with pleasure. Both have readily made friends, on and off the lake. Both have maintained a loving relationship with both parents since the ending of their marriage. Both are outgoing, capable people. Both have strong singing voices which were strongly evident at family gatherings when we would sing a round for grace. Both were taught to swim by our cottage neighbour, Rosemary Bartlett, and both had her for Physical Education at Bedford Park Public School. Both got their high school education at Lawrence Park Collegiate, where the teachers they encountered were a somewhat mixed bag. Both became excellent drivers when they grew up. I could go on, and will probably want to add to the list as it occurs to me.

I almost forgot the United Church camp on Sparrow Lake, a widening of the Severn River and thus part of the Trent waterway across Ontario from the Bay of Quinte to Georgian Bay. Both girls spent several summers there first as campers, then as counsellors-in-training, counsellors and staff with greater responsibility. I have never heard a

*Breffney and Caitlin with 'Grandpa'*

negative comment about these experiences. At least, I believe I am safe in saying that the sources of satisfaction have always outweighed the inevitable unpleasant moments.

One winter when the girls were five and two or six and three, I was playing with them in the snow behind our house, and some problem developed involving Caitlin. Breffney commented, "That's alright, Grandpa, you don't know about children, do you!"

As her reading expanded in scope, Breffney began to read novels with chapters. Her first I remember was by Jean Little called *Different Dragons* which takes place at 264 Woolwich Street in Guelph, the house where the author grew up and where Breff had often visited her grandparents.

When Breffney was about twelve, she and I had a few days together at the cottage at the end of June and the first week of July because she had had chicken pox and couldn't go to Sparrow Lake camp right away. The first day, she caught up on sleep. Then we got playing Mahjong, Dig, and Word Quest—by the hour. We were well matched, although Word Quest is a game where experience of the language is an advantage. Then one day we paddled to the Dales' in Paterson's Bay. It was a paddle I had often done in years gone by, but on this occasion I was out of condition. Paddling there, we had the wind behind us. But, returning, we had a strong head wind and I felt a sense of achievement in just winning around Picnic Point. Throughout, Breff was a strong partner. We stopped briefly to rest at Dead Horse Island where she slipped into the lake. But the weather was warm and she simply found it amusing.

Breffney has graduated from the University of Western Ontario with a degree in Geology. She spent one summer working for DeBeers, the diamond company, collecting soil samples at a centre about 400 kms. north of Thunder Bay. She would be dropped off each morning at her place of work by helicopter. Before being picked up she would have to lug 35 kilograms of soil on her back. At first, she wondered if she could stick it out, especially as the insects were the worst she had ever experienced. But she persevered, developed the necessary muscles, and carried on. It's the sort of experience from which one can't help benefitting.

In 2003, she moved to Calgary, Alberta and entered law school, graduating in the spring of 2006. She worked for a small law firm completing her articles and will soon be called to the bar.

In December 2006, we were invited to Calgary for Christmas with Breffney and Mike. We wouldn't have missed it. We were, of course, introduced to the house Breff and Mike had purchased which was in the early stages of being built. Although it was just half finished, we could imagine the final product when we saw the model. Afterward, Breffney sent us progress pictures by e-mail until June 29th when they were able to move in.

On Christmas Eve, we were taken to a 10 o'clock service at Scarboro United Church where former moderator Bill Phipps was finishing his last year of many in this charge. He had been one of the many people who had remembered my 90th birthday and it was good to greet him in person. (I realized during a carol that he had spotted me in the pews.)

The next afternoon, we were treated to an excellent performance of *The Nutcracker* by the very professional Alberta Ballet Company in the huge South Alberta Jubilee Auditorium.

The day after, we paid our first visit to the town of Banff. Of course, we visited the shops and the local museum. My best attention, however, was taken by the two peaks that dominate the town on the East and the West.

But the best part of our visit had to be our chance to get to know our hosts in a way that is not always possible in a large family gathering.

This summer, during ten days, Breff and Mike spent time at Thirlestane and Breffney used her skill to achieve order in the all-too-handy cupboard under the stairs. This involved a certain ruthlessness where the family was concerned. But we all felt that it was worthwhile.

CHAPTER 107

# Caitlin Anne

Caitlin was our first family computer expert. In June, 2003, when our new computer arrived, she came for a day and put it all together before the professional arrived to do what the firm required. After he had left, the machine was still not ready for use by someone with my level of understanding. So Caity came over from Waterloo for another two hours after which I was able to operate.

Caitlin was a lively baby. When she was two, her father remarked, "I have to realize that there is no limit to her capacity to destroy. It's the way she learns about things." This comment had come after she had ruined a turn-table by ramming the tone-arm down quickly on a record. Around this time, while my bedroom at 264 Woolwich Street was on the ground floor, I carefully retrieved my electric alarm clock when I found her carrying it around. However, all this was a passing phase showing the untrained initiative she had been born with. Six months later, no one had to worry.

A little later, I started playing a table game with the girls. When it exceeded her attention span, Caitlin used an expression learned from her elders to explain her departure: "Right back." Of course, it was not part of her understanding of the expression that she would actually return.

At the age of seven, Caitlin performed a useful service in connection with the new Metro Zoo. I had long remembered the old Riverdale zoo, but had not experienced the new one at Toronto's east end. The Mackay family had often taken it in, using a family membership. So Caity was elected to take me round. On the appointed day, I picked her up at her school

*Caitlin*

and drove her to the zoo. We tramped, it seemed, for miles, seeing the tall giraffes in an open field (I had forgotten how tall they actually were), active dolphins in a pool with windows, and many other species. At last, we were approaching the exit, and Caity sighed, "Well, now you've seen the zoo." Her job was done, and we could go home. She slept soundly in the car.

In the previous chapter, I have listed a number of things that apply to both my wonderful older granddaughters. As little children, I seem to remember the usual children's spats. But during their high school years, they related well to each other. When they visited us at 133 Glasgow Street, they took great pleasure in sleeping together. In her teenage years, Caitlin usually had a job in a ladies clothing store during her holidays where she learned people skills that will always be useful. It was not a surprise that she registered in a business course in university, or that she is doing well.

At Breffney's wedding, Caitlin was, of course, the maid of honour. What some guests may have forgotten, or not known, was that three days before, she had to have her appendix removed. However, she rose to the occasion with a speedy recovery and supported her sister admirably.

In 1999, when Jim got a job in New York City, Esther delayed moving to the US until Caitlin had finished high school. In September, 2001, when Caitlin went off to begin her business degree at Wilfrid Laurier University, Esther moved to New York. In Caitlin's second year, she moved out of residence and rented a house with several of her friends. She also played a leading part in student activities, ultimately heading up the marketing and communication activities for the Peer Help Line as well as working part-time in the computer room at the student centre.

The spring after graduation, with a very close friend, she toured Europe on a student tour. Her study of French came in handy. When the customs official in France inquired on the bus if anyone spoke French, she became the designated interpreter for him and thereafter on the trip.

The following year at Christmas, a number of the Australian students on the Europe tour had invited her to visit and she spent the holiday season down under touring Eastern Australia.

For a couple of summers in a row, she had worked at the Ontario Hydro control centre in Clarkson where her father worked. The job seemed pretty routine until the great power outage on August 16th. She got a firsthand view of disaster recovery procedures as the power went out all along the eastern seaboard from Ontario down to New York State and across as far as Ohio. It was a good thing that it had happened at the end of the summer rather than the beginning as she was called on to provide support in ways that would have been impossible at the beginning of the summer.

After graduating from Laurier, Caitlin did a one year postgraduate diploma course in Advertising at Centennial College followed by an internship at the MacLaren McCann agency in Toronto. She was hired on permanently before her internship was completed and since, has received high praise and a promotion. It would seem that 'the sky's the limit' where she is concerned. We are very proud of her.

CHAPTER 108

# Alexander Mactaggart

In many ways, Alexander's first years were difficult. His difficulty in relating to the concept of eating must have affected his disposition. His extreme allergic reaction to any peanut products must have tempered his normal pleasure in attending birthday parties. (Around the age of one, he ate a cracker with peanut butter on it and he immediately broke out in a violent rash. Subsequently he even had a skin reaction when Morrey gave him a hug after eating peanut butter. There had been some on his moustache.) And having a teacher tell him that he was dumb did lasting harm.

On the other hand, there were times of real happiness. I recall entering the family living room and finding Alexander dancing around the room with great abandon to a tape that was playing. Around this time, a certain song was played often enough to become familiar. His Bloor Street Sunday School teacher was teaching her class about Jesus' death. He mentioned this in the car coming home, and his Dad replied, "But Jesus lives on in our hearts," to which Alexander responded, "My heart's in the Highlands!"

Alexander found that learning to walk was thrilling. One day, his parents sat at opposite ends of the living room, while he walked from one to the other, over and over, till he became exhausted. A whole new world had opened up.

Interest in mechanical things began early. When he was two, his parents took him on a trip to Switzerland. On his return, he pointed up at hydro wires and exclaimed, "cable car".

When Alexander was small, his mother often called, "Come here, Mister". Once at school, when he was asked his name, he replied, "Alexander Mister Mactaggart Ewing!"

The arrival of a baby sister proved hard to get used to. Jealousy set in when parental attention had to be shared, and the

*Alexander & Don*

disagreements were many—sometimes violent. Therefore, his grandmother found a certain incident in Halifax a refreshing departure. The family had made various visits to the Museum of the Atlantic, and some of these had included Alexander before Annie was old enough to go. The first time she was taken, her brother realized that he had something to share. He took her by the hand and said, "Come on, Annie, I'll show you round."

After three difficult years of schooling and the harsh reputation of the second grade teacher he was likely to get, Morrey and Sharon decided to put him in a private school throughout his elementary years.

Alexander often showed a preference for the cottage at Muldrew over the house in Nova Scotia, perhaps because the cottage is on water. When he was about six, I took him rowing in what we call the 'Cockleshell'. At first, we each took an oar and tried to coordinate our strokes, then I let him try to handle both oars. Shortly afterward, we reached Scovils' and, while I visited with grown-ups, Alexander took out Suzi, Trish Scovil's daughter, and "showed" her how to row!

Often Esther has taken Alexander to the Lake for a weekend when there was work to be done. She has found that he is not only a good helper, but enjoys taking responsibility for a segment of the work, and is proud of the result. One year, the cottage was being readied for use after the summer, and windows had to be washed. He took responsibility for the windows of one room and went at it vigorously with a squeegee.

For some years, in the old cottage, Alexander had the habit of leaving the table at mealtimes every time a boat was heard, to go to where he could see it. In the new cottage the table was placed where he could see the lake from the table. By that time, however, the novelty had rather worn off. But he early received instruction in running the motor-boat and has become a very safe driver. Perhaps we should not have been surprised, therefore, that, for three years, he had been given responsibility in connection with the running of the tender for the Mahone Bay Wooden Boat Festival.

Often really attractive children become brats when they reach adolescence. I was never aware of this in Alexander. In fact, he has become more personable as he moved into his teens. He would engage in mature conversation on the phone with his grandparents. One year when Suzanne Perreard arrived at 50 Anderson, Morrey and Sharon were out. Without prompting, Alexander phoned us to be sure we knew this had happened.

Two table games show the change that the years have brought. When Alexander was 4 or 5, we played a game of Sorry. We disagreed about one aspect of the rules. So I consulted the instructions which corroborated my idea. But Alexander almost yelled at me that he KNEW the rules and that I must do it his way. About nine years later, we played chess in Mahone Bay. I might have been playing with a grown-up. Not only had he mastered the rather complicated rules of the game, but my position was always respected.

Alexander has had a variety of jobs. One summer, he worked part-time, in a Cole's bookstore down the road from Acadia University. The pay was not very high, of course. Another year he was employed at a marina on Toronto's water-front. Preparing and sometimes operating boats that people rent is work he has enjoyed. Sometimes he has had to go on rescue missions to bring back people whose motors wouldn't go or who had run out of gas. Having access to his father's car on days off meant that we could enjoy his company at the cottage which is always a delight. More recently he has worked at one of the sailing clubs in Halifax as well as a local radio station. I look forward to more years associating with this great young adult.

CHAPTER 109

# Margaret Anne

Margaret Anne Ewing was born in 1990. She chose at an early age to be called Annie. I have always thought of her as a child with a sunny disposition. She has, of course, endured the usual frustrations. But a smile seems never to be far from her face. I picture her peering around the door to the living-room before a family party with a facial expression that suggested expectation of something she would enjoy.

She has also exhibited positive attitudes. One Christmas, two people managed to give her the same present. Instead of making either donor feel embarrassed, she promptly exclaimed that when a present is that good, she was happy to get two of them.

In the early 90's, we had a house concert on Glasgow Street by the English trio 'Artisan'. Sharon moved about at the back with wee Annie in her arms. Perhaps, with that encouragement, one should not have been surprised to see her—in Mahone Bay and elsewhere—moving spontaneously to a rhythmic recording. In the family van in Nova Scotia I can remember her sitting ahead of me, singing away various songs including Bob Rae's Same Boat Now.

When Annie reached school age, reports on the quality of teaching at the local public school were still not encouraging, and Morrey and Sharon put her in one of a series of private schools. Before long that school was St. Clements, where she has been very happy.

In grade four, she competed in a public speaking contest for students in grades four, five and six, a contest that was usually won by someone in grade six. Her winning speech dealt with various reasons for treating frogs kindly, ending with, "You never know when it is going to turn into a prince!" I can imagine that clear delivery had a lot to do with her win.

For a number of years, Annie declared that art was her favourite subject. When she was about four, Annie produced a painting of a back view of an elephant, a piece that has graced our kitchen ever since. For years, when she came home from school, she would pick up a crayon or another drawing tool. One day I heard her ask her father, "Daddy, when I grow up, may I have the garage for a studio?" Another day, she told her mother that, when she grew up, she would paint every day but Thursdays. "And what are you going to do on Thursdays?" her mother asked. "I'd keep that for sculpture," came the reply. More recently, her interests have become broader and a bit less predictable.

In her first years, when her brother went through the jealous stage, she developed a thick skin. This has not stood in the way of graciousness in meeting adults. But she can be quite frank when things displease her. In Nova Scotia, she has participated happily in a summer choir camp. The first experience, however, was distinctly unhappy. Arriving at the camp on a wet day when the muddy ground was being tracked into every building, she discovered that a special friend had been assigned to a different cabin. She made it very clear to her mother, then and by phone the next day, that this just wouldn't do. However, this proved to be an opportunity for Annie to make new friends and her experience at camp was a happy one.

Annie sings with a very pure soprano voice and has participated in choirs at school and church. Recently, she has been speaking with something of an alto

*Annie kissing a frog*

tone. It will be interesting to see how her voice develops and whether it means that her voice will lower. Annie has had vocal lessons and has competed in the local Kiwanis Festival. In one class, involving musical theatre, she was the winner, and went on to represent the Toronto Festival in a conference in Ottawa of participants from across Ontario.

When she turned sixteen, her grandmother and I commissioned Eleanor Daley to write a song with words which Annie would choose. With Morrey's help, she chose a sonnet by Christina Rosetti. Eleanor was especially glad to be writing for one of the strong members of her intermediate choir. In April, at her singing teacher's class recital in Fairlawn Heights United Church, Annie premiered the song. Her adult voice and style were evident.

In Mahone Bay each summer, Annie has been taking instruction in sailing, a pursuit that she enjoys so much that I imagine she will likely do this all her life. In September 2006, during a school trip to Scotland, one of the host students took her out sailing on the Firth of Forth and she wowed him with her skill in handling a dinghy on the North Sea.

Every year Annie grows into more and more of a young woman, ready to take centre stage in whatever she attempts. How did I deserve such a wonderful granddaughter?

CHAPTER 110

# April 12, 2003— Gala Anniversary

We were told, months in advance, to keep this night, as Morrey would be 50 that week, and the plan was for our immediate family to celebrate that at Alvin Rebick's Bistro 6 that night. We duly marked our calendar. Sometime later, Esther booked our family room for the week of April 13th. We see Esther seldom enough and we accepted that with pleasure.

Then one day I got a peculiar e-mail. It was a copy of one to Esther and Morrey from Susan Francis, a niece of Eleanor's, saying that, because of a previous booking, they couldn't come to the party. "The party?" We should have twigged that something was up. However, a lot of queer e-mails come our way and we left this as a mystery.

On the 12th, Jim Sylph announced that he was driving us to the party. On our way, he told us Morrey had been visiting an art show at Dublin Church and had seen something he thought would interest his mother. Accordingly, we parked at Dublin Church. But Eleanor had seen these art shows before and was not attracted. Her concern was that we get to Bistro 6 on time and she was not getting out of the car. However, I had obediently opened my door, and Jim was able to persuade her to accompany us.

Inside the church, we had to pass through the gym that was set up for dinner and wondered aloud whose wedding was involved. Jim took us to the back door of the sanctuary and took my coat before I entered.

The surprise was complete. My first sensations were the red flash of a camera and the sound of a trumpet. Seconds later, I became aware of a host of familiar faces. We were ushered to

*Head table at Anniversary Gala*

the front where we were seated next to Suzanne Perreard! Eleanor had been trying to phone her for days and had wondered why she had not answered her phone in Geneva.

After we had kissed our grandchildren, the concert began. Gerry Neufeld stood up and led a choir which turned out to be a combination of members of the Guelph Chamber Choir and that of Fairlawn Heights United Church in Toronto. Music had been thrust in front of us, and I gradually became aware that the music had been written specially by Eleanor Daley and that the composer was at the piano!

By this point, we had realized that the occasion was not Morrey's birthday, but our 55th wedding anniversary, celebrated officially the previous December in Mahone Bay, Nova Scotia, but made the excuse for an extravagant tribute to ourselves. At the brief reception following the music, we gradually became aware of just who had made it there. Esther and Morrey, assisted by key people in different walks of life, had invited about 200 people of whom about 130 actually came. I'm sure few married couples enjoy this degree of devotion on the part of their sons and daughters.

We also found out that the initial trumpet fanfare had been

played by Alexander, the music specially written by his teacher. We found out that the movie of the evening, which we were able subsequently to watch, was taken by Alice Milne of Toronto, and that Alice had masterminded the evening's practical organization. We found out that Jim was not only our chauffeur, but the MC of the evening—an exemplary MC, whom we would quickly recommend for other similar occasions. We found that, instead of catering for an intimate family birthday party, Alvin Rebick and his staff had catered a delicious dinner for the whole crowd. And we found out afterward that Esther had arranged seating plans to combine guests who she thought might be mutually stimulating.

At the dinner, the speeches were memorable. Marg Norquay gave a fascinating story in which family background played a big part. Agnes Gelb told of many times she and Eleanor had done things together. Diane Clark recalled being taught music by me in a Burlington school and of many lunches with Eleanor whose support in the church she greatly valued. Mayor Karen Farbridge spoke of our participation in Guelph's culture. Rosemary Bartlett maximized the part we had played in the Muldrew Lake community. Murdo McKinnon knocked down any notion that I was dogmatic in stating my ideas. And Ron Williams probably took the prize as he told of our family relations over 40 years. Finally, Esther stressed that her parents were not only parents but friends, while Morrey introduced poetry appropriate for the occasion.

Eleanor and I did our best to give impromptu responses. Of course, I have always been good at thinking on the way home from a gathering what I should have said there. Afterwards I recalled a sermon my parents and I had listened to by radio in the early 30's. The preacher was Harry Emerson Fosdick of the Riverside Church in New York. The sermon dealt with the importance of believing in the veracity of our finest hours. By way of illustration, he told of a day when he was six years old and had been a real "pain". He had been selfish, rude, disruptive, and many other things. As he told the story, his father would endure only so much of this; then he would begin saying 'Where's Harry? I haven't seen him all day.' The idea was that the real Harry was a delightful child.

What I might have said—after giving our deepest thanks—would have run something like this. "A lot of nice things have been said about us tonight. But I'm sure no one here imagines that we are like that all the time. There are days when we're hard to live with, days when nothing seems to go right. What you have done by your presence and by the things that have been said is to assure us that when we are at our best, that is who we really are. I could only wish someone would do the same for each of you."

A sequel happened in the middle of the following week. Barrie and Sheri Cabena had been unable to come to the party because of duties relating to the annual garage sale of the Guelph Spring Festival. But Barrie delivered his contribution to our celebration. His opus 441 was a suite of piano pieces which he called "Five-and-a-half Winter Potatoes", and which has given us both great satisfaction. In October, 2003, at one of Chalmers Church's noon-hour recitals, I played the 'Potatoes." Barrie was there, and gave full approval of my treatment.

The morning after the party, Esther told us: "I have a confession to make. I booked your accommodation for next week, so that you could put Suzanne there instead." SHE couldn't stay!

# Epilogue

# I—July, 2008

It is now almost five years since the last chapter was written. Since then either my editor or I have been busy with other things, and much has happened in the interval. Esther continues to be busy helping people "build their capability." She has clients in England, in Canada, in the United States—and even in Hawaii! She has given two very successful recitals: one in Toronto in 2003 accompanied by Eleanor Daley; the other in 2008 in New York with Katya Pine. She serves annually as a lay preacher at Muldrew Lake and her many friendships are rich in quality.

Jim continues to be a great strength in the family when he is not touring the world on business. Sometimes, Esther is able to travel with him. Among other places, they have been to India, Singapore, Thailand and more recently, to Egypt. When they return home to Toronto, they will occupy a condominium down on the lake shore.

Breffney graduated from Western University in Geology, spent an energetic summer working for De Beers Diamond Company collecting soil samples in the wilderness of Northern Ontario, and, in 2006, married another Western graduate, Michael Kreitner. The ceremony was conducted in Trinity United Church in Gravenhurst by Reverend Don Gillies. They settled in Calgary, where Mike worked for PetroCanada, and Breffney successfully prepared to be a lawyer. Shortly after she was called to the bar in Alberta (October 2007) Mike received from his company a three-year appointment in Denver, Colorado. And it is there that our first great-grandchild is to be born in December of 2008.

Caitlin graduated from Wilfrid Laurier University with a business degree and has now been employed for two years by an advertising firm, a setting where she continues to shine. She continues to enjoy traveling in her spare time.

Alexander showed his computer knowledge and skills by assembling a computer during his last year in High School. He is now entering his last year as an undergraduate at university. He will be at the Dalhousie campus after spending three years at Acadia. Last summer, he worked on the Toronto waterfront. This summer, he has a similar job in Halifax, plus employment in a radio station twice a week. He continues to be a stimulating conversationalist, by telephone or e-mail.

Annie graduated this year from St. Clement's School and will be attending St. Francis-Xavier University in Antigonish, Nova Scotia. In recent summers, she has studied sailing at the Lunenburg Yacht Club. And she demonstrated her skill during a trip to Scotland. This summer, she is teaching it. She has studied singing for several years, and it has been interesting to notice development from her little-girl voice to adult maturity. It was my privilege to accompany her in "A Wintry Sonnet", a song written for her by Eleanor Daley. We performed it at her grandmother's 90th birthday celebration.

People sometimes ask how I keep going at 91. Part of it is having inherited a healthy body—I sometimes give thanks that I still have two good legs even though my sense of balance isn't as good as it used to be. Part of it is my habit of sleeping through the early part of each afternoon. But another part has been the strength of my hands, which, among other things, allows me to keep at my piano playing.

At the cottage it is sometimes unsocial to practice on the piano located in the living room. I don't tend to use it when anyone is sleeping upstairs, or when the phone is in use, or when people want to visit. A couple of years ago, I rented an excellent electronic keyboard which we keep in the studio. For my 90th birthday, the family turned my rental into a purchase. It is now used for part of every day I am at Muldrew.

# II—Politics

I continue to be active in the NDP, in ways that don't involve door-to-door campaigning. In September, 2006, I was one of several Guelph delegates to the federal party convention in Quebec City. This event was unique in several ways. The party laid on a train any delegate could use to get from Montreal to Quebec. Over 600 travelled that way making it a very long train, so the train had to stop repeatedly to let passengers out at Quebec City's too small platform.

Another element of this event's uniqueness was that the party prioritized its resolutions in a new way. Usually, several hundred resolutions come in while only about 40 to 60 ever make their way to the convention floor for consideration. In the past, a resolutions committee has prioritized them, subject to appeals from the convention floor.

This time, our first sessions were smaller panels, divided according to subject areas. At the panel sessions, a list of resolutions was presented in a certain order. Then followed a motion of approval, which, however, could be amended. I moved an amendment moving mine from 34th to 4th priority and got it passed. That meant that it would almost certainly reach the floor which it did on the Sunday morning.

But three minutes allowed for resolutions to be introduced were totally insufficient to explain an essentially new idea. My motion called for the party, in future, to campaign openly to be elected as the government in every riding, rather than trying to convince the electorate to vote for the NDP only in ridings where we could either win or split the vote. I am convinced that many voters who like our policies, often vote instead, strategically, for another party because they don't believe that the NDP will ever be in government and therefore able to carry them out.

Of course it was easy to get the resolution passed but much harder to get the delegates convinced that we could actually win goverment at Ottawa, since it had never been done. However, an hour and a half later when Jack Layton gave his wind-up address, he said he would "ask the people of Canada to hire him as prime minister". I have followed up by e-mails to Jack Layton along the same lines. Recently, Jack Layton visited Guelph, and while he was shaking hands, remarked that, "Don and I correspond!"

Meanwhile, I have joined many other Canadians in being fascinated by the American election campaign, featuring the emergence of Barack Obama. This has had two results for me. Firstly, I have been forced to renew my understanding of the geography of the United States. Secondly, I am looking forward to the possibility that the US will regain its position in the world of setting a good example for the rest of us.

# III—Recent Celebrations

Following the success of our 55th anniversary party, Esther and Morrey continue to organize outstanding celebrations. At my 90th birthday on November 1st, 2006, there was the usual family gathering at which I was toasted in song. But the lasting item was the book, designed by Jessica Heald, of a compilation of what over 200 relatives and friends tried to put into words what I had meant to them. For instance, Angela Hewitt, who has repeatedly used our piano to rehearse for local concerts, wrote of how I had introduced her to the Poulenc *Intermezzo in A Flat*, playing it for her in our recreation room. She complimented me on "daring to play for her" as she said that most people would be too nervous!

I told Esther that if I lasted to a hundred, she wouldn't need to celebrate because everything would have been said!

But the event that topped them all celebrated Eleanor's 90th birthday in May, 2008. Planned a year ahead by Eleanor herself, it was built around music that she had commissioned to be written by Canadian composers over a period of more than 40 years. The feature of this activity was her choice of Esther's long-time friend, Katya Pine, to set 7 poems from *A Garden Going On Without Us* by Lorna Crozier. This was performed by Esther, Soprano, and the Composer, Katya, at the piano. An additional work, *The Wild Birds*, also to poems by Lorna Crozier, was composed by Katya and performed by Katya on the piano, Esther singing and Doriann Forrester on the flute. Other performers were Annie Ewing, myself and Morrey.

# IV—Jim Allen

In May, 2008, my flute partner of over 50 years, Jim Allen, passed away at the age of 83. In the late 1950's, Jim had inherited a library of flute music from Charlie Armstrong, a brother-in-law who had died at a very early age. He came over to our cottage looking for an accompanist and I got elected. This began a rewarding association of half a century.

In the first years, we practised only in the summer. Jim would walk across the Middle Portage to Memorial Pines where I would meet him in my motor boat. Without significant coordination, we had this meeting timed exactly. As I was slowing for a landing, he would be coming down the hill to the dock.

These summers gave us time to tackle works like the sonatas of Bach and the Hindemith *Flute Sonata*. The music was often a little beyond us technically. But we usually managed to achieve an expression worth sharing. Soon we resolved to give our rehearsals a more immediate objective by presenting house concerts at which these works were performed. Once Jim had the satisfaction of hearing his children humming bits of the Hindemith!

*Jim Allen*

At one point, Jim also began bringing his clarinet. He had used it for jazz, but he gave me credit for starting him on classical clarinet. At another point, we were joined by another flautist, enabling us to do Bach works for two flutes, then by another clarinetist, facilitating other trios.

When Jim retired as a teacher in 1985, he moved to Guelph, and we were able to practise the year round. It also meant that he could join our amateur group, "Pro Musica" which gave us a monthly objective of presenting a piece to the group. Pro Musica is about 15

Guelph people who enjoy monthly meetings where we perform for each other. At this time, we began performing piano and clarinet music. Now our repertoire came to include numbers by Faure and Elgar and our great favourite, the *Bagatelles* by Gerald Finzi. We sometimes added a second clarinet or a second flute for our trios. Thus we never had a shortage of works to try out for this audience of friends.

Our summer programs have also recently been enriched by the participation of Janet Allen on her cello, Don Gillies who joined me for four-hand piano arrangements and Allan Foster who has played at the beginnings and ends of our concerts on the bagpipes.

This year, our concert was given in Jim's memory and a new element was added as 10 year old Max Allen, Janet's son, sang a song and accompanied himself on guitar with his mother on cello. Memories of Jim were shared with us by Ann Armstrong and her sister Joan who recalled how important their uncle Jim had been in the family. Of course, their father was Charles Armstrong who got Jim and me started with his gift of music.

During his last months, Jim's health did not allow him to play as he used to. But the memory of the important way our association has enriched my life will always stay with me.

# End Notes

**1. Fred Nixon,** farmer north of Cobourg, my Grandmother Haig's brother-in-law.

**2. James McLeod** was the younger brother of my grandmother, Maggie McLeod Haig, and he married Lillian Nixon, my Uncle Fred Nixon's sister.

**3. Harry Emerson Fosdick** (1878-1969), a minister in New York, became a central figure in the conflict between fundamentalism and liberal forces in American Protestantism in the 1920's and 30's. He presented the Bible as a record of the unfolding of God's will, not as the literal Word of God.

**4. The Canadian Officers' Training Corps (COTC)** trained university undergraduates for officer commissions in the Canadian Army reserves. The COTC was eventually absorbed by the Regular Officers' Training Program as part of the reorganization of the Canadian Armed Forces.

**5. The United Church of Canada** was founded in 1925 as a merger of four Christian denominations: the then largest and second-largest Protestant denominations in Canada, the Presbyterian Church in Canada and the Methodist Church of Canada, the Congregational Union of Ontario and Quebec, a numerically less significant but historically important denomination of evangelical Protestantism and the Association of Local Union Churches. The Methodists decided centrally that all their congregations would join. The Presbyterians allowed each congregation to vote whether or not to join the union so that at church union, there remained enough congregations to form a Presbyterian Church of Canada which exists to today. In 1968, the Evangelical Union Brethren joined as well and were allowed to keep their own Hymnary.

**6.** In the **Ontario school system** of the time, there were four books (or grades) in elementary school and each was supposed to take two years to study. But first book almost never took two years and second book took two years in Galt but only one year in Oshawa and because we moved from Galt to Oshawa, I had skipped most of second book. My Aunt Muriel, who was a teacher, took me for two weeks in the summer and taught me second book so that I could enter third book in Oshawa (approximately grade five in the current system).

**7. Grade Eight.**

**8. Walter Johannes Damrosch** (1842-1950) was an American symphony conductor. I remember him for NBC's Music Appreciation Hour for schools.

**9. Deems Taylor, American** composer, the narrator of the Disney Film classic, "Fantasia" acted for many years as the intermission commentator on the Sunday afternoon broadcasts of the New York Philharmonic Orchestra.

**10. Ignacy Jan Paderewski** (1860-1940) was a world-famous Polish pianist, who also served his country as president for several months. During this period, he once remarked, "When I miss a day's practice, I know it. When I miss two, my family knows it. When I miss three, my commissars (like cabinet ministers) know it. When I miss four, the whole world knows it!"

**11. *The History of Faith at Work*,** by Karl A. Olsson, M.D. A five part historical series detailing the various aspects of the work and accomplishments of the Reverend Samuel Moor Shoemaker, Jr., DD, STD who was connected to the Alcoholics Anonymous organization. The second part is about Frank Buchman, the Oxford Group and the Four Absolutes: Honesty, Purity, Unselfishness and Love.

**12. "I would be enchanted."**

**13. H. Northrop Frye,** (1912-1991), a Canadian, was one of the most distinguished literary critics and literary theorists of the twentieth century. He was a member of the English teaching staff of Victoria College and the University of Toronto during most of his life. In 1939, he and his wife Helen chaperoned for me a mixed party of students at our cottage on Muldrew Lake.

**14. John D. Robins,** distinguished professor of English at Victoria College. Author of "The Incomplete Anglers" about a canoe trip in Algonquin Park, and "Cottage Cheese" about two weeks spent on Dale Island in Muldrew Lake in 1919.

**15. Edwin J. Pratt,** (1882—1964) a Canadian from Newfoundland who taught at Victoria College and became the foremost Canadian poet of the 20th century.

**16. Leo Smith,** distinguished Canadian cellist, who headed the cello section of the Toronto Symphony for many years. He wrote a much-used text called "Musical Rudiments" and composed works for cello and viol da gamba. He served as an executive with the musicians union where he tended to be a conservative influence. He was a key member of the faculty of music section of the University of Toronto.

**17. Healey Willan,** (1880-1968), known as "the dean of Canadian composers", he was for decades organist and choirmaster of St. Mary Magdalene Church, where he was able to work out his many works for choir and for organ. He was a professor in the U of T faculty of Music. As he, himself used to say, he was "English by birth; Canadian by adoption;

Irish by extraction; Scotch by absorption."

**18.** *Lines Composed a Few Miles Above Tinturn Abbey,* William Wordsworth

**19. George Douglas Atkinson** was born in Carp, near Ottawa and moved to Toronto to pursue his musical studies. To complement his training, he also studied briefly in Leipzig, London and New York. From 1911 until he retired in 1950, he served as organist and choirmaster for the Sherbourne Methodist Church of Toronto. He also taught at the Toronto College of Music and the Royal Conservatory of Music (Toronto), while employed as music director of the Ontario Ladies' College. He is the author of a number of articles on piano technique, instruction and methods of evaluation.

**20.** Originally called the **Chautauqua Lake Sunday School Assembly,** it was founded in 1874 as an educational experiment in out-of-school, vacation learning. It was successful and broadened almost immediately beyond courses for Sunday School teachers to include academic subjects, music, art and physical education. While founders Lewis Miller and John Heyl Vincent were Methodists, other Protestant denominations participated from the first year onward, and today Chautauqua continues to be ecumenical in spirit and practice.

**21. The Honourable and Reverend Henry John Cody,** (December 6, 1868—April 27, 1951) was a Canadian clergyman and President of the University of Toronto from 1932 to 1945. He was the Chancellor from 1944 to 1947.

**22. The Student Christian Movement of Canada (SCM)** is a progressive student movement engaged in social justice and spirituality. Since 1921, students have led the SCM in exploring and challenging the Christian tradition and its meaning in society and culture.

**23. Dr. Russell Ames Cook** from Boston, was the first out-of-state conductor of the Portland Symphony Orchestra with a tenure from 1938-51.

**24. Wilbur K. Howard** became in 1974 the first black moderator of the United Church of Canada, Canada's largest Protestant denomination and served from 1974-1977.

**25. E. A. Corbett** became, in 1935, the first executive director of the Canadian Association for Adult Education. Prior to taking up this position, Corbett was director of University of Alberta's extension division and was the person responsible for founding the Citizens' Forum, Farm Radio Forum and the Banff Centre.

**26.** This was probably a poem by **William Henry Drummond,** who published *The Habitant and other French-Canadian Poems* in 1898. The popularity of the book was such as to bring the poet fame, and a substantial income.

**27. Inter-Varsity Christian Fellowship of Canada,** or **IVCF Canada,** is a Christian organisation which ministers to youth and university students through a variety of ministries, including Pioneer Camps of Canada, high school, college and university ministries. IVCF Canada is a member organization of the International Fellowship of Evangelical Students.

**28. *The Varsity,*** the official student newspaper at the University of Toronto, is the second oldest student newspaper in Canada. Created in 1880, The Varsity is published twice weekly during the school year and three times over the summer months.

**29. George Grube** was a professor of classics at the University of Toronto. In the 1950's and 60's, he was the most sought-after chair of conventions of the CCF and the NDP. According to Margaret Dickson, the Muldrew archivist, George Grube rented the old green cottage to the right of Indian Landing which at one time, was the post office of the lumber camp but had been moved over to a rock south of Indian landing. There have been parts added over the years. Two women, Eileen Boyd and Gladys Armstrong owned it.

**30. Charles Hibbert (Charlie) Millard** (1896 - 1978) was a Canadian trade union activist and politician.

**31. Mitchell Frederick Hepburn** (August 12, 1896—January 5, 1953) was Premier of Ontario, Canada, from 1934 to 1942. He was the youngest Premier in Ontario history, elected at age 37.

**32. George Alexander Drew,** PC, CC, QC, LL.D (May 7, 1894— January 4, 1973) was a Canadian conservative politician who founded a Progressive Conservative dynasty in Ontario that lasted 42 years. He served as the 14th Premier of Ontario from 1943 to 1948.

**33. David Lewis** (1909-1981) was a Canadian labour lawyer and politician. He was national secretary of the Cooperative Commonwealth Federation from 1936 to 1950, and, with Stanley Knowles, founded the New Democratic Party (NDP) in 1961. In 1971 he succeeded Tommy Douglas as leaders of the NDP.

**34. Edward (Ted) Bigelow Jolliffe** (1909-1998) was a Canadian politician and lawyer and the first leader of the Ontario Co-operative Commonwealth Federation (CCF).

**35. Leslie (Richard) Bell,** (1906-1962) was director of music at the Ontario College of Education. Famous as leader of the Leslie Bell Singers, a female choir that grew out of an alumni choir of Toronto's Parkdale Collegiate.

**36. The University of Toronto Schools (UTS)** is a co-educational school affiliated with the University of Toronto, offering specialized curriculum for high achieving students, grades 7 through 12. Created by the University of Toronto in 1910 as a Laboratory School for its Faculty of Education, UTS quickly established itself as a unique school where students excel at learning and innovative classroom practice sets the bar in the field of gifted education.

**37. Alec Templeton,** Welsh-American pianist and composer, divided his recitals between serious performance and humour. In his words, "Good music need not be ponderous to be good. It can be everything from Bach to jazz."

**38. Harvey (Dale) Perrin,** (1905-1999) was an Educator, conductor, violinist, violist, arranger.

**39.** The local canoe building industry began in the late 1850s and early 1860s, when small canoe building operations opened in Peterborough, Lakefield and Gore's Landing. There was sustained growth during the 1870s, and then the industry expanded considerably in the late 1800s. Canoes continued to be a major industry in the Peterborough area right up into the 1960s. The "Peterborough" canoe building industry was actually made up of several different businesses over time. In Peterborough, the principle canoe establishments were the Ontario Canoe Company, the Canadian Canoe Company, the Peterborough Canoe Company, the English Canoe Company and, in Lakefield, The Brown Boat Company.

**40.** Dec 1946 to March 1948, according to Peter Scovil.

**41.** Words & Music by Philip P. Bliss, 1873 who wrote the song for his Sunday school class at the First Congregational Church of Chicago, Illinois.

**42.** Words by Knowles Shaw, 1874. Shaw wrote music for these lyrics, but George Minor's tune is universally used today. Music by George A. Minor, 1880.

**43. Robert Raikes,** successful founder in England in the 18th century of the Sunday School movement, produced a subscription booklet for Sunday School children that became very popular.

**44.** Words: From the *Katholisches Gesangbuch* (Würzburg, Germany: circa 1744) *(Beim frühen Morgenlicht);* translated from German to English by Edward Caswall in Formby's *Catholic Hymns* (London: 1854), & Robert S. Bridges in the *Yattendon Hymnal* (Oxford, England: 1899). And Music: Laudes Domini, Joseph Barnby, in *Hymns Ancient and Modern* (London: 1868) Barnby wrote the tune specifically for this hymn.

**45. John Shelby Spong** (born June 16, 1931 in Charlotte, North Carolina) is the retired Bishop of the Episcopal Diocese of Newark (based in Newark, New Jersey). He is the bestselling liberal theologian of recent times, challenging Christians to rethink the nature of God, Christ, the Bible, and other fundamental doctrines.

**46. The Cooperative Commonwealth Federation (CCF)** was founded in Regina, Sask, in 1933, with J. S. Woodsworth as its first leader. It was an amalgamation of several farm, labour and socialist organizations.

**47.** *The Regina Manifesto* was adopted by the CCF at their first national convention held in Regina, Saskatchewan in 1933. Its primary goal was to eradicate capitalism and replace it with a completely planned economy of socialism.

**48. The Canadian Social Credit Party,** under the leadership of William Aberhart swept the provincial and federal elections in Alberta in 1935. Starting with the premise that all citizens have the right to the wealth they jointly produce, Social Credit was a right-wing party. They were replaced in Alberta, in the 1960's, by the Conservatives.

**49. William Duncan Herridge** in 1939 launched the New Democracy party, which advocated monetary reform and government intervention in the economy. The party's positions were similar to those of the Social Credit Party of Canada. He was R. B. Bennett's brother-in-law.

**50. Henry Herbert Stevens** (1878-1973), was a member of Conservative Prime Minister R. B. Bennett's cabinet who broke with him over the economy in 1935, forming a new party called The Reconstruction Party. Although, in the election of 1935, he won only his own seat of Kootenay East in BC, his party took almost as many votes as the CCF, which was a major reason that the CCF did so disappointingly in its first election.

**51. Richard Bedford Bennett,** 1st Viscount Bennett, PC, KC (July 3, 1870—June 26, 1947) was the eleventh Prime Minister of Canada from August 7, 1930 to October 23, 1935.

**52. Arthur W. Roebuck,** (1878-1971), was attorney-general in the Liberal cabinet of Ontario Premier Mitchell Hepburn from 1934. In 1937, he (together with colleague David Croll) was relieved of his post when he sided with the union in the General Motors strike in Oshawa. He entered federal politics three years later, finishing his career in the Senate.

**53. Joseph W. Noseworthy,** (1888-1956), a popular teacher in Vaughan Road Collegiate who became the successful CCF candidate in the federal by-election of South York in 1942. (See chapter 25.) Some of the media painted him as an "obscure" candidate. They didn't realize how many of the voters had been his students.

**54. Associate of the Toronto Conservatory of Music**

**55.** In May 1942 the **British Columbia Forest Service** concluded an agreement with the Dominion Government to give alternative service work to hundreds of Conscientious Objectors. Their work was to consist of snag falling, road building, erecting telephone lines, fire fighting, and reforestation. Under the arrangement, the Dominion Government paid the Forest Service $2.50 per day per man. Of this amount, the camper was paid 50 cents and the rest was used to take care of his board, lodging, and medical attention.

**56. James Shaver Woodsworth** (July 29, 1874—March 21, 1942) was a pioneer in the Canadian social democratic movement. Following more than two decades ministering to the poor and the working class, J. S. Woodsworth left the church to lay the foundation for, and become the first leader of, the Cooperative Commonwealth Federation (CCF), a social democratic party which later became the New Democratic Party (NDP).

**57. W. Nickel,** a young Canadian Mennonite minister who preached in many of their camps, declared that camp life among other results "taught those, who because of previous isolated church life held the members of another denomination in narrow esteem, to respect and love their brother."

**58. The Macdonald Range** lies west of the Flathead River and east of Wigwam River, just north of US border. The range was named on John Palliser's 1863 map and may have been named after Sir John A. Macdonald, who later became Canada's first prime minister.

**59. *The Beacon,*** with editor, Wes Brown, served to keep the men of the BC Forest Service in communication through its 25 camps. The men were conscientious objectors to World War II. The camps were often in isolated locations, and the paper served to keep the men in good spirits.

**60. Romans 13: 1,** *Let every soul be in subjection to the higher powers: for there is no power but of God; and the powers that be are ordained of God.*

**61. Mount Arrowsmith** is the largest mountain on southern Vancouver Island. It has some of the most accessible alpine and sub-alpine areas for Victoria and other large towns on the Island. The first recorded ascent was made by botanist John Macoun in 1887. Macoun was a botanist to the Geological Survey of Canada. The mountain was named for cartographers, Aaron Arrowsmith and his nephew John Arrowsmith. The mountain was known as "Kulth-ka-choolth", meaning "jagged face", in the Coast Salish language.

**62. Esperanto** is a specially invented language whose name comes from Doktoro Esperanto, the pseudonym under which L. L. Zamenhof first published in 1887. The word itself means 'one who hopes'. Zamenhof's goal was to use language to encourage peace and international understanding.

**63. The Nakusp and Slocan Railway (N&S)** ran between Nakusp,

New Denver, British Columbia and Sandon, British Columbia in the Kootenay region of British Columbia. The railway connected with boats on Arrow Lakes at Nakusp (which connected with the CPR mainline at Revelstoke) and Slocan Lake at Rosebary (which connected with the CPR's Columbia and Kootenay Railway (C&K) at Slocan City). The line was extended to Kaslo with the purchase of the Kaslo and Slocan Railway in 1912. The railway has been abandoned.

**64.** *God Be With You Till We Meet Again,* words by Jeremiah E. Rankin, music by William G. Tomer, 1882, who was, at the time, music director at the Grace Methodist Episcopal Church in Washington, DC. Written as a Christian good-bye, it was deliberately composed as a Christian hymn on the basis of the etymology of "good-bye," which is "God be with you."

**65. John Rowe** decided to go by his middle name, Stan, because there were four other Johns in his office.

**66. George Roy Fenwick,** (1989 – 1970), educator, writer, adjudicator, broadcaster. After studies at the Hamilton Conservatory of Music he became supervisor of music for Hamilton public schools in 1922 and was supervisor and later director of music 1935-59 for the Ontario Department of Education. Leslie Bell said of him, 'His greatest achievement has been the musical development of the rural school' (Toronto Daily Star, 25 Jul 1959). Fenwick's school broadcasts, 'Music for Young Folk,' were popular for 18 years (1946-64) and his competition adjudications were considered kind and fair.

**67. A440** is the 440 Hz tone that serves as the standard for musical pitch. A440 is the musical note A above middle C.

**68.** Field Marshal **Harold Rupert Leofric George Alexander, 1st Earl Alexander of Tunis,** (1891– 1969) was a British military commander and field marshal. He later served as the last British Governor General of Canada.

**69. Freemasonry** is an international men's organization. Although it has religious aspects to its rituals, it is not a religion. It does, however, encourage its members to be involved in their own faith and to live a moral life.

**70.** *The Maple Leaf Forever* is a Canadian song written by Alexander Muir (1830–1906) in 1867, the year of Canada's Confederation. Muir was said to have been inspired to write this song by a huge maple tree which stood on his property: Maple Cottage, a house at Memory Lane and Laing Street in Toronto, Ontario, Canada. The song became quite popular in English Canada and for many years served as an unofficial national anthem. Because of its strongly British perspective it became unpopular amongst French Canadians, and this prevented it from ever becoming an official anthem.

**71.** I seem to remember that 'Sandy McPherson' was his somewhat derisive nickname for the stereotypical bagpiper.

**72.** The **Orff Schulwerk** is an approach to Music Education for children. It was developed by the German composer Carl Orff (1895 – 1982), while he was music director of a school of dance and music known as the Günther-Schule, in Munich. Orff regarded the human body as a musical instrument and devised methods of developing children's natural rhythmic abilities through movement.

**73. The pentatonic scale** is a musical scale with five pitches per octave which are doh, ray, mi, soh and lah as compared to the major scale which has seven pitches.

**74. Keith Warren Bissell,** (1912 – 1992), composer, educator, conductor. He studied Orff's methods in Germany and introduced his methods to the Scarborough Schools. Bissell was also an accomplished composer and his works are still performed today.

**75. Zoltán Kodály,** (1882 – 1967), was a colleague of Bartok in the early collection of folk music in Hungary and neighbouring regions, and made his later career in his own country, where the system of musical education he devised has had a profound effect, as it has abroad. The "Kodaly Method" of music for children employed the system of sol-fa and hand signs to give children a physical sense of the relative intervals. His music was inspired by Hungarian folk music.

**76. Thomas Clement Douglas,** (1904 – 1986), was a Scottish-born Baptist minister who became a prominent Canadian social democratic politician. As leader of the Saskatchewan Co-operative Commonwealth Federation (CCF) from 1942 and the seventh Premier of Saskatchewan from 1944 to 1961, he led the first socialist government in North America and introduced universal public Medicare to Canada. He became the first federal leader of the NDP and served from 1961 to 1971. His wit and ability to mesmerize audiences was memorable and in 2004, he was voted "The Greatest Canadian" of all time in a nationally televised contest organized by the Canadian Broadcasting Corporation.

**77.** This brings me to a story I was told. The Saskatchewan Government asked what kind of gift would be of the greatest help to the flood victims and were told, hip boots. Somebody ordered those boots from Eaton's in Winnipeg and got them! Then, of course, they had to be rebundled and sent back.

**78.** Dictionary of Canadian Artists (McDonald v. 2) gives a brief biography of **Richard Gorman**, who, it says, was one of Bob Norgate's students:

Born in Ottawa, Richard Gorman received his first drawing instruction at Fisher Park High School under Robert Norgate.

**79. Suzanne Butler,** (1917 – ), is the author of 3 bestselling novels for adults and 2 wonderful books for children. She lives in Switzerland.

**80. William Lyon Mackenzie King,** (1874 –1950) was the tenth Prime Minister of Canada from December 29, 1921, to June 28, 1926; September 25, 1926, to August 7, 1930; and October 23, 1935, to November 15, 1948. With over 21 years in the office, he was the longest serving Prime Minister in British Commonwealth history.

**81.** *Ulysses* by Alfred Lord Tennyson

**82.** *Hamlet,* Act V, Scene ii

**83. Lois Wilson** is a minister, ecumenist, educator, author, chancellor, senator, wife, mother of four and grandmother of 12, and a social activist. Dr. Wilson shared team ministry with her husband, Roy, for some 15 years and was Moderator of The United Church of Canada, as well as President of both the Canadian and World Council of Churches.

**84. Allan Emrys Blakeney,** (1925 – ), was the Premier of Saskatchewan from 1971 to 1982, and leader of the Saskatchewan New Democratic Party (NDP).

**85. Donald C. McDonald,** CCF National treasurer who became Ontario CCF Leader in 1953 and continued as NDP Leader from 1962 to 1970. MPP for York South from 1955 till 1982 when he resigned to allow Bob Rae, the new leader, to enter the House. His autobiography, "The Great Fight" showed how deeply aware he was of the degree of corruption and injustice that took place in Ontario in his time. But he was an incorrigible optimist about his party's chances.

**86. Stephen Henry Lewis,** (1937 – ), the older son of David, was MPP for Scarborough West from 1963 to 1977, and Ontario NDP leader from 1970 to 1978. Stephen led the party to achieve the status of Official Opposition in the Ontario Legislature from the Liberals in 1975. In the early 1980's, he became Canada's ambassador to the United Nations. This led to his tenure as United Nations special envoy for HIV/AIDS in Africa. He now leads the Stephen Lewis Foundation, based in Toronto, which supports community-based organizations that are turning the tide of HIV/AIDS in Africa. (www.stephenlewisfoundation.org)

**87.** Mayor of London from 1972-1978

**88. Walter George Pitman,** (1929 – ), is an educator and former Ontario politician. His victory in a federal by-election held in Peterborough, Ontario in 1960 as a candidate for the New Party was a significant catalyst in the movement to re-found the social democratic Cooperative Commonwealth Federation as the "New Democratic Party" (NDP). After his political career, he acted as Director of the Ontario Institute for Studies in Education, President of Ryerson Polytechnic Institute, Dean of Arts at Trent University, and head of the Ontario Arts Council. He has published superb biographies of Ontario musicians.

**89. Gordon Allan Sinclair,** (1900 – 1984), was a Canadian radio journalist and commentator.

**90. David Barrett,** (1930 – ), British Columbia NDP Leader, brought the party to power in 1972, ending the Social Credit government of W. A. C. Bennett. He entered the Legislature in the early 60's. He was Premier of BC for three years between 1972 and 1975, the only Jewish premier in the province's history. In 1988, he won a federal seat on Vancouver Island.

**91. The British Columbia Social Credit Party**, whose members are known as Socreds, was the governing political party of British Columbia, Canada, for more than 30 years between the 1952 provincial election and the 1991 election. For three decades, the SCP dominated the British Columbian political scene, with the only break occurring between the 1972 and 1975 elections when the Premier was NDP Leader, David Barrett.

**92. The Winnipeg Declaration of 1956** (sometimes referred to as the Winnipeg Manifesto) was the program adopted by the CCF at its federal convention of that year, to replace the original Regina Manifesto of 1933. The main change was to abandon nationalization of corporations in favour of regulating their operations. The "Waffle" movement of the following decade was partly a reaction to this development.

**93. Mel Watkins,** (born 1932), is a Canadian political economist and activist. He is professor emeritus of economics and political science at the University of Toronto. He was a founder and co-leader with James Laxer of the Waffle, a left wing political formation within the New Democratic Party that advocated an "independent socialist Canada" and Canadian nationalism.

**94. James Laxer,** (1941 – ), is a Canadian political economist, professor and author. In 1969, Laxer, along with his father Robert Laxer and Mel Watkins, founded the Waffle, a radical left wing group influenced by the New Left, the anti-Vietnam War movement and Canadian economic nationalism that tried to win control of the New Democratic Party. Laxer remains prominent as an author, columnist and commentator.

**95. William Grenville "Bill" Davis,** (1929 – ), was the Progressive Conservative Premier of Ontario, Canada, from 1971 to 1985.

**96.** In 1970, **Quebec nationalists and FLQ** members kidnapped British diplomat James Cross and Quebec provincial cabinet minister Pierre Laporte, who was later murdered. What is now referred to as the October

Crisis raised fears in Canada of a militant terrorist faction rising up against the government. At the request of the Mayor of Montreal, Jean Drapeau, and the government of the Province of Quebec, and in response to general threats and demands made by the FLQ, the federal Liberal government of Pierre Trudeau invoked the War Measures Act. He did this so police had more power in arrest and detention, and so they could find and stop the FLQ members. There was a large amount of concern about the act being invoked as it was a direct threat to civil liberties.

**97. Pierre Elliott Trudeau,** (1919 – 2000), was the fifteenth Prime Minister of Canada from April 20, 1968 to June 4, 1979, and from March 3, 1980 to June 30, 1984. Between 1972 and 1974, when the NDP held the balance of power, Trudeau enacted several progressive measures, including the National Energy policy, an act still strongly criticized in parts of Canada, especially Alberta.

**98. The War Measures Act** (enacted in August 1914, replaced by the Emergencies Act in 1988) was a Canadian statute that allowed the government to assume sweeping emergency powers. The act was invoked three times in Canadian history: During the First World War when many German prisoners of war were interned in camps across Canada, during the Second World War to intern Japanese Canadians and during the October Crisis of 1970 in response to the kidnapping of Cross and Laporte.

**99. Susan Bogert Warner,** (1819 – 1885), the author of Jesus Bids Us Shine, published her words in her novel The Little Corporal (Chicago, Illinois: 1868) under the pseudonym of Elizabeth Wetherell.

**100. Thomas T. Lynch,** (1818 – 1871), published this hymn in 1885. His composition, My Faith it is an Oaken Staff is based on the verse from Ephesians 6: 16-17, "In addition to all this, take up your shield of faith, with which you can extinguish all the flaming arrows of the evil one. Take the helmet of salvation and the sword of the Spirit, which is the word of God."

**101. Dieterich Buxtehude** (c. 1637– 1707) was a German-Danish organist and a highly regarded composer of the Baroque period.

**102. Casavant Frères** is the oldest continuing name in North American organ building. Joseph Casavant Senior built pipe organs in Saint-Hyacinthe where his two sons, Claver and Samuel, established Casavant Frères in 1879. During their lifetime, the brothers Casavant established the finest traditions of craftsmanship among their artisans and a strong organization to carry on those traditions after them. Casavant Frères continues today. (www.casavant.ca <http://www.casavant.ca>)

**103.** See the Appleby United Church history at www.applebychurch.ca/history.html.

**104. Alan Mills** began a successful career as a folksinger on CBC radio in 1947; he sang until 1959 on 'Folk Songs for Young Folks' and 1952-5 on 'Songs de Chez Nous'. Mills's song *I Know an Old Lady Who Swallowed a Fly* (Southern 1951) became popular among folksingers; a Burl Ives performance of the song served as the soundtrack of a 1964 National Film Board (NFB) film of the same name.

**105.** Words by **John G. Whittier,** in *The Atlantic Monthly,* April 1872. The words are from a long narrative poem, *The Brewing of Soma.* "Dear Lord, and Father of mankind, forgive our foolish ways…" Music by: Frederick C. Maker, 1887

**106.** The M1 is Britain's first full-length motorway (it followed the Preston bypass, arguably the first motorway, though this was not to be built any further for a long time). It is also one of the most important, setting off the M6 (Britain's longest and busiest) and linking the north with the south. It begins in London and goes to Hook Moor just east of Leeds.

**107.** York Minster was built between the 12th and the 15th Century and is the largest Gothic church in England.

**108. Arthur's seat,** the remains of a volcano that erupted under water during the Carboniferous Period, is located within Holyrood Park in the centre of Edinburgh. Although only 250m (823 feet) in height, Arthur's Seat is a notable landmark, dominating the city. Seen from the side, it resembles a crouching lion. It takes its name from the legend that has King Arthur riding a lion.

**109. The Scottish Division** is a British Army command, training and administrative apparatus designated for all Scottish infantry units.

**110. Dr. Melville Cook** had been the organist at Leeds Cathedral in the 1960's and shortly after we heard him play in Chester, he moved to Winnipeg to be organist and choirmaster at the largest United Church there. The following year, he moved to Toronto to become the organist and choirmaster at Metropolitan United Church from 1969 until he retired in 1986. He moved back to England then and died in 1991. In 1970, Esther auditioned for and got the job of second soprano soloist in the choir and had five good years of great choral singing experience under his direction.

**111.** *A mighty fortress is our God*

> *A mighty fortress is our God, a bulwark never failing;*
> *Our helper He, amid the flood of mortal ills prevailing:*
> *For still our ancient foe doth seek to work us woe;*
> *His craft and power are great, and, armed with cruel hate,*
> *On earth is not his equal.*

**112.** The **Canadian Centennial** was a yearlong celebration held in

1967 when Canada celebrated the 100th anniversary of the Canadian Confederation. Celebrations occurred throughout the year but culminated on Dominion Day, July 1.

**113. Atikokan,** (2001 population 3,632), is a township in Rainy River District in Northwestern Ontario, Canada. Atikokan (Ojibwa for "Caribou Bones"), was founded over 100 years ago. A small town in Northern Ontario, Atikokan is now known primarily for its beautiful canoe routes and proximity to hunting and fishing locations.

**114.** In the fall of 1964, the principal of Atikokan High School (AHS), a man named Bill Peruniak, created a program to help students mature and reach their full potential. He and his staff realized that they must seek new ways to more effectively promote the growth of individual students, while at the same time, being able to ground the curriculum to the soil of Canada. He wanted to challenge students physically, mentally, and emotionally in the hopes that they would come to realize they were capable of doing much more than they ever thought possible. The Outers Club, based on the Minnesota Outward Bound School model, was established in the fall of 1965. Teamwork and group dynamics would become the key aspects of this program.

**115. Arthur Schultz** ran the general store in Kilworthy, taxied us to catch an early morning train at the end of the summer, and provided many other services in the community. For instance, he drove a school bus and filled the children's mother's grocery orders while they were at school.

**116. George Grube** in 1944 was President of the Ontario CCF. He was the first candidate for parliament I ever supported. Over the years, he was in great demand as a CCF convention chair.

**117. *Julius Caesar,*** Act 2, Scene 2, Calpurnia's speech, *"A lioness hath whelped in the streets; And graves have yawn'd, and yielded up their dead."*

**118.** Esther used to tape the songs for the teachers each month so that teachers who lacked the confidence to learn the songs could learn them from the tape. Some teachers, who felt that they couldn't teach the songs, even used the tapes to teach the children the songs in the classroom. By the time she performed in the schools, many of the children and certainly the teachers already recognized her voice.

**119. Church of Our Lady:** Guelph has one of the most beautiful Gothic churches in Canada. The construction of Our Lady Immaculate began in 1877 under the Irish-Canadian artist Joseph Connolly. The church was consecrated in 1888 by the Bishop of Hamilton. It was funded from Mexico by the Austrian emperor Maximilian.

**120. Tuned Orff instruments** were usually xylophones and glockenspiels and some metalophones in which the bars which were the unnecessary notes were taken off so that the students only played the notes that were in the song.

**121. Tom Lehrer,** (1928 –), taught mathematics at Harvard, MIT and Wellesley College. In addition, he sang and played the piano and created an impressive body of satirical songs inspired by current events. This is his song about pigeons:

> Spring is here, a-suh-puh-ring is here.
> Life is skittles and life is beer.
> I think the loveliest time of the year is the spring.
> I do, don't you? 'Course you do.
> But there's one thing that makes spring complete for me,
> And makes every Sunday a treat for me.
> All the world seems in tune
> On a spring afternoon,
> When we're poisoning pigeons in the park.
> Every Sunday you'll see
> My sweetheart and me,
> As we poison the pigeons in the park.
> When they see us coming, the birdies all try an' hide,
> But they still go for peanuts when coated with cyanide.
> The sun's shining bright,
> Everything seems all right,
> When we're poisoning pigeons in the park.

**122. Yvonne Williams,** (1901 – 1997), was the creator and designer of many beautiful stained glass windows and other installations including windows in Chalmers United Church in Guelph (now installed in Three Willows United Church) and Deer Park United Church chapel in Toronto.

**123.** *The Holly and the Ivy* is a traditional Christmas carol, which is among the most lightly Christianized carols of the Yuletide—the holly and the ivy being among the most familiar plants used for Christmas decoration in churches in England. The music and most of the text was collected by Cecil Sharp from a woman in Chipping Camden, Gloucestershire.

**124.** *The Hymn Book,* published in 1971 by the Anglican Church of Canada and the United Church of Canada.

**125. Casavant Frères** was the organ-building company that manufactured the organ at Chalmers UC.

**126.** *Activating the Passive Church,* by Lyle E. Schaller, Abingdon Press, 1981. It was written for both lay and ordained congregational leaders, and diagnosed the causes of church passivity, and formulated a method for combating the problem.

**127. Catherine Betty Crawford,** (1910 – 2002), graduated with a B.A. from the University of Toronto in 1933. She attended the Ontario College of Education and briefly taught classics at the Ingersoll Collegiate Institute, as it was known then. Her watercolours were evocative and beautiful.

**128. Norah McCullough** graduated from the Ontario College of Art in 1925 and her career began at the Art Gallery of Ontario. In the late 1930s she worked as assistant to Arthur Lismer, one of the original Group of Seven artists. In 1938 she went to South Africa to continue working with the children's art centres Lismer had established in Pretoria and Cape Town. She became inspector of art education in the Cape Town provinces. When she returned to Canada, Ms McCullough worked for the National Gallery of Canada in Prince Edward Island arranging tours and exhibits and setting up art classes for children in Charlottetown. She also worked on behalf of the National Gallery in Quebec and northern Ontario. She was founding executive secretary for the Saskatchewan Arts Board from 1947 to 1956, working tirelessly to promote interest in the arts, in particular in the rural areas. From 1956 to 1958, she travelled in Italy and France studying traditional handcrafts. She became western Canada liaison officer for the National Gallery of Canada between 1958 and 1968, assembling major exhibitions, circulating gallery shows and lecturing. Over the years, Ms McCullough assembled a large private art collection and usually gave friends and visitors to her home an impromptu tour and a lecture. She donated works of Canadian artists to public galleries. One thing I remember about her was that she stressed that when children were introduced to sculpture, they should be encouraged to handle the objects and feel their shape, not merely look at them.

**129. James Crerar Reaney,** 1926 – ), is a Canadian poet, playwright and literary critic. Reaney won his first of three Governor General's Awards for the book of poetry *The Red Heart* in 1949. He received the other two awards for *A Suit of Nettles* (1958) and a joint award for *Twelve Letters to a Small Town* (performed at the Guelph Spring Festival) and *The Killdeer and Other Plays* (1962). Reaney's best-known dramatic work is his *Donnellys* trilogy (1974-1975).

**130. Robert Fleming** (1921 -1976) was a Canadian composer, pianist, organist, choirmaster, teacher. He attended the Royal Conservatory of Music (TCM), which in later years he contributed music to. While at TCM he studied under Healey Willan for composition, Norman Wilks for piano, Ettore Mazzoleni for conducting, and John Weatherseed and Frederick Silvester for Organ. Between 1945 and 1946 he taught at Upper Canada College before joining the National Film Board where he worked in Ottawa and Montreal as a staff composer between 1946 and 1958 before becoming music director between 1958 and 1970. Between those years he was music director for the Ottawa Ballet Festival in 1953 and organist-choirmaster of churches in Ottawa and Ste-Anne-de-Bellevue, Quebec.

**131.** "Nobody in science now believes that sexual orientation is caused by events in adolescence ... Homosexuality is an early, probably prenatal and irreversible preference." Author and geneticist Matt Ridley. Matt Ridley, *Nature via nurture: Genes, experience, and what makes us human*, HarperCollins, (2003). Page 159

**132.** After much heated debate and maneuvering, Council passed a resolution with approximately a 3:1 vote:

> A) That all persons, regardless of their sexual orientation, who profess Jesus Christ and obedience to Him, are welcome to be or become full members of the Church. B) All members of the Church are eligible to be considered for the Ordered Ministry." A strange event had happened. The majority of delegates had come to the Council with a bias against ordaining homosexuals, but with an open mind. They heard the heart wrenching testimonies of devout gay and lesbian church members; many probably met an openly homosexual person for the first time in their life; they debated little else among themselves; they searched their souls and prayed to learn God's will. And most changed their mind! The resolution was subsequently amended to include: "that all Christian people are called to a lifestyle patterned on obedience to Jesus Christ." Another resolution was passed that called for more discussion and examination of "The Issue" and to urge the church to fight discrimination against homosexuals both in and beyond the church.

**133.** *Psalm 46: 4,*

> There is a river whose streams make glad the city of God,
> The holy dwelling places of the Most High.

**134.** South African traditional song.

**135. Harry Fricker** was at one time famous for being the very fine organist at the largest downtown Methodist, then United Church in Toronto, Metropolitan United Church. He was also an outstanding conductor of Toronto's Mendelssohn Choir.

**136.** Source of *Hail to thee blithe spirit*

**137.** Well known folks song, ***The Road to the Isles***

**138.** Ibid

**139.** *Day is dying in the west;*
*Heav'n is touching earth with rest;*
*Wait and worship while the night*
*Sets the evening lamps alight*
*Through all the sky.*

www.ingramcontent.com/pod-product-compliance
Lightning Source LLC
Chambersburg PA
CBHW030329240426
43661CB00052B/1573